"Chicken Side Off First"

A Collection of Humor and
Inspirational stories from around the world!

. . . Beginning in 1958, from
Osceola, Mo. USA

Written and Compiled by:
Richard F. and Neta Ruth
Sunderwirth

Osceola, Missouri USA

The Cover:©

Art work:

All work and design is protected under the laws of copyright and is the property of the authors.

Photos:©

As most of our folks know, we had several thousand wonderful and loyal tour members on our membership list. Most of the photos used in this book were given to us along the way. We certainly wish we had a photo of everyone, because they were like family. We did not pick and choose; we used what we had. We did not use names under the photos because of the possibility of getting a name wrong or leaving one out.
The Author's collection.

Photos are not as we would like. Had we known we were going to write this book, we would have processed them properly.

Layout and Design:©

Layout and interior design of this book completed by L&M Creations, (Linda and Meredith Anderson) Osceola, Missouri. All work and design is protected under the laws of copyright and is the property of the authors.

"Chicken Side Off First"

Most of the stories in this book came from Richard's Fun-Time Tour members through the years. The authors of this book take no responsibility for where they were obtained and have no way of knowing their origin; however, we have noted the authors, if we knew who they were. Most of the stories collected are in the realm of public domain.

Printed in the United States

To Contact the authors:

Richard F. and Neta Ruth Sunderwirth

P.O. Box 543

Osceola, Mo. 64776

Phone: 417-646-5538

To: Neta Ruth

...because she loves to smile

Enjoy!

4-4-14

God Bless!

When I count my blessings

Neta Ruth,

I count you twice...

Keep Smiling!

Neta Ruth Sunderwirth

Dedication

First of all, I want my entire family to know how much I love and appreciate them. They were never hesitant or shy about telling me if they thought something didn't sound quite right, or a funny story might be a little bit close to verging toward indelicate or improper. I would usually listen, tell them thanks, and then go ahead and use my own judgment. I was pleased with their encouragement to continue writing, when I sometimes felt I had tackled a bit too much.

To my loving wife, Neta Ruth, who helped so much, in remembering how some of the funny stories really happened. She never turned me down when I needed her help, and she was also willing to keep the food and liquid going when I got too involved with what we were writing. You will notice, while reading this book; she was my helpmate all through our **"Lifetime Adventures."** It is great when a husband and wife work together.

Yeah! That's me. Don't I look an awful lot like Curly from the Three Stooges?

Now to Mom, who went to be with the Lord in September of 2011 at the age of 98. If she happens to be reading this book, by one of God's special miracles, I want her to know that she was the one who promoted laughter and kept it going while she was raising the family. Much of the time she was laughing with or at my father. He would shake his head and encourage her to continue and that's what she usually did. She is now where she looked forward to being, and is probably keeping everyone laughing, just inside the pearly gates. Her daily prayers were sincerely appreciated and felt by all of our tour members, while our buses, planes, ships, and trains, kept us safely moving on.

And now, to the ones that made it all happen; our tour members. We want to dedicate this book to those wonderful friends who trusted us enough to go with us to so many beautiful parts of this amazing world. The desire to serve others has always been a part of our lives. The ability to make that happen, as much as possible, was given to us; Myself, Neta Ruth, Rick and Laneta by our creator the Lord Jesus Christ. My personal faith is like the old song says, "My hope is built on nothing less, than Jesus' blood and righteousness. I dare not trust the sweetest frame, But wholly lean on Jesus' name." **(Courtesy of Edward Mote & William B. Bradbury)**

We love and appreciate all of you. You were so kind to us, and we could tell by your loyalty, you enjoyed being with us almost as much as we enjoyed being with you. Thank you; and God's richest blessing continue to be with all of you, until we meet again.

"Hang Loose" ... Da Chicken

Retired, but we all loved her!

Welcome to Richard's Fun-Time Tours

Acknowledgments

First of all I want to thank all the wonderful and kind tour members (friends) who were really the ones that made this book happen. They trusted us and believed we could make things come together, and show them a good time. Neta Ruth, Laneta, Rick and I couldn't have done it without them. Many of these friends have departed this life and we truly hope that because of our relationship and their memories, they had a little more fun and joy in their later years, by having been tour members with Richard's Fun-Time Tours.

Thank you, Neta Ruth, for being my wife of 56 years. Thank you for helping me get many of the stories together as correctly as possible, and for all the patience you had and the proof reading you did while putting this book together. You, once again, encouraged me, when things seemed to go so slow.

We're so grateful for our daughter and son-in-law, Rick and Laneta Watts, for their decision to join with us just a few years after we began. They added so much to the operation of our company. We, as well as the tour members, were blessed everyday they were with us, through their love of the people, their prayers for our safety and their hard work that caused everything to come together just right.

I want to thank Meredith and Linda Anderson for their friendship and genuine professional help in producing this book. They were the ones who strongly encouraged Neta Ruth and me to finally write it. Our tour members suggested I do it years ago, and because of Meredith (Andy) and his wife Linda, we accepted the challenge. They pushed my ***"Go for it!"*** button, and made certain we stayed with it. Thank you!

A big thank you goes to Terry Kohnz who worked with us faithfully, through all the ticketing and airline reservations he made on our behalf. Terry helped us in many ways and we sincerely hope and pray for he and his wife as they continue their labors of making Fun-Time Tours the very best.

Thank you to our motor coach drivers, tour escorts, party and office staff, and especially Ruth Grabb for her help when we first started the company. She continued with us on almost every tour and helped make it all happen.

Thank you Willie and Aubrey Williams for the confidence you placed in us when you ask if we'd do our first adult tour to the Albert E. Brumley Gospel Sing in Springdale, Arkansas. You helped us in so many ways, including your prayers on our behalf, and we are extremely grateful. God is real and we know he wants the very best for all of us.

Finally, we thank our Heavenly Father, for Who He is, and how much he helped us along the way. Without God we would be in total darkness.

. . . And, we thank and appreciate YOU, the reader, for having courage enough to start reading our book, and hopefully, finding it interesting enough to finish.

Richard and Neta Ruth Sunderwirth 2014

Neta Ruth and Richard Sunderwirth

Fun-Time Tours

Comments...

Richard,

I have 2 big loves in my life, music, particularly Christian music, and tour buses. I have been operating a charter bus business for 29 years. Before that I was involved in the Christian music production field. I had met and worked with Jim Sunderwirth, Richard's brother in the early 80s', and he told me many things about his 'interesting brother.' Richard. As our bus business grew, I noticed that Richards Fun-Time Tours was growing and taking many wonderful trips with us. Both of my big loves collided when Richard asked us to be his bus company for their tours. Richard took such great care of his customers, knew everyone by name and where they lived and any special transportation need they had to get to their pick-up point. Richard wove humorous stories, with Gospel music on the bus, while taking people all across this Great Nation and Canada, showing them sights and places they had dreamed of seeing, and he brought them to their life. His buses were always full. He packed more sights and activities in a tour than anyone I knew, and with a pace that didn't wear out the Senior travelers. Richard's stories, jokes, songs he sung and narratives stayed with each passenger, but the person -- Richard --was who you wanted to be with; spend some time with, and hear his thoughts. I hope you get to discover and know Richard in this book. You will laugh and shake your head . . . and discover a great American, Missourian, and Christian man.

Danny Newby

President, Crossroad Tours

1320 W. 149th St.

Olathe, Kansas 66061

***

When I think back to the many tour groups that you brought to Cape Cod & Atlantic Canada over the years, a smile comes to my face. You always made it a point to introduce me as part of your team that helped create each unique experience in this area. I would notice how each and every one of your clients felt very special, appreciated and entertained! Richard, thank you for all the years of allowing me to be part of your life, on the road.

Rene P. Poyant

Director – Cape Cod Custom Tours

36 Ocean Street

Hyannis, MA 02601

***

"Chicken Side Off First" will keep you entertained for hours. Story after story of hilarious true events, jokes, and slap-stick comedy will keep you laughing, and turning pages. Richard Sunderwirth can tell funny stories, and this book proves he can write them as well.
Linda Cushman
Author, of "Bittersweet" - "First Train Leaving"-
and "One Rusty Spur"
Books available on Amazon.com

***

It just took a few moments to recollect back to 2002. I was just beginning to work with Richard and Richard's Fun-time tours. I remember Richard, the Tour Director, as a professional individual that took extreme good care of and due diligence to the guests that were traveling with him. Nothing was too complex or too insignificant to distract Richard from doing his professional, courteous, and with a smile on his face, BEST. His keen wit, 'Jokes of the Day', a story here or there, would always brighten up the day for his guests. Remember, Laughter is a good medicine.

In my 40 + years in the travel industry, I've seen two types of tour directors. First, the kind that is there to get a free trip and doesn't care what goes on or happens to the guests. Secondly, the type that is taking his/her duties to heart and doing what is best for the guest. To ensure that every last little detail is handled properly and efficiently and runs smoothly, without letting the guests know there is or was a problem. The latter is the type of professionalism you receive from Richard F. Sunderwirth. He was, and still is the mentor I try to imitate in the tour business and in my life.
Sincerely,
Terry S. Kohnz
Travel Consultant & Tour Operator
Fun-Time Tours

***

In our estimation, there is no one else in this world more uniquely qualified and with the credentials to write such collections of stories! As "Tour Guides in Training" on several of his trips, we watched with amazement as he filled each coach with people who quickly became much more than friends, they became family. That is one of the secrets of his many successes. Richard has that ability to have fun with, provide entertainment for and create an environment that is happy and safe for his passengers. He keeps 'em talking and engaged with each other and that brings them back for more. Many with now over 100 trips in their background, and a few with over 200 trips!

While it is true that no matter who you are, you will pull from your experiences and mold yourself into that person that makes you the most comfortable; having Richard as our initial platform from which to learn, made all the difference in the world. Richard did it all! He provided invaluable input into the workings of the tour industry and had tips that saved us hours and hours of time and resources. Both my wife and I have enjoyed working in the tour industry for the past several years and traveling virtually around the world with three different companies. We owe much of that and many, many thanks to Richard and his ability to work with people.

Randy and Marquita Pace
Tour Directors
Kansas City, Missouri

***

What wonderful, warm memories I have of Richard's Fun-Time Tours! I was fortunate to be their Cape Cod step on guide, and I loved every minute of it. It was so hard to say goodbye to them every year! Richard's humor, friendliness, and his faith were so much a part of each day. The tour was filled with laughter and fun, and Richard never lacked for a story to tell. Before we started on our way each day, Richard led us in the singing of "This is the day that the Lord hath made" and he ended it with "Oh what a beautiful morning". What a wonderful way to start our day! Richard and his wife, Neta Ruth, are special friends. I am so thankful to have been part of their tours!

Beverly LeBlanc
Cape Cod Custom Tour Guide
Hyannis, MA. 02601

***

"The highlight of my tour season was always the arrival of Richard's Fun-Time Tours, and I looked forward to working with Richard each summer. I always learned something from him, whether it was something about Missouri or the easiest way to avoid line-ups at group buffets, and of course, I always learned a new story! It was no wonder his tour members were always so happy and lovely-they had the kindest, most caring, professional, and comical leader in the business! I can't wait to read this

book- even if moving the chicken was never my forte . . ."
Lisa Bullerwell,
Tour Director
Atlantic Tours
Halifax, Nova Scotia

***

Richard; the man with a big heart for us seniors. What a joy to recommend Richard's Fun-Time Tours to the senior world, because I knew they would have a GREAT time, and hear hundreds of fun-packed stories. It is great to be a part of the Sunderwirth generation. God's best to all.
Willie Williams
MR. GOSPEL MUSIC of Kansas City, Mo.
Raytown, Missouri

***

Richard; 1980 was the year I got acquainted with Richard's Fun-Time Tours. I was working part time for Kincaid Coaches Company. Sometimes this included driving the coaches. I always enjoyed that part of the job. That is when I got to know the tour guide that always started the day by singing, "This is the day, the Lord hath made."

That was the day that made me want to sing, "On the road again." My employment with Kincaid was a part-time job that lasted over many years. I always looked forward to the times I would drive for Richard's Fun-Time Tours. The last tour with Richard was approximately 2005. Looking back over the years it was a great time.
Ralph Ferguson
Kincaid Driver
Edwardsville, Kansas

***

Dear Richard & Neta Ruth, We want to tell you how much we appreciate the wonderful trip to NEW YORK.
I know there was a tremendous amount of planning and details to work out to allow all of us to take this trip and we really do thank you for making it possible for us to go and see and do so many exciting things. I was just thrilled to go to the Broadway shows, the other famous places, and the great restaurants. Having both of you with us on this trip really made it special. We thank you.
R & D L,
Independence, Mo.

***

Dear Richard, Thank you so much for a wonderful trip. You were most thorough & more accommodating than any other company I've ever traveled with. We especially want to thank you for going "beyond the call of duty" when B. needed medical attention.

B & PT,
Warrensburg, Mo.

***

Dear Rick & Laneta, Mere words cannot express our gratitude for your thoughtfulness and generosity for the Alaska trip. Looking back, we realize that as great as the trip was, it was being with you two and the group that made it very special. I am thankful we shared Scoop in life and sad that we are sharing him in death, but you all have made our lives brighter and I guess we can thank Scoop for that. I'm glad we could enjoy the moments we had and also thankful that we have each other for some comfort in those moments of sadness.

R & J,
Columbus, Ms.

***

Dear Friends, We enjoyed the great Deep South/Azalea trip with Laneta and Rick so very much. What a truly wonderful time we had . . . all of the beautiful flowers everywhere were such a treat after our cold and snowy winter. At Bellingrath Gardens we almost felt as if we had died and gone to Heaven. Of course, Laneta and Rick are always so delight to travel with!

F & JB
Kansas City, Mo.

***

Dear Laneta, We received your refund check for the FULL amount of the Canadian trip just recently completed. We were so disappointed that we couldn't go. Spent almost 3 weeks in the hospital. We appreciated so much your efforts in obtaining the entire amount of the refund for us, and I know you've gone to a lot of trouble . . . Thanks.

LW,
Independence, Mo.

***

Laneta & Rick, Hope all of you are well and feeling great. Enclosed is a photo of Jean & Judy trying to get my Husky Dog that

I won on the Alaska Tour. We had a good time and had loads of fun. We are looking for another great adventure. Are you having the BIG get together up here in Warrensburg this year!? Tell Richard and Neta Ruth hello. It's always nice to go places with a bunch of people with a Christian atmosphere. God Bless!
B& JA
Warrensburg, Mo.

***

Dear Richard & Neta Ruth, Just a note to tell you we really enjoyed our trip to Nova Scotia and so glad we went when we did. The scenery was breath taking and we enjoyed all the fun we had on the bus. We appreciate how you look out for each and every one on the tour; hope to go on another one with you soon. Thanks again for another great memory.
J& MW
Osceola, Mo.

***

Laneta & Rick, Just wanted to thank you for your concern & prayers. I'm feeling pretty good now, but have to take it easy for a while. I received your check. We never expected to receive such a refund from the Azalea Tour.
NM & NC,
Kansas City Mo.

***

Dear Friends, We enjoyed the great Deep South / Azalea trip with Laneta and Rick so very much. What a truly wonderful time we had . . . all of the beautiful flowers everywhere were such a treat after our cold and snowy winter. At Bellingrath Gardens we almost felt as if we had died and gone to Heaven. Of course, Laneta and Rick are always so delightful to travel with!
F & JB
Kansas City, Mo.

***

Dear Richard & Neta Ruth, We wanted to thank you and tell you how much we enjoyed the Nova Scotia tour! I admit that in anticipation, I was a bit apprehensive about taking a long "bus" tour and I presume my hesitancy was conditioned by the memory of school bus rides. Now that I have "been there, done that", I have no reservations about recommending that tour or others you may

have to everyone!
JR H,
Clinton, Mo.

***

Richard & Neta Ruth, We want to thank you for the wonderful trip to Niagara Falls and New York City. The falls were absolutely awesome. We enjoyed both Broadway shows but especially enjoyed our front row seats at Beauty and The Beast. Also the meals at the United Nations, Tavern on the Green and Arthur's Landing were fantastic. Ooops, forgot the meal at the Skylon tower. The entire trip was truly a once in a lifetime experience for us.
J & JF
Kansas City, Mo.

***

Dear Friends, Thank you so much for a wonderful trip to Louisiana. It was just great. We truly did enjoy being with such a great group of people. I've been on several trips with other tours, but yours is the very best. Thanks again.
JC,
Roscoe, Mo.

***

Laneta, The trip to Mackinaw Island and the train ride into Canada was just beautiful! We thank you for such a great time. Richard's Fun-Time Tours sure are making our retirement special!
SM,
Blue Springs, Mo.

***

Hi, Rick & Laneta, Just wanted to let you know how much I've enjoyed all the tours on my way to 100 (100 trips that is). You've played a big part and I thank you so much. I'm sure the next hundred trips will be just as great. Thank you for everything.
BM,
Lee's Summit, Mo.

***

My friends, I have been reflecting on all the trips I have taken with you. The mountains, canyons, streams, lakes, waterfalls, awesome oceans, beautiful foliage; our great American historical sights, fabulous food and fellowship, and all these were made possible for me by God's grace. I'm so grateful to God and to you, my dear friends of Richard's Fun-Time Tours, for giving me this opportunity.
DC, Kansas City, Mo.

***

The following tribute was written by one of our tour members and presented to us sometime near our retirement. We will always be grateful for their kind words and expression of love as is shown here.

. . . Richard's Fun-Time Tours . . .

How does one say thank you, To the guy who always sings. "This is the day the Lord has made" and other beautiful things? How does one say thank you for all the silly jokes, and all the funny stories you find to tell all of us folks? How does one say thank you for the specially planned event, like the evening down in Warrensburg where a fun-filled night was spent? And how does one say thank you for the time you take to plan, the trips we look so forward to with our wild and wonderful man? And how does one say thank you, you're really quite unique, especially when the gorgeous blonds you do so well critique! And what a wonderful way to work, with family along for the ride, Your daughter and that gorgeous blond, Neta Ruth, close by your side. Well, guess I'll just say thank you for all the good you do, And say, Oh, what a beautiful morning, when God blessed us with you!

. . .

"We all know that Neta Ruth is not a blond, but she did play one in one of our skits. She did a good job, too."

BON VOYAGE!
WELCOME
ABOARD!
It is our company policy ...
To celebrate all GREAT events!

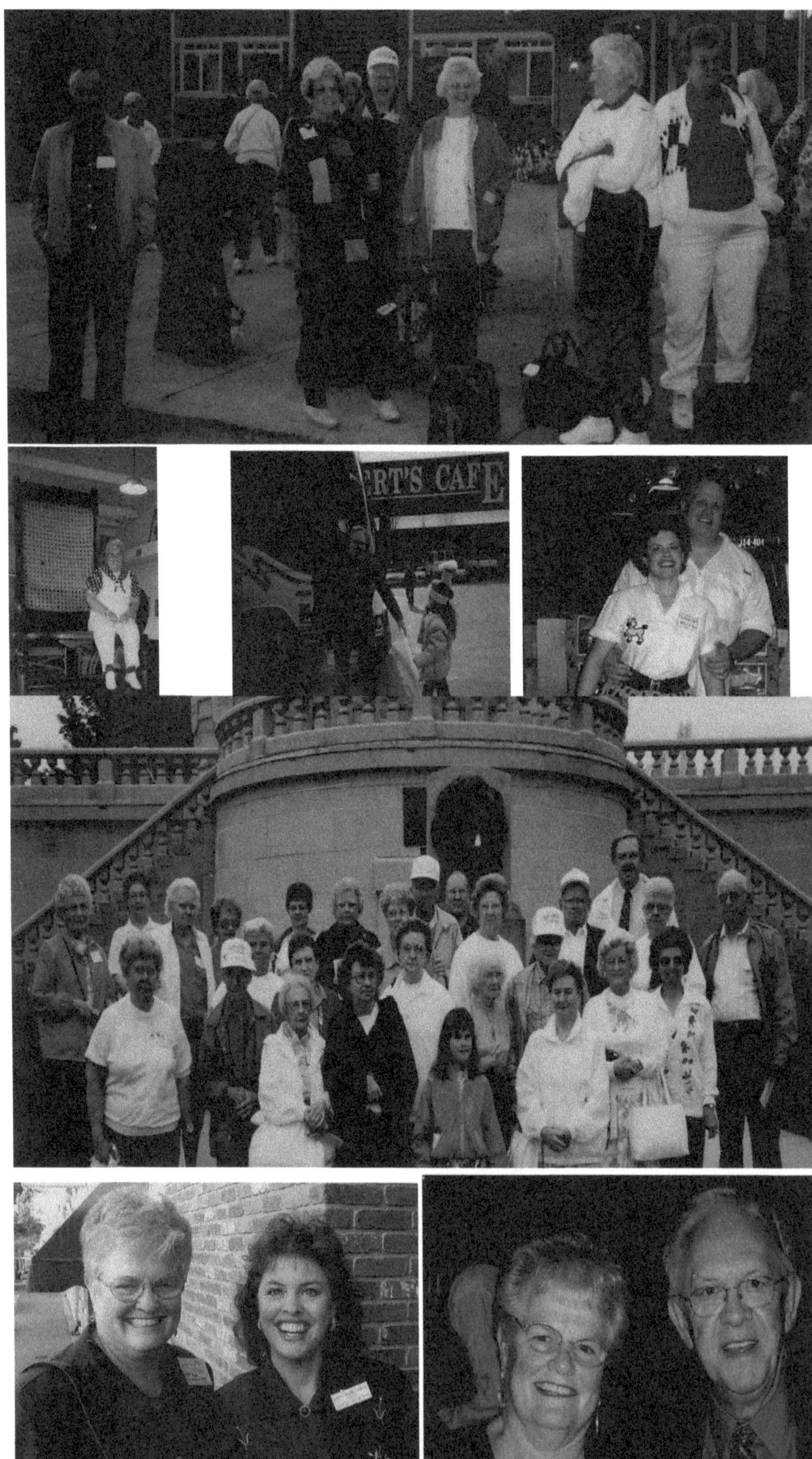

Foreword...

This book was written for **You** . . . the reader. It was written to be a lifetime book or a resource book for about anything regarding humor in any way, form or fashion. It is for you and anyone, in times of joy, sadness, loneliness, despair, and maybe in times of death. This book, for sure, is one for the coffee table.

This book; was basically written and designed to bring much **JOY,** and **LAUGHTER**, to as many people as possible, because it is filled with really funny stories . . . many stories that will truly give your spirit a shot in the arm. There are some one-liners, but mostly stories that will lift you out of the miry clay, as the lyrics from one beautiful song say, "It will put a **NEW** song in your heart to stay!"

If you happen to be a minister, story-teller, a public speaker or a tour guide, there are stories that can be used for fun, illustration, and inspiration. There are many true stories, funny anecdotes, and also a mini-autobiography of my life, outlined in chronological order of businesses, etc. and things in general that Neta Ruth and I have done and been involved in through the years.

One of the first persons to look at the original manuscript told me, THIS BOOK could, very easily, be the best book ever compiled for HUMOR and INSPIRATION. Why? Because it is a collection of happenings and humor, from the files of doing tours around the world for over 18 years. As a tour escort keeping the folks laughing was almost better than keeping them fed. Most of the stories within these pages have been told on our tours starting in 1959 and forward. I really believe you will be blessed in various ways as you read and absorb the entire contents.

This book will never be noted for its' brilliant writing, its' perfect English, or its' totally correct punctuation. The literary authors will probably never have this in their library, because they are too busy selling their own books and critiquing others . . . but that's alright, because they are, in most cases, really nice folks also.

The reason for the title *"Chicken Side Off First"* will be explained later in the book.

Many of the humor stories do not have paragraphs indicated. The reason for this is to save space throughout the book.

"I feel better all over than I do anywhere else," is an old expression but many have expressed it through the years. "When you laugh, the whole world laughs with you," is also a known phrase. The good Lord implanted the 'FUNNY BONE' on the inside of us; just like he did all the other bones. We really wouldn't be worth a plug nickel without it. If you love to laugh; if you REALLY enjoy laughing . . .

THIS BOOK IS, WITH OUT A DOUBT, FOR YOU!

Over 1300 stories

"Give me a sense of humor,
Lord, give me the grace to see a joke,
to get some humor
out of life, and pass it on to other folk."
(Author unknown)

Richard's Chickens - All named "Hang Loose"

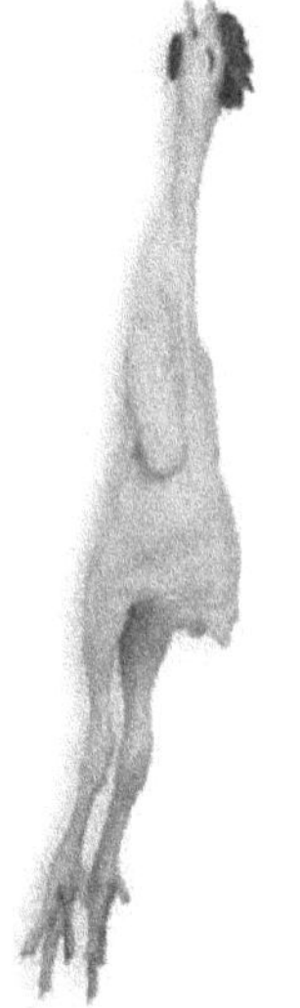

Richard & Neta Ruth Sunderwirth

"A YOUNG BOY'S DREAM"

A time-line of adventures in the "opportunities" market!

Once upon a time, many miles ago, there was a very young boy who really liked to work and tell funny stories. At 9 years of age he decided he would go into business for himself. He made real nice pot holders, and sold them all over town for 10 cents apiece. These pot holders were made from two paper plates. One whole plate for the back and one half paper plate for the front. The plates were held together by various colors of yarn.

By now, I'm sure you realize I'm talking about myself, Richard F. Sunderwirth, and the beginning of my working career. This little story is not meant to be a life story, **(that would fill several books)** only the different stages of working, leading up to "Richard's Fun-Time Tours" and a little beyond.

My next financial adventure, at 10 years of age, was negotiating with my dad, to work in my folks's grocery store. The deal was, I would work every day after school, in the store, until closing time. Then on Thursdays I would stay as long it took to stock the shelves. Each week on Thursday was the day the big truck would bring in our main supplies. On Saturday I would work all day, and sometimes until midnight.

In the summertime we would have the Courtyard Follies on the courthouse lawn, and the town square would be filled to overflowing with folks just to hear the fabulous 'hillbilly, Gospel and country music.' We were closed on Sunday. My starting salary was $^{\$}1^{50}$ per week, and believe it or not, I thought that was great.

I can't remember if we were in the 3rd or 4th grade but one of my very best friends, Susan 'Scott' Anderson, and I went into business for ourselves. Susan's dad and mom had a charge account down town at a local grocery store. I think Susan or maybe it was me; at least one of us, or maybe both, decided we would go down and get one pound of sliced lunch meat and one pound of sliced cheese; and also 1 or 2 large loaves of sliced bread. We took those three items back near the school and sold meat, cheese and bread sandwiches. I think we sold sandwiches, every school day, for about one month. We only got 10 cents per sandwich, but we could clear about $^{\$}2^{00}$ to $^{\$}3^{00}$ between the two of us, and this was a pretty good profit, because we really didn't have any cost. It was all profit. At the end of the first month we were forced out of business. Mr. Scott, I think, sorta accused his wife of hoarding lunch meat and cheese, but the mystery was finally solved and we immediately went into bankruptcy; however, we did fairly well for 4 great weeks. My dad said he always wondered why it took 30 minutes for me to get from school to Sunderwirth's IGA grocery store to work; well, I was selling sandwiches.

My sister, Gail, played the accordion. She and I would sing at the follies and that would usually bring in some extra money. "Windy", Bill Smith would have a drawing at the end of the 'so-called' concert, and we'd always get a little cash. One day, when I was about 62, Bill stopped me at the post office and said, "Richard, do you remember when you and Gail sang and played at my Courtyard Follies? I said, "Of course Bill." Bill replied, "Well, folks seemed to enjoy it when really young folks would entertain. Gail would play the accordion and the both of you would sing." "Yeah, you're right on," I said. Bill continued, "If you remember we had a drawing at the end of each show. I would give $^{\$}1^{00}$, $^{\$}2^{00}$, $^{\$}3^{00}$, $^{\$}4^{00}$, and $^{\$}5^{00}$, each week. Well, each Saturday night you kids would always get something, once in a while, even the $^{\$}5^{00}$. At the end of the evening's music, I would draw your name, even if it wasn't on the ticket. People liked to hear you kids sing, and I for sure wanted to keep you coming." Bill said, "Don't tell anyone about this until I'm through the Pearly Gates." Bill if you are reading this, I saved it until now!

Very few stores, in any small town, stayed open on Sunday. That was the day for church, a big dinner at someone's house, or a potluck at the church. After dinner my sister, Gail, and I would spend most of the afternoon sitting on the front porch of our house, waiting and watching cars and trucks miss the corner, just west of the Catholic Church. Very few Sundays would go by without something going over the big embankment. We still have the church, the embankment, and the big curve today, but now the main highway goes around our town, and we're all aware of the bad curve, so no one goes off anymore.

I gave very little thought to playing with the other kids. You know? Cowboys and Indians and such; all I could really think about was earning enough spending money; but I really did like to work. My allowance was 25 to 50 cents through grade school and put that with the $1.50 salary, plus the singing and the sandwiches, I was doing pretty well.

By the time I reached 12 years of age, it was time to re-negotiate with my dad again. We decided that $3 a week would be fine. After all that was doubling my wages and that was good in those days. The allowance was increased to 75 cents.

I can't remember how I worked this next adventure into my grocery store job, but I did. I sold Grit magazines for 1 year. After the 1st year I found out my bicycle expenses ate up my profit, in addition to the criminals who wouldn't pay their Grit bill. (You know who you are!) It was good experience that probably saved me from getting too ripped off in the future.

At 14, my freshman year in school, we reached another milestone. I would work in the store for $15 per week with the following agreement. My folks were to feed me (not snacks), provide my bed, and buy my necessary clothing. All other items I would pay for. Dad would have made me a much better deal, but I felt that was fair. I even told him if I run short of money I would borrow from him, and I wanted to pay him interest. It was exciting as a got my first experience in the business world, I thought.

About the middle of my freshman year I purchased an upright, really attractive, popcorn machine from Burt Lair, (He owned a drug store just off the north side of the town square.)

The machine cost me $200. It took me almost 2 years to pay for it. My dad helped me push that big machine, on little wheels, all the way from our grocery store for 2 blocks up town. For the next 3 years I sold popcorn at the Follies on Saturday night, and during the day on Thursday's I would sell popcorn at Pasley's Sale Barn in Osceola. When I finally got my driver's license I took my popcorn machine to the big Springfield Fair in August, for 2 years. I'll never forget the first night I was at the fair. I ran over a huge four inch water main, with my little pickup truck. The water valve was located about a foot or so behind the concession stands. Most of the folks working in the little stands either slept in the stand or behind it. The water shot 30 or 40 feet in the air. A whole bunch of folks got really wet before they got it shut off. No one saw me do it, and I knew I couldn't do anything about it, so I just quickly drove back to my little stand, where I had a cot and went to bed. I sat on the side of the cot and watched all the excitement. The next morning at breakfast I visited with Emmett

Kelly. (I played piano for him during his performance with the big circus.) During breakfast Mr. Kelly and I tried to help figure out who ran over the water main the night before. I didn't offer much information

I can't quite remember, but one year I worked for Bill Durnell at the Missouri State Fair, in Sedalia also. While there I expanded the merchandise in my stand and added hotdogs and soda pop.

A few of the days there, mom and dad would feel sorry for me and come up and help for a few hours.

I picked up a little extra cash when I leased my popcorn machine to the school on special events. Mr. Remington, my High School Superintendent, said he wouldn't pay but $25, but I knew how much profit there was in popcorn, so, I said, "Nope, $50, or no deal, but I did operate it during the basketball tournaments and he paid me the $50. I definitely wanted to operate it, to avoid some kid tearing it up. When I graduated from High School I figured it was time to sell my popcorn machine and the other stuff to Mr. Earl Baker, a local businessman. He wanted it real bad, so I made a sacrifice and sold it to him for $700. I think on that deal I cleared a pretty good profit.

I received several scholarships my senior year in music, but I decided I would not go on to college. I had a burning desire to buy a business and start earning my way, rather than going to school for four or more years. Most people in town thought my folks had money, but they were mistaken. Dad and Mom, I found out too late, had some people working for them that carried most of their profit out the back door. I was the one that discovered it was happening, but it was too late to do much good. My folks always owed a balance on their home, wherever they lived, and never got it paid off until my wife and I, my sister and brother, paid their balance after we were adults.

I'll never forget how my Dad cried at the time we did it for them. In his 80's he was finally out of debt.

A short time after graduating I was walking around the square one Sunday afternoon and I saw a sign in the Bus Station Café window that said, **FOR SALE**. Well, I really liked their hamburgers, their chocolate sundaes, which I never got enough of, and I especially wanted to know what all the junk was in the back room. I think there was stuff back there that had accumulated for 50 years or more. **(Definitely valid reasons for buying a café!)**

I walked into the café, and asked Mr. John Alsbaugh what he wanted for it, and he said "$4,000." I didn't have it, so I walked up to Boyd and Lena Gover's house and said to Boyd. "Boyd, **(I could call him Boyd, rather than Mr. Gover, because when my folks first moved to Osceola in 1937 we lived with he and his wife, Lena, for a few years, when I was just a baby).** "I need to borrow $5,000, today." Boyd said, "Richard, what in the world do you want that much money for, and what's the hurry?" I said, "I just bought the Bus Station Café for $4000. I gave him a check, and I don't have the money to cover it. I need the extra $1,000 to use for operating money." **(I don't know how I knew that, but I guess it just sounded good to me.)** He said, "Do you have any collateral?" I said, "Nope, I don't think so, what is that? But I'll try and get some as soon as possible." He got his check book out and wrote me a check for $5,000. I walked back to my folk's home, and told my Dad and Mom that I had just purchased the Bus Station Café. I thought Dad would probably scold me and Mom would faint, but both said, "If that is what you want to do, it is alright with us." My agreement with John was that if I bought it he would take his very personal items out and leave that afternoon. He did that; I can't remember, but I think we opened the next morning, with Mom by my side and we sold a lot of good food for several years. Here I was, owning a business the very first year out of high school, and owing $5,000. That was a ton of money back in 1956-57. It didn't seem to bother me too much because I was excited, and I was ready to go to work and I knew I could make a success of it. **(I guess if I hadn't made it, I would have had to go back to selling 10 cent potholders.)**

The Bus Station, during the time of our ownership, was a real Bus Station. We had anywhere from 8 to 10 buses for rest stops every day; however, on Friday evenings we would sometimes have 4 buses out in front at the same time. Many folks used the buses to travel to Kansas City, to Springfield and other cities going back and forth to work, so on Friday evenings and Sunday evenings we were extremely busy. Most of the stops had time built in for sandwiches, a piece of pie, coffee etc. Each stop stayed for around 20 to 25 minutes.

I built up a fantastic relationship with most all of the drivers during this first year. We got along fine and many times, since I wasn't married at that time, I would ride the bus to Kansas City, maybe eat a bite up there and catch the very next bus back to Osceola, just in time to open up again. I really enjoyed riding the bus and, even way back then, anytime I was in a crowd I liked to tell a funny story now and then and visit with the folks on the bus. I probably wasn't supposed to do that, but I do remember hearing the driver's laugh every once in a while in route, and that just made me search for more good stories.

Well, all of a sudden it was April of 1958, and I was dating my future wife, Neta Ruth. Prior to our marriage Neta Ruth worked for the Daily Democrat Newspaper, as a teletype operator, in Clinton, Mo. She was there from 1956 through most of 1958. She typed the entire daily Democrat newspaper and the weekly Warsaw paper. She earned a total of $26 a week. We often have laughed about that, because when she quit they had to hire 3 people to take her place. **(SHE WAS GOOD!)**

Neta Ruth and I got married in August of 1958. We were very young and we had a great time going here and there during that first year, mostly after closing time at 10 p.m. We were open 7 days a week; and so, it was really great having a Mom that could step in, even more than her regular hours, to fill in when we needed to be gone. Neta Ruth jumped in, from the beginning of our marriage, and began working just like she owned the place, (well, she did). She and I worked together while we were in the Bus Station; from that point forward we worked side by side in every other business we owned through the coming years. One exception; she worked for the St. Clair County Courier Newspaper, also as a teletype operator, for two years in 1968-1970.

Our first child, a son, Richard Wayne, was born in October of 1959. Even while Neta Ruth was pregnant she worked hard in the café. Richard Wayne would sit in his little rocking chair and watch the folks come and go, during the day, when we were both working.

I remember one day we'd been to Clinton and were rushing home to get back to work. At that time Neta Ruth was pregnant with Richard W. Evidently her door was not completely closed and when we turned the corner in front of the café, she fell out. She hit the pavement, but yet was hanging on to the swinging door. We've never forgotten that experience because while she was in limbo I made a brilliant remark. I simply said, "Well, get up." She could have been killed, but like the stupid things men many times do, I had my mind on getting us back to work. I think she's finally forgiven me for that remark.

One thing we both enjoyed doing was going somewhere different, for a little outing, and, of course, it had to be after closing time, 10 p.m. Most of the time we would get out of town and drive 6 miles, all the way to Lowry City, and stop at a little restaurant and service station along highway 13 north. We could each get a big thick ham sandwich, **(A big baked ham was always sitting in the window leading into their kitchen)** and a cup of coffee, and the total bill was $1. We couldn't go any further than Lowry City, because we had to be back at the restaurant the next day by 5:00 a.m. because we opened at 6:00 a.m.

During this time I was also serving on the local fire department. Every time we'd get a call I'd say, "Neta Ruth, Mom, one of you get on the grill, I'll be back shortly."

One more thing, Gay Fulton was a faithful friend. She sat in the front of the restaurant, where she waited for taxi customers, and when she was not busy with that, she sold bus tickets; we did that also.

For the last few years of operating the café in Osceola, my brother, Jim Sunderwirth, and I delivered the Springfield Leader and Press Newspaper. Every Sunday morning, after throwing the papers, we'd go to Boyd and Lena's home and have the best fried tenderloin, in the country; that also came with biscuits and gravy. I had a nice, practically new, red and white convertible. I would drive and throw the papers to the customers, and Jim would roll them, as we drove the route, and he would also walk the square and make downtown deliveries. He always likes to joke and tell people that when payday rolled around we'd split the profit; I'd give him his 25% and take my 75%.

In 1962, our first daughter, Laneta Kay (Sunderwirth) Watts, was born. She was truly a blessed addition to our family.

One short story –

My uncle said, "Just so you can learn from it."

My aunt and uncle lived in Rockville, Mo. for many years. They owned and operated a general merchandise store. They decided to get out of the business by having an auction and selling, not only the merchandise and fixtures, but the building as well. They had the auctioneer and someone to clerk the sale, but no one was available to be the cashier. My uncle called me one day, in our early stages of operating the Bus Station Café, and said, "Richard, would you be interested in being the cashier for our big sale coming up in two weeks?" I was thrilled that he had enough confidence in me to ask, so I said, "Yes" without giving the offer a lot of thought. He said he would pay me $15 for the day. Keep in mind, Neta Ruth and I combined, made an average of $85 a week, so an additional $15 sounded pretty good

The day came; I jumped in my car and headed for Rockville. The sale went good, for those days. During the sale day I handled checks and cash in the amount of $33,000. That was more money than I'd seen in my life or even could think about.

The money came in fast and furious; everyone was in a hurry to leave once they make their purchase. When the sale was over, the clerk and I got together to balance the books. She said to me that according to her records, which we tallied twice, I only had $32,997. Well, we counted and balanced one more time and I was still $3 short. I should have known being only $3 off from handling that much money was an absolute miracle. $30, or $300, wouldn't have been too terribly bad, considering the fast pace of the transactions.

I went to my uncle feeling really bad, and I hated to tell him I was short $3. He didn't say much, but he walked over to where my aunt was standing. I couldn't hear what they were saying, but I knew it couldn't be good. They both walked back to where I was, and he said, "Richard, you did really well today; however, **just so you can learn from it**, we're going to deduct the $3, from your $15. I was disappointed, but I was still proud that they would even ask me in the first place. I drove back to Osceola and when I told Neta Ruth what happened, I'm telling you, **the %*)#*@$* hit the fan**. I won't tell you what she said, but it wasn't good. Now, there's usually a good ending to most stories, if we just hang in there for a while.

My uncle died, and several years later my aunt died, and I was the administrator of their estate. Really I did love both of them, but I want you to know this; beyond question, I got my $3.00 back with a "Whole bunch" of interest. **End of this story**

Sometime in the latter part of 1958 one of our bus drivers mentioned to me that there was a company down in the boot heel of the state, called Robbins Educational Tours, that could probably use somebody like me, since I had that natural gift of gab.

I found out more about the company and called the owner, Mr. Medford Robbins. He interviewed me over the phone and told me if he was interested in me he would call me someday. I didn't hear anything from him at all until February or March of 1960. I figured the tour business was out the door; however, he called me one day and said, "Richard, be in Memphis, day after tomorrow, and you can go with me on a 6-day trip to the Gulf Coast and New Orleans. We'll pick you up at the Continental American bus station in Memphis, Tennessee at 7:00 a.m."

By the time I got some clothes ready it was time to leave on the late bus for Memphis. It took me about an hour to convince Neta Ruth that I really needed to go. I figured when an opportunity came up, I needed to jump on the wagon. (I mean the bus)

Keep in mind that our son was only about 5 months old, and there I was leaving all that work and responsibility to a young wife and a tired mother.

After riding the bus all night, **(At least, I knew the drivers well enough I didn't have to buy a ticket.)** I arrived in Memphis; got on Mr. Robbins' bus, and worked for his company for the next several years. These were high school senior trips that I was escorting. I traveled from March thru May on the tours, and worked in the winter, selling these tours to seniors in schools, in Missouri, Illinois and Arkansas.

Every moment I was home I still had to work and keep the café open and give the girls a little rest. I was homesick when I was gone; Neta Ruth was crying, running the restaurant, and taking care of a new baby boy at the same time. We were making about $85 a week at the restaurant, and, the weeks I worked on the tours, we made an additional $75. Even though I had to pay all of my travel expenses, while calling on the schools, we still thought financially, we were in tall clover, even though we still struggled, and I mean struggled, to pay our bills.

After working with Robbins Educational Tours for a year or so, Mrs. Robbins called me and gave me the horrible news that Mr. Robbins had passed away. She asked if I would be a pallbearer at his funeral; she also told me that he had requested that I become the new operator of their company.

After the funeral and considerable discussion, I agreed to take that position. It was a very difficult decision to make because Mr.

Robbins had 10 or 11 trained and faithful lady tour escorts that worked for his company, and here I was, having only been with the company for a much shorter period of time, coming in and being their boss. I met with the ladies and all went well. I stayed with them for about 4 more years, but during that time I had the opportunity to learn a lot about tour and travel. Each year we had tours to Florida and the Gulf Coast, New Orleans, Chicago, and a trip or two to Washington, D.C. The miracle in all of this was that I was only 19 when I started conducting tours for Robbins Educational Tours, Inc. I was only 2 or 3 years older than the students, but I never let them know that.

One Quick Story - "I ruined his senior class trip."

I had one tour where the teachers could not handle the discipline of the kids on the tour. They were young teachers; not as young as I, but nearly. We had one boy that got drunk, the first night out. I called him aside and told him one more of those incidents and I would, without question, send him home on a Trailways® bus. I told him, "We're going to a very dangerous city tomorrow, New Orleans, and anything could happen, and no one should even think about alcohol." He smarted back to me, and I told him, "I will not argue with you, but I will send you home."

Not only was he ruining the trip for himself, but for his teachers and classmates as well. We arrived in New Orleans and sure enough, he got drunk. I didn't know about it until the next morning when one of the sponsors told me. I had already checked on the bus schedules and I was ready, just in case. I called his mother and told her to expect him in St. Louis at 7:30 p.m. that day. Well, the trip, from that point forward, was great. We had 3 more days to go and I didn't think about the incident until the last 30 or so miles going into his local town, just east of St. Louis, Mo. I talked to our bus driver and said to him, "Mitch, I know who we'll meet when we get to the school yard. It will be his mother, coming down the hill to meet and greet me." Well, she was and her little boy was with her.

She let me know in no uncertain terms; I had ruined his senior class trip that he had worked for and planned on for four years. Yes, she greeted me and let me know that she was really upset, and that she was going to call the company. I was the company, but she didn't know that. I had no idea what to say that would please her; however, before I really knew what was happening I said, "Mrs. Rodgers, I couldn't do for your son in 3 days, what you and your husband failed to do in 17 years." She didn't say a word; she went back over the hill, and we never heard any more from her. I firmly believe God was responsible for the answer I gave her!

After owning and operating the Bus Station Café in Osceola for four years, we were offered an opportunity to be a big part of a brand new restaurant in Collins, Mo. called "Lake Gate Restaurant." This opportunity was given to us by Mr. and Mrs. Byron Remington. Mr. Remington was the Superintendent of Osceola Independent School District and Mrs. Remington taught music in high school. These folks were two of the best friends I ever had. I respected them personally and in their professional career as well.

Mr. and Mrs. Remington came to me one day and asked me if I would consider being the operator of a new restaurant and service station in Collins, Mo. After consideration, we accepted his proposal. He built the buildings and Neta Ruth and I operated them. We continued to operate the Bus Station for another two years, while at the same time operating "Lake Gate Restaurant," and a Texaco Service Station. We were there from 1962 through 1967. We had a very successful business, and met and served many new friends. We were extremely blessed for having so many wonderful customers and employees, both in Osceola and Collins, and from the surrounding communities.

After leaving the restaurant in Collins, I went to work for a new motor club in Springfield, Mo. and worked there for a little over a year.

In 1968 several men in the Osceola area became business associates and we started Travel-Aid & Safety Assn. (TASA). I was President of that company for several years. This business was similar to AAA except with a much larger financial benefit to its members. We sold (TASA) to a similar company in Texas and it was operated in that state for several years.

1968 was also the year our youngest daughter Tina Renea (Sunderwirth) Leiber, was born. Once again, another wonderful blessing came into our lives. Just a few short years after their marriage, we were blessed again, with a granddaughter Krystal Rylee Leiber and grandson James Race Leiber.

Chicken Side off first...

As mentioned earlier in 1959 our son Richard Wayne was born. We were blessed when he and his wife, Sherri, brought another blessing, a grandson, Richard (Scoop) Dobin Sunderwirth.

Then in 1985 our grandson Scoop passed away, as a result of an accident, and then his father, our son, Richard Wayne passed away in 2005, during an Esophagus operation.

In the beginning stages of (TASA), we also owned and operated, S & H Mobile Home Sales and Service in Osceola. That operation was sort of a challenged undertaking. Someone told me I couldn't sell mobile homes, so, like a ding-bat, I took the challenge and was one of the top producers of the Star Mobile Home and Bendix factories. During the first year in business, we won an 8 day, all-expense paid cruise on the S.S Emerald Seas. On that particular voyage the sea was so rough it's a wonder we ever took another cruise . . . but we did . . . many of them, once we started Richard's Fun-Time Tours.

I also stopped selling mobile homes due to the fact we purchased another business in 1978; Osceola Cheese Company. This company was originally built in 1944 by Mr. and Mrs. W.K. Scott.

It was a wonderful, successful and well known company for many years before we purchased it, and continued with growth until we sold it in 1989. During the tenure there the buildings were completely re-decorated and increased in size by 5 times, and the sales increased also by over 5 times. We sold cheese both retail and wholesale and enlarged the mail-order business considerably. We sold Osceola Cheese Company to Mike and Marsha Bloom. It has continued to be a great business for Osceola and employs many people. The sale of that business worked out really well. Mr. and Mrs. Bloom were looking for a good retail business to buy, and we were looking for a good buyer, that was capable of operating that type of business. Everything worked out fine for Mr. & Mrs. Bloom and for the Sunderwirths.

Richard & Neta Ruth Sunderwirth

"The Beginning of "Richard's Fun-Time Tours"

We thought we retired in 1989. Little did we know, we would be getting in to the largest business we would ever own. One day I was approached by Mr. Willie Williams who, knowing that I had been in the tour business many years before, asked me if I would consider doing a tour to the Albert E. Brumley 3-day Gospel Quartet Sing in Springdale, Arkansas. I thought about it for a few minutes, checked with Neta Ruth, and said that we would do it.

Shortly after making the decision to do the tour to Arkansas, my sister, Gail, and I did a Gospel Concert in Windsor, Missouri, and while there I told a small audience we were going back into the tour business, with adults mainly this time, rather than high school seniors. I said if they would put their name and address on my little note pad, I would put them on a mailing list for "Richard's Fun-Time Tours."

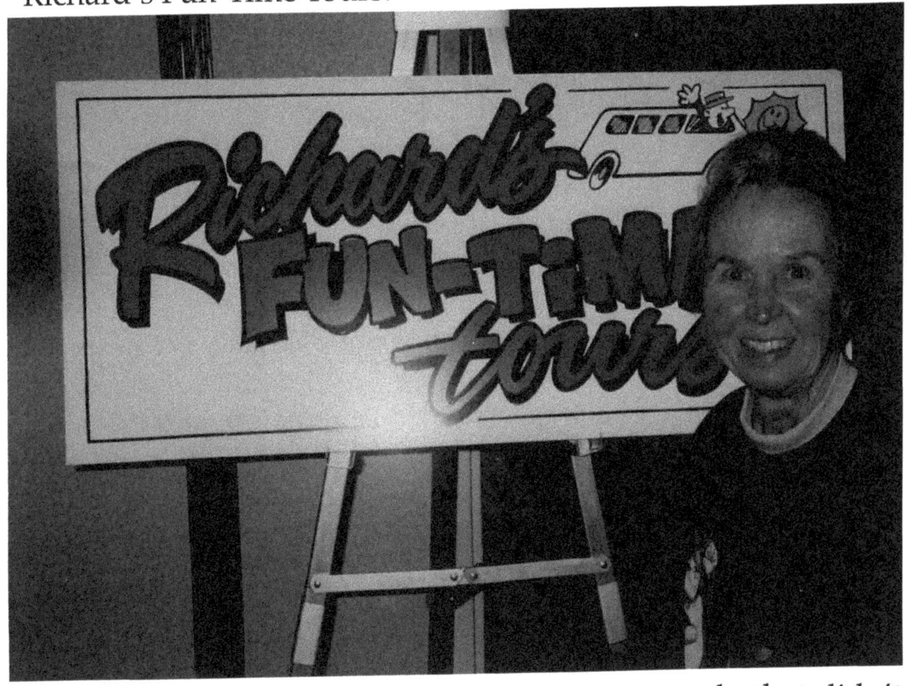

At that time, we planned to do 1 tour a month; that didn't work out the way we planned, because we were on the road constantly for the next 12 years. We were blessed with many wonderful folks who wanted to go around the world . . . and boy, did we ever do it. Wow! as mentioned, Neta Ruth and I continued to work together. She went with us on the tours she wanted to go on, and kept me in clothes and also another suitcase was always ready, so that I could come in at night and leave early the next morning on another tour.

Within a year we had taken quite a few tours, and had over 1,000 on our mailing list, as mentioned. We only really planned to do 10 or 12 tours a year; however, we ended up doing 30 to 40 tours each year thereafter. By the 10th year we had over 10,000 on our mailing list. We literally traveled all over the world. We did tours by bus, train, airplane, and, of course, cruise lines. We used Kincaid and Crossroads buses, and at times we had to use buses from other companies, in order to handle our volume. We used mostly Princess Cruises and Royal Caribbean. We never used newspaper, magazine, phone book or any other form of advertising except brochures directly to our own mailing list. This list was comprised of folks going with us, or their friends asking to be put on the list.

All of our tours were very popular. The most popular steady tours were the 'Short Mystery Tours' and the cruises. We never ceased being amazed at how our business grew. Some of our tours would leave home with anywhere from 150 to 250 on a waiting list. We were blessed with wonderful tour members, which will be our close personal friends for the balance of our lives. From the very beginning our method of operating was based on the 4 basic principles:

Give our tour members the lowest price possible, yet maintain quality.
Present the best sights and attractions, have the most fun, and tell the best stories within reason.
Never lie to any tour member or to our suppliers.
Love them to pieces, and listen to their funny stories.

Of course, the above principles could be, and should be, applied to any business operations.

"A Merry Heart Doeth Good
Like A Medicine"

Proverbs 17:22

Richard & Neta Ruth Sunderwirth

Every tour we took started off with prayer. After the prayer we sang this little song, ***"Oh what a beautiful morning; oh what a beautiful day. We've got a wonderful feeling, everything is going our way."*** If we didn't start with prayer and the little song, it just didn't seem right, so we made it happened on each tour.

At the close of every tour, about 15 minutes before arriving home, thanks to Roy Rogers and Dale Evans, we would sing, ***"Happy trails"*** and then finalize the tour; thanks to Carol Burnett, we would sing the song, ***"I'm so glad we had this time together."***

Richard with Roy Rogers

Tour member with Roy Rogers's Son ... Roy Dusty Rogers

Roy admires Osceola Cheese gift.

Most of the time during one or both of those songs, I would see a few tears trickle down most of the tour members faces. I would save mine until I was alone, on the way back to Osceola. We truly loved these people.

When we did our first adult tour with 2 buses, it was Neta Ruth and I, plus our drivers and a really good associate; her name was Ruth Grabb. She was one that we all grew to love and appreciate; she worked with us and stayed very active for the entire 10 years.

Another one that was with us quite a lot, and gave me the strength to hang in there when things might be a little crazy, was Willie Williams. It seemed like between he and Ruth Grabb, they knew almost every senior citizen in greater Kansas City area.

Willie was a lot of help; he was a great tour promoter and he thought everyone should go on "Richard's Fun-Time Tours." Neta Ruth and I became very close to Willie and his lovely wife, Aubrey, through the years. Willie was well liked wherever he was. He and Aubrey owned and operated KEXS Gospel radio station for many years. He was the host of the popular ***"Southern Gospel Time"*** TV show on Channel 50 in Kansas City, Mo. He and I worked together on a telethon or two. He also worked with the "Youth for Christ" organization, and that's just the beginning of his great ministry through-out Missouri.

As the years passed our business grew rapidly. We were working our fingers to the bone, it seemed, sometimes, but God always came through; help was just around the corner.

Our daughter, Laneta, and her husband, Rick Watts joined with us in 1994. They worked in the tour office, conducted tours as tour escorts and enhanced our operations, more than we could have ever imagined. They were a tremendous asset to the company. Everyone enjoyed them immensely. Rick and Laneta commented as follows:

"It's such a joy to see some of God's most beautiful creations with one of His greatest generations!"

"Hang Loose" the chicken, was our tour mascot. This chicken was a long skinny one, but some of our tour members, kept it dressed in a beautiful bright yellow pant suit. ***Through the 10 years it hung on the inside front windshield of the bus, and would change from side to side every time we stopped. By using this method "Hang Loose" would let us know which side was***

to get off the bus first. One side got off first and then the next side the next time. This worked pretty well for us; however, there was always someone yelling, "Richard, don't forget to change the chicken."

We found in the tour business we also used "Hang Loose" as an expression; like in Hawaii, the symbol means, don't worry, be carefree. In life, and on tours, sometimes the storm winds will blow. If you're rigid, and unbending, you'll break. If you'll take it easy and relax, everything will be alright, and will usually work out for the best . . . So, **EVERYBODY . . . HANG LOOSE!**

Neta Ruth probably worked as hard or harder than any of us. She worked in our office, drove shuttle buses to and from the departures and return trips, helped with escorting, kept Richard on the straight and narrow, baked cookies, and was known thru-out the tour company as: "THE STUFF WATCHER." She even had a gold badge with **Stuff Watcher** printed on it. It was an inside joke with all of us, but what that job meant saved many tour members from getting lost, and also saved stray hand-held pieces of luggage from being left behind. No one outside of the company had the foggiest notion of what it meant. If you ever come in contact with Neta Ruth, she just might tell you all about it.

This book contains MOST of the jokes, comments, articles, quips, and Inspirational material etc. that we used on the tours. Richard, Rick and Laneta were known for their ability to tell a funny story and they themselves started laughing even before the punch line. (**Neta Ruth would usually get to hear the new stories in advance and give her opinion whether they were OK to tell.)** Many stories and humorous bits and pieces of information came from our tour members, and sometimes, they were just a wee bit too explicit. That really made it rough on us, because we loved a good story, and we loved to pass them on . . . but, once in a while we couldn't do it. I usually had a list of new jokes for every tour. I think this book was meant to be, because; for all the years we were in business, I kept all the funny stories in a file.

BEING A TOUR OPERATOR IS NOT FOR EVERYONE

First of all it is a must that you love people and love to be around people.

You must be a person that is blessed with patience.

You must be willing to give of yourself and be more than willing to go the extra mile.
You will need specialized training in the travel industry.
You will need to learn the ways of the computer.
You must know or be willing to learn much about geography, history, accounting, communications, sales and general business management.
You must love to travel and enjoy getting up early and staying up late.
You must develop a good memory and know everything you can about your tour members, particularly their likes and dislikes.
You must be an organizer and be able to plan programs that will work and be able to judge time frames.
You must be able to anticipate what is coming and be able to adapt to any situation. You must be a problem solver. You must be able to negotiate well and be good in general purchasing.

You must always live by the 4 rules plan;

1. **GIVE THE TOUR MEMBER ALL YOU CAN GIVE THEM FOR THEIR MONEY.**
2. **GIVE THEM THE BEST TIME THEY'VE EVER HAD.**
3. **LOVE THEM NO MATTER WHAT.**
4. **NEVER LIE TO THEM**

If you can learn all of the above and like it . . . then you're on your way to becoming a GOOD tour operator. ***(RFS)***

FOOD FOR THOUGHT

(Ten Commandments, For All Travelers)

1. Thou shall not expect to find things precisely as they are at home . . . for thou hast left home to find things different.
2. Thou shall not take anything too seriously, for a carefree mind is a basis for a good vacation.
3. Thou shalt not let other tour members get on thy nerves . . . for thou art paying good money to enjoy thyself.
4. Thou shalt not worry . . . he that worries hath little joy and the tour hast an escort to do that for you.
5. Thou shalt not judge all the people of a country or area by one person with whom thou hast had a problem.
6. Blessed are they who hunger and thirst for a short period of time . . . for the waitress is busy and we are a large group.

7. Thou shalt rotate thy seat . . . all of God's creatures have the right to be first. 8. Blessed are those who can wait and smile for they shall surely enjoy themselves. 9. Thou are welcome in every place . . . treat they host with respect and thou shall be an honored guest. 10. Bless thy escort and driver for surely they deserve it.

Written by a tour member

***

THE TOUR MEMBERS'S PRAYER

Heavenly Father, look down on your humble tour member who travels this earth mailing postcards, walking around in drip-dry underwear, carrying armfuls of souvenirs, and looking for the john.

We beseech you that our bus be on time, that we receive our very own luggage, and that our overweight luggage go unnoticed, and the ones that carry it be very understanding, especially when they win the hernia award.

Dear Lord, we pray for our safety on this entire tour; that the phones work, there is no mail waiting from home causing us to cancel the rest of our trip, and Oh Lord, please let the ice machines work; the pop machines give us our change, and please Lord . . . no stairs. Oh, by the way, with regard to the ice machines; make certain we don't have to walk very far to get ice, but we want them far enough away so that when someone else is getting ice we can't hear the noise.

Lead us to good quality inexpensive restaurants, where the tips are included in the price of the meal and the coffee is not too strong to drink. Dear Lord, I mean the meals that we have to pay for ourselves while on the trip. The included meals should be in really nice places, with fantastic gourmet meals. Maybe even a little out the ordinary.

Give us strength to visit museums and theatres and cathedrals, and allow us to have that long afternoon nap yet, Oh Lord, make certain that we miss absolutely nothing . . . and please, please, we really do prefer, at all theatres, to sit in the center section at about the 4th row back . . . and oh yes, we all want the end seat, of course . . . only if you see fit.

Let us never say an unkind word, but also have mercy on us for our flesh is weak, especially that which is just below the nose.

Protect our wives from bargains they cannot afford. Lead them not into temptation for they know not what they do.

Keep our husbands from looking at beautiful women and comparing them to us. Save our husbands from making fools of them-selves wherever they go, and please do not forgive them their trespasses for they, in this situation, know EXACTLY what they do.

And, oh Father, when our tour is over, please grant us the favor of finding some poor soul who will look at our photographs, videos, and listen to our stories. We ask all this in the name of Wal-Mart, Shoney's Inns, Master Card, Visa and the government of this land.

Amen and Amen !

One Big Tour Party . . . Every year at the University

Every year we had a "Thank You" party for our tour members in Hendrick's Hall at Central Missouri State University in Warrensburg, Missouri. The building would seat 1,400 people, so we had to make the stipulation that the first 1,400 tour members that showed up could come in. A few more could have been squeezed in but the fire marshal said, "No." We had a 3 hour show that was always pretty good.

We brought in David Sandy's Magic Production; The Blackwood Brothers Gospel Quartet; several comedians from Branson and Lake of the Ozarks, Missouri; Dr. Carl Hurley, "America's Funniest Professor" from Lexington, KY; a special attraction from the Wisconsin Dells area; the Barbara Fairchild Show, and many other top notch acts from around the country. Our family usually helped with entertainment as well. My sister, Gail Ingle, was always faithful on the grand piano and helped in other ways also. My brother, Jim, was a guest artist at times. Other friends from Osceola and the Kansas City area also helped us. Over the years it became a great production, and we always had full houses every year, I truly believe everyone had a good time.

During the evening we would call many of our tour members to the stage and give out special awards and would also give away about $3,000 in prizes by winning tickets. Richard, Neta

Richard & Neta Ruth Sunderwirth

Ruth, Rick and Laneta Watts, Gail Ingle, J.R. Leiber, my two small grandchildren, Rylee and Race, my brother, Jim Sunderwirth helped with the party. Neta Ruth even came up with a blond wig and tried to be my 30 year old blonde for the evening. I used the 30 year old blonde in many of my stories. Even, once in a while, we'd have an extra special attraction that would steal the show.

Chicken Side off first...

Richard and Neta Ruth's Grand Children

We would talk about new tours. Willie Williams would open the event with prayer, and then we'd be off and running until about 10:30 p.m. It was a nice party and everyone always seemed to have a great time of fun and fellowship. In addition to all the

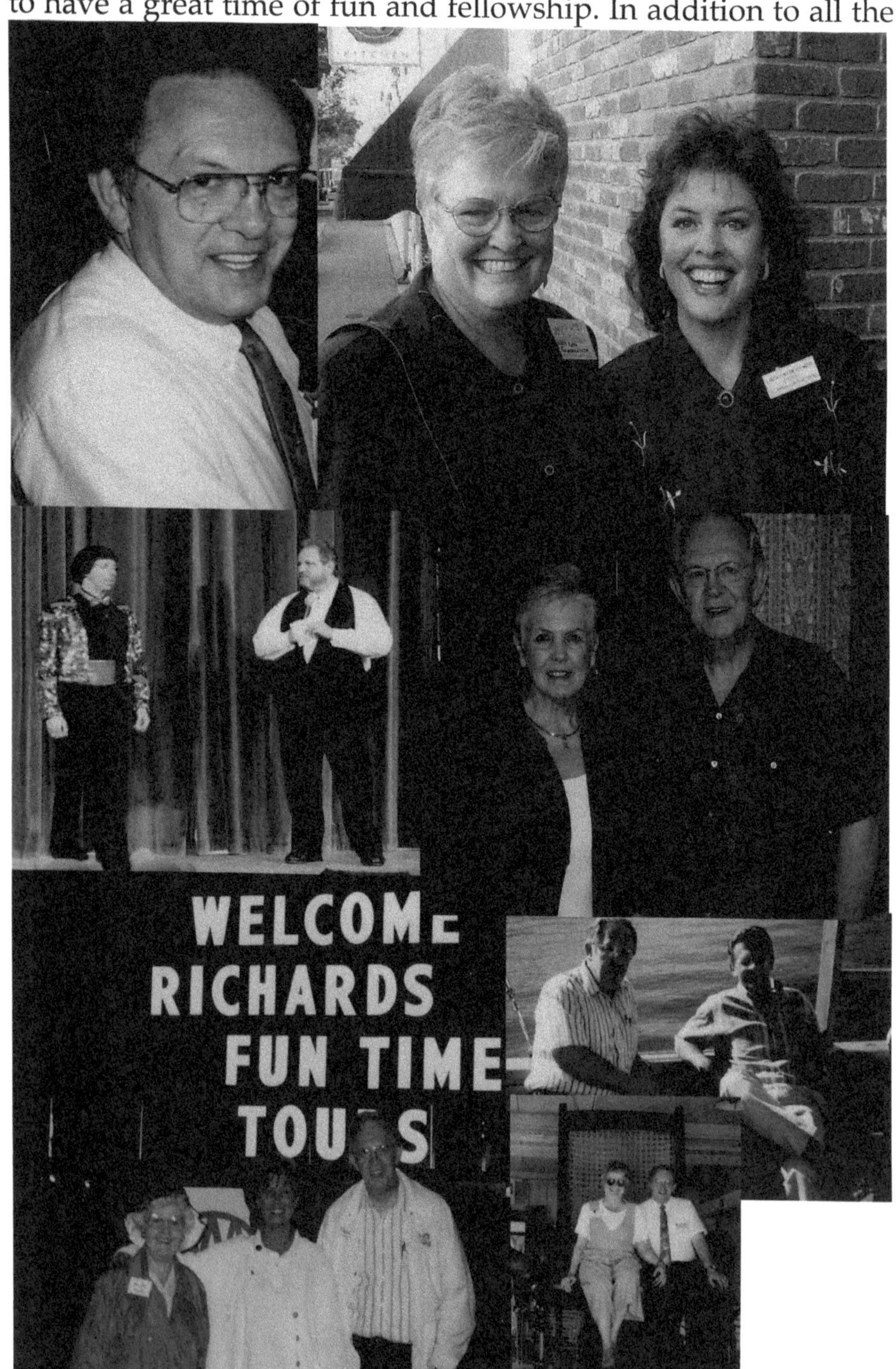

cars parked everywhere we usually had 8 or 9 big buses lined up and down the streets, and, of course, we always tried to have the best drivers that we could possibly get. Most of these drivers all became very personal friends, as well as great drivers.

One of the great highlights of our tours was the "Cavalcade of Comedy" featuring Carl Hurley and Jeanne Robertson. Richard's Fun-Time Tours always attended their live productions, wherever they were held each year. We also, on every tour, used their DVD productions, as TV comedy entertainment, when we traveled along between major sightseeing events.

If you want great, hilarious, good-natured comedy for your tours, or for personal comedy of Carl or Jeanne at home contact: Mike McKinney at McKinney Associates, P.O. Box 5162, Louisville, KY 40255-0162. Or preferably, if you need a good laugh really quick, get in touch with Mike on your computer; www.carlhurley.com or www.mckinneyspeakers.com **"YOU WILL NOT BE DISAPPOINTED!"**

We operated "Richard's Fun-Time Tours" until 2000. We sold the tour company to Terry Kohnz who was one of our associates that handled all of our airline travel each year, and many other operations of the tour company. He works hard and is dedicated to see that you have a great tour at a fair price. As of the publication date of this book Mr. and Mrs. Terry Kohnz are going strong in their company now called "FUN-TIME TOURS" and would be more than happy to include you as a new tour traveler. They can be reached at: Mr. Terry Kohnz, "Fun-Time Tours", P.O. Box 387, Waterloo, IL 62298, or 1-800-315-1386. **Get in touch today, for the latest "Fun-Time Tours" brochures.**

I worked for Terry a couple of years after selling the business to him. Rick and Laneta also worked with Terry for a period of time after Terry began operations.

After retirement I went to work with Sheldon's Funeral Home in Osceola, Mo. While working with Sheldon's Funeral Home, I worked, for a period of time, as supervisor in charge of training in 5 Missouri counties, for the United States Census Bureau.

Also during my retirement years I did CD and DVD duplication in addition to filming 85 local Senior Citizens of which most had been born in the area. Each film was approximately one hour in duration. I love to remember and benefit from the knowledge of our blessed senior citizens. They have so much information and most of the time they are willing to share it with anyone who will request it. I always try to treat them with the dignity they deserve.

We sincerely hope that you enjoy this book. It has certainly been a pleasure traveling with all the wonderful people that we have worked with and have known through the years in the tour business. They are the ones that made it all happen.

ONE MORE IMPORTANT THING

I'm sure there are a few stories that could possibly be a little offensive to some readers. If so, I'm extremely sorry if in any way I've offended you by putting them in this book. It's amazing how many have been given to me, through the years, which I have chosen to leave out. One or two or three, may have slipped through. I have always enjoyed telling a good, funny story!

As I previously mentioned; it was amazing how many really funny stories were given to me by tour members, that in no way I could tell on the bus. And they knew that when they gave them to me. Once in a while when they were on board I would, for a few moments, pretend I was going to tell one, and, oh my, would they ever squirm. I was getting back at them for giving me a story they knew I could not repeat.

Richard & Neta Ruth Sunderwirth

In Loving Memory

Richard Wayne Sunderwirth Born 1959 - Passed 2005
Richard Dobin (Scoop) Sunderwirth
Born 1985 - Passed 2001

We thought of you today, but that's really nothing new. We thought of you yesterday and the days before that too. We think of you in silence; we often speak you names. We have our precious memories; your photos in our frames. Our love for both of you; from which we'll never part. We know God has you in his arms, we hold you in our hearts.

Richard Dobin (Scoop) Sunderwirth 1985-2001 Grand Son	Richard Wayne Sunderwirth 1959-2005 Son

Chicken Side off first...

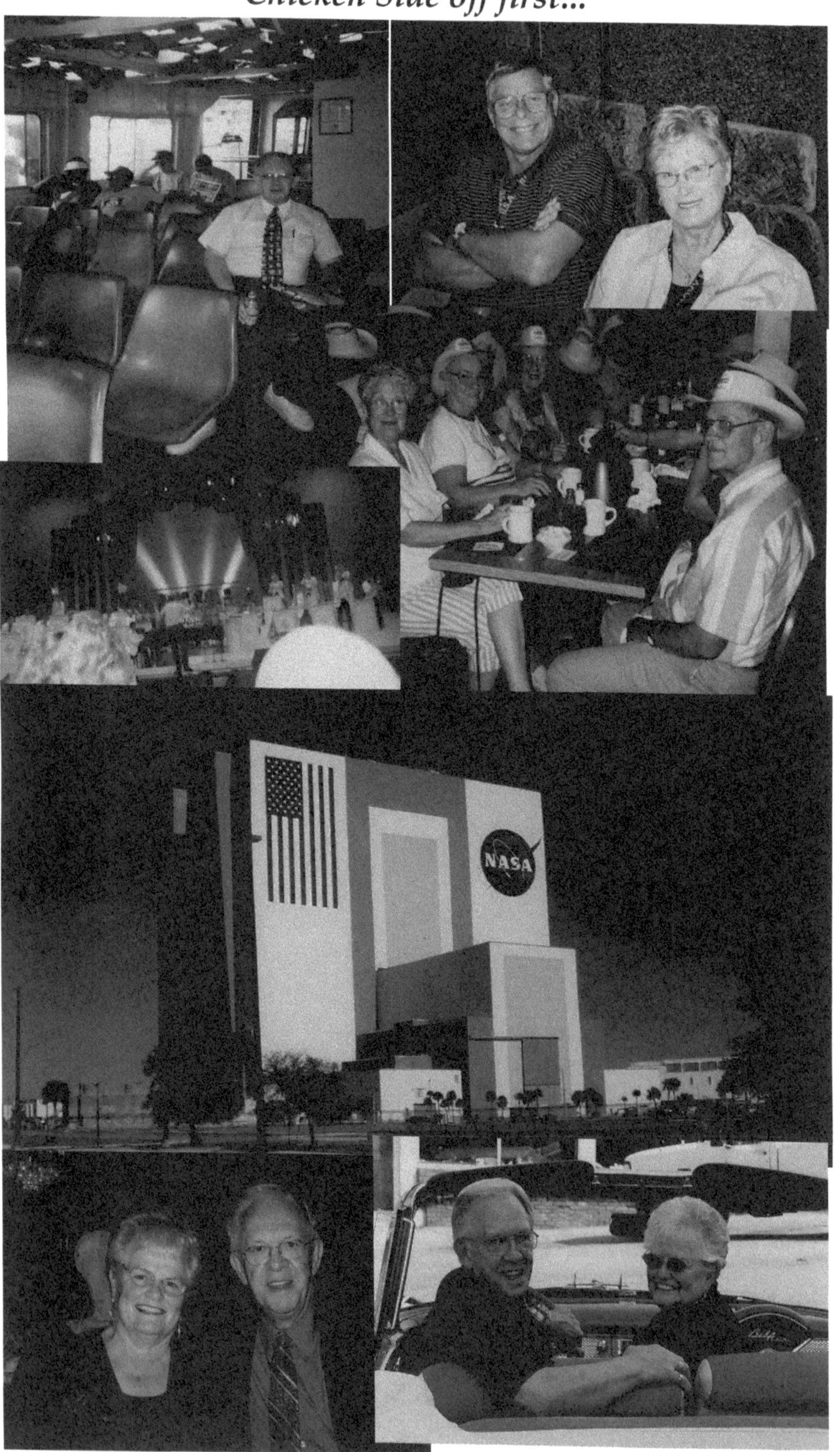

Richard & Neta Ruth Sunderwirth

"Around the world . . . with God's finest folks!"

By: Rick and Laneta Watts

To begin this segment from my husband, Rick and myself, (Laneta, daughter of Richard and Neta Ruth), we want to say a big **THANK YOU** to those of you who were part of our 8 ½ years with Richard's Fun-Time Tours. What a time we had, touring around the world with some of God's finest folks. You were a blessing to us then, and many of you are still in touch with us today. Words cannot express the blessing you are to us. There are others, who didn't have the opportunity to travel with us, but have become friends through other encounters. Blessings are on you as well. If we haven't met, I feel we'll soon know each other through the joy of this book.

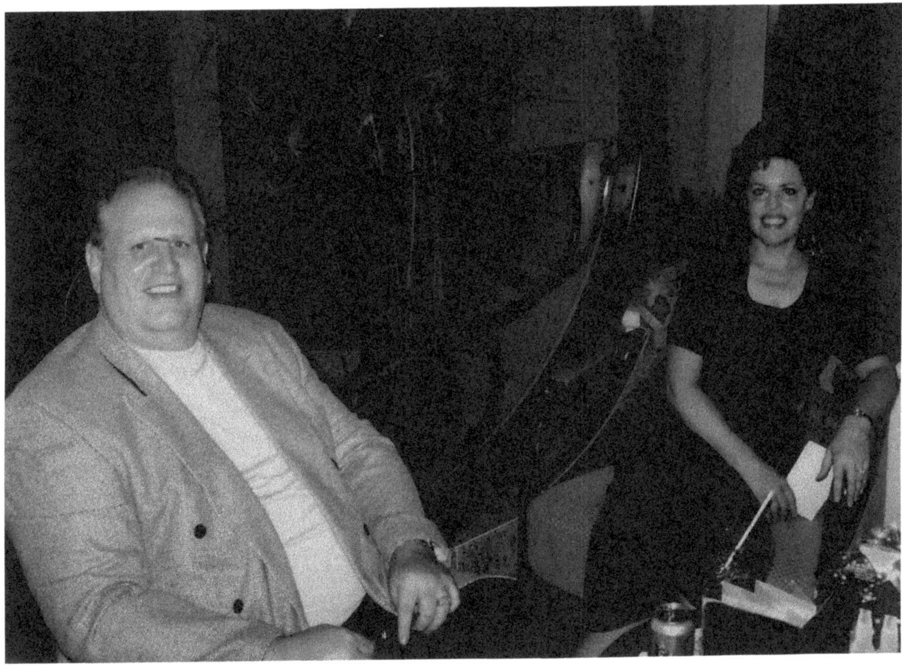

I began as a tour escort with much trepidation. You see, my father is the best tour guide in the world. I believed it then, in 1994, and still believe it today. You also knew he was the best, and I knew you felt that way, proving it by your actions of going on trip after trip with us. I did not want anyone disappointed that I was going to be the tour guide, so I endeavored to be a 'little Richard.'

I couldn't be just like him, of course, though people have told me we are a lot alike . . . while I can't carry as heavy a suitcase, the traveling days certainly made me expand my joke repertoire. I finally quit telling any great, new funny story I heard, to Mom & Dad. I wanted the opportunity to tell it on the bus first!

And you, cream of the crop people, made it so easy. My hubby told me to 'just be myself' and that you would love me, and he was right. Having been used to THE BEST on the tours, you gave us a chance, accepted, trusted, loved us, and didn't we have fun? Whether it was touring a place you'd waited a lifetime to visit, or waiting in line 20 deep for the restroom, we were laughing, enjoying life together.

My 'entertainment' portion on the bus finally evolved into not quite so much joke telling, but reading uplifting stores, poems and presenting the occasional brain teaser. Rick rarely told a story, but when he did, it was usually an event in itself. A friend who lives in Osceola still mentions one story of Rick's any time we meet. Oh, the memories. **The next 4 or 5 pages of memorable material, is just some of what we shared along the way.**

***

A young girl, Sally, went to school one day and the teacher told the class that she wanted the children to tell what their father did for a living and then they would discuss it. She called on Sally to begin. Sally stood at the front of the class and announced "My father is a popcorn salesman." The teacher said "That's good, Sally, Can you spell that for us?" Sally hesitantly said "P O O P," and the teacher stopped her and said, "No, that's not right, Sally. Please think about it and begin again." Sally thought and thought and even more slowly began, "P O   O P," and again the teacher stopped her. Sally waited a bit more, and began once again , "P O . . . and finally a little boy at the back of the room slammed his hand on the desk and said, "My father's a bookie and I'll lay you 3 to 1 odds she's going to spell POOP again!

***

A little boy walked down on the beach, and as he did, he spied a matronly woman sitting under a beach umbrella on the sand. He walked up to her and asked, "Are you a Christian?" "Yes," she replied. "Do you read your Bible every day?" She nodded her head, "Yes." "Do you pray often?" the boy asked next, and again she answered, "Yes." With that he asked his final question, "Will you hold my quarter while I go swimming?"

***

Mother mouse said to baby mouse when they saw a cat, "BARK, BARK!" Now honey, see how important it is to know a foreign language!"

***

A traveling salesman's car broke down. He saw a farm in the distance and asked the lady of the house if he could stay the night. She answered "Yes, but I must tell you, we have no daughters, no animals and my husband and I have a wonderful marriage." The traveling salesman said, "Oh, sorry. I must be in the wrong joke."

***

A young man felt called to be a monk. After reporting to the monetary the head monk informed him of the rules. "Here we enjoy the beauty of silence. Every 10 years you will be permitted to say 2 words." 10 years went by. The new monk was called in and given the opportunity to speak his 2 words. "Cold food," and then went on about his business. Another 10 years passed and it was time for his 2 words. "Hard bed," he spoke and continued on. 10 more years passed and once again he was given the opportunity to speak. Without hesitation he said, "I quit!"

***

An elderly lady liked sitting at the park feeding the pigeons. One day she brought with her a whole loaf of bread to feed her daily company. She fed each pigeon with joy. Suddenly a man rained on her parade by telling her that she shouldn't throw away good food on a bunch of pigeons when there are a lot of people starving in Africa. Without hesitation she snapped back at him. "Well you dummy, I can't throw that far!"

***

Two old men were visiting on the front porch. A frog hopped up and said, "Kiss me and I'll turn into a beautiful princess and be yours forever." The old man picked up the frog and put it in his pocket and said to his friend, "At my age I'll have a lot more fun with a talking frog!"

***

Did you hear about the poor snakes that were jealous of their hoity, toity snake neighbors? They were overheard saying, "I remember when they didn't have a pit to hiss in!"

***

Man to wife; "You've been with me when I had my car wreck, when I lost my job, my cancer . . . now that I think about it, you're bad luck!"

***

A drunk stumbles into a confessional booth. The priest keeps knocking on the door. Finally the drunk says, "There's no use to keep knocking. There's no toilet paper in here either."

***

The man who can smile when things go wrong has already thought of someone he can blame it on.

***

Retirement: Twice as much husband, one half as much money

***

Troublemaker: A guy that rocks the boat then persuades everyone else there is a storm at sea.

***

A miser isn't much fun to live with, but makes a wonderful ancestor!

***

Work for the Lord: The pay may not always be great, but the retirement plan is 'out of this world!'

***

There are some people you hate to take advice from because they seem to need it so badly themselves.

***

The following is a poem, and song, that folks always seem to enjoy!

I've never made a fortune and it's probably too late now, but I don't worry about that much, I'm happy anyhow. As I go along life's journey I'm reaping better than I sowed. I'm drinking from my saucer 'cause my cup has overflowed.'

Ain't got a lot of riches, sometimes the goings rough, but I got 2 kids that love me, that makes me rich enough. I just thank God for their blessings, and the mercy He has bestowed, I'm drinking from my saucer 'cause my cup has overflowed.'

And I remember times when things went wrong, and my faith got a little thin, but then all at once the dark clouds broke and the old sun broke through again. So Lord, help me not to gripe, about the rough row I had hoed. I'm drinking from my saucer 'cause my cup has overflowed.'

And if God gives me strength and courage, when the way gets steep and rough, I won't ask for other blessings, I'm already blessed enough. And may I never be too busy, to help another bear his load. Then I'll keep drinking from my saucer 'cause my cup has overflowed.'

***

And now, for a few of Rick's stories.

There once was a man visiting a very famous, large, fancy resort. He was having a wonderful time, but this particular day woke up not feeling well. He had to stay close to the restroom for several hours, then felt he'd be OK to go exploring around the hotel. He was wrong. Within a few minutes he again desperately needed a bathroom, but couldn't locate one. He asked and received directions to, "go down this long hallway, turn to the left, go about halfway down the corridor and take a right, go just a little ways and you'll see some steps. Go up the steps, then go down another hallway eventually curving to the left and then back to the right, and just a few steps further and you'll see the restroom." He had only gone a few steps when he couldn't hold back any longer. He was so sick. Finally he made it down the hall to the left, to the right, up the steps, another hallway to the left and to the fight, and finally, in the door of the fancy bathroom. After a short time there was a knock at the door. "Yes, may I help you?" he asked. "Hello, I'm the head bellhop and Mr. Johnson sent me to tell you to not worry about a thing. I've cleaned up behind you, down the long hallway, to the left, to the right, up the steps, on the next hallway and to the left and to the right. Mr. Johnson sent some clothing for you and I am to take yours to be cleaned. Mr. Johnson says we understand that this could happen to anyone. Mr. Johnson says we so appreciate your patronage through the years and hopes you won't be embarrassed and will return with your family again and again. Mr. Johnson says we'll have your clothing returned good as new this evening. Mr. Johnson hopes you'll be feeling better soon, and again, please do not feel any embarrassment. That's what Mr. Johnson says. I say; next time you get sick with diarrhea, STAND STILL!"

"This could be embarrassing. Beware of Mr. Johnson!"

(Part of the reason Rick's stories were so funny was that he embellished them. When he had the sick man looking for a bathroom, he had the poor guy going up and down and around corners, and well, it would have had to been a LARGE hotel similar to the Grand Hotel on Mackinaw Island. And the bell-hop, he spoke with a speech impediment and got very animated when he said, "That's what Mr. Johnson said!" It's one of those 'you need to be there' to get the full effect, but definitely memorable.)

***

(One of Ralph's favorites (Ralph was our main bus driver) was a true story that happened to Rick's grandparents.) Grandpa had false teeth, but didn't like to wear them. Granny decided to pull a prank one day. She had found another pair of dentures somewhere and switched them with the ones Grandpa had soaking. Then she popped popcorn, knowing that was one time Grandpa always put his dentures in. Sure enough, the smell of popcorn woke Grandpa from his nap and he stumbled in to the bathroom and put in his dentures. He entered the kitchen with a funny look on his face, working his jaw around this way and that. Finally he said, "Osta, I think I've had a stroke." It finally dawned on him a prank had been played. He said, "That Mack." Mack was rick's dad, and as far as we know Rick's Grandfather never did know that Granny is the one who switched the teeth.

***

One more, and even if you're heard this joke before please read to the end. We were in the town of Fredericksburg, Texas. We always told the people that it was a good place and the right time of year to buy nuts, and we'd point out some places to purchase them. When everyone was back on the bus getting ready to depart Rick decided he'd tell a 'nut' story. "There was an old, old man who crippled up to the druggist to order an ice cream sundae. The young lady looked at him and asked, "Crushed nuts?" and he replied, "No, arthritis." That's the way the story is supposed to go. Rick got it turned around. "The young lady asked, "Arthritis?" And the old man said, "No, Crushed Nuts?" I was in the back of the bus and hollered to Rick, "No, no. You reversed the punch-line." Meanwhile it was pandemonium in the bus. At our next rest-stop, a gentleman that had been with us on many trips, handed Rick a $20^{00} bill and said that was because he hadn't laughed like that in a long time, and that was the best he had ever heard that story!

***

I hope you've enjoyed some of our reminiscing of wonderful times together. We would like to give a quick update of what's happening in our lives. Many of you have prayed for us through many years of Rick's undiagnosed health problems. And so many sent encouraging cards our way. Thank you, thank you, thank you; Rick has been steadily getting stronger for about the last 6 or 7 years. He had a radio program for a little over 2 years called "Man in the Middle." He's not broadcasting at present, but has been concentrating on building a website, that as you are aware, can reach all around the world. The website is almost finished. There will be audio, pictures, articles, a place to post prayer requests, music and interviews with various characters. Everybody has a story, and it's so interesting and encouraging to hear what God has done and is doing in the lives of those around us. You can find us on the internet maninthemiddle.org We would appreciate your logging on and telling your friends about the site so they can log on also.

Remember that, "A merry heart doeth good like a medicine." It truly, truly does. Thanks for being such wonderful friends. May God richly bless you and yours.

Rick and Laneta Watts

***

"A few of our most cherished incidents . . . that happened on our tours."

(Most of the personal names have been changed to protect the innocent . . . and the guilty.)

One morning about 5:30 a.m., my phone rang and it was one of our nice tour ladies. She was frantic; she said, "Oh Richard I'm really in trouble. I thought my eyes were getting a bit weak last evening but I never thought my eyes would get this bad this quick. I replied, "What is going on." She said, "I got up early; drank one cup of coffee and then I put my glasses on and everything is worse than without the glasses. Really I can't see worth a crap, I don't know what I'm going to do. I may have to go home; I can't go on like this." I asked her, "Myrtle, where is your roommate?" "She's taking a shower, and I didn't want to bother her." I looked through her glasses and "Wow", they were as strong as I've ever see. Well, about that time her roommate started to come out from the shower area, and as she started through the door she saw me and said, "I'm so glad you are here, by the way, why are you here so early in the morning? I said, Myrtle called me and told me she thought she was going blind. About that time Maggie put on her glasses and said, "My gosh, I'm in trouble too, maybe we'd better call the office and tell them that there is some kind of something in this room that has affected our eyes." I thought maybe I knew the answer because this same thing has happened before. I said, "Why don't you switch glasses and see what happens. Maggie said, "No need doing that because these are my glasses. I talked them into switching glasses and everything was back to normal. Their glasses were exactly the same design and color and they just knew for sure it wasn't that . . . but it was. In one tenth of a second everything was back to normal.

***

On one of our tours to London a tour member asked me this question. I'm sure she was serious about it so I didn't make a joke out of it; I didn't want to embarrass her in front of the group. She asked me if we had time could we stop to see the pyramids while we were there, and on which day of our tour would it be open. I don't remember, for sure, what I told her, but we managed not to get anywhere near Egypt. She was satisfied when I told her we would definitely see them if at all possible. I got through it without a lie or with her being disappointed.

***

Most of the breakfast meals were included at the motels. When we stayed at a nice new hotel usually I provided a regular American buffet breakfast. Well, the day before this particular incident, I told the group that we would not have a normal motel provided breakfast. I told them that we had included something special, since they had all been so good and behaved themselves. Well, this particular lady happened to be one that did quite a lot of talking, a lot of the time. So, she missed the part where I told them to be in the restaurant at a certain time and enjoy the included big meal. The next morning I was loading luggage and I met her in the hall. I ask her if she was going to enjoy our breakfast. Knowing that we did not have the normal motel breakfast included, here is what she said to me. "Oh no, Richard, I'm just not really hungry this morning; I've been eating so much I think I'll just skip breakfast today." I knew, from that remark, she had missed my instructions, so I replied to her, "Mrs. Paddlefish, you really don't want to miss this one. We have a full American buffet included today, not the normal motel type breakfast, but a really great one." "You probably didn't catch what I said last evening on the bus. You'd better get in there and help yourself." She said, "Oh no, I'm really not too hungry." I went back up the hall and stopped and peeked around the corner and then slowly went back after a couple of minutes, and stuck my head in the door, and told the folks we'd be having a little bit of a late lunch. (I'd already told them that, but I wanted to verify what I thought would happen.) I met her as she cleared the end of the buffet line and, you wouldn't believe it, but she had enough food on two plates that looked a lot like 2 satellite dishes. She looked me straight in the eye, and said, "I changed my mind, have you had your meal yet? It sure looks good doesn't it?" I said, "You have a good day now." I just kinda giggled to myself and finished taking the luggage to the bus. I didn't even go back to see if she had the third plate. In spite of that little blunder, she was really a sweet lady.

***

Ralph Sullivan was our steady bus driver for 9 years. He was really a good driver and liked by all who knew him. He passed away in 2011 and it was a shock to everyone. He was still young and still had many miles in him, but the Lord called him home.

One day he asked me, "Richard, sometimes I have really good tips and then sometimes they are really bad; do you have any idea what causes this? I replied rather bluntly, "Well Ralph, I think once in a while you say something that maybe upsets our folks a bit. I heard you tell a lady a couple of weeks ago, that she looked like she was gaining weight. That's not a good thing to do." "I didn't really mean it," he said. "Yes, I replied, "but she didn't know that, and it might have offended her, and she told the others and they all cut back a little on their tip. We have to be really careful and not say things that might be taken the wrong way." The next week I met the bus; Ralph got off the bus and we greeted each other, and about that time two of our tour ladies drove up and got out of their car. The ladies started toward the bus and Ralph, trying to be really nice helped them with their luggage, and then trying to be complimentary went over to one of them and said, "It's a good morning; it is good to see you, and you don't look near as fat as you did on the last trip." Well, once again that didn't help his situation. Thank goodness, most of the times; however, his tips were good and he really did appreciate them.

***

I probably have already mentioned this somewhere in this book, but just in case I haven't, here it is again. Every once in a while we would get a letter like this and it would just really make us laugh. The letter would go kinda like this; we enjoyed the last trip, we really had fun, etc. Then close to the end they would write, if for some reason you don't get this letter please let us know and we'll send you another one because we really want to get on the mystery trip or whatever tour they had in mind. We got quite a few similar to that one, but here's the one that took the cake; I think we even saved this one. I intended to send a deposit for the (whatever tour), but I'd already sealed the envelope so, go ahead and put me down for (whatever tour), and I'll send you the money next week. Thanks a lot.

***

Our first night out was in Memphis, TN. I handed out the room keys; then I started to help with the luggage. One 30 year old blonde came running up behind me and said, "Richard, come here quick and check my room; there is a man sleeping in my bed." I said, "Oh Hilda, you must have gone to the wrong room." She, in an instant replied, "Well, if that is true, how come my key worked?" That was a pretty good thought to bring up, so I said, "Let's go to your room and see what we can do." On the way back around to the other side of the corridor she said to me, "Richard, I'll tell you one thing; if he gets to stay then I want one also." I think she was kidding, but she sure sounded like she meant it. We got it all straightened out, and neither one of them got the fellows.

***

We spent two nights on this tour in Biloxi, Mississippi. Everything went well through the evening; however, the next morning Sarah met me at breakfast and said, "Richard, can you move me a little closer to the ice machine? Last night, and the two nights before, I've been all the way at the other end of the hall, and it's a long ways to walk." I said, "Well Sarah, if they have an extra room and if we can get it switched I'll sure take care of that for you." Guess who met me at breakfast the next morning? Sarah said, "I wish I'd stayed where I was. I didn't have to walk very far to the ice machine, but I just barely got a wink of sleep. Every time someone got ice, it sounded like a freight train, CLUNK, CLUNK, CLUNK. "I stuck my head out the door once and told them to hold their bucket under the ice when it dropped. Well, that was even worse; the empty bucket made more noise than when the ice dropped all the way to the bottom of the machine." I think every night from then to the end of the tour I just simply gave her a room away from the ice machine and everything was fine from that point forward.

***

In the early years of our senior class tours, on the Gulf Coast and New Orleans tour, we would always spend Monday evening at the Roosevelt Hotel in New Orleans, Louisiana. As one of our attractions, we would always go to the beautiful Blue Room dinner & show lounge while there. Many folks around the nation would listen to WWL radio, which played live music from the Blue Room. It was called "Leon Keltner," and his fabulous Blue

Room orchestra, live from the Roosevelt Hotel in downtown New Orleans.

Upon arriving in town, I would get off the bus, while the group was doing the city tour, with a special local guide, and check to make certain everything was set for that evening dinner and show. The second time I was in New Orleans, I got a bright idea, and believe it or not it worked. I would meet with the manager of the show lounge and find out who was going to be our special evening entertainment. The first time it happened to be Jimmy Durante. I obtained his room number from the Blue Room manager, and gave him a call. (Security in those days was nothing like it is today.) I told him I was a tour director from Missouri, and I had a senior class bus tour and would be coming to the evening show. Sometimes we would have as few as 1 bus and other times we would have as many as 8 buses at a time. I needed all the help I could get to make me appear to know a few special people, along the way, so I asked Mr. Durante if sometime during the show he would come over to our group of tables and pretend he had known me for quite a while and I him. He appeared to like the idea and right in the middle of the show he stopped, and made his way over. Well, that went over really good and I was "King Kong" for the rest of the tour. I did that every Monday evening during the entire spring touring season. I was blessed to meet and visit with Jimmy Durante, Mitzi Gaynor, Les Paul & Mary Ford, Dick Shawn, Vaughn Monroe and many others during those years of touring with the seniors and their sponsors. This was just a typical adventure that I was always getting into, and for a young whippersnapper, I was making a little money, doing a lot of traveling and having a ball.

***

On our Gulf Coast tour which included Pensacola, Florida we took the time to spend most of one afternoon at the beach. On this tour since 95% were senior citizens they were happy to be able to pull off their shoes, roll up their slacks, and spend an hour or so walking on the beach, picking up shells, and wading in the beautiful blue gulf water. When we arrived I would give them their instructions, departure time, etc. and then I would get my shoes off and roll up my britches, even before they were all off the motor coach. I told them that I was meeting a couple of my good friends and when they were ready, come on down to the water's edge, and I would introduce them and they could take a photo of my friends and me to put in their scrapbook.

Now here is what I never told them; however, they probably figured it out in a few minutes. When they arrived it was fun watching the expression on their faces when they saw me with my arms around two beautiful girls in very skimpy bathing suits. What I would do was quickly get to the beach, and since it was usually spring break somewhere, there were always a large number of girls to choose from, that would go along with an old fat ugly tour director's request. I would select 2 of the prettiest girls I could find and tell them what I wanted, and they would always go along with the joke. I would stand between the two of them, with my arms around their waist and be visiting with them, like I'd known them for years, when my group arrived. The lady tour members would get a kick out of taking our pictures and telling me they were going to send them home to my wife. After everyone had seen us and had the photos they wanted, I would bid the girls farewell and then we would go on with our fun in the water. The girls would walk away and usually be laughing at what had just happened. Just another day in the life of a tour director.

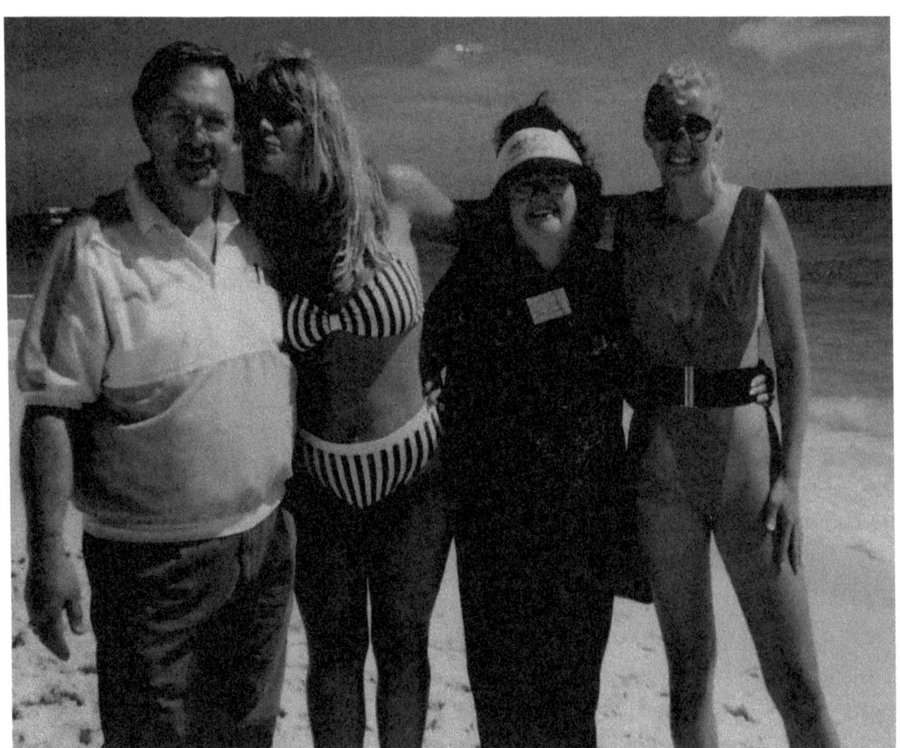

Richard & Neta Ruth Sunderwirth

***

On one of our tours to Israel we were standing in front of where the guide was telling us all about David's tomb. After his presentation he asked if anyone in our group had a question. One of our ladies spoke up and said, "Yes, I have a question. Who is buried in David's tomb?" Politely he responded, "Well, there was King David, and many other well-known folks of the day." She was happy with that and away we went on to the next site.

***

On another tour of Israel we had just arrived in Jerusalem to begin our touring. The first night one of our nice ladies forgot to set her alarm with the new time change. At midnight the alarm went off. She got out of bed without waking her husband and took a shower, fixed her hair, put on her makeup, had a cup of coffee, and then woke her husband. He looked at her with a puzzled look and said, "Hey, what in the world are you out of bed all dressed and ready to go for?" She said, "Well, you'd better get up and ready yourself because we have breakfast in about 30 minutes." He got up; looked at his watch, which had the correct time, and said, "Oh, my goodness, go back to bed; you're up about 6 hours too early." "She was so upset she just stayed up the rest of the night and made the best of it. She was really tired that day. You'll never guess what happened the next night. She did exactly the same thing; however, she realized it without waking her husband. She didn't want to tell him so she just stayed up again for the rest of the night and, I think she said she read a book. I don't know whether she got much out of the next touring day or not. I was afraid to ask her.

***

My wife almost killed one of our tour escorts. We had two buses and the tour escort on the other bus was a feller. We were in Florida at Silver Springs, and while there we attended the Ross Allen reptile farm and show. He milked the rattlesnakes. He went through quite a bit of dialog and played around with these huge snakes before he started milking them. Almost everyone, including my wife, wouldn't even get close to the area with the snakes, but close enough to see what he was doing. The other escort picked up a really big rubber toy snake and just as Mr. Allen started doing the milking he threw the rubber snake around her neck. She went into a panic attack; started swinging her arms and we came very close to having a murder right there in front of our entire group of tour members. I don't know for sure what she said to him, but I'll guarantee he never ever even considered doing that again. Yes, just another day in the life of touring.

***

We did quite a number of cruises around the world. We always had enough people in our group to have our own private welcome party. We would serve all types of soft beverages, and lots of different snacks. Well, I'd done this enough times, even though we had a big private sign at both entrances to our party, to know we'd have usually 12 to 15 other cruise members come in and join us. I guess they figured we wouldn't notice them and they'd get in on the free stuff. I really didn't care if they came in, but I had a funny thing planned for them. Our tour members all knew what I was going to do and they could hardly wait until I went into action. About 10 minutes after they came in, and before they got up to serve themselves to the goodies, I would get up in front of the whole group and say, "Good evening everybody; I'm so glad you could all make it to our "Richard's Fun-Time Tours" welcome aboard party. Before we get started with all the prizes and special things for y'all, I want to take about an hour and tell you what Amway has done for me." **(Now, I don't want to get in trouble with our Amway friends, so I'll say they really do have good products.)** Anyway our tour members, at this point, would be beginning to breakout in a big laughing spasm. What was really funny was watching our party breakers slowly rise and sorta shuffle their way toward the exit. Usually before they got there they realized we'd played a funny on them, but they left anyway. Just another part of a fun-filled day.

***

On one tour we went to Kansas City and saw a really great play. The guest star was Don Knotts. I had made reservations several months in advance and one of the requests I made was that my wife and I would get to visit with "Barney" after the play.

The group sales lady said that wouldn't be possible because, at his age, by the time the play was finished he just couldn't stand in line and visit with the groups. Well, since I had two busloads of tour folks, and I was spending quite a lot of money with the theatre, I felt they could probably persuade him to meet with just the two of us. She said she would try to arrange it, just as long as I didn't mention to anybody until the buses were loaded for departure, and basically everyone was gone. After the play, my people went to the bus and Neta Ruth and I went backstage and visited and took pictures with Don.

"Richard and Barney Fife looking for an arrest."

It would have been really nice if I could have had him come to the bus, but I just couldn't push to far. It was really a nice experience. During our visit, I mentioned the "Andy Griffith Show" and he told us that it was probably the most fun he ever had in filming. He also said that little Opie gave them many suggestions as to what little boys would say in real life and he told us that most of the time they would change the script to what Opie thought made more sense. We really enjoyed our visit with good ole Barney Fife.

***

As the tour was making its way to the Dead Sea, on the Israel tour, the escort was giving all the instructions about what they were going to see and do while there. He had told the night before to be sure and bring a bathing suit, because everyone always wants to spend a little time in the Dead Sea.

He gave almost every possible detail about the minerals in the water. Also, because of all the salt, you couldn't sink; you'd just sorta roll around. He continued on about all the wonderful healthy material in the water, etc. One lady, we'll call Matilda, held up her hand, and held it up for a long period of time before the guide noticed her. Finally he said, "Young lady, do you have a question?" She replied, "Yes I do, with all that good stuff in the water, are we supposed to sit in it, or are we supposed to drink it?" Well, the day just kept getting better and better.

***

"Neta Ruth. Bring my bathing suit! Neta Ruth, Neta Ruth!"

***

We were in Cape Cod, MA. On this particular late afternoon we went on a whale watching tour. Our on board guide told us that we probably wouldn't see any whales on our way out, but on the way back, the water would get extremely rough and then the whales would really begin to move around and come up out of the water. All the tour members were really excited and everyone's desire to see whales up close was fulfilled. Nowhere on the boat were there any sharp edges due to the possibility of getting shifted around when the whales moved, etc. We had one beautiful blond lady, I think around 30 years of age that had a skin problem that if she would happen to rub up against, even a smooth area of stainless steel, it could still very easily cause the skin to slide around and really bleed. Well, the whales really started to move, and the ole boat began bouncing up and down, sideways, and every other maneuver it could make. All of a sudden the 30 year old blond slid a bit on the metal and rubbed skin off of her ankle bone. The only thing, at that time, that I had to stop the bleeding was some thick gauze, some disinfectant, and some good white tape to hold it on. The only problem was that she was wearing panty hose and the wound was about 4 inches by 6 inches in size. Well, we all decided that I had to cut out an area, from the panty hose, a little bigger than the 4 by 6, in order to apply the necessary bandage. I cut out the hose; took some gauze and cleaned the wound, applied the disinfectant, the gauze, and put the tape around it. By this time everyone had calmed down a bit, and even the whales began to back away. We finished the whale watching tour and came to shore and then headed to the motel. Out local guide and I, took the 30 year old nice lady to a 24 hour medical clinic and got the proper medicine. I even got her a discount on her medicine, and we headed to the motel. After I got to my room

I called my wife, Neta Ruth, and told her how the day was going. Just before I hung up I said to her, "The only thing that happened

was we had a little accident while on the boat, and I had to cut the panty hose off the 30 year old blond. I then told her I'd give her the details when I got home." Well, my wife figured out who she was, the 30 year old blond, and she came back very quickly and said, "Richard, I don't care if it is almost 10:00 p.m. you're going to give me all the details right now. Well, I did and then, before I knew it, it was morning and time to leave again. My wife got over it, the blond got over it, but I'm still trying to figure out why I couldn't wait until morning to tell my wife what happened.

***

We were in Hawaii on the Island of Maui at the Royal Lahina resort. Everybody was in a hurry to get into their rooms and off to the beach. We were going to a big party that night and wanted to swim for a while before getting all dressed up. Most of our group was on the 11th floor. I did not go for a swim because I had several things to get confirmed and there would be plenty of time the next day. I came through the lobby and headed up to my room. When I reached the 11th floor and the elevator door opened I heard two of our ladies hollering and really laughing. I started to ask them what was going on but they seemed to be in a hurry. Well, here's what had just happened. They came up from the beach and went to their room #1105 to bathe and get ready for the party. Ruby got in the shower first and lost about 10 lbs. of sand rather quickly. She was just about ready to get out, and she heard Patty say, "Ruby, Ruby, hey Ruby; someone has stolen all of our clothes." Then she heard a correction. Patty said, "Let's get out of here as quick as we can; the closet is filled with men's clothing." In about 15 seconds they realized they were in the wrong room. They put their bathing suits back on, opened the door, and made a bee line to their correct room which was 1110. Just as they were going in to their room they said they heard some men get off the elevator and go into room 1105. How lucky they were, because they just missed being caught by a few seconds. No telling what the men thought when they found at least 10 lbs. of sand in the shower, a really damp floor, the bed wrinkled and the TV on. They went to the room by accident because they really thought they were in 1105 but it, for sure, was 1110. I talked with the girls briefly and then I went back down to the lobby and asked the clerk why did key number 1110 work in room number 1105? The lady just smiled and said, "Oh, once in a great while that will just happen." It didn't seemed to bother her one bit, but it sure did start the girl's two days at the Royal Lahina off with a bang. I didn't rat on the ladies, I didn't think I should, but I'll tell you this much, everybody on our tour really had fun with this story.

***

This story is on the boss-man himself. We were on a South American cruise and we took a little side trip up the Amazon River toward Peru. We stopped at a little village to see their lifestyle in action and to visit with the REAL natives of that part of the country. That night we were to have a cultural floor show in the ship's main auditorium. It seated about 12 to 15 hundred people, and there were two shows each night as usual. Well, that night the cruise director asked me to sing a new song that I had written, "DROP YOUR DRAWER'S BLUES" This song always went over pretty good on the cruises because it was a comedy song about what you go through when you are in the process of taking radiation. I was recovering from prostate cancer when I wrote the song. Everyone connects with the song so they usually would give a pretty good round of applause, because either they have had cancer, will have cancer or know someone that has it. Well, that night the director told me to stand at the edge of the stage but back in the side curtains area. He said that I would be on right after he welcomed everyone to the show. He said he would say, "Here's one of our tour directors singing a new song that he'd had just recently written." Make welcome . . . blah . . . blah . . . etc. Ok, I was ready to go on stage; the opening music from the orchestra was just starting. I heard some rustling behind me and felt several bumping in to me. Boy, this for sure, was a cultural show from the Amazon. Next to me stood six beautiful, rather dark skinned ladies with absolutely nothing on but a little G-String; nothing on their tops whatsoever. Just as I turned and noticed them, I was introduced and I had to walk on to the stage, with a big music orchestra playing my accompaniment. This song has five verses and five choruses. I made it through the first verse and choruses and then, I guess it dawned on me what I had just seen, and I completely wrote two brand new verses that I'd never even heard myself. I looked down and saw my wife and a big bunch of my tours folks sitting together and Neta Ruth was looking at me like she thought I'd seen a ghost. I could tell she was telling the folks that she'd never heard those verses yet. Well, I finally gained my composure, and finished the song. I barely made it through the first show but I did OK on the second one. I sang that time with the correct lyrics. After the folks in the auditorium saw what I saw they understood why I wrote new words, and barely made it on and off the stage. It really was a pretty good show, but they sure didn't have to spend much money on costumes.

***

Here's another one, and it just again happens to be on me again. We were on a 12 day eastern tour going to Washington, D.C. Philly, Lancaster, Richmond and a bunch of other places as well. We stopped our third night at Bedford, PA. This was a nice little motel that offered a huge hot tub, swimming pool, and nightly bingo. I didn't want to play bingo but most of our tour members did. There was one couple that thought they would just walk around and take pictures, and I just thought I'd maybe get in the hot tub. The folks all went to bingo, except this one couple; I got in the hot tub. I'd been in there about 30 minutes when a big 18-wheeler pulled up into the motel's parking lot, which was clearly visible from the hot tub. About the time the truck pulled in, the couple that was going to take pictures had come out and they were standing talking to me. The door of the truck cab came open and a lady, probably in her 40's jumped out and we heard her say to her husband, or possibly boyfriend, "Honey, I think I'll get in the hot tub, is that OK with you? He said, "Sure."and here she came. I looked at the couple from the tour and they looked at me, and we all thought, what is she going to use for a bathing suit. Well, she didn't do anything. Remember now, I was the only one in the hot tub. She got about 10 feet from where I was, and took all of her clothes off except her under-garments. Both garments were bright red, I think, and she just jumped right in and said, "How you doing tonight?" I replied, "I think I'm doing alright." I looked over at my tour couple and they were taking movies of me and the lady. I was about ready to get out when they drove in but I waited too long. I stayed there for a while longer, I didn't know whether to try and get out or not. She stayed in an additional 30 minutes and then she climbed out. Boy oh boy, those bright red scanty garments sure knew how to make them-selves smaller when they got wet. I tried to turn my head, without embarrassing myself and my tour couple, but of course, they just kept on taking pictures. That's the last time I ever got in a hot tub without a crowd of folks with me. I think probably my face was redder than her garb.

***

We were in Williamsburg, Virginia touring all the beautiful and historic sites. I heard the sirens going off and, for some reason, I looked at my wife, Neta Ruth, and said, "I don't know why, but I have a feeling it is probably one of our tour members in trouble." Well, we ran up to where the commotion was and sure enough, one of my ladies appeared to be having a heart attack. We got her in the ambulance and headed to the local hospital. Her room-mate went with her so she wouldn't be alone in case it was her heart and she had to stay. I couldn't go in the ambulance so my driver took me to the hospital in our big bus. Since it was time to take our group to lunch I told him to go on and take them and I would call him when I had some news and was ready to be picked up. It was a heart attack and she was really in a bad way. I found out later, when I called her son, she was supposed to be in the hospital at home. He told me she was, but knowing she had paid for her trip, she just checked herself out and came on the trip without telling him. Well, I told you all of that just to lead up to the funny part.

I got all of her paper work finished, made arrangements for her room-mate to stay, and I went out in the hall and called my driver to pick me up on the way out of town. He said they had finished their meal and it would be about 20 minutes before he would get there. About the time I finished the call, a rather large black lady was coming in the door, close to where I was sitting. She was really a nice lady, so we began visiting a bit. She asked me why I was there and I told her I was waiting on a bus to pick me up. I didn't say anything to her about my tour lady in the hospital. She quickly informed me, "They ain't no bus coming here; this shore ain't no bus station. I works here so I know." I replied, thinking I would have some fun with her. I said,"Yeah, I know the bus will pick me up right here, at this door." Once again, with a little more fervor she said, "I'm a telling you now boy, I been working here a long time; there ain't no buses run down these here streets to pick people up. You is gonna be here from now on if you believes a bus is gonna pick you up." I had about 5 minutes left before I thought he would be pulling up so, I said again, "I'll just bet you a coconut pie that a big bus will be here, if he's on time, to pick me up right away." She laughed and said, "I'll take that bet boy, but where's we gonna get us a coconut pie." I told her I'd just pick it up the next time I came back, and about that time my tour bus pulled up smak-dab in front of where we were sitting. She slapped her leg, stood up and all she could say was, "Well, I'll be **7^%7# ed." She looked at me once again, slapped her leg, and just walked on down the hall shaking her head. Well, just another day on one of our tours.

***

This story is not a funny one, but it is one that makes a fellow feel really good. We were on a tour in San Francisco, CA and we were getting ready to go on a scheduled boat over to Alcatraz Island for a tour of the facility. I always pay for our tickets to attractions way in advance, because I can get better prices doing it that way. We had a full bus, but four of our folks decided not to go at the last minute. Our tour members were all standing in line ready to board so, while I was waiting for them to start boarding I walked around in front, where the walk-up passenger tickets were being sold. Since I could not get a refund on the tickets, I decided to do what I've done on several occasions, when I had unused tickets for attractions. I watched the line for a bit and I noticed two young couples standing back away from the ticket window counting their money and discussing something. I suppose, whether they could make the trip or not. The tickets were very expensive, but it was a really fantastic tour. We never went to S.F. without going. I walked over to the couples and said, "Are you planning on going to Alcatraz this morning?" All four of them spoke almost in unison and said, "We were really looking forward to it, but the price is way more than we expected." "I looked at them and said, "Well, it looks like this is your lucky day. I have four tickets paid for that I'm not going to use. Here they are and you guys have a wonderful day! I think they did . . . and I, for sure had a great day! This was just another fantastic day on one of our tours.

***

We were in Hollywood doing a part of our tour and I saw quite a commotion in front of one of the big fancy theaters. I ask my driver to pull over to the curb. Normally there would be no room at that spot, but there just happened to be on that particular day. There was a young man out in front who appeared to be selling tickets, of some kind, for a show. Well, I was curious so I got out and went over to talk with him. He was really a nice friendly fellow. He said there was the annual live sports award show being televised there that evening. I asked him what he was doing there in front. He said, you know we have these similar type shows going on here in Hollywood all the time. Sometimes it is hard to get a full crowd, because we need movie and TV stars to be here, especially in the front 8 or 9 rows, to make it look good on television.

My mind began to come alive when he said that because we did not have a planned activity for that evening. I said to him, "Do you have any room left for the show, and if so, how much are the group tickets? He said to me, "Oh, we have plenty of tickets and we don't charge anything. We just want to have a crowd.

Now I was getting excited at that point; my old mind was really clicking. He said there are gold passes, silver passes, and green ticket passes. I can give you all the green ones you want. They will be about 12 or 15 rows back because the stars get the up-front seats which are the silver and gold ones. I told him I would take 58 tickets and when could I get them. He said, "If you'll be here at 6:00 p.m. or even a little earlier, I'll be here and give them to you. I was in tall clover. I asked him if he did this type of work all the time and he said to me, "Nope, just part of the time; in my steady job I'm the house keeper for Desi and Lucille Ball. That's about all I could take in one visit with him. I jumped back on the bus and told my folks what we were going to be doing that evening after dinner. I think I even forgot to tell them that I got the tickets for free. I did say that we were not going to be up close, like we usually had in Branson, but they would still be good seats. I found out as the young fellow mentioned, this was a live show and would be broadcast at 9:00 p.m. in our home towns. We all called our relatives and told them to tune in.

Well, when we got to the theatre that evening about 5:45, I picked up the tickets and most of them were the gold ones, and the rest were silver, and they were scattered tickets, so we were all sitting in and around the TV and Movie Stars. Two rows in front of me, on the aisle, was Tim Conway, and a few seats over was Muhammad Ali (Cassius Clay), and Doris Day was sitting over in the next section close by, and one of our tour membes was sitting by her. We were in high society that night and it didn't cost us one penny. The MC for the show was Bob Saget. There were stars everywhere and I figured they were mighty fortunate to meet the folks with Richard's Fun-Time Tours. Just another evening on one of our tours.

***

This story is not directly connected to the tours, but it shows that through the years laughter was a big part of our family. Every day something started with a laugh and ended with a laugh, and a whole bunch of laughter in between. One day the three of us, Mom and Dad's three kids Richard Sunderwirth, Gail (Sunderwirth) Ingle and Jim Sunderwirth just happened to be at our parent's home at the same time. This was a rare thing, because we were all very busy and going different directions all the time. I was busy with the tours and out of the country most of the time; Gail was St. Clair County Treasurer, and Jim was Minister of Music at a large church in Port St. Lucie, Florida. We were sitting around and visiting. As Mom's do, sometimes when no one else is around, and this is what she did that particular day. She said," Kids I'm so proud of you. Gail you're the county treasurer, and you're been involved with your music here in Osceola and everywhere; Jim you've traveled all over the world in Christian Music Ministry for many years; and she started to say something to me, along those same lines, but; I had just gotten off from a tour the night before. I don't remember what had happened but something had gone terribly wrong with a reservation or something like that, and I was really down in the dumps. I felt I had messed up big time somewhere. She said, "Richard, you've done about everything in the world you ever wanted to do, and you've;" well, right then I butted in and said, "Mom, I don't feel like I've really done anything right, I feel like I'm the dumbest person in the world." She butted in and she really made me feel good; she said, "Richard I don't think you could get any dumber." Jim jumped in and said, "Mom, you don't mean that." She replied, "Yes, I really do, what did I say?" We told her what she said and we all got a big laugh out of it, and I started feeling better right away. That day ended up being a good one, once again with lots of laughter.

***

On one of our high school senior class tours we started our pickup in Rolla, Missouri. We were going on what we called the; 6-day, "Deep South Tour, including New Orleans." On this particular tour we had two different schools because many of the senior classes did not have enough students to fill a bus. From Rolla we went on to the boot-heel of Missouri and picked up the second group. That morning we loaded the first group at 6:00 a.m. Included in the group were 3 sponsors, myself as the tour escort; our driver and 22 students. Everyone was accounted for so we headed south.

About halfway to our morning destination I noticed that one of the lady sponsors didn't have much to say to the other two. It seemed as if they hadn't known each other for very long or something. We picked up our other tour group about 10:30 a.m. and proceeded to our lunch stop in Memphis. We didn't get a lot done during the first half of the day due to the fact we needed to wait until both groups were on board. As a matter of fact we didn't even do introductions until later. When we got to our cafeteria, this lady, that I was a little concerned about, came up to me and said, "Thanks so much for the ride to Memphis." I felt something was a bit fishy and I found out really soon what it was. This lady heard our driver talking at the Coffee Cup Café, prior to our arriving for our pickup, and since she was trying to find a way to Memphis, she figured we were her best plan yet. I thought she was one of the sponsors, since I'd never met them before; the bus driver also thought she was one of the sponsors, and the sponsors thought she was the bus driver's wife. Well, that started the day off with a bang; we all had a great laugh but I suppose she had the best laugh, because she got a free ride from Rolla to Memphis. And that is just part of another day on the tours. Oh, by the way, we all agreed she was a ratty mess, but none of us said anything to each other because we didn't want to offend anyone that we were going to be riding with for 6 days on a tour.

***

When I was in training for my first tour in 1959 I rode with Mr. Robbins, the owner of Robbins' Educational Tours. Back in those days there were very few places for buses to use for rest stops. Many times we would stop at an intersection where there was a service station on each corner. We would tell the high school seniors to split up and a few go to different corners to use the restrooms and maybe buy a soda pop or something for refreshment. Very few chain restaurants, fast food places, and very few chain motels or hotels. After we left Memphis heading south on I-55 **(which just happened to be brand new)** Mr. Robbins told me to watch and listen to what he did. In those days there were few highway markers and hardly any street markers at all. He told me to use buildings, homes, big trees, etc. to identify sites when we were about to see one. We passed through Grenada, Mississippi and he said to me, "Richard, do you see that big old silo over on the left about a quarter mile down the road?" "Now, do you see that little sheep shed across from it on the right?" I said, "Yep, shore do". He told me to make a note of that because when I came with my own tours over the next several weeks I could look for those 2 markers and just beyond the sheep shed there would be a herd of Brancusi cattle. This is a brand new breed of cattle; a breed bred from an Angus and a Braham.

Well, I wrote all of that down while he went ahead and told the story and pointed them out to the tour group. His description of the new breed was great. Everyone was excited to see them. The next week I had my own group of seniors and after we left Grenada I watched for the old silo and the sheep shed. Well, I saw them both, so I told them the story of the fantastic new breed of cattle. Everyone got up on the edge of their seats and watched. I pointed out the sheep shed and told them to look just a few feet after seeing the shed. They did, and I said, "Ok, guys and gals, get ready for a wonderful new site. We passed the sheep shed and guess what? There were 2 old jersey cows standing there all by themselves. I suppose they moved the Brancusi cattle to another location, but every time it got a little bit quiet, someone on the bus hollered out, "And on the right, Brancusi." I didn't get off to a very good start that day.

***

During those early tours I was only about 2 or 3 years older than the high school seniors I was taking. There will be a lot more information about those early years in chapter one of this book.

One of the fun things we did on this tour; a 6-day tour to the

Gulf Coast and New Orleans, was to go the Lake Ponchartrain Amusement Park. This was one of the largest amusement parks in the entire country. They had a roller-coaster called the Zephyr that would just blow your socks off. On this particular tour I had two buses and there was about half of the group boys and half girls. I described this as one of the biggest and fastest and scariest anywhere. I challenged the girls and said if any of you will ride this monster with me I'll be brave and ride it with you. Well, I didn't think that, well, I didn't think period, that but a few would take me up on it. The ride was included in the price of the ticket and one could ride as many times as they could stand it. If I remember correctly, 39 of the girls lined up and I had to ride with every one of them. When that was over I for sure, made no more challenges on anything to anyone.

This same evening the main music attraction at the park was Debbie Reynolds. She was only 23 or 24 at that time in her career. I felt it was my duty to go and visit with her after her show because, after all, I did bring a bunch of business with me that night, and so I felt justified in doing so. We visited and she was very nice and, of course, I enjoyed being able to meet her. If you happen to meet her sometime, tell her I said "Hello!" It's only been 50 years.

After we left the amusement park we went down to the old "World Famous" French Quarter and had French beignets and strong chicory coffee, blended with hot milk. Very few really slept well that night because we weren't in the habit of drinking coffee that strong, especially after 2 or 3 cups; it was very delicious. The Morning Call Coffee Stand has been open 24 hours a day since 1870.

***

One of my very first tours was to Osceola and Monegaw Springs, Missouri. This was a senior citizen group from just east of Kansas City, Missouri. One of the attractions was going to the bluffs overlooking the Osage River where the so called "Outlaws", the Younger Brothers' and the James Brothers' would hide, when necessary, from law officials.

We arrived at the bluff's hideout cave and I described what it was all about. I hired a couple friends, Rick Reed and his friend to portray Jessie and Frank James. They rode in on their horses, robbed us, and made that portion of the tour rather exciting. A few days prior, I went to the cave and, in addition to the other names that were carved all over the front of it, I carved "Minnie did it here, 1939."

I knew Minnie was going to be on the tour so I set her up. A

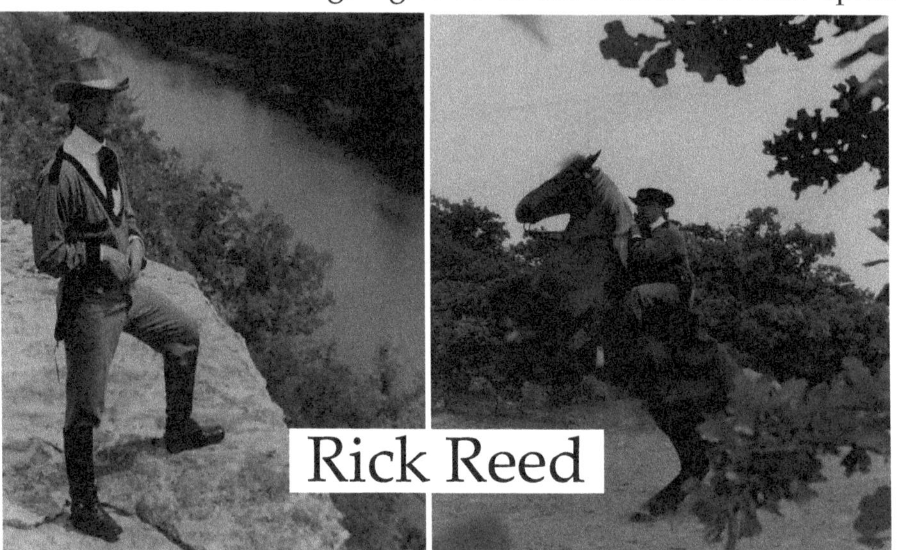

Rick Reed

little information about Minnie was that Minnie and her three sisters lived in the Osceola area and went to high school there. I knew that for little mini-adventures, while dating, etc . . . she might have, while going to school in the late 30's she would possibly have come to the cave just for something to do, like I did when I attended school in Osceola. Now, this lady I had known for many years. She was really a nice person; however, anything she wanted to say she said it. She didn't hold back and you never knew for sure what was going to come from her mouth. Well, as I was pointing other names, carved on the cave walls, I just happened to come upon what I had carved earlier, and I said to Minnie, thinking she would just probably blow a gasket when I pointed it out to her. "Gee Whiz Minnie! I found your name carved up here on the wall." And then I continued on for the benefit of the tour group. "Didn't you and your 3 sisters go to high school in Osceola in the late 30's? She said, "Yes, we did." Is there a chance you might have come out here on a date one time or another? She answered, "Yes, we could have." Then I said, "What do you have to say about this; it says, 'Minnie did it here, 1939?'" She stood and thought for 10 or 15 seconds, kinda shook her head, and then said, "WELL, . . . I probably did." The tour group burst out in laughter 'big time'. The joke turned out to be on me rather than Minnie. Everyone got quite a kick out of the little incident that I tried to pull on Minnie that day. She's been dead for many years now, but she was a good ole gal, and we had a lot of fun on the tour that day.

***

On one of our Nashville tours we were staying at a Ramada Inn a very short distance from Murfreesboro Pike. The Inn was just up over a high bank from the Pike within close walking distance from it. Back in those days the walking and running craze was in full throttle. One of our tour members, Gene Reding, had a brand new blue and white striped jogging suit. Most of the time he would get up an hour or so ahead of anyone else on the tour to start jogging.

Well, this one morning about 5:30 a.m. he put on his suit, and walked over the high bank down to Murfreesboro Pike, so he could walk along the roadway. He did not take any identification with him. He basically knew very little about the city of Nashville and could not communicate with anyone about where he was really located, except the fact that it was a nice motel in Nashville.

He was jogging along the highway and all of a sudden a couple of Nashville Police cars, with lights a flashing, pulled up close to him; one in front and one in back. They took much precaution and ask for his identification, which he did not have, and also many other questions that he could not verify. You see, just over the other side of Murfreesboro Pike was a state penitentiary; and their uniforms just happened to be blue and white striped. They thought he had escaped from the facility. With no way to prove he was not a criminal his situation was getting worse by the second. His only salvation was the fact that he was wearing his Richard's Fun-Time Tours Cap, that we furnished all of the tour members. He pointed up over the hill to where the big bus was located and described it to the police officers. He had no cell phone or any other way to call anyone, because he had no number memorized. And besides that he really hated to call anyone at 5:45 a.m. in the morning.

Finally, after quite a lot of continued questioning he convinced them he really was on a bus tour. They finally let him go; they told him the next time he jogged in a new city be sure and carry some identification, and maybe he should have a red and white dotted suit rather than blue and white striped. One thing for certain he should never ever take off his cap. We had fun with him for the next several days once we heard the story and he regained his composure.

***

A little short story, but it shows a sample of what we always tried to do to make certain no one was cheated on a tour. We were on a trip to the canyons and mountains of Colorado. We were to pick up several tour members in Osceola and my wife, Neta Ruth, was to shuttle them to meet the bus, for a very early departure. That particular morning one lady was running late getting to Osceola. My wife had the list of tour members who were to be there; however, after waiting and calling everyone she could think of to find out why and where she might be, she had to go ahead and leave her in order for the others to make the bus connection. Neta Ruth just barely met us and we left on schedule, but we had to leave without this one tour member. Neta Ruth came on back to Osceola and the lady, by then, had arrived at the original pickup point. My wife called me and we decided there was nothing else we could do but for her to bring the one lady cross country, all the way to Garden City, Kansas. She drove hard for a lot of miles, and we all joined together at the motel there for the first night out. The lady was happy that she made the tour. I don't remember now why she was late, but my wife spent that first night of the tour with me, and then headed all the way back to Osceola by herself. I really hated to have to ask her to do that, but we knew that was the only thing we should do. We felt that things like this would continue to help build our tour business . . . and it WAS the right thing to do.

***

One more little story; one evening while we were in New York City we went to the second Broadway show of our tour. Normally I would have had time to get down to the show prior to the starting time and make some arrangements with the police who were on guard in front of the theatre; before our bus would be arriving. No, I didn't bribe them to save a spot for our bus in front of the theatre, but this time there was no possible way for me to make my wishes known. Well, you might as well know why I wanted to get there early. I did this many times all over the USA. I would just simply tell the police that if it just happened to be possible that my bus ended up right in front of the theatre, I would certainly show my appreciation. Each time this happened it was, for sure, worth the 100 bucks of appreciation that I showed them. However; this night it was not the case. We had to park about a block and a half away. That wouldn't have been too bad, but after we reached the theatre, sat down, and the musical started, it starting raining cats and dogs. I noticed the side door from where we were sitting. I left the show and went outside and found the exact location of our bus in relationship to where the side door was. I went outside and found a little fellow up the street selling umbrellas. He asked me if I would like to purchase one. Since we had 56 tour members I knew we'd need 28 umbrellas (one to a couple). I said to him, "No, I'd like to buy 28 umbrellas." He had 28 of them, we made a deal, and then I had 28 of them. He put them in a nice plastic bag for me and I went back to the show. At intermission I told my group to be sure and go out that side door, and try to leave the building as much in a group as possible. I remember telling them to be sure and use the restrooms before the show was over. After the last curtain, the side door opened and here came my folks. The rain coming down was worse than any other time. My tour group had no idea what I'd done. As they came out the door I handed each couple an umbrella and told them to make a right turn and the bus would be just one block away. Since it was a beautiful sunny evening before the show started none of my tour members had their umbrella with them, and nobody else did either. I could have sold every one of them . . . for a pretty good price, but I didn't. I think my folks talked about the umbrella deal more than they talked about Niagara Falls, the dinner at the United Nations, or even the meal at Tavern on the Green. Sometimes small things get more attention than big things, if done for the right reason.

***

One last tidbit; We were in Nashville one evening and I was asked to be in a skit on stage at the Roy Acuff Theatre with Louise Mandrell. It was very difficult for me to make the decision to do it, but I decided, to make her happy, I would go ahead, Ha Ha! We had great seats for the show and four of my tour members were sisters and were sitting together in the center of the third row, with the rest of the group around them. The four sisters had on Richard's Fun-Time Tours visors, all with little blinking lights. Before we started the skit Louise asked me if these folks were part of my tour. I said "Yes," and she asked them if I'd been good to them on the trip; they said, "pretty good," and the skit started.

Through the years I've had the privilege of being on stage in many theatres with great wonderful entertainers. I've talked, sung, danced and even been a dancing Christmas tree several times. Well, I mentioned that to tell you this; most of the time, no matter who it was that had the same opportunity to be on stage, when the event was over, the star, would give their volunteer a little kiss on the cheek. When they use folks from the audience stars DO NOT kiss on the lips; that is a no no in show business.

This particular skit was a dandy. I had on a rubber mask some of the time, as was necessary in the skit. We did our thing; laughed quite a lot, and I acted my normal self and was a bit crazy in what I was doing. She got a little wild herself; **(Thank goodness, they filmed this skit and I still have a copy.)** When it was all over Louise thanked me and before she realized it she gave me a big kiss . . . smak-dab on the lips. The second it happened she looked like she was going to faint, and I felt like I was sorta boiling over. She wasn't supposed to do that but she did. Well, just another day in the life of a lucky tour escort.

"You're from where?"

Richard & Neta Ruth Sunderwirth

"Here We Go!"

"If you are depressed, you are living in the past. If you are anxious you are living in the future. If you are at peace, you are living in the present."

Laotzu

***

An Amish boy and his father visited a beautiful new mall. They are amazed by almost everything they saw, but especially by two shiny, silver walls that moved back and forth. The young boy said to his father, "My, what a fantastic attraction this is." The father responds, "Son, I have never seen anything like this in my life. Don't know what it is." While the boy and his father watch wide-eyed, an old lady in a wheelchair rolls up to the moving walls and presses a button. The walls open and the lady rolls between them into a small room. The walls close and the boy and his father watch small circles of lights with numbers above the walls light up. They continue to watch the circles light up in the reverse direction. The walls open up again and a beautiful 24 year-old woman steps out. "Son," the father says, "quick, go get your mother."

***

"Always remember that your present situation is not your final destination. The best is yet to come?

***

A sales company has particular trouble selling Bibles in their location. They are always looking for someone to break through to their market and make a real difference. One day, a man comes in with a job application and says, "I-I-I-I'd L-L-L-like t-t-t-t to b-b-b-b-be a B-B-B- Bible s-s-s- salesman, s-s-s- sir." Initially, he doesn't want to give the job to this man, but his conscience got the better of him. He decided to try him out. After three weeks, the manager is looking at the sales figures and realizes that the new guy is selling the most copies, Amazed, he calls him into his office. "You've only worked here for three weeks and you've already sold more copies than anyone else here! How do you do it?" "W-w-w-w-w-well, I g-g-g-g- go up t-t-t-t- to th-the d-d-d-door and d-d- I-I-I- I s-s-s-s- say, w-w-w-w- would y-y-y-y- you l-l-l-l-like t-t-t-t- to b-b-b-b-b- buy a c-c-c- copy o-o-o- of th-th-th-th- the B-B-B-B- Bible, or w-w-w-w- would y-y-y-y- you l-l-l-l-like m-m-m- me-me-me t-t-t- to r-r-r-r- read it t-t-t-t to y-y-y-y-you? D-d-d-d- dey u-u-u-usually b-b-b-b- buy one."

***

"Dear Algebra, Please stop asking us to find your X. She's never coming back and don't ask Y."

***

David received a parrot for his birthday. This parrot was fully grown with a bad attitude and worse vocabulary. Every other word was a really a bad one. Those that weren't bad were, to say the least, rude. David tired hard to change the bird's attitude and was constantly saying polite words, playing soft music, anything that came to mind. Nothing worked. He yelled at the bird, the bird got worse. He shook the bird and the bird got madder and then really said a bunch of bad words. Finally, in a moment of desperation, David put the parrot in the freezer. For a few moments he heard the bird squawking, kicking and screaming and then, suddenly, all was quiet. David was frightened that he might have actually hurt the bird and quickly opened the freezer door. The parrot calmly stepped out onto David's extended arm and said, "I'm sorry that I offended you with my language and actions. I ask for your forgiveness. I will try to check my behavior." David was astounded at the bird's change in attitude and was about to ask what changed him when the parrot continued, "May I ask what the chicken said or did, before he went in the freezer?"

***

"Be thankful for the bad things in life. For they opened your eyes to the good things you weren't paying attention to before!"

***

"To one who has faith, no explanation is necessary. To one without faith, no explanation is possible."

***

In an adult Sunday school class the lesson from Genesis centered on Abraham who lived for a time in Beersheba. A class member asked the teacher, "Please tell me how far it is in actual miles from Dan to Beersheba. I've always heard the expression 'from Dan to Beersheba.' Another member said, "Do you mean to tell me that Dan and Beersheba are places? I always thought they were husband and wife, like Sodom and Gomorrah."

Dear Santa, "I don't want much for Christmas, I just want the person reading this to be happy. Friends are the fruit cake of life; some nutty, some soaked in alcohol, some sweet; but mix them together and they're all my friends."

***

Not a funny . . . but a really great story.
An eye witness account from New York City, on a cold day in December, some years ago: A little boy, about 10-years-old, was standing before a shoe store on the roadway, barefooted, peering through the window, and shivering with cold. A lady approached the young boy and said, "My, but you're in such deep thought staring in that window?" "I was asking God to give me a pair of shoes," was the boy's reply. The lady took him by the hand, went into the store, and asked the clerk to get half a dozen pairs of socks for the boy. She then asked the clerk if he could give her a basin of water and a towel. He quickly brought them to her. She took the little fellow to the back part of the store and, removing her gloves, knelt down, washed his little feet, and dried them with the towel. By this time, the clerk had returned with the socks . . . Placing a pair upon the boy's feet, she purchased him a pair of shoes. . . She tied up the remaining pairs of socks and gave them to him . . . She patted him on the head and said, "No doubt, you will be more comfortable now . . ." As she turned to go, the astonished kid caught her by the hand, and looking up into her face,

with tears in his eyes, asked her; "Are you God's Wife?"

***

"Charm is good, for about 15 minutes; then you better know something!"
Toni's Walk Talk

***

A tiny but dignified old lady was among a group looking at an art exhibition in a newly opened gallery. Suddenly one contemporary painting caught her eye. "What on earth, she inquired of the artist standing nearby, is that?" He smiled condescendingly. "That, my dear lady, is supposed to be a mother and her child." "Well, then," snapped the little old lady, "why isn't it?"

***

"Do you know why it's hard to be happy? It's because we refuse to let go of the things that make us sad."

***

It's always difficult to bring sad news, but I thought you should know. Today, there was a great loss in the entertainment world. The man who wrote the song "Hokey Pokey" died. What was really horrible was that they had trouble keeping his body in the casket. They'd put his left leg in and . . . Well, you know the rest.

***

"We are not human beings having a spiritual experience. We are spiritual beings having a human experience."
(www.trueactivist.com)

***

An English professor wrote the words, "Woman without her man is nothing." on the blackboard and directed his students to punctuate it correctly. The men wrote: "Woman, without her man, is nothing." The women wrote: Woman! Without her, man is nothing."

***

"If a cluttered desk is a sign of a cluttered mind, of what, then, is an empty desk a sign?"
Albert Einstein

***

Teacher: What happened in 1809? Student: Lincoln was born. Teacher: What happened in 1812? Student: Lincoln had his third birthday.

***

"It is better to walk alone, than with a crowd going in wrong direction."
Diane Grant

***

A teacher told her student to write a one hundred word essay on cars. One boy handed in his essay which read, "Once my dad bought a new car and took me for a ride. We went about twenty miles and the car broke down and wouldn't start." End of essay, with a footnote, "That's only twenty-four words. The rest was not fit to print."

***

"The mind replays what they heart can't delete."

***

After the teacher finished his rather long lesson he asked, "Are there any questions?" One little fellow in the back of the room, who was a bit tired of the lesson asked, "Yep, I got one, what time is it?"

***

"You cannot hang out with negative people and expect to live a positive life."

***

Six year old Johnny was a disruptive influence in his Sunday school class week after week. Finally one Sunday the teacher could take it no longer. She said, "Johnny, you are incorrigible." Not knowing the meaning of the word, Johnnie said, "No, I'm not. I'm a Presbyterian."

***

When asked why they managed to stay together for 65 years, the woman replied, "We were born in a time where if something was broken, you fixed it . . . not throw it away."

***

A teacher in the Prime-timer's class came home from shopping one afternoon and opened a large package. Taking out the lampshade she said to her husband, "Isn't it beautiful, George. It only cost fifty dollars." George looked at it and said, "That's an outrageous hat. If you wear it to church I'll tell you one thing for sure, you'll go alone."

***

Little Raymond returned from Sunday school in a happy mood and said to his mother, "The teacher said something awfully nice about me in her prayer today." "That's wonderful, what did she say?" Well, she said in her prayer, "O Lord, we thank thee for food and Raymond."

***

The Sunday school teacher told the story of how Elijah on Mt. Carmel built an altar, put wood on it, cut the bullock in pieces and laid them on the altar. "And then he commanded the people to fill four barrels with water and pour the water over the altar. Now, can anyone tell me why the water was poured over the bullock?" One lad piped up and said, "To make the gravy."

***

Here's the reason baby diapers have brand names such as "Luvs" and "Huggies", while undergarments for old people are called "Depends". When babies poop in their pants, people are still gonna Luv'em and Hug'em. When old people poop in their pants, it "Depends" on who's in the will! Boy, I'm sure glad to get that straightened out.

***

Mystery Solved

It seems that when the good Lord was making the world, he called man aside and bestowed upon him 20 years of normal sex life. Man was horrified, but the Creator refused to budge. Then the Lord called the monkey and gave him 20 years. "But I don't need 20 years," said the monkey. "Ten years is plenty." Man spoke up and said; "May I have the other 10 years?" The monkey agreed. The Lord called on the lion and also gave him 20 years. The lion too, wanted only 10. Again, man spoke up. "May I have the other 10 years?" "Of course," said the lion. Then came the donkey, who was also given 20 years. Like the others, 10 years was enough for him. Man again asked for the spare 10 years, and he got them. This explains why man has 20 years of normal sex life, 10 years of monkeying around, 10 years of lion about it and 10 years of making a donkey out of himself.

***

George and Sam were enjoying an afternoon sitting on a part bench in the park. George asked Henry "Do you remember that stuff they used to put in our coffee way back during the war to make us forget about women?" Henry said, "I think you mean salt peter!" "Yeah, replied George, "that's it." After a few minutes George said, "I think it's beginning to work!" (Copied)

***

"With self-discipline most anything is possible."

Theodore Roosevelt

***

Walking on the grass is good for you!

The room was full of pregnant women with their husbands. The instructor said, "Ladies, remember that exercise is good for you. Walking is especially beneficial. It strengthens the pelvic muscles and will make delivery that much easier. Just pace yourself, make plenty of stops and try to stay on a soft surface like grass or a path. "Gentlemen, remember; you're in this together. It wouldn't hurt you to go walking with her. In fact, that shared experience would be good for you both." The room suddenly became very quiet as the men absorbed this information. After a few moments a man, name unknown, at the back of the room, slowly raised his hand. "Yes?" said the instructor. "I was just wondering if it would be all right if she carries a golf bag while we walk?" (Kinda brings a tear to your eye and a lump to the throat. This kind of sensitivity just can't be taught.) (Copied)

***

A little girl was saying her prayers before going to bed. She finished but then she remembered something else, She said, "Dear God, please, please send clothes for all those poor ladies on Grandpa's computer. Thank you so much God; Amen"

***

At a 60th high school reunion, he was a widower and she a widow. They had known each other for a number of years being high school classmates and having attended class reunions in the past without fail. This 60th anniversary of their class, the widower and the widow made a foursome with two other singles. They had a wonderful evening, their spirits high; the widower throwing admiring glances across the table; the widow smiling back at him. Finally, he picked up courage to ask her, "Will you marry me?" After about six seconds of careful consideration, she answered, "Yes . . . yes I will!" The evening ended on a happy note for the widower. But the next morning he was troubled. Did she say "Yes" or did she say "No?" He couldn't remember. Try as he would, he just could not recall. He went over the conversation of the previous evening, but his mind was blank. He remembered asking the question but for the life of him he could not recall her response. With fear and trepidation he picked up the phone and called her. First, he explained that he couldn't remember as well as he used to. Then he reviewed the past evening. As he gained a little more courage he then inquired of her. "When I asked if you would marry me, did you say "Yes" or did you say "No?" "Why you silly man, I said 'Yes, Yes I will.' And I meant it with all my heart." The widower was delighted. He felt his heart skip a beat. Then she continued. "And I am so glad you called, I couldn't remember who asked me!" (Copied)

***

Richard & Neta Ruth Sunderwirth

(Be sure and read the directions. It is funny!)

1 or 2 quarts of rum . . . 1 cup butter . . . 1 tsp. sugar . . . 2 large eggs . . . 1 cup dried fruit . . . 1 tsp. baking powder . . . 1 tsp. Lemon juice . . . 4 cups brown sugar . . . 1 cup of chopped nuts.

BEFORE YOU START: sample the rum to check for quality. (Good isn't it?) Now go ahead, select a large mixing bowl, measuring cup, etc. Check the rum again; it must be just right. To be sure rum is of the highest quality; pour 1 level cup into a glass and drink it as fast as you can. Repeat . . . With an electric mixer, beat 1 cup of butter in a large fluffy bowl. Add 1 seaspoon of thugar and beat again. Meanwhile, make sure the rum is of the highest qualitty. Try another cup (open the second tuart, if necessary). Add 2 arge legs and 2 tups of fried druit and beat till high. If the druit gets struck in beaters, just pry it loosey with a drew scriver. Sample the run again; checking it for tonsicistcy. Next, sift 3 cups of pepper or salt: (it really doesn't matter.) Sample the run again. Sift a pint of lemon uice; fold in schopped butter and strained nuts. Add to babblespoons of brown thugar, of whatever color you can find, mix mell. Grease oven and turn cake pan to 350 gredees. Now pour the whole mess into the boven and ake; Check the run again, then go to ged. Mary Christmas!

***

An agitated patient was stomping around the psychiatrist's office, running his hands through his hair, almost in tears. "Doctor, my memory's gone. Gone! I can't remember my wife's name. Can't remember my children's names. Can't remember what kind of car I drive. Can't remember where I work. It was all I could do to find my way here." "Calm down." said the psychiatrist, "How long have you been like this?" "Like what?" replied the patient.

***

A dog ran into a butcher shop and grabbed a roast off the counter. Fortunately, the butcher recognized the dog as belonging to a neighbor of his. The neighbor happened to be a lawyer. Incensed at the theft, the butcher called up his neighbor and said, "Hey, if your dog stole a roast from my butcher shop, would you be liable for the cost of the meat?" The lawyer replied, "Of course! How much was the roast?" The butcher replied, "$7.98." A few days later the butcher received a check in the mail for $7.98. Attached to it was an invoice that read; Legal Consultation Service: $150.

***

Chicken Side off first...

There was a competition to cross the English Channel doing only the breaststroke, and the three women who entered the race were a brunette, a redhead and a blonde! After approximately 14 hours, the brunette staggered up on the shore and was declared the fastest breaststroker. About 40 minutes later, the redhead crawled up on the shore and was declared the second place finisher. Nearly 4 hours after that, the blonde finally came ashore and promptly collapsed in front of the worried onlookers. When the reporters asked why it took so long to complete the race, she replied, "I don't want to sound like I'm a sore loser, but I think those two other girls were using their arms."

***

"I know that you believe you understand what you think I said, but I'm not sure you realize that what you heard is not what I meant."

(Robert McCloskey)

***

(This one is neat. I would have liked to have been there.)

You can never underestimate the innovativeness of American Farm Boys. At a high School in Kansas, a group of male students played a prank. They let three goats loose inside the school. But before turning them loose, they painted numbers on the sides of the goats; 1, 2 and 4. School Administrators spent most of the day looking for No. 3 . . . Now that's funny, I don't care who you are. And you thought there was nothing to do in Kansas!

***

A cowboy rode into town and stopped at a saloon for a drink. Unfortunately, the locals always had a habit of picking on strangers, which he was. When he finished his drink, he found his horse had been stolen. He goes back into the bar, handily flips his gun into the air, catches it above his head without even looking and fires a shot into the ceiling. "Which one of you sidewinders stole my hoss?" he yelled with surprising forcefulness. No one answered. "Alright, I'm gonna have anotha beer, and if my hoss ain't back outside by the time I finish, I'm gonna do what I dun in Texas! And I don't like to have to do what I dun in Texas!" Some of the locals shifted restlessly. He had another beer, walked outside, and his horse is back! He saddles-up and starts to ride out of town. The bartender wanders out of the bar and asks, "Say partner, before you go . . . what happened in Texas?" The cowboy turned back and said, "I had to walk home."

***

THINK YOU'RE HAVING A BAD DAY? THINK AGAIN . . .

The following was taken from a Florida newspaper:
A man was working on his motorcycle on the patio and his wife was in the kitchen. The man was racing the engine and somehow the motorcycle slipped into gear. The man, still holding the handlebars, was dragged through a glass patio door and, along with the motorcycle, dumped onto the floor inside the house. The wife, hearing the commotion, ran into the dining room and found her husband on the floor, cut and bleeding, the motorcycle lying next to him and the patio door shattered. She ran to the phone and called for an ambulance. Because they lived on a hill, the wife ran down several flights of sidewalk steps to the street to direct the paramedics. After the ambulance departed, the wife uprighted the motorcycle and pushed it outside before driving the family car to the hospital. Seeing that gas had spilled on the floor, she took paper towels, blotted up the gasoline, and threw the towels in the commode. The husband was treated and released. After arriving home, he looked at the shattered patio door and the damage to his motorcycle. He was a bit despondent when he went into the bathroom, sat on the commode and smoked a cigarette. After finishing the smoke, he flipped it between his legs into the toilet bowl. The wife heard a loud explosion and screaming. She ran into the bathroom and found her husband lying on the floor. His trousers had been blown away and he was suffering burns. The same ambulance crew was dispatched and the wife met them at the street again. The paramedics loaded the husband on to the stretcher and began carrying him down the stairs to the street. One of the paramedics asked how her husband had been burned. She told him and the paramedics both started laughing so hard that one of them tipped the stretcher and dumped the husband out. He fell down the remaining steps and broke his arm. Now that's having a bad day!

***

THE DIFFERENCE BETWEEN CATS

Chicken Side off first...

AND DOGS . . .

What is a Cat?

Cats do what they want. They rarely listen to you. They're totally unpredictable. They whine when they are not happy. When you want to play, they want to be alone. When you want to be alone, they want to play. They expect you to cater to their every whim. They're moody. They leave hair everywhere. They drive you nuts and cost an arm and a leg. CONCLUSION: They're tiny little women in fur coats.

What is a Dog?

Dogs lie around all day, sprawled on the most comfortable piece of furniture in the house. They can hear a package of food opening half a block away, but don't hear you when you're in the same room. They can look dumb and lovable all at the same time. They growl when they are not happy. When you want to play, they want to play. When you want to be alone, they want to play. They are great at begging. They will love you forever if you rub their tummies. They leave their toys everywhere. They do disgusting things with their mouths and then try to give you a kiss. **CONCLUSION:** They're tiny little men in fur coats.

***

There was once a snail that was sick and tired of his reputation for being so slow. He decided to get some fast wheels to make up the difference. After shopping around a while, he decided that the Datsun 240-Z was the car to get. So the snail goes to the nearest Datsun dealer and says he wants to buy the 240-Z, but he wants it repainted "240 S. "The dealer asks, "Why the 'S'?" The snail replies," 'S' stands for snail. I want everybody who sees me roaring past to know who's driving." Well, the dealer doesn't want to lose the unique opportunity to sell a car to a snail, so he agrees to have the car repainted for a small fee. The snail gets his new car and spent the rest of his days roaring happily down the highway at top speed. And whenever anyone would see him zooming by, they'd say "Wow! Look at that "S"-car go!"

***

The teacher gave her 5th grade class an assignment. They were to get their parents to tell them a story with a morale at the end of it. The next day the kids came back and one by one began to tell their stories. "Johnny, do you have a story to share?" asked the teacher. "Yes Ma'am, I sure do; my daddy told me about my Aunt Carol. Aunt carol was a pilot in Dessert Strom and her plane got hit. She had to bail out over enemy territory and all she had was a small flask of whiskey, a pistol and a survival knife. She drank the whiskey on the way down, so it wouldn't fall into enemy hands, and then her parachute landed right smak-dab in the middle of 20 enemy troops. She shot 15 of them with the gun 'till she ran out of bullets; killed four more with the knife, 'till the blade broke and then, she killed the last one with her bare hands." "Good Heavens," said the horrified teacher, "What kind of moral did your daddy teach you from this horrible story?" "Well," said Johnny, "One thing; he told me to stay away from my Aunt Carol when she's been drinking."

***

A French guest was staying in a really nice hotel in Edmonton, France. She phoned room service for someone to get some pepper up there as soon as they could. The concierge asked the lady, "Ma'am do you wish to have black pepper or white pepper?" Very quickly she replied, "No, you dummy, 'toilette pepper', toilette pepper.'"

***

Did you ever wonder why lemon juice is made from artificial flavoring, while dish washing liquid is made from real lemons?

A really tough day!

I had the toughest time of my life. First, I got angina pectoris and then arteriosclerosis. Just as I was recovering from these, I got tuberculosis, double pneumonia and phthisis. Then they gave me hypodermics. Appendicitis was followed by tonsillectomy. These gave way to aphasia and hypertrophic cirrhosis. I completely lost my memory for a while. I know I had diabetes and acute indigestion, besides gastritis, rheumatism, lumbago and neuritis. I don't know how I pulled through it. It was the hardest spelling test I've ever had!

***

A plumber attended to a leaking faucet at the neurosurgeon's home. After a 7 or 8 minute job the plumber demanded $150 in payment. The neurosurgeon exclaimed, "I don't charge that amount, even though I am a surgeon." The plumber replied, "I agree, you are right. I too, didn't either, when I was a surgeon. That's why I switched to plumbing." "Like most surgeons' say, it ain't what you do, it is what you know to do that makes the cost a little higher."

***

Two friends meet in the street. Jim looked forlorn and at most, on the verge of tears. The other man, John, said, "Hey man, how can you look like the whole world caved in?" Jim said, "Let me tell you; 3 weeks ago an uncle of mine died and left me $40,000." "That's not bad," said John. "Hold on, I'm just getting started; 2 weeks ago, a cousin, I never knew, kicked the bucket and left me $80,000 free and clear." "Boy," said John. Jim came back with this, "Last week my grandfather passed away; I inherited almost a quarter of a million dollars from him." "Gee whiz man, how come you look so glum and frustrated?" said John. "Well, this week I didn't get nothing," said Jim, with tears running down his cheek.

***

One day Bill and Tom went to a restaurant for dinner. They ordered their steaks and before long the waiter brought out their 2 steaks. Bill quickly picked out the biggest steak for himself. Tom wasn't happy about that; "When are you going to learn to be polite." Tom said, "If you had the chance to pick first, which one would you have picked?" Bill replied, "Well, the small one, of course." Tom said, "What are you whining about then, the small piece is what you would have picked, and that's what you got, so shut up and enjoy it."

***

A film crew was on location deep in the desert. One day, during the filming, an old Indian went up to the director and said, "Tomorrow rain." The next day it rained. A week later, the Indian went to up to the director again and said, "Tomorrow storm." Sure enough the next day there was a terrible hail storm. The director said to his secretary, "This old Indian is incredible, he's good." The old Indian said to the director, "Tomorrow, warm nice day." Sure enough the next day was beautiful. The director called to his secretary and said, "Hire the old Indian to be our weather man." After several weeks of predicting the weather correctly, the old Indian failed to show up. Then in two weeks here he was back.

The director said, "Good to see you; what is the weather going to be tomorrow? I have a really big scene to film and I need your prediction, I am depending on you." The old Indian shrugged his shoulders and said, "Me don't know, radio is broke."

***

A crusty old bird

There was a crusty old corporal in the base hospital, who was, beyond question, a real stinker. Nothing they did pleased him. He got really mad at everybody for everything. One day one of the nurses came in and decided she had had it. This guy was rude, nasty talking and she'd had all of it she could take. She decided before she quit working there she would at least get even in some way, so she came up with a plan. She said to the old bird, "Roll over, it's time to take your temperature." Well, he rolled over and she did what she had to do. She left the room and left him lying on the bed having his temperature being taken, he thought. She also left the door wide open. There were lots of people going up and down the hall. He growled to one; "What's the matter, haven't you ever seen anybody getting their temperature taken?" "Yes, Sir!" they said. "But never with a flower."

***

Bob was showing off his hunting dog to his friend Bill. They went down towards the lake and Bob said to the dog. "How many ducks are there boy?" The dog raced off to the lake, came back a couple of minutes later, and barked twice. Seconds later, two ducks floated into view. "That was unbelievable, can he do it again?" Bill asked. "Sure," responded Bob, "How many ducks are there boy?" The dog raced off again, came back, and barked four times. Four ducks flew in and landed on the pond. "I have to have that dog." Bill said. "I'll give you $5,000 and all of my hunting dogs." They agreed to the deal, and Bill took the dog home to show it off to his wife. Bill and his wife took his new dog down to the lake and Bill said, "How many ducks are there boy?" The dog raced off, came back, grabbed a stick, shook it, and threw it over his shoulder. "Bob gypped you," his wife said. "You are such a fool." Bill protested. "But I saw it work," let me try again. "How many ducks are there boy?" Again the dog raced off; came back, grabbed a stick, shook it, and threw it over his shoulder. "Oh my" Bill said, "This dog is useless." Then, after selling the dog, he went back and told the story to Bob. After hearing that Bill had sold the dog, Bob cried, "YOU FOOL! That dog was telling you there were more ducks than you could shake a stick at!"

***

Bubba and Junior were standing at the base of a flagpole, looking up. A woman walked by and asked what they were doing. "We're supposed to find the height of the flagpole," said Bubba, "but we don't have a ladder." The woman took a wrench from her purse, loosened a few bolts, and laid the pole down on the ground. Then she took a tape measure from her pocket, took a measurement, and announced, 18 ft. 6 inches, and she just walked away. Junior looked at Bubba and said," Golly, some folks think we're a bit stupid, that woman was supposed to give us the height of the flag pole and all she gave us was the length."

***

Jimmy's mom dragged him in front of his dad during the football game. "Talk to your son," she said. "He refuses to obey a word I say." The father turned to Jimmy angrily and said, "Jimmy, how dare you disobey your mother. Do you think you're better than you own father?"

***

There was a young Scottish boy, called Angus, who decided to try life in Australia. He found an apartment, in a small block, and settled in. After a week or two his mother called from Aberdeen to see how her son was doing in his new life. "I'm fine," Angus said, "But there are some really strange people living in these apartments. One woman cries all day long; another lies on the floor moaning; and there is a guy next door to me who bangs his head on the wall all the time. "Well, ma laddie," says his mother, "I suggest you don't associate with people like that. "Oh," says Angus, "I don't Mama, I don't. No, I just stay in my apartment all day and night practicing on my bagpipes."

***

A story about man's best friend; Sex!

When I went to the City Hall to renew my dog's license, I told the clerk I wanted a license for Sex. He laughed and said, "I'd like one too lady, but we don't sell that type of a license." Then I said, "But this is a dog." He said he didn't care what she looked like. Then I said, "You don't understand, I've had Sex since I was 9 years old." He winked at me and said, "You must have been quite a kid."

When I got married and went on my honeymoon, I took my dog with me. I told the hotel clerk I wanted a room for my wife and me, and a special room for Sex. He said, "You don't' need a special room for Sex. As long as you pay your bill, we don't care what you do." I said, "Look mister! You don't seem to understand. Sex keeps me awake at night." The clerk said, "Funny, I have the same problem."

Well, one day, I entered Sex in a contest, but before the competition began, the dog got loose and ran away. Another contestant asked me why I was just standing there, looking disappointed. I told him I had planned to have Sex in the contest. He said, "Wonderful! If you sell tickets, you'll clean up!"

Well, my wife and I decided to separate, so we went to court to fight for custody of the dog. I said to the judge, "Your honor, I had Sex before I was married." The judge said, "The court is not a confessional. Please stick to the facts." Then I told him that after I was married, Sex left me. He said, "Me, too."

Well, last night Sex ran away again, and I spent hours looking all over town for him. A cop came over to me as asked, "What are you doing in this alley at 4 o'clock in the morning?" I said, "I'm looking for Sex." My case comes upon Friday, but I'll tell you once thing for sure; if I ever get another dog I sure ain't gonna name him Sex!

***

"If builders built buildings, the way programmers write programs, the first woodpecker that came along would destroy civilization!"

***

A group of seniors were sitting around talking about their ailments. "My arms are so weak I can hardly hold this cup of coffee," said one. "Yes, I know. My cataracts are so bad, I can't even see my coffee," replied another. "I can't turn my head because of the arthritis in my neck," said a third, to which several nodded weakly in agreement. "My blood pressure pills make me dizzy," claimed another. "I guess that's the price we pay for getting old," winced an old man as he shook his head. Then there was a short moment of silence, "Well, it's not that bad," said a woman cheerfully. "Thank God we can all still drive."

Sunny Susan, in Arizona

***

"Oh what a tangled web we weave, when first we practice to deceive!"
(Sir Walter Scott)

***

A man was mowing his front yard when his attractive, blonde, female neighbor came out of the house and went straight to her mailbox. She opened the mailbox, and stormed back into her house. A little later, she came out of her house again, went to the mailbox, again opened it, and again slammed it shut. Angrily back into the house she went. As the man was getting ready to edge the lawn, the blonde came out again. She marched to the mailbox, opened it and then slammed it closed harder than ever. Puzzled by her actions, the man asked her, "Is something wrong?" She replied, "There certainly is! My stupid computer keeps telling me I have mail."

***

After his return from Rome, Willy couldn't find his luggage at the London Gatwick airport baggage area. So, he went to the lost luggage office and told the woman there that his bags hadn't shown up on the carousel. She smiled and told him not to worry because they were trained professionals, and he was in good hands. "Now," she asked, Willy has your plane arrived yet."

***

A father was examining his son's report card. "One thing is definitely in your favor," he announced. "With this report card, you couldn't possibly be cheating."

***

"My girlfriend takes advantage of me." "What do you mean?" "I invited her out to dinner, and she asked me if she could bring a date.

***

A husband is about to leave on a business trip. "Honey, if my business requires me to stay longer in that town, I'll send you a telegram," he said. His wife replies, "Don't bother, darling, I've read it already; it's in the pocket of your coat."

***

You know, if brains were dynamite, she wouldn't have enough to blows her nose!

***

How do you milk an ant? First, you get a very low stool . . .

***

HERE IS OLD AGE AT ITS' BEST!

George and Sam, two friends, met in the park every day to feed the pigeons, watch the squirrels and discuss world problems. One day George didn't show up. Sam didn't think much about it and figured maybe he had a cold or something . . . But after George hadn't shown up for a week or so, Sam really got worried. However, since the only time they ever got together was at the park, Sam didn't know where George lived, so he was unable to find out what had happened to him. A month had passed, and Sam figured he had seen the last of George, but one day, Sam approached the park and . . . lo and behold . . . there sat George! Sam was very excited and happy to see him and told him so. Then he said, "For crying out loud George, what in the world happened to you?" George replied, "I have been in jail." "Jail!" cried Sam. What in the world for?" "Well," George said, "You know Sue, that cute little 30 year old blonde waitress at the coffee shop, where I sometimes go?" "Yeah," said Sam, "I remember her. What about her?" "Well, one day she filed rape charges against me; and, at 89 years old, I was so proud that when I got into court, I pleaded guilty; the darn judge gave me 30 days for perjury."

***

Chicken Side off first...

Women over 60 don't have babies because they would put them down and forget where they left them.

***

A man woke up to find himself in a Catholic hospital with nuns taking care of him. As they nursed him back to health, one of the nuns asked him if he had health insurance. "No," He replied, "No health insurance." "Do you have any money in the bank?" asked the nun. "No, no money in the bank." The nun asked, "Do you have any relatives you could ask for help?" The man replied, "I only have a spinster sister, who is a nun." At this the nun became irritated. "Nuns are not spinsters. Nuns are married to God!" "OK, don't get all shook up, said the man. Just send the bill to my brother-in- law.

Richard & Neta Ruth Sunderwirth

Chicken Side off first...

"The best way to forget all your troubles is to wear tight shoes."

***

The older you get, the tougher it is to lose weight because by then, your body and your fat are really good friends.

Sometimes I think I understand everything, then . . . I begin to regain consciousness.

I had to give up jogging for my health because my thighs kept rubbing together and setting my pantyhose on fire.

Skinny people irritate me? Especially when they say things like, "You know, sometimes I just forget to eat." Now I've forgotten my address, my mother's maiden name, and my keys, but I've never forgotten to eat. You have to be a very special kind of stupid to forget to eat.

A friend of mine confused her Valium WITH HER BIRTH CONTROL PILLS. She had 14 kids, but she doesn't really doesn't care.

I know what Victoria's Secret is. The secret is that nobody older than 30 can fit into their stuff.

Just when I was getting used to yesterday, along came today.

***

An old gentleman complained to his doctor that his right ear was giving him trouble; he couldn't hear out of it. So the doctor checked, checked, checked, listened, listened, and said, "Oh, you know your ear problem is just an age problem. Your ear is getting old and that's all, that's why you can't hear." The gentleman said, "Nonsense, nope that doesn't make any sense, because it is exactly the same age as my left ear, and I sure don't have any problem with it. Try something else Doc."

***

A couple was invited to a swanky masked Halloween party. The wife got a terrible headache about an hour before they were to leave. She told her husband to go to the party alone. He, being a devoted husband, protested but she argued and said she was going to take an aspirin and got to bed, and there was no need of his good time being spoiled by not going, so he took his costume and out he went.

The wife, after sleeping for about an hour, awakened without pain, and as it was still early, she decided to go to the party. In as much as her husband did not know what her costume was, she thought she would have some fun by watching her husband, to see how he acted, when she was not with him.

She joined the party and soon spotted her husband cavorting around on the dance floor, dancing with every nice chick he could, and sporting a little feel here and a little kissy there. His wife, sidled up to him and being a rather seductive babe herself, he left his partner high and dry and devoted his time to the new gal that had just arrived.

She let him go as far as he wished; naturally, since he was her husband. Finally he whispered a little proposition in her ear and she decided no, that would mess up her joke on him. Just before unmasking at midnight, she slipped away and went home and put her costume away and got into bed, wondering what kind of explanation he would make for his behavior.

She was sitting up reading when he came in. She asked him what kind of a time he had at the party. He said, "Oh, the same old thing; you know I never have a good time when you're not with me." And then she asked, "Did you dance much." He replied, "I'll tell you, I never danced one dance. When I got there, I met Pete, Bill Brown and some others, so we went into the den and played poker all evening. But I'll tell you this . . . the old boy I loaned my costume to sure had a really good time."

***

One day at school the first grade teacher was reading the story of the 3 little pigs to her class. She came to the part where the first little pig was trying to accumulate some building materials for his home. She read . . . and so the pig went up to the man with the wheelbarrow full of straw and said, "Pardon me sir, but may I have some of that straw to help build my house?" The teacher paused and then asked the class, "What do you think that man said?" One little boy raised his hand and said, "I think he said, "Holy smokes, a talking pig."

***

His wife had just bought a new line of expensive cosmetics abso-

lutely guaranteed to make her look years younger. She sat in front of the mirror for what had to be hours applying the "miracle" products. Finally, when she was done, she turned to her husband and said, "Hon, honestly now, what age would you say I am?" He nodded his head in assessment, and carefully said, "Well, honey, judging from your skin, Twenty. Your hair, mmmm, eighteen. Your figure, twenty-five." "Oh, you're so sweet! Oh, you're so nice!" "Well, hang on, I'm not done adding it up yet."
Copied

***

It is well documented that for every mile that you jog, you add one minute to your life. This enables you, at age 85, to spend an additional 5 months in a nursing home at $5,000 per month.

1. My grandmother started walking 5 miles a day when she was 60. She is now 97 and she must still be walking some where, because we don't know where she is.
2. I joined a health club last year, spent about $400. Haven't lost a pound. Apparently you have to show up.
3. I have to exercise early in the morning before my brain figures out what I am doing.
4. I don't exercise at all. If God meant us to touch our toes, he would have put them further up our body.
5. I like long walks, especially when they are taken by people who annoy me.
6. I have flabby thighs, but fortunately my stomach covers them.
7. The advantage of exercising every day is that you die health -ier.
8. If you are going to try cross country skiing, start with a very small country.
9. And last, but not least, I don't jog, it makes the ice jump right out of my glass.

***

"Never be bullied into silence, never allow yourself to be made a victim. Accept no one's definition of your life; define yourself."

Harvey Fierstein

***

Three good laws

Never get into fights with ugly people, they have nothing to lose.

If you dance with a grizzly bear, you better let him lead.

When putting cheese in a mousetrap, always leave room for the mouse.

***

EDUCATION!

A crying 6-year-old told his mother that his little sister had pulled his hair. "Don't be angry," his mother said. "She doesn't realize that pulling hair hurts." A short while later, the mother heard more crying. When she walked into the room, she saw her daughter crying. The little boy looked up at his mother and said, "She knows now."

***

PRAYER!

A small boy pleaded with his father for a baby brother. "Why don't you pray for a little brother every night before you go to bed," his dad suggested. The little boy prayed every night for several weeks. During that time, his wish wasn't granted, and he eventually gave up. Several months later, the boy's father said, "We're going to the hospital to see your mother. We have a big surprise for you." When they walked into the room, the boy saw his mother holding three babies. "Well, what do you think about your triplet brothers?" Father asked. The boy thought for a moment, then replied, "I bet you're glad I stopped praying when I did." Helen

***

THE ONLY WEIGH!

A woman noticed her husband standing on the bathroom scales sucking in his stomach. "I don't think that is going to help," she commented, thinking he was trying to weigh less. "Sure it will," he said. "It's the only way I can see the numbers." Christeen

STUCK!

Dr. Carver was called to the Tuttle house to examine Mrs. Tuttle, who was experiencing terrible pain. Dr. Carver went in to check her out. He came back out shortly and said, "Mr. Tuttle, do you have a hammer?" Mr. Tuttle answered, "Sure do," so he went to the garage and returned with a hammer. The doctor thanked him and went back to his patient. A few moments later he appeared again. "Do you have a chisel?" the doctor asked. Once again, Mr. Tuttle got the tool for the doctor. Over the next 10 minutes, Dr. Carver asked for and received a pair of pliers, a screw-driver and a hacksaw. Finally, Mr. Tuttle asked, "What are you doing to my wife?" Not a thing," said the doctor. "I can't get my instrument bag open." Rosalie

***

TOP TEN REASONS WHY GOD CREATED EVE

10. God worried that Adam would always be lost in the garden because men hate to ask for directions.
9. God knew that Adam would one day need someone to hand him the T.V. remote. Man don't want to see what's ON tele vision, they want to see WHAT ELSE is on!
8. God knew that Adam would never buy a new fig leaf when his seat wore out and would need Eve to get a new one for him.
7. God knew that Adam would never make a doctor's appoint ment for himself.
6. God knew that Adam would never remember which night was garbage night.
5. God knew that if the world was to be populated, men would never be able to handle childbearing.
4. As "Keeper of the Garden," Adam would never remember where he put his tools.
3. The scripture account of creation indicates Adam needed someone to blame his troubles on when God caught him hid ing in the garden.
2. As the Bible says, "It is not good for man to be alone!" And the number one reason God created Eve. . .
1. When God finished the creation of Adam, He stepped back, scratched His head and said," I can do better than that."

***

Six-year old was trying to thread a needle. "Come on now, Say AHHHHHHH."

***

We used to have a bowling alley in Osceola until someone stole the ball.

***

Three friends die in a car accident and they go to an orientation in heaven. They are all asked, "When you were in your casket and friends and family are mourning you, what would you like to hear them say about you? The first guy says, "I would like to hear them say I was a great doctor of my time and a great family man." The second guy says, "I would like them to say I was a wonderful husband, and school teacher who made a huge difference in our children of tomorrow." The third guy says, "I would like them to say, hey look, he's moving."

***

A magician working a summer cruise ship had a pet parrot that would very often spoil his act. The parrot would always say to the audiences. "He has the card in his left pocket, or the cards up his sleeve, or it went thru a hole in his top hat." The ship sank one day and the parrot and the magician found themselves together on a raft. For 4 days the parrot stared silently at the magician. Finally, on the 5th day the parrot said, "Okay, wise guy, I give up, what did you do with the ship?"

***

Mable told this story about her son David . . . Here's how the story goes!

Mable's son David just couldn't find a job, he hated to live at home because he was 28 years of age. He talked it over with his mother and together they thought it would be nice if he would move to New York City and attempt to get a job there. Well, that's what he did; he moved in just a few days. His mother, of course, worried about him but at the same time she really felt it was time to do so. After a few weeks he called home and said to his mother, "Mom, I got a good job, pays well, I have a nice reasonably priced apartment, and I've got a really great room-mate." His mother was so excited; she promptly asks him about his roommate. He said, "Mom, before you get all shook up I've got to tell you something, her name is Stephanie." Well, that didn't go over very good. She questioned him quite a bit about the fact that it was a girl. He told her it was only platonic and that there was no real closeness between them, but it sure helped out because they split the rent. Mom finally picked herself up off the floor and went along with him to a degree. In about 3 weeks she decided she was going to visit him and see how he was getting along. Of course it was a great surprise to both David and Stephanie. The first night there Stephanie fixed a wonderful meal of turkey, gravy, dressing, and all the basic stuff. Mother thought it was a very good meal. She stayed a few days and went home fairly satisfied, but yet still a bit worried. A day or so later Stephanie said to David, "Honey, have you seen the sterling silver gravy ladle, you know, the one that belonged to my grandmother; I can't find it since your mother was here for a visit. I don't know if she accidentally took it with her or not." "I'm not saying what happened, I'm not saying she did or she didn't, but I can't find it." "Well," said David, "But I'm sure if she did it was just an accident." "I'll give her a call and see if she knows anything about it." Stephanie said, "You know how much that means to me and I would really appreciate you doing that, you know I'm not saying she did or she didn't but I really want to find it." David replied, "Oh honey I know how much it means to you." He made the call and talked to his mummy. "Mom, you know when you were her to visit we had turkey, gravy and the works; well, we can't find Stephanie's precious sterling silver gravy ladle." "Is there a chance you might have accidently taken it home with you?" Mom said, "Oh no David, I wouldn't do that, but I will tell you this." "I don't know if you did or you didn't, what I mean is, I really don't think you're sleeping with Stephanie or not; but, if you'll go in and pull the covers back on her bed you'll find the gravy ladle . . . **END OF STORY, FOR NOW!**

***

"Don't go around thinking the world owes you a living. The world owes you nothing. It was here first."

Mark Twain

***

A young girl was engaged to be married. "But Dad I really don't want to leave Mother." "Honey, I don't want to stand in the way of your happiness; take her with you."

***

"What were your father's last words?" "He didn't have any. Mother was with him till the very end."

***

The doctor said to his patient, "The check you gave me came back." "Well, don't worry about it Doc, so did my lumbago."

***

Great SPECIAL today! We have 75 percent off on all parachutes. "What's the matter with them?" "Oh, they work fine." Only one little hitch, they only open on impart."

***

Two little boy were having a disagreement. Johnny says, "Yep, the first man in the world was Hoss." "No, No says Jimmy." "Yes, it was, cause I've seen lots of those "Bonanza" shows on TV and I know it was Hoss." Jimmy says, "I still know you're wrong, it was Adam." "Oh gosh, well, I knew it was one of those Cartwright boys."

***

"Well, I'm not saying that her fiancée is, cheap," whispered the office gossip. "But every time I get close to her engagement ring, I have an overwhelming desire for some cracker jacks."

***

"My wife and I had words the other night." "Did you get everything worked out?" "I don't know I still got mine." "You still got what?" "Words, I never did get to use mine."

***

Jim and Ralph were talking about things they had said to their wives that sometimes didn't go over to well. Jim said, "Yeah, I didn't mean for it to come out this way but when she walked out of the bedroom I said, 'Haven't you got anything that looks better than that."

***

"To learn who rules over you, find out who you are not allowed to criticize."

Voltaire

***

Richard & Neta Ruth Sunderwirth

"You know, my wife has got 10 closets full of clothes and nothing to wear. She's got a pair of shoes with every dress. We were going out to eat and she said, "Which shoes are you going to wear?" I said, "Both of them, these..." Carl Hurley

***

I got a cousin that came to visit last week. He got arrested. He went to court and got all dressed up. I said to him, "Joe what do folks say when you get all dressed up." "Well, most of the time they say, would the defendant please rise." Carl Hurley

***

Not too long ago, some of you might remember, our city council decided to put up a one-way street sign. Well, it worked pretty good until we started home. We all got out of town and couldn't get back.

***

My wife and I went out to a patty pig supper. We drove about 60 miles to get there. It was quite a few miles just for supper. We walked in the door and I told my wife, "I wished I'd brought my TV." "Why would you want to bring your TV?" she said. "Welllllllllll, that's where I left our tickets laying." Carl Hurley

I really liked Mickey Mouse when I was a kid. My folks figured out that Mickey lived in Orlando, Florida. We decided we'd drive down and see Mickey. We did just that, but when we got there we saw a big sign over the inter-state that said "Mickey Mouse Left." Well, we turned around came home. Carl Hurley

***

The other day a fellow came up to me and ask if I could give him $20 to help bury a Politician. I said, "I sure can as a matter of fact; I'll give you $200 and you can bury 10 of them."

***

My friend went into a bank and asked the loan officer for a loan. The officer said, "Well Sam, I think we might be able to arrange that. What do you do?" Sam said, "Oh, this and that? "Where do you work?" "Here and there." "When do you work?" "Now and then." "Sam said to the officer, "When do you think I might be able to get this loan?" The bank officer replied, "Oh . . . by and by." Carl Hurley

***

About three weeks ago my wife told me I ought to buy me a suit with two pairs of pants. Well, that made sense because I always wore out the one pair of pants first. I went out and bought me a nice suit with two pair of pants. Do you know what the first thing I went and did? I burnt a hole in the coat!

***

"Only a life lived for others is a life worthwhile"

Albert Einstein

***

I don't wear my artificial teeth no more because the last time I tried it I put them in upside down and durned near chewed half my head off.

***

I guess you've heard about folks that carry a lighter that won't light? I got a worse problem. Mine won't go out.

***

I've always had bad luck. Even when I was a little boy going to school, my voice was so high I had to sing with the girls. By the time I got old enough to appreciate it, my voice changed.

***

With my kind of luck if they cut a beautiful woman in half and offered to share with me, I'd get the part that eats.

***

I even have trouble with my clothes. I don't know which is the most aggravating; my pants falling down or my shorts creeping up.

***

The other day my wife bought me a new bicycle. I guess she thought I needed the exercise. I was riding down the street and I saw a boy out in his front yard sitting on a nice lawn mower. I figured he just might want to trade his mower for my new bike. I ask him if he would trade and he said yes. I said to him "Does it run alright?" He said, "Well, the last time I started it up it sure did." So we traded, fair and square. He got the bike and I got the mower. I took it home and in a few days I started to mow the grass. I jerked and I jerked on the starter cord and, sure enough, my luck, it wouldn't start. Finally I went back down to find the little boy and told him my mower wouldn't start. "Well," he said. "You have to cuss it for a while, then it will. "You don't understand son. I'm a Preacher and I've forgotten how to cuss." The little boy looked me straight in the eye and said, "If you keep trying long enough it will come back to you."

***

"Patriotism means to stand by your country. It does not mean to stand by the President or any other political official." Theodore Roosevelt

***

A thirty year old gal got on the airplane and immediately sat down in first class. The flight attendant came up and said to her, "Let me see your ticket? You do not have a first class ticket. You'll have to go back to the next section of the plane." The young lady said, "I'm 30 years old, I'm blond, I'm beautiful, I'm going to Chicago and I'm going to sit in first class." "No, honey, you can't sit in first class without a first class ticket." Once again she shouted out, "I'm 30 years old, I'm blond, I'm beautiful, I'm going to Chicago, and I'm going to sit in first class." The flight attendant called the supervisor and told her the problem. The supervisor bent over and whispered in the gal's ear and she politely got up and moved back to the next section of the plane. The attendant asked the supervisor what it was she said. The supervisor said, "No big deal, I just told her that first class wasn't going to Chicago."

***

TRUE STORY: I had a gentleman call me one day and ask me if I would speak to their group about the book that I had written, the "Burning of Osceola, Missouri," I said, "Yes, I would be happy to." He said he especially wanted a couple of things, first he wanted to know about the burning and secondly he only wanted about 20 minutes. Well that was one I turned down. I've never been able to speak about anything for only 20 minutes. For me to speak for that short of time is sorta like trying to nail Jello® to the wall. I just can't do it.

Chicken Side off first...

***

Buster was driving down the road with his license plate just barely hanging on to the back of his car and every little bit it was bouncing on the roadway. The police stopped him and told him of the situation. Buster said, "Golly, I'm sure glad you stopped me. I borrowed that from my neighbor's car so I could go down and re-apply for my driver's license." Before the policeman could say anything Buster's wife spoke up, "Don't believe anything he tells you because he was half drunk when we left home."

***

A fellow went into a restaurant and ordered 6 big farm eggs, 6 slices of bacon, 4 pieces of fried sausage, and a big bowl of fried taters with white cream gravy on the top. Another fellow was sitting across the aisle from him and really told him in no uncertain terms that a breakfast like that would kill him. He told him too much fat, sugar, etc. "Don't you know that your arteries carry blood to the heart, but with that junk in them they can't do their job." The man eating the breakfast said to the gentleman giving the advice. "My daddy lived to be 97 and I'm going to do the same. The stranger said, "Well, he lived to be 97 probably because he ate proper food in proper amounts." The fellow eating the breakfast said, "Nope, he lived to be 97 because he minded his own business."

***

"I have a simple philosophy; fill what's empty, empty what's full; scratch where it itches."

Alice Roosevelt Longworth

***

Do you know that we guys say things we shouldn't say to our wives sometimes? Yep, I sure messed up the other day." "My wife said she just finished setting her hair," and I jumped in and said, "What time is it supposed to go off?" I shouldn't have done that.

***

Some of these jokes are so old that when Adam told them to Eve she said she'd already heard them.

***

Did you hear about the actress who married a director and longed for children? Her husband told her he didn't want to have children, so she divorced the director and married a producer.

***

A college education seldom hurts a man if he is willing to learn a whole bunch after he graduates.

***

"Natural ability without education has more often raised a man to glory and virtue than education without natural ability." Cicero

***

This guy's wife retired and she came home the first day of her retirement and told her husband there had to be some changes made around the house. She told him to white wash the yard fence, and then she got mad when he started asking questions. So he didn't finish asking and because of that when he finished the fence she really got mad at him. He said I tried to ask you what color you wanted it and you told me to shut up. It's your fault.

***

The other day a fellow came up from Osceola to Clinton. He had quite a financial problem so he went down to apply for some assistance to help feed and clothe his family of 7 kids and 1 wife. He hadn't had an opportunity to work for a long time. He sat there in his ragged and dirty overalls. He didn't even have enough money to by soap to wash his clothes. Eventually the social worker came in and started asking him some questions. "Now what assets do you have that you are now living on. Do you have very much in stocks and bonds and if so do you have your retirement set up on annuities or just cash in insurance policies?" She went on with a bunch of questions similar to the last one. "What assets are you living on now she asked again." He answered her with; "Well, I have 5000 shares in stocks with Phillips Oil, 500 shares in G. M. and 1500 in Conoco Oil." "Do you own a house?" "Yes, I live in a two story house with a full basement and a swimming pool." "I guess the house must be about 3400 sq. ft. "Oh, yes and I also have 3 homes that I rent out. One is on 500 acres of top farm land." "Do you have a car to get you around in?" "Why yes, I have a 2012 Lincoln Continental that I use for everyday and a new Ford pickup when I go shopping." "A friend brought me up here today, because I had no available cash to buy gasoline for my vehicle." At that point she said to the gentleman. "You've got to be kidding?" He said, about as quick as he could get it out of his mouth, "Well, you started it.

***

"Do you know what you get when you cross a lawyer with a politician?" "A Chelsea"

***

Well, there's at least one advantage to being poor . . . the doctor will certainly cure you faster.

***

"Doctor, Doctor, come here quick, my little Gary has swallowed my razor blade." "Now don't get too excited Mr. Conn," replied the doctor, don't panic." "So, Mr. Conn, what are you doing about it so far?" "Well, I've been using my electric razor."

***

Dr. Lucas was helping to train a young intern who frankly wasn't too bright. As they were looking at the x-rays of a patient, Dr. Lucas said, "You notice there that the pictures show that one of the patient's legs is longer than the other, which explains his limp. Now Tom, the doctor inquired, what would you do in a case like that?" After deep deep thought, Tom finally replied, "I guess doctor I would probably limp also."

***

"Honesty is the first chapter in the book of wisdom."

***

One of the ladies who makes a habit of swimming at the city swimming pool was talking to one of her friends, "Mable what do you think about this, I was told that one of the local boys took a leak in the city community pool." "Well, Susie I'm pretty sure that happens to everyone that ever swims once in a great while." "Well, you're probably right, but really! From the high dive?"

***

"Hey John, would you help me out with the blinker lights on my car? I can't tell from the inside if they are working." Ok Fred, start working them, yep, nope, yep, nope, yep, nope, the best I can tell is they're working only about half of the time."

***

The State Restaurant Inspector came into Jim's Hot Shot Café. "Jim you've got way too many roaches in here." "Ok," said Jim, how many am I allowed?"

***

"Hey, Ramona, don't you think it is about time your mother found a place of her own; she's been living here with us for almost 20 years?" "What do you mean, my mother, I thought she was yours."

***

"You don't have to be great to start, but you do have to start to be great."

Zig Ziglar

***

The nice young couple was getting married. When they got the part where the minister asked this question, "Do you take this man for richer or poorer?" The bride said without blinking, "For richer, I wasn't born yesterday."

***

A little boy was telling his daddy about sleeping with his mommy. He said, "Daddy me sleep with mommy." "No son, you must say, I slept with mommy." Little boy said again, "Daddy no, me sleep with mommy." Once again, daddy said, "No son, you must say, I slept with mommy," "Well daddy if you say so, but if you did, you got out before I got in."

***

"Honey, you remind me of the sea." "Oh darling, I know why," She replied, "I'm beautiful, I'm so wild and so romantic." "Nope, most of the time you make me sick."

***

The old man and his lady were sitting on the porch swing. He tried to get a bit romantic even though he couldn't she couldn't hear very well. He said, "Darling, I love you, you're tried and true." She responded, a little bit angry, "Well, I'm tired of you too."

***

"Did you know you shouldn't eat pinto beans and onions at the same time," "Well, why is that, said the lady?" "I heard they will give you tear gas."

***

The elderly lady called her daughter and told her she was starting to date again. The daughter said, "Mom, don't you realize you're 80 years old?" "Yep, said her mother, "I know that." "Well, what's the big deal then, is he rich, or good-looking, or famous?" "Nope, he ain't none of those things." "What is it then," said her daughter. "Well, if you really have to know, he can drive after night."

***

Mrs. Jones went to her doctor and told him that she was having night-mares, horrible ones. "What are they about?" said the doctor. "I keep dreaming there are lots of snakes under my bed" The doctor said, "I think I know how to take care of that, where do you live Mrs. Jones?" She gave him her address, paid her bill, and went home satisfied that he would do what was necessary. The next night she had no dreams about snakes under her bed. The next morning she called her best girlfriend and said the doctor took care of my problem with the snakes. "What did he do for you?" asked her friend. "Oh he just cut the legs off of my bed, where they couldn't get under there anymore."

***

"A word to the wise ain't necessary; it's the stupid ones that need the advice!"

Bill Cosby

***

The farmer lost his prize bull, so he went and got another one. It was the worst cross-eyed bull he'd ever seen. He took the bull to the vet to see if he could straighten the bull's eyes. The vet got a rubber hose and stuck it the bull's rear-end and blew like crazy. "How's the eyes doing he asked the farmer." The farmer said they were completely straight. It really shocked the doctor because he was only joking. "Here, he said to the farmer, you blow and let me look at his eyes." "What in the world are you doing," said the vet to the farmer. The farmer replied, "I'm changing ends on this hose, you don't expect me to blow on the same end where you had your mouth, do you?"

***

" A hole is nothing at all, But you can break your neck in it."

***

This fellow went on vacation in Florida. He decided it was time to eat so he went into one of the nicest places he could find. He ordered his drink and it was only 19 cents. He ordered a cheeseburger, thinking they would make up the price on it, only to find it was 59 cents. He asked the waiter, "How about a T-bone steak." Well, it was only $^{\$}1^{25}$. He said, "How in the world can you make any money selling this food so cheap. Does your boss really know the price you are selling it for?" "Nope, he's on vacation in the Bahamas with my wife . . . and I've got an idea he's doing to her about the same thing I'm doing to him right now."

***

This couple rented a room in a pretty nice hotel. After they got in the room the fellow decided to go down to the lobby and get a coke. I don't think this guy was the brightest person in the room. He asked his wife, "Honey, how in the world do they expect me to get out of here. There are only 2 doors and one says restroom and the other do not disturb?"

***

HERE'S A DANDY ABOUT THE NEW PHONES WE'RE SUPPOSED TO USE TODAY.
If you are calling from your touch-tone telephone PRESS One. If you have been in an accident, PRESS Two. If you are having a heart attack and have difficulty breathing, enter your Social Security number and PRESS the pound key on the lower right side of your phone. Please hold for the next available operator. If he or she is not readily available you may PRESS the STAR button and then enter your telephone number and she or he will be more than happy to return your call at their earliest convenience. Thank you so much for using our services today, and we certainly hope you enjoyed the music.

***

"A helping word to one in trouble is like a switch in a railroad track... an inch between wreck and smooth, rolling prosperity." Henry Ward Beecher

***

Everybody thought my uncle Vernon was dumb, only going to the 3rd grade. He went to the bank one day to see if he could get a loan. He asked to borrow a dollar. He wanted to do it proper so he said to the clerk, "Would you please hold this note for one year?" At the end of the year he came back with a dollar and the banker said he owed him 11 cents interest. My uncle told him thanks and started to walk out of the back. The banker said to my uncle, "Why did you only borrow a dollar." "Well, said Vernon, I went down to this other bank down on the corner, and they wanted $25.00 bucks to get a safe deposit box to hold that there note, and you did it for 11 cents.

***

"Do you talk to your wife when you make love?"
"Only if there is a phone handy."

***

People today want economy, and they'll pay almost any price to get it.

***

Winter is the time of year when you try to keep your home as warm as it was in the summer when you complained about it.

***

A friend of mine walked into a first-class hotel in New York and asked if there were any vacancies. "What kind of room would you like, sir?" He encouraged the fellow to go ahead and register and then my friend asked, "What have you got for around $25.00?" The clerk replied, "You're holding it."

***

A frazzled mother was ordering a beverage for her youngest child when the waitress asked, "What size drink do you want for your child?" The mother answered, "Whatever size you'd like to clean up.

***

"A heavy burden does not kill on the day it is carried."

Kenyan Proverb

***

Two prisoners were put into one cell. One asked, "How long are you in for?" The second one said, "50 years. The first prisoner said, "I'm in for 75 years, why don't you go ahead and take the bed nearest to the door since you're getting out first."

***

An amorous boyfriend asked his new girlfriend, "How about some good old-fashioned loving?" The girlfriend answered, sure thing, I'll call my grandmother."

***

Give a man a fish and you feed him for a day. Teach him how to fish and you will get rid of him on the weekends.

***

A heavy snowstorm closed the schools in one town. When the children returned to school a few days later, one grade school teacher asked her students whether they had used the time away from school constructively. "I sure did, teacher," one little girl replied. "I just prayed for more snow."

***

An elderly man had a complete physical examination. "My good man," said the doctor, "You're as sound as a dollar bill. You'll live to be 80 years old." "But I'm 80 years old now." The doctor said, "See, what did I tell you."

***

"A happy person is one whose arithmetic is at its best when they are counting their blessings."
Copied

***

Minnie Pearl told this one:
Lady celebrating her 100th birthday. The gentleman doing the interview asked, "What do you contribute your long life to?" She answered, "Good health." "You mean you haven't been bed ridden in 100 years,
"Oh sure sonny, probably several times; even once in a buggy."

***

The wife gained a few pounds. She squeezed into a pair of old blue jeans. She wondered if her added weight was noticeable, so she asked her husband, "Honey, do these jeans make me look like a side of the house?" "No dear, not at all, our house isn't blue."

***

The wife and her husband were reminiscing about their dating days, when he mentioned that she used to have a coke bottle figure. "Honey, I still have coke bottle figure, can't you tell?" "Yeah I sure can," said her husband, "Only now it's a two liter."

***

One night after dinner John and Judy decided to take a walk before the sun went down. Judy said to her husband, "Sweetie, do these jeans and yellow shirt look ok on me?" "Honey," he replied, "you still look great, and besides, it's going to be dark soon."

***

During the depression, at great financial sacrifice, my parents bought a piano for me and my twin sister and arranged for us to take piano lessons. For many years, Mom and Dad glowed with pride as their little twins played duets at various community functions. Some 30 years later, dad and mom came over for dinner and asked me to play the piano. Warning that I hadn't played for a long time, I still agreed to do so. As I played I noticed tears running down dad's cheek. I turned to him and said, "Was it that good dad." He sadly shook his head and replied. "All that money shot to thunder."

***

My pet peeves are numerous, but there is one that really bugs me. It is by those who offer free gifts as a part of their sales pitch. Late one night, I was in bed when the phone rang. The voice congratulated me and said, "Sir, you've just won a free burial plot, including a beautiful vault." I said, "Well, go ahead and send them both over." Then I hung up and went back to sleep.

***

How Much?
A woman goes into Wal-Mart to buy a rod and reel. She doesn't know which one to get, so she just grabs one and goes over to the register. There is a Wal-Mart associate standing there with dark shades on. She says, "Excuse me, Sir . . . Can you tell me anything about this rod and reel?" He says, "Ma'am, I'm blind, but if you will drop it on the counter I can tell you everything you need to know about it from the sound that it makes. She didn't believe him but dropped it on the counter anyway. He said, "That's a 6′ graphite rod with a Zebco 202 reel and 10 Lb. test line. It's a good all-around rod and reel, and it cost $20." She says, "It is amazing that you can tell all that just by the sound of it dropping on the counter. I think it's what I'm looking for, so I'll take it." He walks behind the counter to the register; she bends down to get her purse and lets out a pretty big toot. At first she is embarrassed but then realizes that there is no way he could tell it was her. Being blind, he wouldn't know that she was the only person around. He rings up the sale and says, "That will be $25.50." She

says, "But didn't you say it was $20?" He says, "Yes ma'am, the rod and reel is $20, the duck call is $3, and the catfish stink bait is $2.50. And thank you for shopping at Wal-Mart.

***

"Did you hear about what happened to me last Halloween?" "Well, one kid showed up at our door dressed as an IRS agent. It looked very authentic, and it was verified when he took over 40 percent of my candy."

***

"Your present circumstances don't determine where you can go; they merely determine where you start."

Nido Quebin

***

Boy, this one is different. I called the airlines to make reservations for a trip. I was immediately put on hold. After several minutes of taped music and several recorded messages another message came on and said, "If you've been waiting longer than 10 minutes, please press 8 wait 2 minutes and then press 4. "This will not speed up your call, but it will give you something to listen to while you are waiting."

***

"The nerve of it all, I got a registered letter from the sewer dept. They said they'd had just about enough out of me."

***

"To me women are like computers, I can't turn either one of them on."

***

Arnold complained to a co-worker that he didn't know what to get his wife for her birthday. She already has everything you could possibly think of, and anyway she can buy herself whatever she likes. "Here's an idea," said the co-worked. She continued on, "Make up your own gift certificate that says, "Thirty minutes of the greatest loving anyway you want it. I guarantee she'll be enchanted." The next day, Arnold's co-worker asked. "Well, did you take my suggestion?" she asked. "Yes, said Arnold," "Did she like it? "Oh yes, she jumped up, kissed me on the forehead and ran out the door yelling, 'See you in 30 minutes."

***

Arriving home from work, I was greeted in the driveway by our pregnant dog. As she waddled toward me, I called out, "How are you doing, Fatso?" From next door over the fence our neighbor was pulling weeds and she hollered back. "Oh, just fine, you stupid xytejpl37."

***

Some friends of mine celebrated the birth of their fourth child by giving a back-yard barbecue. I stood by the grill, chatting with the host who remarked, "After four kids, I think it's time to go for the big V." "Yeah, I don't blame you; you're going to get a vasectomy?" "Oh no," said the host, "we're going to get a big van."

***

There was a millionaire who left a lot of money in the attic. He said to his wife, "Leave it there until I die and when I'm leaving I'll grab it on the way up." After his death his wife happened to find the money one day while cleaning. She said, "I told him he should have put that box of money in the basement."

***

If you don't know how to do something go ahead and start anyway. There will a lot of people come by and tell you exactly how to do it.

***

Some friends were talking one day about the price of folk's brains after their death. They decided that a doctor's brain would be worth $10,000; a lawyer's would be $20,000; a top notch scientist's would be $50,000 and a tour director's would be $100,000. One asked, "Why would the tour directors' be so high?" "Well, because it is brand new, it's never been used."

***

Just getting out of the driveway was a major problem during last year's snow and ice storms. One guy was relating how he used his seven year old son's baseball bat to smash the slick coat of ice on his driveway. He said he got really cold one morning and went inside for a cup of coffee before attempting to clear the car. A few minutes later, his 7 year old son, who had been outside with him came in and said "Dad, I got the ice off the car." "How did you do that," the father said, "The same way you did dad, with the baseball bat."

***

A grandson asked his grandfather for some advice. "Granddad, you know I'm getting married right away?" "Yes," said the grandfather. "Where did you and Grandma go on your honeymoon?" said the boy. Grandpa answered. "Well, it didn't cost us very much son, we just went upstairs for a couple of days."

***

A guy came home from work one day, really tired. He pulled off his clothes and went to bed. He started rubbing his feet, as he said, "feet go to sleep, legs go to sleep, tummy go to sleep, thighs go to sleep," and then he did it all over again, and finally he was asleep. About the time he got to sleep real good his wife walked in from the bathroom with a really thin red negligee on. She gently patted him on his shoulder and said, "Honey, I'm home," He sat straight up in bed and began to slap his legs, feet, tummy, & thighs and began to holler at the top of his voice, "Ok you guys, everybody up up up let's get up boys, time to get up up up."

***

"Crime today is getting so bad . . . so bad. The other day a guy was run over trying to steal the hub caps off of his own car that was being stolen."

***

Life from the seat of a tractor

I was reading these words of wisdom and a couple names just popped into my head,

An old farmer's words of wisdom most of us could live by. Your fences need to be horse-high, pig-tight and bull-strong. Keep skunks and bankers at a distance. Life is simpler when you plow around the stump. A bumble bee is considerably faster than a John Deere tractor. Words that soak into your ears are whispered . . . not yelled. Meanness doesn't just happen overnight. Forgive your enemies; it messes up their heads. Do not corner something that you know is meaner than you. It doesn't take a very big person to carry a grudge. You cannot unsay a cruel word. Every path has a few puddles. When you wallow with pigs, expect to get dirty. The best sermons are lived, not preached. Most of the stuff people worry about, "ain't ever gonna happen" anyway. Don't judge folks by their relatives. Remember that silence is sometimes the best answer. Live a good and honorable life, then when you get older and think back, you'll enjoy it a second time. Don't interfere with something that ain't bothering you none. Timing has a lot to do with the outcome of a rain dance. If you find yourself in a hole, the first thing to do is stop digging. Sometimes you get, and sometimes you get got. The biggest troublemaker you'll probably ever have to deal with, watches you from the mirror every morning. Always drink upstream from the herd. Good judgment comes from experience, and much of that comes from bad judgment. Letting the cat "outta" the bag is a whole lot easier than putting it back in. If you get to thinking you're a person of some influence, try ordering somebody else's dog around. Live simply, love generously, care deeply, Speak kindly, and leave the rest to God. Don't pick a fight with an old man. If he is too old to fight, he'll just kill you.

***

"Did you know that 95% of most men die before their wives do?" "Is that right," his buddy said, "Why is that?" First guy said, "Well, because they want to."

***

"I can't change the direction of the wind, but I

can adjust my sails to always reach my destination."

Jimmy Dean

***

"Did you hear about the guy that exercised his chickens" "No, why is that." Well, because they kept laying deviled eggs."

***

A man met a pretty girl at a dance only to discover that she had been married three times. When asked about her first two husbands, she replied, "They both died from eating poison mushrooms." "Oh, that's too bad," said the man. "What happened to the third husband?" "Well, he died from a skull fracture." "No kidding," remarked the man. "Yeah, he wouldn't eat his mushrooms."

***

"Did you hear about the guy that sold eggs for $^{\$}1^{20}$ a dozen?" Another guy said, "I can get bigger eggs for $^{\$}1^{10}$ from the man down the street." The guy said," Well, you'd just better go on down the street and get your ***BIGGER*** eggs from him. I'm not going to get my hens all stretched out of shape for a dime."

***

At the party this guy got up and introduced his wife and said, "This is my beautiful wife, she's 53 years of age and the mother of three." He did this every time they went anywhere; at every party, every get-together of any kind. After many times of doing this she really got sick of hearing of it so she decided to get even with him and maybe it would shut him up. At the next party he got up and said the same ole thing . . . "and the mother of three." Well, she got up and said, "This is my wonderful husband, he's 65 years of age and the father of two." Yep, that stopped his introductions from that point forward.

***

"I'll bet you five dollars you can't recite the first three words of the constitution of the United States of America." "Well, I most certainly can. I'll take that bet." He said," I pledge allegiance to the flag, etc." "Golly," the other man said, here's your five dollars, I didn't think you knew it."

***

Life really begins when the last kid leaves home and the dog dies.

***

Old man looked over and saw a dog sitting down, and he was hollering something terrible. "What's the matter with that dog," the old man asked. The owner said, "Well, he's my politician dog." The old man says, "What's that got to do with it?" The owner replied back, "You see, he's sitting on a patch of cockle-burs and he'd rather just sit there and holler than get up and do something about it."

***

Somebody ask the bus driver a question. He answered the question and then ended by saying, "Yep, all my troubles are behind me."

***

When you got it . . . you got it!

Two old bachelor brothers lived way up in the hills of Kentucky. This story takes place in 1932. They lived together, and they went to town every Saturday morning to get supplies, etc. They drove a 1929 Model A Pickup. These were pretty dependable automobiles but they kinda bounced around a lot, especially if the roads were rough with ruts, etc. Well, one Saturday morning Clem and Clifford took off to the store, it was about 8 miles, or so. When they got there they started picking up what they needed and a new sign caught their attention. Now back in those days there were metal signs that hung on the walls of most of the "Lum and Abner" type stores of that day, many metal signs even on the outside of the buildings; signs like Prince Albert Smoking Tobacco, Calumet Baking Powder, Old Judge Coffee, etc. This new sign said, Exlax, "makes you feel so much younger." Clem said, "Clifford, have you ever heard of that before?" Clifford answered with a puzzled look on his face, "Nope, never did hear of that one. It must be something new. I don't know about you Clem but I think as old as we're getting we ought to get a couple big bars of that stuff, what do you think?" Clem said, "Yep, I'm game for anything that will make a feller feel younger." So they each bought a big bar of Exlax, loaded their supplies and headed home. By this time it had started to rain and the roads were getting really bad. About half-way home Clem said to Clifford, "Clifford, I think it's about time for us to try that there Exlax stuff." "Me to", said Clem. "Why don't we try your bar first and see how it goes." "OK" said Clem. They tore open the package and each took a big bite of Exlax. As they traveled down the road the bouncing got much worse. Clem looked over at Clifford and said, "Clifford, are you feeling any younger?" "Nope," he said. "I don't think we ate enough of it, so they finished one bar and about half of the other one. By now their old car was really bouncing up and down and shaking things all around. Clifford said, "Clem, are you feeling any younger? "Nope," replied Clem, "I think we mighta got took." "I don't know," said Clifford, "Why don't we jest finish it off." Well, they did. As they started down this last big hill toward home, Clem, with a little redness to his face said, "Clifford are you feeling any younger?" Clifford answered and said, "No, Clem, but I can tell you one thing. . .for sure, right now I'm doing a mighty childish thing." Well, that ends the story except I must tell you this, It's a good thing they had a two hole out-house, because Clem and Clifford spent the next two days in there down over the hill. I don't think either one of them ever bought Exlax again. Told at a Carl Hurley Cavalcade of Comedy in Lexington, Kentucky, by one of their great entertainers

***

"A sound head, an honest heart, and a humble spirit are the three best guides through time and eternity" Sir Walter Scott

***

Here's a good 30 day diet plan. A beautiful 30 year old gal came to the door. "If you can catch me within 30 days you can have me," she said. All the way till the 29th day, this fellow was really doing well. He told himself by tomorrow I think I can catch her. The next day a really ugly, 350 pound gal was at the door and she said to him, if I can catch you they say I can have you. You've got to think about this one for just a second.

***

The cow and the Quaker

The Quaker and the cow, between the two of them kept turning over the bucket of milk. Finally after about 4 turnovers the Quaker said to the cow, "Oh cow, Thou knowest that I cannot curse thee, old cow, Thou knowest that I cannot physically harm thee, but what Thou doesn't know is that I can sell you to my Baptist neighbor and he can literally knock the stuffing out of you."

***

While we were waiting in our tour bus for some stragglers to show up, a man, obviously not with our group approached the bus and was about to board. How would our driver handle the situation we wondered. Straight-faced he leaned toward the door and asked, "Sir, are you going to the nudist colony?" "Oh no," replied the would-be passenger, retreating quickly. "Works every time," the driver said.

***

One time a woman fainted in our downtown shopping area. It caused quite a commotion. One flustered fellow asked the crowd, "Does anyone here know VCR?"

***

"I hurt all over, everywhere I touch hurts," Says the little lady. She touches several parts and hollers every time. Finally she went to the doctor's office and he takes a full body X-ray. He finds that the only thing wrong with her is simply a broken finger.

***

This guy went into a local bar and spotted a really beautiful lady. They had a few drinks and he went home with her. They sat and kissy kissy awhile and so on and before he knew it, it was 6:00 a.m. "Oh, my wife will kill me." He says to the lady, "Do you have any baby powder?" She gave him the powder and he rubbed some on his hands and headed home. When he got to the door it was locked. He beat on the door and finally his wife came to the door and said, "Where in the world have you been." He said, "I found this beautiful lady, went home with her and spent the night making kissee kissee." The wife said, "Let me look at your hands. You bum, you're lying to me again. I know what you've been doing, you've been bowling again."

Chicken Side off first...

***

Three famous surgeons were visiting. The first surgeon said, "A man came in to me with his hand completely cut off, I fixed it back just like new and he is now a famous violinist." The second doctor said, "A man came to me with both legs cut off. I stitched them back on and today he is a marathon runner." "That's nothing," said the third doctor, "I came upon the scene of a terrible accident. There was nothing left but a horse's posterior and a pair of glasses. Today that man is seated in the United States Senate."

***

A tourist passing through South Dakota stopped at a blood bank to make a donation. Afterward, he was resting on a cot and saw another donor who appeared to be a Native American. The tourist struck up a conversation and asked. "Do you live in the Sioux Reservation?" "Yes," the man replied. "Are you a full-blood Sioux?" "Well, actually, no," he said. "Right now I'm about a pint low."

***

A couple had been married for over 50 years. "Things have really changed," she said. You used to sit very close to me." "Well," Her husband replied, "I can remedy that," he said moving next to her on the couch. "She said, "And you used to hold me tight." How's that?" he asked, as he gave her a big hug. "Do you remember you also used to nudge my neck and nibble on my ear lobes?" He jumped to his feet and left the room. She said, "Where in the world are you going?" He answered, "I'll be right back, I've got to go get my teeth."

***

The English, the American and the Polish. Teams of two were hired to put telephone poles in the ground and paid according to their individual quality of work and their speed in which they did their work. The first day's work; American 22, the English 20, and the Polish only 2. The boss asked why the Polish guy did so poorly? He said, "Golly, I thought I did pretty good, did you see how much of their poles they left out of the ground?"

***

The youngster advised his younger brother that he could be

spared much agony and toil by refusing to learn to spell the first word. "The minute you spell cat you're trapped," He said, "After that, the words just get harder and harder."

***

"Linda, dear," said a mother to her little daughter. "Run across the street and see how old Mrs. Green is this morning." A few minutes later Linda returned, "Momma," she reported, "Mrs. Green says it's none of your business how old she is."

***

An irate voter said to the man running for office. "I wouldn't vote for you if you were St. Peter himself." "If I were St. Peter," said the candidate, "You couldn't vote for me, "You wouldn't be in my district."

***

A rookie cop was asked in an examination what he would do to break up a crowd. He thought for a minute and wrote, and you can tell by his answer that he knew lot about the knowledge of human nature. He said, "I'd take up a collection."

***

Henry's mother, Mabel, has four children, that is all. The first one's name is Summer. The second one's name is Fall. Winter is the third one, and that leaves just one more. Can you guess the name of the final babe she bore? (answer on page 285)

***

A hotel has a posted sign in each room. It says: Please be courteous to our employees. They are harder to get than guests.

***

Two grandmothers were bragging about their grandchildren and one, quite impressed, asked, "How old are your grandsons." "Well, replied the other, the doctor is two and the lawyer is 4."

***

A father of five came home with a new toy. He summoned his children and asked, "Which one of you should be given the present? Who is the most obedient, never talks back to mother, and who does everything he or she is told?" There was a silence and then chorus of voices said, "You play with it daddy."

***

There is a real difference between intelligence and wisdom. For example: Intelligence is when you spot the flaw in your wife's reasoning. Wisdom is when you refrain from pointing it out.

***

An elderly lady and man was going to town. The old man was riding the mule and the lady was walking. I stranger walked by and said, "My goodness man, why are you riding and your wife is walking?" "Well," he said, "she doesn't have a mule."

***

Three ladies decided to stop in a downtown restaurant for a spot of tea. "I want a glass of weak tea," said the first lady. The second lady said, "I'd like tea too but very strong, with lemon." The third lady said, "Well, for me I'd like tea also, but please would you make sure the glass is absolutely clean?" "Ok," said the waiter. He came back with the tea and politely said, "Which one of you gets the tea in the clean glass?"

***

A lot of men are willing to split the blame for a failed marriage, half his wife's fault, and half her mother's fault.

***

Changing a diaper is like getting a present from Grandma. You don't know for sure what's inside, but you know you're probably not gonna like it.

***

The maid kept knocking on my door. It doesn't do any good to hang up **DO NOT DISTURB** signs on the doorknob. She kept knocking and finally, after she said she wanted to come in and clean up, I let her in. Well, she came in, took a bath and left.

***

My cousin is with the FBI. They finally caught him last week.

***

These diets are something else. I joined another health club to lose weight and after about 6 weeks, I found out I weighed about $350 less.

***

Did you ever notice that every time congress hammers out a budget we're the ones who get nailed?

***

This guy was really an avid golf player. He and his buddy were out playing and they saw a hearse go by. One remarked to the other. "My goodness isn't that a sad situation," Yeah," it sure is," said his buddy. That's my wife there in the hearse. If she'd lived until tomorrow we'd have been married 22 years."

***

During the course of a baseball game the umpire happened to glance at the stands and noticed medics carrying a woman out on a stretcher. Walking over to the manager of one of the teams, he asked, "What happened, heart attack?" "No," said the manager, whose team was losing. He snarled and said, "No, you called ONE right and she fainted."

***

"My wife says if I don't give up golf she's going to leave me." "Gee, that's tough luck." said his golfing buddy. "Yeah , it sure is. I'm really going to miss her."

***

This guy went into a bar and saw this beautiful lady sitting at the counter. She looked rather lonely so, just to be nice, he went over and sat down by her. She looked at him and said, "I'll do anything you want for $200 if you can say it in three words." The guy looked a bit startled, thought for a moment and said to her, "Paint my house."

***

The old man and his wife were sitting in a swing on the front porch. All of a sudden the lady just knocked the fire of him and he went rolling off the porch. He picked himself and said to his wife, "What in the world was that all about?" "Well," she said. "I just got to thinking. That was for 40 years of bad loving." After a bit he reached over and knocked the soup out of her. She rolled off the porch, picked herself up, climbed back in the swing, and said, "What was that for." "Well, I just got to thinking; that was for knowing the difference."

***

Once upon a time there was a big train robbery. The robber jumped on the train and said, "I'm gonna rob all the men and kiss all the women." Some of the men jumped up and said, "Ladies we're gonna save you." One little old lady said, "Hold on now guys, he's the one robbing this train."

***

Newly Weds . . .

The husband hadn't talked to his new wife for a couple of hours so he called her from the office. When she answered the phone he said, "What's my little honeybun wife doing this fine morning?" "Well, sugar plum, I've been filling the salt shaker." He said, "You've been doing what?" She replied, "I said I've been filling the salt shaker." The husband replied back and said, with a little different tone of voice. "You've been all morning filling our one little salt shaker?" "Yes, dear, it is rather difficult. I bet you've never tried getting salt in through them little holes before." He said, "Have a nice day."

***

What a fine looking bunch of folks we have here today. I tell everyone that, but this time I really mean it.

***

Yes sir'ree; They're gonna have me back to talk to them again sometime in January, and how do I know? Well, they said it would be a cold day . . .

***

This feller was quite an admirer of the human body. He went by the shop where he heard they were painting folks in the nude. He walked into the gallery, and one the ladies said to him, "Would you like to paint me in the nude?" He kinda stuttered and then replied, "Well, I'd be delighted to do that but I'd kinda like to keep my socks on, so I'd have somewhere to wipe my brushes."

***

This young boy was working and this nice beautiful bashful young lady sorta waltzed by. He said to her, "Would you like to take a little walk with me? She said, "Oh no, I couldn't do that because you might try to kiss me." He said, "No I didn't mean today, I'm busy. You see I'm watching this pig for a farmer and I'm giving these chickens a bath in this wash tub. I'm too busy to try and kiss you." She said, "I'll tell you what, if you put the chickens under the tub, I'll hold the pig and we can still go ahead take a walk today."

***

A man was travelling across the country in a big balloon. He spots a farmer working in the hay. He shouts to the farmer, "Hey there, do you know where I am?" The farmer replied, "Ha, ha, you can't fool me, you're up there in that little basket under that big balloon."

***

It's really a good day when you get up and nothing new hurts.

***

"Now that you've won a million dollars in the lottery," said the reporter, "What do you plan to do with all your money?"

"Well, I guess I'll keep on farming until the money's all gone."

***

"Where's all your cards bubba? Daddy says you're not playing with a full deck."

***

The secretary saw ants running up the telephone cord. She quickly called her boss and said, "Get over her quick, we've been bugged."

***

Husband and wife were going across country. They stopped in a little town where they'd never been before to get a bite to eat. The husband said to the waiter, "Sir will you help me and tell me where we are?" The waiter got out his pad and pencil and said,

"I'll even do better than that, I'll spell it for you. It is B U R G E R K I N G! The wife said to her husband, "Honey, maybe we better get out of here while we still have a chance."

***

"I'm going on a 30-day diet." said his wife. "Yep, I'm gonna start in 30 days."

***

"Did you hear about the hummingbird and doorbell that fell in love? They got married and had a little humdinger."

***

A friend of mine just recently spent about $6,000 on a young registered Black Angus bull. He put him out with the herd but he just ate grass and wouldn't even look at a cow. He was beginning to think he had paid more for that bull than he was worth. Anyhow, he had the Vet come and have a look at him. He said the bull was very healthy, but possibly just a little young, so he gave me some pills to feed him once per day. The bull started to service the cows within two days, all his cows! He even broke through the fence and bred with all of his neighbor's cows! He's like a machine! He don't know what was in the pills that the Vet gave him. . . but my friend said they taste a lot like licorice.
Copied

***

While John was reading the newspaper, his wife asked. "John, will you still love me when I'm old and gray and grumpy?" "Sure I do," he mumbled.

***

Ladies don't forget the rummage sale today. It's a good chance to get rid of those things not worth keeping around the house. Be sure and bring your husbands.

***

To celebrate their silver anniversary, a couple went to Niagara Falls and asked a motel clerk for a room. "We only have the honeymoon suite available." The couple told the clerk, "We've been married 25 years," the man said, "We don't need the honeymoon suite." "Look, Buddy, replied the clerk. I might rent you Yankee Stadium, for a bargain, but that doesn't mean you have to play ball in it."

***

The wedding ceremony had just concluded. The groom thrust his hand into his overalls pocket and asked the preacher what he owed him. In these parts, we don't charge for this service," the reverend replied, but you may pay according to your bride's beauty." The groom handed the reverend a dollar bill. The pastor then raised the bride's veil, took a look and dug quickly into his own pocket and gave the guy 50 cents in change.

***

A woman went through a red traffic light and crashed into a man's car. Both of their cars are demolished but amazingly neither of them is hurt. After they crawled out of their cars, the woman said; "Wow, just look at our cars! There's nothing left, but fortunately we are unhurt. This must be a sign from God that we should meet and be friends and live together in peace for the rest of our days." The man replied, "I agree with you completely. This must be a sign from God! The woman continues, "and look at this, another miracle. My car is completely demolished, but my bottle of wine didn't break. Surely God wants us to drink this wine and celebrate our good fortune." Then she hands the bottle to the man. The man nods his head in agreement, opens it, drinks half the bottle and then hands it back to the woman. The woman takes the bottle, and immediately puts the cap back on, and hands it back to the man. The man asks, "Aren't you having any?" She replies, "Nah. I think I'll just wait for the police."

***

"Whether you think that you can, or think that you cannot, you are usually right." Henry Ford

***

This guy went to jail. His only means of income was from his potato crop. His wife wrote to him and said, "Do you expect me to dig up the 5 acres and plant the potatoes?" He wrote back and said, "Please honey, don't dig up the 5 acres, that's where I hid all the money." She wrote back and said, "I think someone is reading our mail, someone dug up the 5 acres, now what do I do?"

Her husband quickly wrote back and said, "NOW PLANT THE POTATOES."

***

A young man applied for a job at a supermarket. The manager said, "Yes I'll give you a job. Sweep out the store. "But," said the young applicant," "I'm a college graduate." The manager quietly replied," Oh, that's all right. I'll show you how."

***

An Englishman heard an American say, "The happiest years of all my life, were spent in the arms of another man's wife . . . Lucy, my mother." The Englishman thought that was worth repeating to a friend of his. His version was, "The happiest years of all of my life, were spent in the arms of another man's wife, Er, ah, oh, by golly, right now I forgot her name!"

***

"I find the harder I work the more luck I have."

Thomas Jefferson

***

Demonstrator No. 1: "There's one thing about this 'down with the government' demonstration what worries me." Demonstrator No. 2: "And what's that?" Demonstrator No. 1: "How are we going to get our unemployment checks and food stamps after we overthrow this lousy government?"

***

A family's little dog gave birth to 5 little puppies. The mother of this little boy said, "Honey, go out and see whether they are little boys or little girls." "The little boy ran out to the small room in the barn, and came running back rather quickly, he said, "Mommy, I turned them all over to look, but somebody took all their labels off."

***

Claude and Maude went to the doctor for their annual checkup. The doctor checked Claude first, so he went on home. The doctor checked Maude over and said, "Maude, I've got some bad news for you. The tests show that you're pregnant." Maude said, "Doctor that can't be true, I'm 81 and Claude is 88, Oh Doc, what do you think I should do?" The doctor said, "You'd better call Claude up right now and give him the news." "OK," she said. So Maude went to the pay phone and put in her dime and called Claude. Claude answered the phone, and Maude said, "Claude, Claude, Claude, you got me pregnant," Claude said, "Who is this?"

***

Henry had never jumped from a plane. He'd plan too but never did get around to it. So one day he decided it was time. He went out to the airport to the place that offered parachute jumps and told them he was ready to go. They told him all that all he had to do was pull on the rip cord and the chute would open and then when he got to the ground just try to land and keep walking. They got everything ready and out the door he went. He did free fall for some time and then he decided it was time to pull the cord. He did, and nothing happened. He pulled it again, and nothing happened. By now he was getting a bit worried. About that time he met some guy, but he was going up rather than down. He hollered to the other guy and said, "Hey there, do you know anything about parachutes? The guy hollered back, and said, "No, I sure don't, do you know anything about gas stoves?

***

"Be nice to people on your way up, because you'll for sure meet them, on your way down." Jimmy Durante

***

"Yes, my relatives have done quite well." said Bryan, "How about yours?" "No, I don't think so, my dad ended up in the state prison. He robbed a bank and got caught, and he's been there ever since. "Oh, that's too bad," said Bryan. "How about your mother?" "Well, she wanted to be a lawyer but the first thing out of the bag she shot her first client, and ended up in the hospital for mentally retarded." "Oh my, did you have any brothers or sisters?" Yes, George said, I had a sister but she went to work for the fire department, she always liked fires, and she ended up burning down the station, so they put her away for destroying public property." "Oh yeah," said George, "I did have a brother that went to Harvard University." Bryan said, "Well, it seems like, at least, you had one pretty sharp relative. What is he studying to be?" "George answered, "He ain't studying nothing, they're studying him."

***

President George W. Bush went to Israel on a guided tour. He was really excited about all the wonderful things he saw. When he went to bed the first night out, he had a dream. He dreamed he saw Moses. In his dream he went up to him and said, "Aren't you Moses? My name is Bush." The man said, "No, I'm not Moses." President Bush said, "Come on now, I think you're Moses." The man again replied, "No, I'm not Moses." President Bush said, "I know you are Moses so why don't you say that you are?" Finally Moses said, "Well, Mr. Bush, to tell you the truth the last time I spoke to a bush, I spent 40 years in the wilderness, is that a good enough reason?"

***

The young man and his date went into a really nice restaurant for dinner. The head waiter met him at the door and said, "Young man, you must be wearing a tie to come in here." "You've gotta be kidding, replied the young man." "No, I'm not kidding but I will tell you this; across the street there is a variety store that sells about everything, maybe you can get one over there." "Ok, said the young man," He and his girlfriend ran across to the store and asked the clerk if he sold ties." The clerk said, "No, but I sell jumper cables and sometimes people come over here needing a tie and I sell them a set of cables, and they wrap them around their neck making a bow tie. A tie is a tie you know. It has always worked in the past." Well, as much as he hated to, the young man purchased the jumper cables, wrapped them around his neck and it sorta looked like a bow tie. They went back across the street. The waiter said, "Well, a tie is a tie, so I'm gonna let you come in, but . . . Don't you dare START NOTHING!

***

This little old man never in his life had much of our worldly goods. He reached 81 years of age and he passed away. All of his life he'd always wanted a halo statue but never could afford one. Everyone that he knew had one, but he him himself never had the opportunity. He'd used them a few times and he thought they were just wonderful. When he got to the pearly gates St. Peter greeted him and said, "Pedro, you finally made it. We've been looking for you. Everyone that makes it to Heaven gets to ask for anything he's always wanted, now it's your turn." "Oh, wonderful," said Pedro. "Yes, that's true, anything you've ever wanted," replied St. Peter. "Well," said Pedro, "are you sure I can have anything?" "Yes, that's what I said." "Ok, I've always, all my life, want a halo statue, replied Pedro." St. Peter said, "You want a what?" "I want a halo statue, that's all I want." St. Peter said, "Ok, I'll take you around and see if you find one you like, but I've never heard of one called a halo." Pedro said, "Oh, you know, everybody's got one and some have got two or three." St. Peter took Pedro all over Heaven but could find nothing like Pedro wanted. St. Peter said to Pedro. "I'm puzzled. I have no idea what it is you are wanting." Pedro was getting a bit discouraged. He looked St. Peter in the eye and said, "All you have to do is pick it up, put part of it to your mouth and part of it to your ear, and say 'halo statue." All Pedro ever wanted was a nice new telephone so he could say, "Hello, is that you."

***

What a Truck!

Several years ago there was a huge gasoline explosion in downtown Houston, Texas. Every fire department in and around Houston went to the fire and could not in any way get a grip on getting the fire put out. It seemed that it was getting bigger all the time.

The Mayor finally put out an all-points bulletin to many of the cities in Texas. There just happened to be a medium sized community about 90 miles north of Houston that had a small group of Mexican volunteer firemen and they had one, fairly decent sized truck, but their manpower was a little shy. The Houston Mayor said if anyone thought they had any idea that might work to put out the fire, they would be welcome to try, and they would be honored in some way. Well, the fire-chief in this little town got together with his men and said, "Boys I think we can do it. I think we can go in to the center of that fire and put it out. Anybody else besides me willing give it a try?" Believe it or not every member of the small department said, "Let's give it a shot,

I think we can do the job."

They called the Mayor and told him to give them a police escort and clear the way. The mayor questioned him a bit about why he thought they could do it and the chief said, "We've got the determination and the guts to pull it off." The mayor said, "Come on down boys, we're desperate." Well, the boys filled their tires with air, un-plugged the battery charger, put all the water and foam they could get on the truck, turned on their sirens and headed out of town for Houston. The entire town was out to see them off; they were so proud of their boys.

About a mile from down-town Houston the chief threw the old truck into double over-drive and let her rip. Even though a couple of the boys thought they were going a bit fast, they couldn't get the message to the chief. He was going in with all that he had.

Believe it or not they went to the center of the fire, emptied all of their water and foam and put out the fire. Everyone was thrilled and so thankful to the Mexican crew from up north. A few days later the Mayor called the fire-chief and told him and his boys to come to Houston for a big celebration.

The Major presented them with a huge plaque and a check for $1,000. The mayor asked the chief what they planned to do with the money and the chief said, "Well, the first thing we're gonna do is get the darn brakes fixed on our truck."

Richard & Neta Ruth Sunderwirth

"Fun-Time Friends helping Richard and Neta Ruth celebrate their 50th wedding anniversary."

Chicken Side off first...

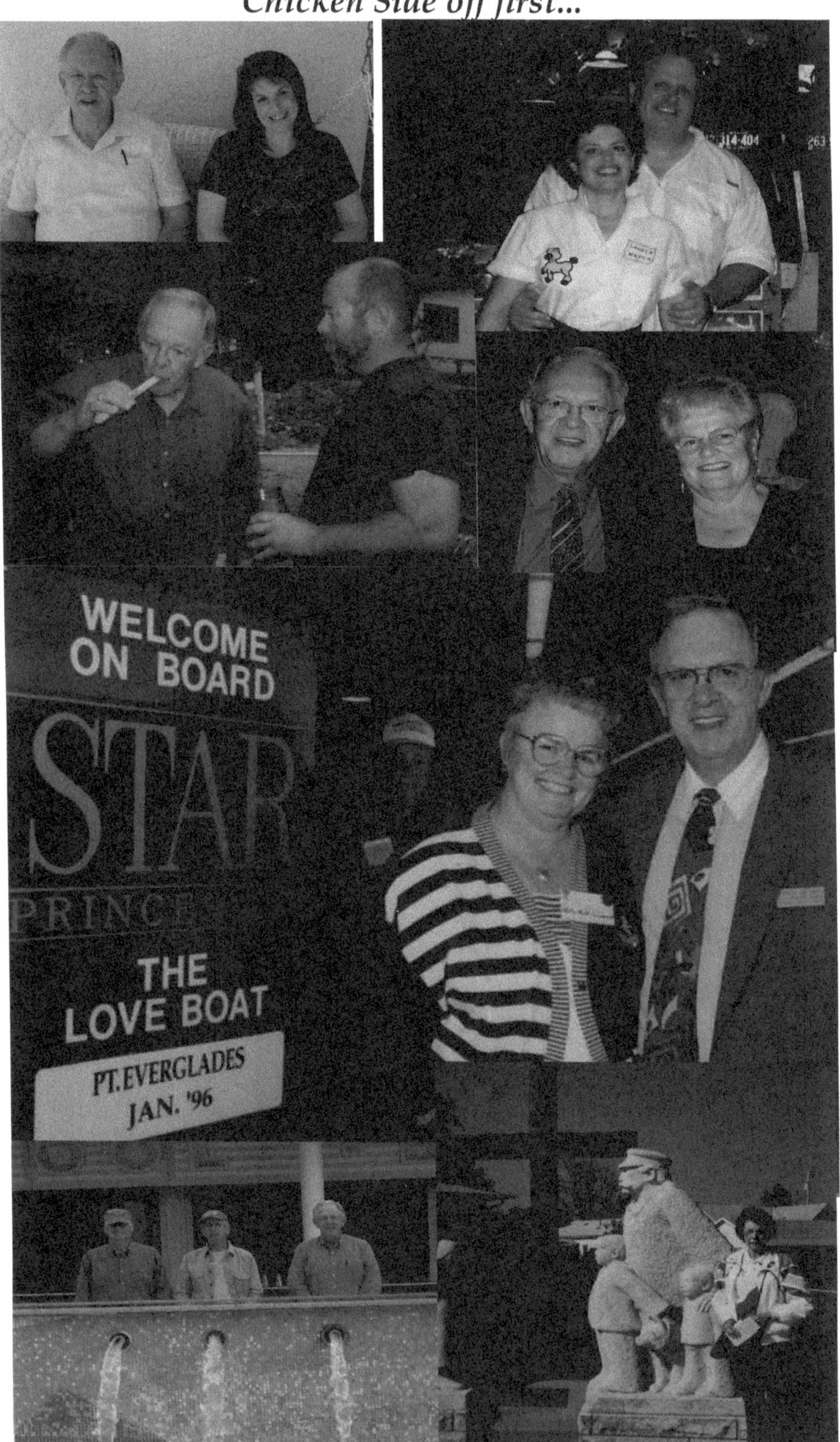

Richard & Neta Ruth Sunderwirth

A true story, almost to the letter!

We lived in a house where mom and dad's bedroom was in the opposite end of the house from my sister's bedroom. My bedroom was just off the kitchen, but it was real close to my sister's room. Every night, everyone would go to bed, and without exception, would say "goodnight" to everyone else. I didn't go to sleep because I knew what was coming. After about 15 minutes my 13 year old sister, Gail, would say to my folks, "Goodnight". They would say, "Goodnight", back again. Yep, I knew what was coming. In about another 5 minutes my sister would say, "Goodnight," and my dad (I knew it was coming) would say, "Gail, go to sleep." "Ok daddy," Our dad was angry and I was laughing my head off. In another 5 minutes, "Goodnight," "Gail, if you don't go to sleep I'm going to come in there and blister you." "Ok daddy, goodnight." In about 10, here we'd go again. This would honestly go on for at least 3 or 4 more times. "Goodnight daddy," "Gail, Gail, Gail, (silence for a moment then,) "D-aaaaa-dy when you come in here to blister me, would you bring me a drink of water?" I lived for every night, because I knew what was going to happen."

***

Philip's grandmother had a serious problem. She was failing pretty fast because of her age and the fact that she was a bit mentally challenged. Philip began searching for a nice place that his Granny could live. A place that could help her, and yet at the same time a place that she would enjoy. Well, the first place he went to changed his mind about doing that and he decided he would go to a nice assisted living home. Well, that's what he did and it worked out fine. Here's what happened that caused him to change his mind. He went in and the supervisor took him through the first floor of the institution and as they were walking through the facility he heard someone call out in a horrible tone of voice. This fellow over in the corner was shouting out, "LuLu, Lulu, Lulu, Lulu," I ask the attendant what was going on and he said, "This gentleman had gone with a girl in high school that had jilted him and he has never gotten over it. He's been going on that way for years." I said to the attendant, "Oh my, that's terrible, I feel so sorry for that fellow." We went up to the second floor and started looking around and we heard another fellow crying out "Lu Lu, Lu Lu, just about the way as the fellow on the first floor. I said, "What in the world is going on now? That guy is calling out the same name," the attendant replied, "Yeah, he's got a problem that's similar but totally different, he's the one that got her."

***

Old Mrs. Johnson really liked pinto beans. Some folks call them old fashioned brown beans, but either one of them she really enjoyed, especially in the spring of the year when the green onions were fresh out of the garden. With the beans and the onions and good ole slab of corn bread she would have a real feast. Well, this particular day the guy that worked at the grocery store got in a case of shotgun shells. He was putting them up on the top shelf and he accidently dropped a small box of the shells, which split apart, into a barrel that was full of dry brown beans. He looked up and the boss was coming in the front door so he jumped down and shook the barrel, so the boss wouldn't notice that he had dropped the shells. They filtered down in through the beans. About that time, Mrs. Johnson came in the front door and went over and scooped up 2 lbs of the beans into a paper sack, paid for them, and went home and started them cooking. About 5:30 in the afternoon the beans were ready to eat and boy did she eat a bunch of them. Wow! And were they ever so good. She ate so many of the beans that they really worked her over during the night. The next morning she went over to her neighbor's house and said, "Mildred, the funniest thing happened to me on the way over her today. I walked out my back door; I bent over to pet the dog, and I shot my cat."

***

This extremely negative young man, didn't like to work, didn't like to do anything that was difficult. He decided he would possibly join the Army, but there was too much walking. He checked about the Marines, too much fighting. He checked about the Air Force, and there was too much flying and jumping out of airplanes. He said, "I don't know what I'm going to do to make a living. Just as sure as I joined the Air Force I'd jump out of a plane, pull the rip-cord, and the truck, that was supposed to pick me up, probably wouldn't even be there."

***

A couple of 80-year-olds got married. At the afternoon reception, the bride was asked where they were going on their honeymoon. "Not very far," she replied. "Henry doesn't drive after dark."

***

I sometimes wonder what the Ten Commandments would have been like if Moses had been a member of Congress!

***

Little boy couldn't sleep, He woke his mommy up about midnight and said, "Mommy, tell us a story mommy." "Wait a minute son. Your daddy will be home in a few minutes and he'll tell us both a good one.

***

"My wife has tried every diet invented. Her latest is coconuts and bananas. That's all she eats." "Is she losing any weight?" "No, but I'll tell you one thing, she can sure climb a tree."

***

A guy told his buddy, "I've had it, I'm going to commit suicide. I'm going to hang from my waist." His buddy said, "Well, if you really have decided to do that you ought to hang from you neck, if you want it to work." The guy said, "I done tried that, but I couldn't breathe."

***

I don't know for sure, but I think I might get me a Ross Perot watch; it runs awhile and then stops . . . No, I think I'll get a Bill Clinton watch; it sells for \$3.98 plus tax, plus tax, plus tax, plus tax, etc.

***

This lady went in to the newspaper office and asked for the obit dept." I can only spend about \$2.00 for this ad," she said. "Well," said the office clerk," I can't do a \$2.00 ad but I can give you 5 words for \$3.00, would that be ok?" The lady said, "That will be fine, here's what I would like, SMITH DEAD, CADILLAC FOR SALE."

***

Grandpa Jones said to Roy Acuff, "Roy what do you do when your wife gets out of line?" Roy said, "That's no big deal; I just grab her, pull her dress up over her head, throw her over my lap and spank her real good. That will keep her in line." Next day Roy saw Grandpa going in the back door of the Grand Ole' Opry building and he said, "Grandpa, did that work with your wife?" Grandpa replied, "Well, Roy it didn't work at all. I pulled her dress up over her head; threw her over my lap, looked down, and by golly I couldn't remember why I was mad."

***

"Grandpa, would you please go and kick the ball?" said grandson Charley. "Well, said Grandpa, "Why are you in such a hurry?" Charley replied, "Momma said, when you kick off we'll be rich."

***

A couple of guys were playing golf. There were quite a few ants running around; their lives were in danger. One ant looked at the rest of the ants and said, "If we're gonna survive this ordeal we'd better get on the ball."

***

There was a little boy who allowed his dog to get really dirty. He went to one of his friends and said, "What is the best way to get my dog clean, he's just filthy?" "Well," his friend said, "I think my mother washes our little dog in tide." "Thanks a lot, I'll try that," said the boy with the dirty dog. Next day the two boys ran into each at school and the boy with the tide remedy said, "Did you get your dog clean with the tide?" "Yeah, I got him clean alright, but he died." "He died, what in the world happened to him?" "I really think the spin cycle got him."

***

A lady came running into the doctor's office and boy was she sick; she was foaming at the mouth. The doctor says, "Lady, I think you've got the rabies, and I don't think you're going to make it." The lady said, if that's the case help me make out my will." The doctor agreed to help her. They worked on it for a while and the doctor say's, my goodness that sure is a long will." Yes, it appears to be that way, but I'm making out a list who I intend to bite."

***

"My goodness what an ingenious invention; I think it's better than the computer, and maybe even the television." His friend said, "Well, what in the world is it?" "The thermos bottle," "How could that be so good," asked his friend. "It keeps some things hot and some things cold." "What makes that so great?" "Well, how do it know?"

***

Mr. Gorsky; A True Story
On July 20, 1969, as commander of the Apollo 11 Lunar Module, Neil Armstrong was the first person to set foot on the moon. His first words after stepping on the moon, was "That's one small step for man, one giant leap for mankind." This was televised to Earth and heard by millions. But just before he re-entered the lander, he made the enigmatic remark: "Good luck, Mr. Gorsky." Many people at NASA thought it was a casual remark concerning some rival Soviet Cosmonaut; however, upon checking, there was no Gorsky in either the Russian or American space programs. Over the years many people questioned Armstrong as to what the "Good luck Mr. Gorsky" statement meant, but Armstrong always just smiled. On July 5, 1995, in Tampa Bay, Florida, while answering questions following a speech, a reporter brought up the 26 year old question to Armstrong. This time he finally responded. Mr. Gorsky had died and so Neil Armstrong felt he could now answer the question. In 1938, when he was a kid in a small Midwest town, he was playing baseball with a friend in the backyard. His friend hit a fly ball, which landed in his neighbor's yard by the bedroom windows. His neighbors were Mr. and Mrs. Gorsky. As he leaned down to pick up the ball, young Armstrong heard Mrs. Gorsky shouting at Mr. Gorsky. "Sex! You want sex? You'll get sex when the kid next door walks on the moon!"

***

"Oh honey, I'm so sorry, our divorce was a terrible mistake. Can you ever forgive me? You're the most beautiful lady in the world, and the kindness also. Oh, by the way, congratulations on winning the lottery."

***

Johnny, was a little boy that had lived in an orphanage most of his life. He came in when he was 1 year old and he left at age 6. While there he, along with the other boys and girls only took a bath 2 times a week, due to the large number of children. Finally a wonderful couple came along and adopted Johnny. He was really happy to have new parents. He went with them and started his new life. About the only thing different about where he was living now, other than his own bedroom and his loving parents, was the fact that he had to take a bath every evening before going to bed. He didn't like that because he was not in the habit of taking one that often. About 3 months after leaving his first home the folks from the orphanage came to visit and see how he was doing. They all visited a while and finally the folks who came to visit him took him off to the side and said, "Johnny, how are things going here; are they treating you alright, etc?" "Oh yes," said Johnny. They are really great parents, and I really like it here, but I have to take a bath every night. Just between you and me and think what they really wanted was a duck."

***

Things that irritate a sane person

A piece of foil candy wrapper makes electrical contact with your filling.

You set the alarm on your digital clock for 7: p.m. instead of 7: a.m.

The radio station doesn't tell you who sang that song.

You rub on hand cream and your hand is so slick you can't turn the bathroom doorknob to get out.

People behind you in a supermarket line dash ahead of you to a counter just opening up.

Your glasses slide off your ears when you perspire.

You can't look up the correct spelling of a word in the dictionary because you don't know how to spell it.

You have to inform five different sales people in the same store that you're just browsing.

You had the pen in your hand only a second ago and now you can't find it.

You reach under the table to pick something off the floor and smash your head on the way up.

You go to the store just after putting your 3 loose pennies in the last store's little penny jar by the register. Then you go to the next store and find that after your purchases you are one penny short and they make you break a $20 dollar bill to get it.

Richard & Neta Ruth Sunderwirth

No more lipstick

A middle school in Quebec was faced with a unique problem. A number of girls were beginning to use lipstick and would apply it in the washroom. That was fine but after they put the lipstick on they would press their lips to the mirrors leaving lip prints on the glass. Finally the principal decided something had to be done. She called all the girls to the washroom and met them there with the custodian. She explained that the lip prints were causing major problems for the custodian who had to clean the mirrors every day. To demonstrate what a hard job that was, she asked the custodian to go ahead and clean a mirror. He proceeded to take out a long-handled brush, dip it into the nearest toilet and scrub the surface of the glass. You may not believe this, but there have been no further lip prints on the mirrors.

***

The Blonde and the TV

A blonde went to the appliance store sale and found a bargain. "I would like to buy this TV," she told the sales person. "Sorry, we don't sell to blondes," he replied. She hurried home and dyed her hair, then came back and again told the salesman, "I would like to buy this TV." "Sorry, we don't sell to blondes," he told her. "He recognized me," she thought. She went for a complete disguise this time; haircut and new color, new outfit, big sunglasses, then waited a few days before she again approached the sales person. "I would like to buy this TV." "Sorry, we don't sell to blondes," he replied. Frustrated, she exclaimed "How do you know I'm a blonde?" "Because that's a microwave, "he replied.

***

More Evidence That This World Is Full Of Complete Idiots

Police in Wichita, Kansas, arrested a 22-year-old man at an airport hotel after he tried to pass two (counterfeit) $16 bills.

A company trying to continue its five-year perfect safety record, showed its workers a film aimed at encouraging the use of safety goggles on the job. According to Industrial Machinery News, the film's depiction of gory industrial accidents was so graphic that twenty-five workers suffered minor injuries in their rush to leave the screening room. Thirteen others fainted and one man required seven stitches after he cut his head falling off a chair while watching the film.

Chicken Side off first...

The Chico, California City Council enacted a ban on nuclear weapons, setting a $500 fine for anyone detonating one within city limits.

A bus carrying five passengers was hit by a car in St. Louis, but by the time police arrived on the scene, fourteen pedestrians had boarded the bus and had begun to complain of whiplash injuries and back pain.

Swedish business consulting Ulf at Trolle labored 13 years on a book about Swedish economic solutions. He took the 250-page manuscript to be copied, only to have it reduced to 50,000 strips of paper in seconds when a worker confused the copier with the shredder.

A convict broke out of jail in Washington, DC; then a few days later accompanied his girlfriend to her trial for robbery. At lunch, he went out for a sandwich. She needed to see him and thus had him paged. Police officers recognized his name and arrested him as he returned to the courthouse in a car he had stolen over the lunch hour.

Police in Radnor, Pennsylvania, interrogated a suspect by placing a metal colander on his head and connecting it with wires to a photocopy machine. The message, "He's lying" was placed in a copier, and police pressed the copy button each time they thought the suspect wasn't telling the truth. Believing the "lie detector' was working, the suspect confessed.

When two service station attendants in Ionia, Michigan refused to hand over the cash to an intoxicated robber, the man threatened to call the police. They still refused, so the robber called the police and was promptly arrested.

***

Joe's Barber Shop

A man walked in to Joe's Barber Shop for his regular haircut. As he snips away, Joe asks "What's up?" The man proceeds to explain he's taking a vacation to Rome. "ROME?" Joe says, "Why would ya want to go there? It's a crowded dirty city full of Italians? You'd be crazy to go to Rome! So, how you getting there?" "We're taking TWA," the man replies. "TWA?" yells Joe. "They're a terrible airline; their planes are old, their flight attendants are ugly and they're always late! So where are ya staying while you're there?" The man says "We'll be at the downtown International Marriot." "That DUMP?" says Joe. "That's the worst hotel in the city! The rooms are small, the service is surly and slow and they're overpriced! So, what ya doing when you get there?" The man says "We're going to go see the Vatican and hope to see the Pope." "Ha! That's rich!" laughs Joe. "You and a million other people trying to see him. He'll look the size of an ant. Boy, good luck on THIS trip. You're going to need it!"

A month later, the man comes in for his regular haircut. Joe says, "Well, how did that trip to Rome turn out? Betcha TWA gave you the worst flight of your life!" "No, quite the opposite," explained the man. "Not only were we on time in one of their brand new planes, but it was full and they bumped us up to first class. The food and wine were wonderful and I had a beautiful 30 year old blond flight attendant who waited on me hand and foot!" "Hmmm," Joe says, "Well, I bet the hotel was just like I described." "No, Quite the opposite! They'd just finished a $25 million remodeling. It's the finest hotel in Rome, now. They were overbooked, so they apologized and gave us the Presidential suite at no extra charge!" "Well," Joe mumbles, "I know you didn't get to see the Pope!" "Actually, we were quite lucky. As we toured the Vatican, A Swiss guard tapped me on the shoulder and explained the Pope likes to personally meet some of the visitors, and if I'd be so kind as to step into this private room and wait, the Pope would personally greet me. Sure enough, after 5 minutes the Pope walked through the door and shook my hand, I knelt down as he spoke a few words to me." Impressed, Joe asks, "Tell me, please! What'd he say?" "Oh, not much really, just, 'Where did you get that awful, terrible, sorry-looking haircut?'"

***

Humor keeps you healthy!

A typical 4 year old does it up to 500 times a day! The average adult does it only 15 times. It increases the heart rate, eases tension, and promotes muscle tone. A few seconds of this does the body as much good as a few minutes of physical exercise. It actually causes the brain to release endorphin, the body's natural pain-killer. It helps us cope with problems, aides in dealing with change, helps with learning retention, and it's biblical. What in the world is it?

It's Laughter !

"How many laughs have you had today?"

Chicken Side off first...

Laughter can make you feel better !
Laughter is a "social lubricant."
Laughter is good for reducing stress!
Laughter is an "Emotional weight-loss technique."
Laughter is free! Does not require batteries!
Humor can help you cope with difficult situations!
Non-polluting, Non-taxable, Non-fattening, & No cost!

***

A life-long city man , tired of the rat race, decided he was going to give up the city life, move to the country, and become a chicken farmer. He found a nice, used chicken farm, which he bought. It turns out that his next door neighbor was also a chicken farmer. The neighbor came for a visit one day and said, "Chicken farming isn't easy. Tell you what. To help you get started, I'll give you 100 chickens." The new chicken farmer was thrilled. Two weeks later the new neighbor stopped by to see how things were going. The new farmer said, "Not too good. All 100 chickens died." The neighbor said, "Oh, I can't believe that. I've never had any trouble with my chickens. I'll give you 100 more." Another two weeks went by, and the neighbor stops in again. The new farmer says, You're not going to believe this, but the second 100 chickens died too." Astounded, the neighbor asked, "What did you do to them? What went wrong?" "Well," says the new farmer, "I'm not sure. But I think I might be planting them too close together."

***

"I have come to the conclusion that politics is too serious a matter to be left to politicians."

(Charles de Gaulle)

***

Doughboy Dead at 71

Veteran Pillsbury spokesman Pop N. Fresh, died yesterday of a severe yeast infection. He was 71. Fresh was buried in one of the largest funeral ceremonies in recent years. Dozens of celebrities turned out including: Mrs. Butterworth, the California Raisins, Hungry Jack, Betty Crocker and the Hostess Twinkies, The gravesite was piled high with Flours and longtime friend, Aunt Jemima, delivered the eulogy, describing Fresh as a man who "Never knew how much he was kneaded." Fresh rose quickly in show business, but his later life was filled with many turnovers. He was not considered a very smart cookie, squandering much of his dough on half-baked schemes. Still, even as a crusty old man, he was a roll model for millions. Fresh is survived by his second wife, Sweet Bread. They have two children and one in the oven. The funeral was held at 3:50 for about 20 minutes.

***

The Cost

Walking up to a department store's fabric counter, a pretty girl asked, "I want to buy this material for a new dress. How much does it cost?" "Only a kiss a yard." replied the smirking male clerk. "That's fine," replied the girl. "I'll take ten yards." With expectation and anticipation written all over his face, the clerk hurriedly measured out and wrapped the cloth, then held it out teasingly. The girl snapped up the package and pointed to a little old man standing beside her. "Grandpa will pay the bill," she smiled, and walked away.

***

The Open Grave

A man was walking home late one night from work, tired and hungry. He took a short cut across a cemetery; stumbled and fell into an open grave. He screamed and called out for help, finally resigning to the fact that no one would hear or help him at this late hour, and he would have to wait until morning when surely the grave diggers would return. So, he nestled himself into a corner of the grave. Soon after, another man also walking home from work, taking the same shortcut, stumbled and fell into the same grave. Frantically, he screamed for help, tying to claw his way out, as the first man watched. Finally, the first man said to him, "You'll never get out of here."- - But he did!

***

The District Attorney requested all the robbery victims to come to the police station to study a lineup of five people. He placed his suspect at the end of the line. Then he asked each to step forward and say, "Give me all your money . . . and I need some change in quarters, nickels, and dimes." The first four did it right. However, when it was the last man's turn to recite, he broke the case by blurting out, "That isn't what I said."

***

In Joplin, Tennessee, Henry Johnson was on trial for the armed robbery of a convenience store in a district court this week when he fired his lawyer. Assistant district attorney Martin Polson said, #47, was doing a fair job of defending himself until the store manager testified that Johnson was the robber. Johnson jumped up, accused the woman of lying and then said, "I should have blown your cotton-picking head off." The defendant pauses, then quickly added, "If I'd been the one that was there." The jury took 20 minutes to convict Johnson and recommended a 30 year sentence.

***

"Politicians are people who, when they see light at the end of the tunnel, go out and buy some more tunnel." (John Quinton)

***

Pay-back time: Spoil your grandchildren rotten next time they visit. It will take their parents weeks to get them back to normal.

You know you're getting older when you're sitting in a rocker and you can't get it started.

It's hard to be nostalgic when you consider the alternatives.

"When I was younger," Mark Twain said, "I could remember anything, whether it happened or not."

Last will and testament: Being of sound mind, I spent all of my money.

It's a sign of old age when you feel like the day after the night before and you haven't been anywhere.

Old age is not so bad, when you consider the alternatives.

You know you're getting older when the candles cost more than the cake.

Middle age is when a narrow waist and a broad mind begin to change places.

"When I was young, the Dead Sea was still alive," said Mr. George Burns.

Old age is when everything starts to wear out, fall out or spread out.

Richard & Neta Ruth Sunderwirth

Old age is the period of life when a man begins to feel friendly towards insurance agents.

The years between 60 and 80 are the hardest. You are always being asked to do things, and yet, you are not decrepit enough to turn them down, and make it sound sincere.

Old age is when candlelit tables are no longer romantic because you can't read the menu, or the bill, or even figure why the candle is even lit.

***

The Company Commander and the First Sergeant were in the field. As they hit the rack for the night, the First Sergeant said, "Sir, look up into the sky and tell me what you see?" The Commander said, "I see millions of stars." First Sergeant said, "And what does that tell you, sir?" Commander replies, "Astronomically, it tells me that there are millions of galaxies and potentially billions of planets. Theologically, it tells me that God is great and that we are insignificant. Meteorologically, it tells me that we will have a beautiful day tomorrow. What does it tell you, Pop?" First Sergeant replies, "Well, sir, it tells me that somebody stole our tent."

***

A great Story!

On a flight from Johannesburg a middle-aged, well-off white South African Lady has found herself sitting next to a black man. She called the cabin crew attendant over to complain about her seating. "What seems to be the problem Madam?" asked the attendant. "Can't you see?" she said, "You've set me next to a kafir. I can't possibly sit next to this disgusting human. Find me another seat!" "Please calm down, Madam." The flight attendant replied. "The flight is very full today, but I'll tell you what I'll do, I'll go and check to see if we have any seats available in club or first class." The woman cocks a snooty look at the outraged black man beside her (not to mention many of the surrounding passengers). A few minutes later the flight attendant returns with the good news, which she delivers to the lady who cannot help but look at the people around her with a smug and self-satisfied grin. "Madam, unfortunately, as I suspected, economy is full. I've spoken to the cabin services director, and club is also full. However, to answer, the attendant continues . . . "It is most extraordinary to make this kind of upgrade, however, and I had to get special permission from the captain. But, given the circumstances, the captain felt that it was outrageous that someone should be forced to sit next to such an obnoxious person." Having said that, the flight attendant turned to the black man sitting next to the lady, and said. "So if you'd like to get your things, sir, I have your seat ready for you . . ." At which point, apparently the surrounding passengers stood and gave a standing ovation while the black man walked up to the front of the plane to first class. The lady just sat there in total amazement. As far as we all could tell no one spoke to her at all during the flight.

***

The Loan (Another True & Great Story of Compassion)
A New Orleans lawyer sought an FHA loan for a client. He was told the loan would be granted if he could prove satisfactory title to a parcel of property being offered as collateral. The title to the property dated back to 1803, which took the lawyer three months to track down. After sending the information to the FHA, he received the following reply. **(Actual letter below)**

"Upon review of your letter adjoining your client's loan application, we note that the request is supported by an Abstract of Title. While we compliment the able manner in which you have prepared and presented the application, we must point out that you have only cleared title to the proposed collateral back to 1803. Before final approval can be accorded, it will be necessary to clear the title back to its origin."

Annoyed, the lawyer responded as follows. **(Actual letter below)**

"Your letter regarding title in Case No. 189156 has been received. I note that you wish to have title extended further than the 194 years covered by the present application. I was unaware that any educated person in this country, particularly those working in the property area, would not know that Louisiana was purchased by the U.S. from France in 1803, the year of origin identified in our application. For the edification of uninformed FHA bureaucrats, the title to the land prior to US S. ownership was obtained from France, which had acquired it by Right of Conquest from Spain. The land came into possession to Spain by Right of Dis-

Columbus, who had been granted the privilege of seeking a new route to India by the then reigning monarch, Isabella. The good queen, being a pious woman and careful about titles, almost as much as the FHA, took the precaution of securing the blessing of the Pope before she sold her jewels to fund Columbus' expedition. Now the Pope, as I'm sure you know, is the emissary of Jesus Christ, the Son of God. And God, it is commonly accepted, created this world. Therefore, I believe it is safe to presume that He also made that part of the world called Louisiana, He, therefore, would be the owner of origin. I sincerely hope . . . you find His original claim to be satisfactory. Now, may we have our . . . loan?" ***"THEY GOT IT"***

***

Coat Hanger Angel

A woman was at work when she received a phone call that her daughter was very sick with a fever. She left her work and stopped by the pharmacy to get some medication for her daughter. When returning to her car she found that she had locked her keys in the car. She was in a hurry to get home to her sick daughter; she didn't know what to do, so she called her home and told the baby sitter what had happened and that she did not know what to do. The baby sitter told her that her daughter was getting worse. She said, "You might find a coat hanger and use that to open the door." The woman looked around and found an old rusty coat hanger that had been thrown down on the ground possibly by someone else who at some time or other had locked their keys in their car. Then she looked at the hanger and said, "I don't know how to use this."

So she bowed her head and asked God to send her some help. Within five minutes an old rusty car pulled up, with a dirty, greasy, bearded man who was wearing an old biker skull rag on his head. The woman thought, "Great Goodness. This is what you sent to help me?????" But, she was desperate, so she was also very thankful. The man got out of his car and asked her if he could help. She said, "Yes, my daughter is very sick . . . I stopped to get her some medication and I locked my keys in my car, I must get home to her. Please, can you use this hanger to unlock my car?" He said, "Sure?" He walked over to the car, and in less than one minute the car was opened. She hugged the man and nice man." The man replied, "Lady, I am not a nice man. I just got out of prison today. I was in prison for car theft and have only been out for about an hour." The woman hugged the man again and with sobbing tears cried out loud . . . "Thank you, Lord, for sending me a professional."

***

Only in America

Only in America . . . can a pizza get to your house faster than an ambulance.

Only in America . . . are there handicap parking places in front of a skating rink.

Only in America . . . do we leave cars worth thousands of dollars in the driveway and leave useless things and junk in the garage.

Only in America . . . do banks leave both doors open and then chain the pens to the counters.

Only in America . . . do we use answering machines to screen calls and then have call waiting so we won't miss a call from someone we didn't want to talk to in the first place.

Only in America . . . do we use the word "politics" to describe the process so well? "Poli" in Latin means "many" and "tics" meaning "blood-sucking creatures."

"We hang petty thieves and appoint the great ones to public office." (Aesop, Greek Author)

Richard & Neta Ruth Sunderwirth

***

Yep, this is a good one too!

I heard the story told recently about a king in Africa who had a close friend that he grew up with. The friend had a habit of looking at every situation that ever occurred in his life (positive or negative) and remarking. "This is good!" One Day the king and his friend were out on a hunting expedition. The friend would load and prepare the gun for the king. The friend had apparently done something wrong in preparing one of the guns, for after taking the gun from his friend, the king fired it and his thumb was blown off. Examining the situation the friend remarked as usual. "This is good!" To which the king replied, "No, this is NOT good!" and proceeded to send his friend to jail.

About a year later, the king was hunting in an area that he should have known to stay clear of. Cannibals captured him and took him to their village. They tied his hands, stacked some wood, set up a stake and bound him to the stake.

As they came near to set fire to the wood, they noticed that the king was missing a thumb. Being superstitious, they never ate anyone that was less than whole. So, untying the king, they sent him on his way. As he was returning home, he was reminded of the event that had taken his thumb and felt remorse for his treatment of his friend. He went immediately to the jail to speak with his friend. "You were right" he said, "It was good that my thumb was blown off." And he proceeded to tell the friend all that had just happened. "And so I am very sorry for sending you to jail for so long. It was bad for me to do this." "No," his friend replied, "This is good!" "What do you mean, This is good?" How could it be good that I sent my friend to jail for a year?" "If I had not been in jail, I would have been with you."

***

"Never under estimate the power of . . . termites."

***

"A penny saved . . . is not much."

***

"Laugh and the whole world laughs with you . . .

cry and . . . you have to blow your nose."

***

Once upon a time, a woman had a wonderful, faithful cat. One day, a man ran over the cat accidentally with his car. So, the man went to the old woman and said, "I'm terribly sorry about your cat. I'd like to replace him." "That is so nice of you!" said the old woman, deeply touched. "So how good are you at catching mice?"

***

"Do you believe in life after death?" the boss asked one of his employees. "Yea, sir" the new recruit replied. "Well, then, that makes everything just fine" . . . The boss went on. "After you left early yesterday to go to your Grandmother's funeral, she stopped in to see you."

***

A nursery school teacher was delivering a station wagon full of kids home one day when a fire truck zoomed past. Sitting in the front seat of the fire truck was a Dalmation dog. The children fell to discussing the dog's duties. "They use him to keep crowds back," said one youngster. "No," said another, "He's just for good luck." A third child brought the argument to a close. "They use the dogs," she said firmly, "To find the fire hydrant."

***

Burma-Shave Story, "The Verses By The Side of The Road"

Years ago, the Burma-Shave shaving cream company put up road signs all over the United States and other parts of the world. The signs were spaced a few hundred yards apart and were designed to be read one line after the other as the vehicle proceeded down the highway. They became very popular as they were often both safety oriented and humorous. Six hundred different slogans were known to line our highways. Poet Laureate, was shaving cream inventors son, Alan Odell.

By the 1950's when long distance motorists were lucky to average 30 miles an hour, (according to Detroit News) Odell had 7,000 quintets of signs strung along U.S. roadsides. Once, when Odell himself had run out of ideas, he commissioned a nationwide contest which produced not only volumes of sappy sonnets, but also an advertisers dream . . . universal brand awareness.

By the 1960's the shaving cream that smelled like soap, and

it's little white-on-red highway signs of silly verse, had fallen by the wayside. The entire history of the Burma-Shave signs and a complete listing is available in a book, "The Verse by the side of the Road." Written by Frank Rowsome, Jr. Published in 1965 by Stephen Green Press. This book was reprinted in 1990 in paperback by Penguin Books. Penguin Books forward was written by Bob Dole. **(FOLLOWING IS ONE DOZEN OF THE SIGNS)**

If harmony-is what-you crave-then get a "tuba" **Burma Shave.**

Paw likes the cream-Ma likes the jar-they both like the price-so there you are. **Burma Shave**.

Fire, fire-be brave-grab your pants-and your, Burma Shave.

Cattle crossing-means go slow-that old bull is some cow's beau. **Burma Shave.**

Fuzzy Wuzzie was a bear-Fuzzy Wuzzie had no hair-so Fuzzy Wuzzie-wasn't Fuzzy! Wuzzie! **Burma Shave**.

The monkey took-one look at Jim-and threw the peanuts back at him. **Burma Shave**.

A nut at the wheel-a peach at his right-curve ahead-salad tonight. **Burma Shave**.

College Boys!-your courage muster-shave off that Fuzzy cookie duster. **Burma Shave.**

Do not pass-on curve or hill-if the cops don't catch you-the morticians will. **Burma Shave**.

If you pass-on yellow line-hope the funeral's yours-not mine. **Burma Shave**.

Don't take a curve-at sixty per-we'd hate to lose-a customer. **Burma Shave.**

There'd be more traffic-in the air- if we could put-these signs up there. **Burma Shave**.

***

Seeing eye dog . . . A true story!

I was flying from San Francisco to Los Angeles. By the time we took off, there had been a 45-minute delay and everybody on board was ticked. Unexpectedly, we stopped in Sacramento on the way. The flight attendant explained that there would be another 45-minute delay, and if we wanted to get off the aircraft, we would re-board in 30 minutes. Everybody got off the plane except one gentleman who was blind. I noticed him as I walked by and etly underneath the seats in front of him throughout the flight. I could also tell he had flown this very flight before because the pilot approached him and, calling him by name, said, "Keith, we're in Sacramento for almost an hour. Would you like to get off and stretch your legs?" Keith replied, "No thanks, but maybe my dog would like to stretch his legs." Picture this . . . all the people in the gate area came to a completely quiet standstill when they looked up and saw the pilot walk off the plane with the seeing eye dog! The pilot was even wearing sunglasses. People scattered. They not only tried to change planes, they also were trying to change airlines! (Douglas V. Taylor)

***

"Those who are too smart to engage in politics are punished by being governed by those who are dumber." (Plato)

***

MY MOTHER TAUGHT ME . . .
LOGIC. . . ."If you fall off that swing and break your neck, you can't go to the store with me."
MEDICINE . . . "If you don't stop crossing your eyes, they're going to freeze that way."
TO THINK AHEAD . . . "If you don't pass your spelling test, you'll never get a good job!"
ESP . . . "Put your sweater on, don't you think that I know when you're cold?"
TO MEET A CHALLENGE . . . "What were you thinking? Answer me when I talk to you . . . Don't talk back to me!"
HUMOR . . . "When that lawn mower cuts off your toes, don't come running to me."
BECOME AN ADULT . . . "If you don't eat your vegetables, you'll never grow up.
GENETICS . . . "You are just like your father!"
ROOTS . . . "Do you think you were born in a barn?"
WISDOM OF AGE . . . "When you get to be my age, you will understand."
ANTICIPATION . . . "Just wait until your father gets home."
RECEIVING . . . "You are going to get it when we get home."
JUSTICE . . . "One day you will have kids, and I hope they turn

out just like you . . . then you'll see what it's like."

***

A 50/50 MARRIAGE

A Young man saw an elderly couple sitting down to lunch at McDonald's. He noticed that they had ordered one meal, and an extra drink cup. As he watched, the gentleman carefully divided the hamburger in half, and then counted out the fries, one for him, one for her, until each had half of them. Then he poured half of the soft drink into the extra cup and set that in front of his wife. The old man then began to eat, and his wife sat watching, with her hands folded in her lap. The young man decided to ask if they would allow him to purchase another meal for them so that they didn't have to split theirs. The old gentleman said, "Oh no, We've been married 50 years, and everything has always been and will always be shared, 50/50." The young man then asked the wife if she was going to eat, and she replied, "Not yet, it's his turn with the teeth."

***

PRACTICE RANDOM ACTS OF KINDNESS

Laugh out loud often and share your smile generously.

If you know someone who is going through a bad day or a difficult time in life, make it better by doing something. . . anything to let him or her know someone cares . . . and don't let on who did it.

Buy a big box of donuts or chocolates for the office next door, or the UPS person or the mail carrier.

Slip a $20 bill into the pocket . . . pocket book . . . of a needy friend or a stranger.

Visit a neighbor with a bouquet of flowers for no reason at all.

Let the person behind you in line, at the grocery store, go ahead of you.

Write a card thinking a service person for his or her care and leave it with your tip. Be sure to include a very specific acknowledgment: "I appreciate the careful way you cleaned the room without disturbing my things." "Your smile as you served me dinner really made my day."

Give another driver your parking spot.

When someone is trying to merge into your lane in traffic, let

Chicken Side off first...

All of you reading these words have loved someone, have done someone a kindness, have healed a wound, have taken on a challenge, and have created something beautiful. Never doubt how precious, how vitally important you are. Every moment you make a difference. Today, appreciate yourself as a random act of kindness.

Thank your church choir members for their music.

Take five minutes to have a conversation you don't have to have.

Share your umbrella with someone.

Write letters to an ill child.

Invite someone to celebrate a holiday at your house.

Give a stranger a compliment.

Leave a note telling neighbors how much you enjoy their garden.

Listen to a friend who needs a friend . . . don't' give advice, just care.

Buy an extra bag of groceries and give to someone out of work.

Send your minister's family a note of thanks.

Be polite when someone dials your phone number by mistake.

Entertain someone's child for them while standing in a checkout line.

Greet your driver when you get on and off the bus.

Cook, clean or do laundry for someone who is ill.

Keep a hot dish and a dessert in your freezer and give to someone when an emergency occurs.

Read a book to a child . . . then -- ***SMILE ! ! !***

***

FOR THOSE OF US WHO REMEMBER!

These great questions and answers are from the days when Hollywood Squares' game show responses were spontaneous, not scripted, as they are now!

Question: Do female frogs croak? Answer: Paul Lynde: If you hold their little heads under water long enough.

Question: If you're going to make a parachute jump, at least how high should you be? Answer: Charley Weaver: Three days of steady drinking should do it.

Question: True or False, a pea can last as long as 5,000 years. Answer: George Gobel: Boy, it sure seems that way sometimes.

Question: You've been having trouble going to sleep. Are you probably a man or a woman? Answer: Don Knotts: That's what's been keeping me awake?

Question: According to Cosmopolitan, if you meet a stranger at a party and you think that he is attractive, is it okay to come out and ask him if he's married? Answer: No, wait until morning.

Question: Which of your five senses tend to diminish as you get older? Answer: Charley Weaver: My sense of decency.

Question What are 'Do it,' and 'I can help,' and' I can't get enough'? Answer: George Gobel: I don't know, but it's coming from the next apartment.

Question: As you grow older, do you tend to gesture more or less with your hands while talking or driving? Answer: Rose Marie: You ask me one more growing old question sonny, and I'll give you a gesture you'll never forget.

Question: Paul, why do Hell's Angels wear leather? Answer: Paul Lynde: Because chiffon wrinkles too easily.

Question: When you pat a dog on its head he will wag his tail. What will a goose do? Answer: Paul Lynde: Make him bark?

Question: If you were pregnant for two years, what would you give birth to? Answer: Whatever it is, it would never be afraid of the dark.

Question: According to Ann Landers, is there anything wrong with getting into the habit of kissing a lot of people? Answer: Charley Weaver: It got me out of the army.

Chicken Side off first...

Question: Back in the old days, when Great Grandpa put horse-radish on his head, what was he trying to do? Answer: George Gobel: Get it in his mouth.

Question: Who stays pregnant for a longer period of time, your wife or your elephant? Answer: Paul Lynde: Who told you about my elephant?

Question: Jackie Gleason recently revealed that he firmly believes in them and has actually seen them on at least two occasions. What are they? Answer: Charley Weaver: His feet.

Question: According to Ann Landers, what are two things you should never do in bed? Answer: Paul Lynde: Point and laugh.

The audience laughed so long on some of these question and answers it took up almost half of the show !
We Don't Stop Laughing Because We Grow Old, We Grow Old Because We Stop Laughing. . .

***

The Vet's Bill

One day an old lady's dog passed out on her floor. She was used to her dog playing dead, so she thought nothing of it, but three days passed and still the dog didn't move, so she became worried. She took the dog to her local veterinarian. The vet set the dog on an observation table and began examining the dog. A couple minutes later, the vet left the room. Then he returned with a cage and inside the cage was a cat. He set the cage next to the dog and let the cat out. The cat walked around the dog six times then went back into his cage. A few minutes later the vet came to the old lady and said, "I'm sorry, but your dog is dead. That'll be $250 dollars." "250 dollars! for what?" shouted the old lady. "Well, 50 dollars for the examination, and $200 dollars for the cat scan."

***

15 things to remember!

1. You should not confuse your career with your life.
2. No matter what happens, somebody will find a way to take it too serious.

individual who perceives a solution and is willing to take command. Very often that person is crazy.

4. Nobody cares if you dance well. Just get up and dance.
5. Never, ever, ever lick a steak knife.
6. Take out the fortune before you eat the cookie.
7. One of the most powerful forces in the universe is gossip.
8. You will never find anyone who can give you a clear and compelling reason why we observe daylight savings time.
9. There comes a time when you should stop expecting other people to make a big deal out of your birthday. That time is age eleven.
10. The one thing that unites all human beings, regardless of age, gender, religion, economic status or ethnic background, is that, deep down inside, we ALL believe we are above average drivers.
11. The main accomplishment of almost all organized protests is to annoy the people who are not in them.
12. A person who is nice to you but rude to a waiter is not a nice person.
13. Never, under any circumstances, take a sleeping pill and a laxative at the same time.
14. There is a fine line between "HOBBY" and "MENTAL ILLNESS."
15. If you want something to happen, start a rumor.

***

Grandfather's Dinner

A frail old man went to live with his son, daughter-in-law, and four-year old grandson. The old man's hands trembled, his eyesight was blurred, and his step faltered. The family ate together at the table. But the elderly grandfather's shaky hands and failing sight made eating difficult. Peas rolled off his spoon onto the floor. When he grasped the glass, milk spilled on the tablecloth. The son and daughter-in-law became irritated with the mess. "We must do something about Grandfather,"said the son. "I've had enough of his spilled milk, noisy eating, and food on the floor !" So, the husband and wife set a small table in the corner. There; Grandfather ate alone while the rest of the family enjoyed dinner. Since Grandfather had broken a dish or two, his food was served in a wooden bowl. Sometimes they saw a tear in his eye as he sat alone. Still, the only words the couple had for him were sharp admonitions when he dropped a fork or spilled food. The four-year-old watched it all in silence. Then; one evening before supper, the father noticed his son playing with wood scraps on the floor. He asked the child sweetly. "What are you making?" Just as sweetly, the boy responded, "Oh, I am making a little bowl for you and Mama to eat your food in when I grow up." The four-year-old smiled and went back to work. The words so struck the parents that they were speechless. No word was spoken but tears streamed down their cheeks and both knew what must be done. That evening the husband took Grandfather's hand and gently led him back to the family table. For the remainder of his days he ate every meal with the family. And for some reason, neither husband nor wife seemed to care any longer when a fork was dropped, milk spilled, or the tablecloth soiled.

Children are remarkably perceptive. Their eyes ever observe, their ears ever listen, and their minds ever process the message they absorb. Remember the saying, "Children are like sponges; they absorb everything and anything that is put in front of them." Never forget to show others how much you love them and never forget that little eyes are watching.

***

A guy walks into a post office one day to see a middle-aged, balding man standing at the counter methodically placing "Love" stamps on bright pink envelopes with hearts all over them. He then takes out a perfume bottle and starts spraying scent all over them. His curiosity getting the better of him, he goes up to the balding man and asks him what he is doing. The man says "I'm sending out 1,000 Valentine cards signed, 'Guess who?'" "But why?" asks the man. "I'm a divorce lawyer," the man replies.

***

HOW TO MESS WITH THE IRS!

Always put staples in the right hand corner. Go ahead and put then down the whole right side. The extractors who remove the mail from the envelopes have to take out any staples in the right side . . . Never arrange paper work in the right order, or even facing the right way. Put a few upside down and backwards. That way they have to remove all your staples; rearrange your paperwork and re-staple it (on the left side) . . . Line the bottom of your envelope with glue and let it dry before you put in your forms, so that the automated opener doesn't open it and the extractor has to open it by hand . . . If you're very unfortunate and have to pay taxes use a two or three party check . . . On top of paying with a three party check pay one of the dollars you owe in cash. When an extractor receives cash, no matter how small an amount, he has to take it to a special desk and fill out a few nasty forms . . . Write a little letter of appreciation. Any letter received has to read and be stamped regardless of what it is or what it's on . . . Write your letter on something misshapen and unconventional. Like on the back of a Kroger sack . . . If you send 2 checks they'll have to staple your unsightly envelope to your half destroyed form . . . Always put extra paper clips on your forms. Any foreign fasteners or the like have to be removed and put away . . . Sign your name in ink on every page. Any signature has to be verified and then date stamped . . . When you mail it, mail it in a big envelope (even if it's just a single EZ form) . . . Big envelopes have to be sorted differently than regular business size ones. An added bonus to the big envelope is that they take priority over other mail, so the workers can hurry up and deal with your mess . . . NOTE: These are just a few of the fun and exciting things you can do with the man. These methods are only recommended when you owe money.

***

From RICHARD'S DESK
"DID YOU KNOW?"
(A sample of each week's story)
A typical story From RICHARD'S DESK each week in our local Osceola, Mo. weekly St. Clair County Courier newspaper!

PURE COUNTRY SORGHUM; MYTHS AND TRUTHS ABOUT THIS WONDERFUL PRODUCT. HOW IT IS MADE AND FROM WHAT; WHERE IT IS MADE AND BY WHOM. YES, OSCEOLA FAMILIES KNOW HOW TO MAKE PURE SORGHUM AND THEY HAVE BEEN DOING IT SINCE EARLY 1900. THIS PURE COUNTRY SORGHUM IS MADE IN THE OSAGE HILLS BY THE FAMILY OF L. GARRISON & SONS. . . "AND BOY IS IT EVER GOOD."

Way back in the Ozark hills (Bear Creek area, down by the old Corbin store, 12 to 15 miles east of Osceola on 82 highway.) in the early 1900s, Levi Garrison decided it was time to make sorghum. Sorghum had been around for a long time but Levi thought he and his sons could make it just as good as anyone else and probably even better.

(Levi was the father of Mahlon Garrison, whose son is Edward Garrison, and his son is Ronnie Garrison.) Currently Ed and Ron are the main ones still making the sorghum; however, Ed's sister Joyce Bacon, from what I saw, is probably one of the hardest workers of all. Sometimes Jim Carnahan gives a big helping hand as well as other friends and neighbors. Usually it takes the whole family to get the job done, even the girls, Noelle and Livie are smak-dab in the middle of it all. I think Shelley takes care of the labeling, filling jars and whatever else is needed. As most folks in this area know there is a ton of Garrison cousins, brothers, sisters, uncles, and so on, and I'm sure if they were needed to help with a good big crop all Ed and Ron would have to do is give a holler.

Many folks think that anything marked sorghum is the real stuff, but that is not necessarily true. For many years there were no laws with regard to labeling products so just about anyone could call it sorghum and get by with it. Now days if it is marked pure sorghum it had better be, or you can be in big trouble. If it is called sorghum blend, or sorghum molasses, or sugar cane molasses, you're not getting the real stuff. All of it still tastes pretty good but for the pure sorghum lovers, it just ain't the same. Many folks say, "You either like it or you don't like it, there is usually no middle ground."

Sorghum syrup and molasses are not the same. Molasses is a by-product of the sugar industry. Sorghum is the juice from the sorghum cane that is boiled, or some call it cooked, to produce the syrup. By cooking it the water is separated from the sorghum syrup.

Sorghum is made from sweet sorghum cane, not sugar cane or grain sorghum. It can be used as table syrup or can be used in baking. You can put sorghum syrup on pancakes, corn bread, or toast. You can use it in baked beans, cookies, BBQ sauce, make popcorn balls with it and even make sorghum suckers. (The kids love the suckers).

Sorghum is a healthy food. It contains iron, calcium, potassium as well as antioxidants, and is sorta just like Maxwell Coffee, "good to the last drop." Sorghum syrup can be substituted for molasses and corn syrup in all recipes as well as for sugar in many others (with some allowance made for reducing liquid in other ingredients). Sorghum does not need to be cold. It does not mold like maple syrup, but could sugar. If this happens, just reheat it back to liquid form by placing the jar into a bigger pan of hot water until it returns to a good liquid form.

Once the crop is cut down you have to get right with it and start squeezing, and cooking. You can't wait until you feel like it. You gotta start and keep going until you are finished, and sometimes it takes more hours and more help than normal. Everyone has got a special job; cutting and hauling the cane; chopping and feeding the cane into the press; stoking the cooker; boiling, skimming and straining the juice; filtering it several times, making sure everything in the process is working correctly, and then finally bottling and labeling it for sale.

Sorghum cane grows 12 to 15 feet tall. It is usually planted in the spring, around the first of June, like most grasses, and is harvested in late summer, usually in late September or the middle of October. Seed from the head of previous crops is where the seeds come from to plant the next crop. Ron usually plants several acres each year.

Once it is determined that it is time to cut down the cane you have to get right with it. First you cut the stalk down by hand with a corn knife, then within 2 or 3 days you knock off the leaves, cut off the head to obtain the seeds for the next year, load the stalks on to a trailer and transport to the press, (rather than press some call it the sorghum mill.)

Upon arriving at the squeezing press you begin the process of feeding the cane into the press. The old time press was run by horses pulling a devise in a circle causing the gears to engage the press. You can still use the horse power but it is easier to use a tractor or a gasoline motor. The Garrison press has been in their family for many years; however, they have chosen to use the gasoline motor as their means of power.

As the sorghum syrup is squeezed from the cane it is funneled into a long tube or pipe, heading down the hill that leads to the first straining tank. The syrup is strained 3 times before reaching the cooking vat. The first and second times through with cheese cloth and then a stainless steel screen.

Upon reaching the cooking vat, which has been properly

heated to the correct temperature, the syrup runs into the vat and as it is cooked it is constantly stirred to prevent scorching. Another part of the job that keeps someone busy is stoking the fire with wood to keep an even heat.

There has to be water in the vat at all times when it is being heated in order not to burn the pan. As the sorghum syrup flows into the pan for cooking the water is pushed to the opposite end and forced out through an opening in the end of the vat. The syrup is forced to stay at the hottest end so the cooking process can continue until it is finished.

Once the sorghum syrup is ready to leave the vat it is poured into 5 gallon buckets and then from there into pints, quarts, and half gallon containers, ready for sale.

When the first batch of Sorghum is ready then they have to have an official taster which this time just happened to the author of this article.

Since last year I kept sorghum in my cupboard all the time which meant going back to Ron's house and getting more quite often. Every chance I get I spread a spoon of sorghum on a couple of biscuits or 2 or 3 slices of toast, along with some good ole creamery butter, and even some times I add a dab of peanut butter; and that's what I call living high on the hog; so to speak.

Ron says they usually can produce about 30 gallons of sorghum a day. That sounds like a lot, which it is, but they only cook for 2 days. Next year, they plan to produce a total of 100 gallons, and if you make a mad dash to Ron's house, or pick it up at Bear Creek Methodist Church some Sunday morning, I think you'll be hooked on pure country sorghum from that time forward. Just in case you're wondering; they don't have shelves of sorghum in church; I think Ron keeps his vehicle loaded, just in case.

For inquires on sorghum contact: **Ron Garrison, 2380 N.E. 1021 Rd. Osceola, Mo. 64776**

***

HAS THIS EVER HAPPENED TO YOU?

One night at about 3 a.m. my wife was getting up from the toilet to return to bed when she heard a little noise. It was a suspiciously rodent like sound that seemed to be right in the bathroom with her. She, of course, froze and listened attentively for any further sign of invaders. After a moment, satisfied that she was alone, she took a step for the door. Rodent scratchy sounds again! She froze, not breathing. Silence; her heart beat fast as she, once again, tried to retreat from the bathroom. This time the noise was accompanied by something touching the back of her leg! That was, of course, too much to bear. She literally flew the 8 feet to the bed, clearing the foot board by a couple feet, to land screaming by my side. This is not a pleasant way to wake up. Scrambling into consciousness, now scared half to death myself, I managed to get the light on. The culprit was right there in plain sight, a trail of toilet paper neatly marked the path from the bathroom to the bed.

***

Reaching the end of a job interview the human Resources Person asked a young Engineer fresh out of MIT, "And what starting salary were you looking for?" The Engineer said, "In the neighborhood of $125,000 a year, depending on the benefits package." The interviewer said, "Well, what would you say to a package of 5-weeks vacation, 14 paid holidays, full medical and dental, company matching retirement fund to 50% of salary, and a company car leased every 2 years; say a red Corvette?" The engineer sat up straight and said, "Wow! Are you kidding?" And the interviewer replied, "Yeah, but you started it."

***

Albert Einstein's mother said, "But, Albert, it's your senior picture. Can't you do something about your hair? Styling gel, mousse, something . . . ?"

George Washington's mother said, "The next time I catch you throwing money across the Potomac, you can kiss your allowance good-bye!"

Jonah's mother said, "That's a nice story, but now tell me where you've really been for the last three days?"

Superman's mother said, "Clark, your father and I have discussed it, and we've decided you can have your own telephone line. Now will you quit spending so much time in all those phone booths?"

Thomas Edison's mother said, "Of course I'm proud that you invented the electric light bulb. Thomas; Now, turn off that light and get to bed!"

Mona Lisa's mother said, "After all that money your father and I spent on braces, Mona, that's the biggest smile you can give us?"

Abraham Lincoln's mother said, "Again with the stovepipe hat, Abe? Can't you just wear a baseball cap like the other kids?"

Napoleon's mother said, "All right, Napoleon. If you aren't hiding your report card inside your jacket, then take your hand out of there and prove it!"

***

This lady and her husband where living quite well; however they never ever seemed to have enough money to meet all their needs. Also, every once in a while they would fuss and fume over this and that, just sorta like most marriages now days. One day the lady won 5 million dollars. Her husband came home from work, and as usual he was complaining about he didn't have enough room in the house for his things. It seems like her things took all the room. When she told her husband that she'd won the lottery she immediately said, "Honey, pack your clothes, pack your summer and winter ones, pack them all." He said, "Pack all my clothes, what are we going to do . . . move? She replied, no buster, as of matter of fact, as of this moment, you're out of here."

Heathcliff and Gertrude were discussing what a job it must for her to lay an egg. She agreed and said, "Yeah honey, it really is quite a chore, but nothing like what the mayor is going to do this next week. I read in the paper where he is going to lay a corner stone at our church building site next Sunday." Heathcliff replied, "Wow, I'm sure glad you don't have to do something like that."

***

There was an old maid school teacher who was about to retire. After devoting her entire life to the children in her classroom she felt lost and didn't know what to do, so she decided to put an ad in the local newspaper. "Retired school teacher seeks refined gentleman to help her find the playground before the bell rings."

***

An ambitious lawyer, wanting to impress a prospective client with his importance and wealth, buzzed his secretary on the intercom. "Miss Jones," he barked, "Get me my broker." She replied, "Stock or pawn."

***

The surgeon does everything, but doesn't know anything; the Diagnostic medical man knows everything, but doesn't do anything; the Psychiatrist doesn't know or do anything; and the Pathologist knows everything but it's too late.

***

George always wanted to ride in an airplane. He and his wife, Mable, noticed there was an offer to ride in an airplane absolutely free with only one condition. "I'll take you and your wife up and if I can do my flying the way I want to, and you never scream or make any kind of a noise, I'll do it for nothing, but if you holler you've got to pay me full price which is $50." If you don't make a sound then I'll pay you $50." George looked at his wife and said, "I think we ought to take him up on that, what do you think?" Mable replied, "Good, I'm ready to go, $50 is $50 "Ok," said George, we're ready to go." Well, they got in the plane and they took off. He flipped upside down, did a couple of reverse rolls, did two or three dives, and headed back to the airfield. George said nothing. When they got down, the pilot said, "Well, George

I guess I owe you $50, you never made a sound." George said, "Yeah you're right, but I almost hollered on that last roll when Mable fell out, but like we said, "$50 is $50.

***

A little boy and his father went shopping together at the grocery store. As they were walking around the store there was a really large lady walk in front of the little boy. "The boy said to his father, "Look there dad, that ole gal is bigger than a dump truck." The father said, "Son, you shouldn't say things like that, it is not polite, if she hears you it will make her feel bad." "Ok," said the boy. They continued shopping and when they got in line at the check-out counter the large lady was right in front of dad. Just when they got real close to the lady, the Pepsi® truck that had pulled up in front of the store starting beeping. The little boy screamed, "Dad, look out, she's backing up."

***

Two old maid sisters, Mable and Maude, were going down the road toward town. Maude couldn't hear worth a flip so Mable did the driving. They got pulled over by a cop. He said, "Could I see your driver's license please," Maude hollered real loud, "What did he say?" Mable said, "He said he wanted to see my driver's license." Maude groaned, "OK." The cop looked at her license and said, "Oh, I see you're from Osceola, Missouri." "Yes, replied Mable," Maude hollered loudly, "What did he say?" Getting pretty disgusted with Maude, Mable said, "He says he sees that we're from Osceola." Maude says, "OK, Then the cop said to Mable, "You'll never believe this but, many years ago I lived in Osceola and I knew a gal there that was probably the ugliest and meanest ole gal I'd ever seen in my life." Maude said, "What did he say?" Mable replied, "Oh shut up Maude, he thinks he knows you."

***

Three guys were talking, and one said, "By the way, what did you get your mother-in-law for Christmas last year." Charlie answered and said, "Well, I got mine a cemetery lot." "Golly," said Sam, "What are you going to get her this year?" Charlie said, "I ain't getting her nothing, she didn't use what I got her last year."

***

What do you get when you cross a pigmy with a bat? "I don't know," said Smitty, "But I'll bet you one thing for sure, I'll bet it was a short little sucker.

***

Excuses sent to schools by parents; for real

My son is under the doctor's care and should not take P.D. today. Please execute him.

Please excuse Mary for being absent. She was sick and I had her shot.

Dear School: Please exkuse John for being absent on Jan. 28, 29, 30, 31, 32, and 33.

Please excuse Gloria from Jim today.

John has been absent because he had 2 teeth taken off his face.

Chris will not be in school because he has an acre in his side.

Please excuse Tom for being absent yesterday. He has diarrhea and his boots leak.

Please excuse John for being. It was his father's fault.

Please escus Jane. She had been sick and under the doctor.

Sally won't be in school a week from Firday. We have to attend a funeral.

Please excuse my son's tardiness. I forgot to wake him up and I didn't find him until I started making the beds.

Please excuse Harriet from school yesterday. We forgot to get the Sunday paper off the porch, and when we found it on Monday, we thought it was Sunday.

Please escuse Ray from school. He has very loose vowels.

***

The old man was setting on his porch, when a young man walked up with a pad and pencil in his hand. "What are you selling, young man?" he asked. "I'm not selling any thing, sir," the young man replied. "I'm the census taker." "A what?" the man asked. "A census taker. We are trying to find out how many people are in the United States." "Well," the old man answered. "You're wasting your time with me, I don't got no idea."

***

Johnny, age 5, was being taught to be neat and clean and to pick up after himself. One evening after taking his bath his mother asked him if he had picked up and taken care of his dirty clothes. He replied, "Yes Mom, I picked them up and put them right in the hamster."

***

Excerpts from actual letters sent to landlords . . .

1. "The toilet is blocked and we cannot bathe the children until it is cleared."
2. "This is to let you know that there is a smell coming from the man next door."
3. "I am writing on behalf of my sink, which is running away from the wall."
4. "I request your permission to remove my drawers in the kitchen."
5. "Our lavatory seat is broken in half and is not in three pieces."
6. "Will you please send someone to mend our cracked sidewalk. Yesterday my wife tripped on it and is now pregnant."

***

A couple was married for 45 years and raised a brood of 11 children, and were blessed with 22 grandchildren. When asked the secret for staying together all that time, the wife replies, "Many years ago we made a promise to each other; the first one to pack up and leave has to take all the kids."

***

Mary Siegel was almost crazy with her three young kids. She complained to her best friend. "They're driving me nuts! Such pests. They give me no rest and I'm half way to the funny farm." "What you need is a playpen to separate the kids from yourself," her friend said. So, Mary bought a playpen. A few days later, her friend called to ask how things were going. "Superb! I can't believe it." Mary said, "I get in that pen with a good book, a chocolate bar, and the kids don't bother me for hours!"

***

The hostess (with a daughter of marriageable age, of long duration) sent out an invitation to an officer (who was supposed to be the prospective suitor of her daughter's hand.) "Mr. and Mrs. Dabney request the pleasure of Captain Black's company at dinner on the 16th of September." She was somewhat dismayed to receive the enthusiastic reply: "With the exception of four men on leave, and two sick, Captain Black's company accepts with much pleasure your invitation to dinner on the 16th of September."

***

Nominated best joke of the year . . .

A Russian arrives in New York City as a new immigrant to the United States. He stops the first person he sees walking down the street and says, "Thank you Mr. American for letting me come into this country, giving me housing, food stamps, free medical care, and a free education!" The passerby says, "You are mistaken, I am from * * * * * " The man goes on and encounters another passerby. "Thank you for having such a beautiful country here in America." The person says, "I not American, I Vietnamese." The new arrival walks farther, and the next person he sees he stops, shakes his hand, and says, "Thank you for wonderful America!" That person puts up his hand and says, "I am from Middle East, I am not American." He finally sees a nice lady and asks, "Are you an American?" She says, "No, I am from Africa." Puzzled, he asks her, "Where are all the Americans?" The African lady checks her watch and says, "Probably somewhere working."

***

Carjacking foiled

An elderly lady in Atlanta, Georgia, went Christmas shopping at a major mall. Her sister assured her that it would be a safe place to go. Just in case, she brought a 38 caliber revolver along in her handbag. After shopping all day, she walked back to the parking lot carrying her bag and packages. As she approached her car, she noticed two men sitting in it. She put the bags on the ground, pointed a finger and shouted, "You men get out of my car." Still nothing happened, the men just sat there. So, she opened her purse and took out her .38 revolver, pointed it at the men and shouted. "You men; I've told you twice to get out of my car. Get out and I mean RIGHT NOW." This time the doors flew open and the two men ran like jack rabbits.

The lady put the gun into her purse, retrieved her packages, placed them in the back seat of the car, and got behind the steering wheel. When she put her key into the ignition it would not turn. Suddenly, she realized that she was not in her car. She looked around to see if anyone was watching, carefully opened the door, took her packages and walked to her car, which was parked about four spaces away. As she was leaving the parking lot she noticed several security guards and honked and waved to get their attention. She called out to them saying. "I need to tell you about something that just happened to me." One of the guards replied, "Lady, we don't have time to chat. There's a little old lady with a pistol out in the parking lot hijacking cars." She drove to the police station. The sergeant to whom she told the story nearly tore himself in two with laughter and pointed to the other end of the counter, where two pale white males were reporting a carjacking by a mad elderly white woman. No charges were filed.

***

Some Thoughts

I was thinking that women should put pictures of missing husbands on beer cans.

I have found at my age going bra-less pulls all the wrinkles out of my face.

I was thinking about how people seem to read the Bible a whole lot more as they get older; then it dawned on me, they were cramming for their finals.

You know when people see a cat's litter box, they always say, "Oh, have you got a cat?" Just once I wanted to say, "No, it's for company!"

The man that takes the funeral notices around through town says this happens all the time. At least 3 or 4 times per trip; he says when he lays the folder on the counter someone usually says, "Oh, did they die." When that happens he said he would really like to say . . . . . . !

I thought about how mothers feed their babies with little tiny spoons and forks so I wonder what Chinese mothers use? Perhaps toothpicks?

Employment applications blanks always ask who is to be notified in case of an emergency. I think we should write . . . A Good Doctor!

Why do they put pictures of criminals up in the Post Office? What are we supposed to do . . . write to these men or women? Why don't they just put their pictures on the postage stamps so the mailmen could look for them while they deliver the mail? Or better yet; why don't they just hang on to the person right after they take the picture.

Richard & Neta Ruth Sunderwirth

I thought about being rich and it really doesn't mean so much . . . Just look at Henry Ford, all those millions, and he never owned a Cadillac!

If you jogged backward . . . would you gain weight?

Wonder what you call a pocket calculator in a nudist camp?

I wonder if Adam ever said to Eve. "Watch it! There are more ribs where you came from!"

I have decided that Nostalgia is the VCR of our minds.

I'd kill for a Nobel Peace Prize.

Love may be blind, but marriage is a real eye-opener.

Hell hath no fury like the lawyer of woman scorned.

Bills travel through the mail at twice the speed of checks.

Hard work pays off in the future. Laziness pays off now.

Eagles may soar, but weasels aren't sucked into jet engines.

Borrow money from a pessimist; they don't expect it back.

***

Life is a Theater. . .

Invite Your Audience Carefully! Read carefully.

Not everyone is healthy enough to have a front row seat in our lives. There are some people in your life that need to be loved from a distance. It's amazing what you can accomplish when you let go of, or at least minimize your time with draining, negative, incompatible, not going anywhere relationships/friendships.

Observe the relationships around you . . . Pay attention!

Which ones lift and which ones lean?

Which ones encourage and which ones discourage?

Which ones are on a path of growth uphill and which ones are going downhill?

When you leave certain people do you feel better or feel worse?

Which ones always have drama or don't really understand, know or appreciate you?

The more you seek quality, respect, growth, peace of mind, love and truth around you, the easier it will become for you to decide who gets to sit in the front row and who should be moved to the balcony of your life.

"If you cannot change the people around you, change the people you're around."

***

Woman shot in her own driveway

Chicken Side off first...

Linda Burnett, 26, a resident of San Diego, was visiting her in-laws and, while there, went to a nearby supermarket to pick up some groceries. Later, her husband noticed her sitting in her car in the driveway with the windows rolled up and her eyes closed, with both hands behind the back of her head. He became concerned and walked over to the car. He noticed that Linda's eyes were now open and she looked very strange. He asked her if she was okay, and Linda replied that she had been shot in the back of the head and had been holding her brains in for over an hour. The husband called the paramedics, who broke into the car because the doors were locked and Linda refused to remove her hands from her head. When they finally got in, they found that Linda had a wad of bread dough on the back of her head. A Pillsbury biscuit canister had exploded from the heat, making a loud noise that sounded like a gunshot, and the wad of dough hit her in the back of her head. When she reached back to find out what it was, she felt the dough and thought it was her brains. She initially passed out, but quickly recovered. The defective biscuit canister was analyzed and the expiration date was from 2008.

***

The mother of three notoriously unruly youngsters was asked whether or not she'd have children, if she had to do it all over again. "Sure," she replied, "But not the same ones."

***

As part of the admission procedure in the hospital where I work, I ask the patients if they are allergic to anything. If they are, I print it on an allergy band placed on the patient's wrists. Once when I asked an elderly woman if she had any allergies, she said she couldn't eat bananas. Imagine my surprise when several hours later a very irate son came out to the nurses' station demanding, "Who's responsible for labeling my mother 'bananas'?"

***

Doctor's Statistics

Number of physicians in the US: 700,000. Accidental deaths caused by physicians per year: 120,000. Accidental deaths per physician: 0.171.

Number of gun owners in the US: 80,000,000.

Number of accidental gun deaths per year (all age groups) 1,500. Accidental deaths per gun owner: 0^{00}00188

Statistically, doctors are approximately 9,000 times more danger-

ous than gun owners.
"FACT: Not everyone has a gun, but everyone has at least one Doctor."

***

I've Learned, and Believe me, I've Learned that . . .

1. . . . the best classroom in the world is at the feet of an elderly person.
2. . . . when you're in love, it shows.
3. . . . just one person saying to me, "You've made my day!" makes my day.
4. . . . I feel better about myself when I make others feel better about themselves.
5. . . . having a child fall asleep in your arms is one of the most peaceful feelings in the world.
6. . . . what we have done for ourselves alone dies with us. What we have done for others and the world remains and is immortal.
7. . . . a sincere apology is worth more than all the roses money can buy.
8. . . . words harshly spoken are as difficult to retrieve as feathers in a gale.
9. . . . being kind is more important than being right.
10. . . . you should never say no to a gift from a child.
11. . . . I can always pray for someone, when I don't have the strength to help him in some other way
12. . . . no matter how serious your life requires you to be, every one needs a friend to act goofy with.
13. . . . sometimes all a person needs is a hand to hold and a heart to understand.
14. . . . life is like a roll of toilet paper. The closer it gets to the end, the faster it goes.
15. . . . we should be glad God doesn't give us everything we ask for.
16. . . . money doesn't buy happiness or class.
17. . . . it's those small daily happenings that make life so spectacular.
18. . . . once a relationship is over, if you experienced more smiles than tears, then it wasn't a waste of time.
19. . . . Under everyone's hard shell is someone who wants to be

appreciated and loved.

20. . . . never to humiliate another person. Always give him an honorable way to back down or out of something and still save face.
21. . . . the Lord didn't do it all in one day. What makes me think I can?
22. . . . if you are still talking about what you did yesterday, you haven't done much today.
23. . . . to ignore the facts does not change the facts.
24. . . . when you plan to get even with someone, you are only letting that person continue to hurt you.
25. . . . you view other people's children in a whole different light when you have some of your own.
26. . . . the older I get, the smarter my parents and grandparents become.

***

Albert Einstein

When Albert Einstein was making the rounds of the speaker's circuit, he usually found himself eagerly longing to get back to his laboratory work. One night as they were driving to yet another rubber-chicken dinner, Einstein mentioned to his chauffeur (a man who somewhat resembled Einstein in looks and manner) that he was tired of speech making. "I have an idea, boss" his chauffeur said. "I've heard you give this speech so many times; I'll bet I could give it for you." Einstein laughed loudly and said, "Why not? Let's do it." When they arrived at the dinner, Einstein donned the chauffeur's cap and jacket and sat in the back of the room. The chauffeur gave a beautiful rendition of Einstein's speech and even answered a few questions expertly. Then a supremely pompous professor asked an extremely esoteric question about anti-matter formation, digressing here and there to let everyone in the audience know that he was nobody's fool. Without missing a beat, the chauffeur fixed the professor with a steely stare and said, "Sir, the answer to that question is so simple that I will let my chauffeur, who is sitting in the back, answer it for me."

Richard & Neta Ruth Sunderwirth

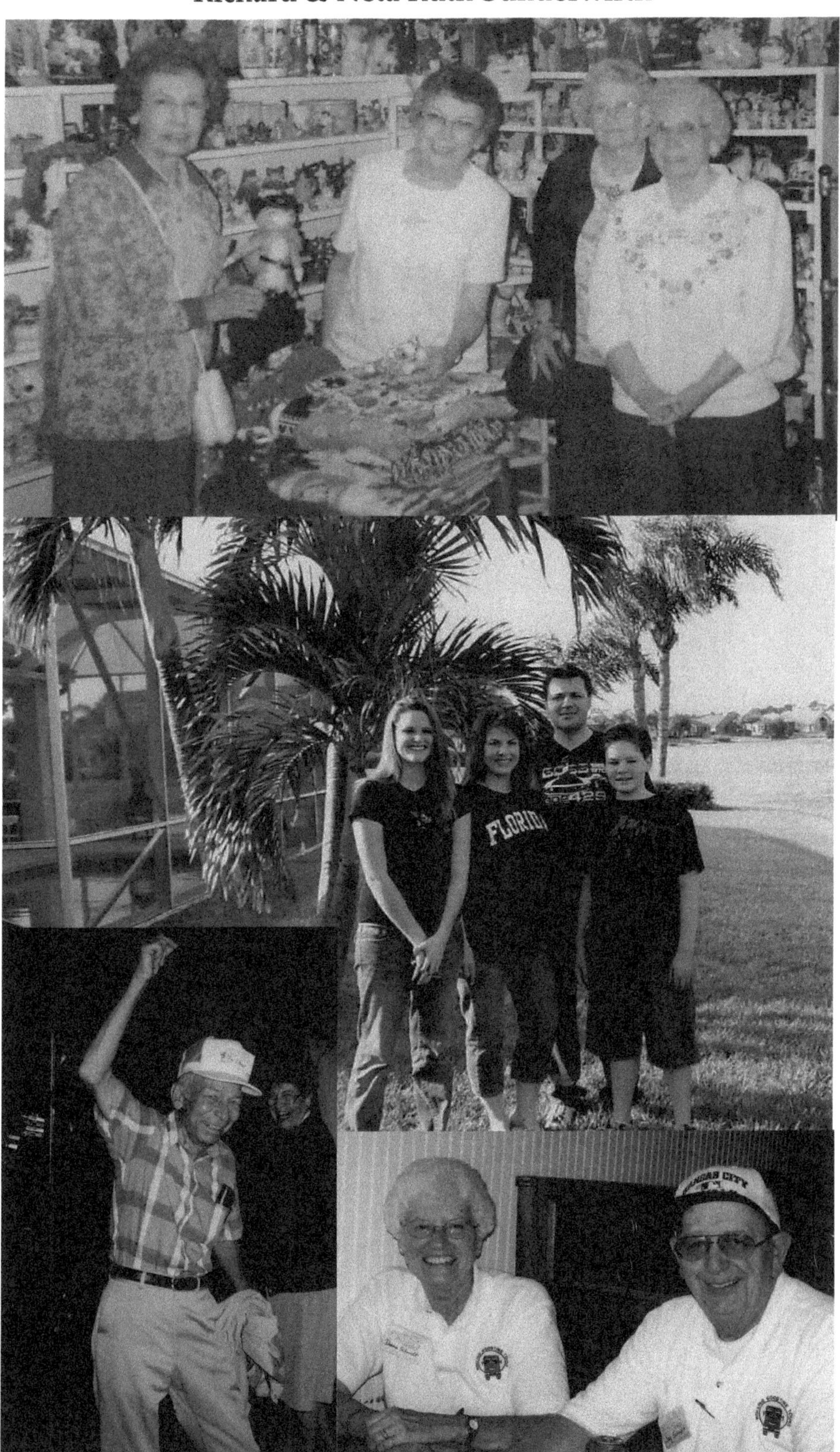

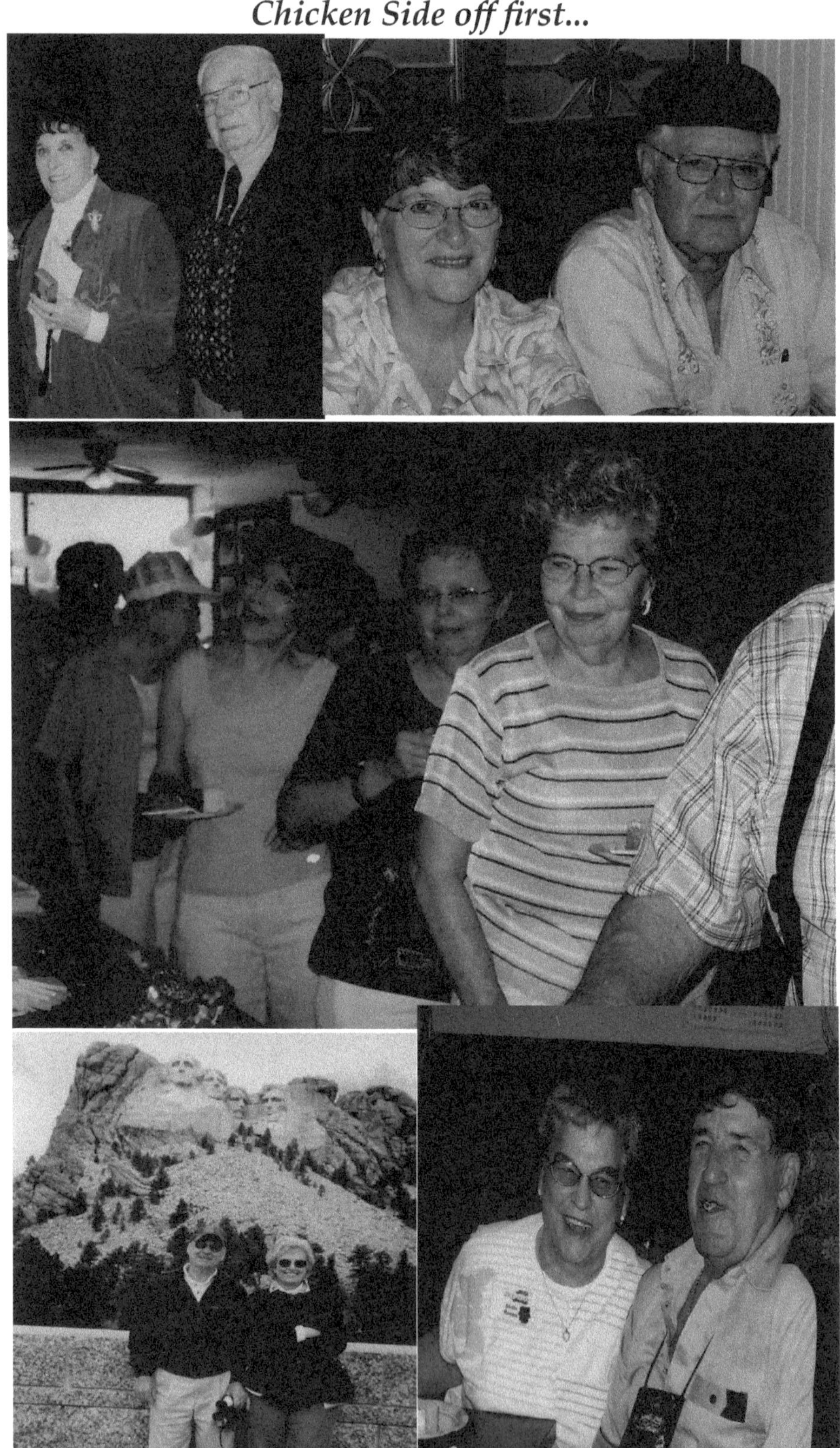

"You know you're wearing too much cologne when you out-skunk a skunk." Bob Lang

***

This elderly gentleman was down town standing on the street corner; he was moaning and carrying on something terrible. A fellow came up to him and said, "What's the matter old timer?" The old man replied, "Well, I should be OK but I'm not. I've got a lot to be thankful for. You see, I just got married again to this beautiful 30 year old blonde. She really loves me. She cooks for me. She rubs my feet. She says sweet things to me and a whole bunch of other wonderful things." The stranger said to the old fellow, "It sounds like, to me, that you've got it made." The old man replied, "Yeah, if I could only remember where I live."

***

Quite a few people live in all-electric homes these days. Folks even drive electric cars. But the really sad part about all of that is the fact that everything in the house and even in the garage is CHARGED!

***

Winners and Losers

The Winner is always a part of the answer. The loser is always part of the problem.

The Winner always has a program. The loser always has an excuse.

The Winner sees a green near every sand trap. The loser sees 2 or 3 sand traps near every green.

The Winner Says, "Let me do that for you." The loser says, "That's not my job."

The Winner sees an answer for every problem. The loser sees a problem in every answer.

The Winner says, "It may be difficult, but it is possible." The loser says, "It may be possible, but it's too difficult." **Don Greenwell**

***

I wrote this book during the winter. One morning as I was writing I just happened to look out the window and I couldn't believe my eyes. I called my wife and told her to look outside. There was a teen-age boy with his pants pulled up.

***

ENTHUSIASM

Enthusiasm is the greatest business asset in the world. It beats money and power and influence. Single-handed, the enthusiast convinces and dominates where a small army of workers would scarcely stir a speck of interest. Enthusiasm tramples over prejudice and opposition, spurns inaction, storms the citadel of its object, and like an avalanche overwhelms and engulfs all obstacles. Enthusiasm is faith in action; and faith and initiative rightly combined remove mountainous barriers and achieve the unheard of, and miraculous. Set the germ of enthusiasm afloat in your business; carry it in your attitude and manner. It spreads like a contagion and influences every fiber of your industry. It begets and inspires effects that you did not even dream of. It means increase in production and decrease in costs. It means joy and pleasure and satisfaction to your workers. It means life real and virile. It means spontaneous bedrock results. It means all the vital things that pay dividends. It also helps each one of us to have a more inspirational spirit. **Don Greenwell**

***

Oley wanted to take his cousin from out west to go ice fishing on a thick, frozen Minnesota lake. They cut their holes and dropped their lines in. Oley kept reeling in fish, while his cousin wasn't even getting nibbles. "How do you keep getting so many bites?" the cousin asked. "Hrmmp" mumbled Oley. "What was that, I didn't understand you," the cousin replied. "Hrmmph!" Oley mumbled through clenched teeth again. "I'm sorry, I still didn't catch that." Oley put his hand in his mouth and pulled something out, and then spoke again, "You have to keep your worms warm."

***

The angry wife met her husband at the door. There was alcohol on his breath and lipstick on his collar. "I assume," she snarled, "There is a very good reason for you to come waltzing in here at six o' clock in the morning?" "Abbbb so luteley, there is," he replied. "Breakkkkfast."

***

The boss returned from lunch in a good mood and called the whole staff in to listen to a couple of jokes he had picked up. Everybody but one girl laughed uproariously. "What's the matter?"

grumbled the boss. "Haven't you got a sense of humor?" "I do have a sense of humor, but this time I don't have to laugh," she replied. "I'm leaving Friday."

***

A new business was opening and one of the owner's friends wanted to send him flowers for the occasion. They arrived at the new business site and the owner read the card, "Rest in Peace." The owner was angry and called the florist to complain. After he had told the florist of the obvious mistake and how angry he was, the florist replied, "Sir, I'm really sorry for the mistake, but rather than getting angry, you should imagine this . . . 'Somewhere there is a funeral taking place today, and they have flowers with a note saying, 'Congratulations on your new location.' "

***

I hate my job day!

When you have an 'I hate my job day,' even if you're retired, you sometimes have those days where you stop at your local pharmacy and go to the thermometer section and purchase a rectal thermometer. Be sure you get the brand by 'Johnson & Jones'. When you get home lock your doors, draw the curtains and disconnect the phone so you won't be disturbed. Change into some very comfortable clothing and sit in your favorite chair. Open the package and remove the thermometer. Now, carefully place it on a table or a surface so that it will not become chipped or broken. Now, the fun part begins. Take the literature from the box and read it carefully. You will notice that in the very small print there is a statement. "Every rectal thermometer made by 'Johnson and Jones' is personally tested and then sanitized. Now close your eyes and repeat out-loud 5 times, "I'm so glad I do not work in the quality control department at 'Johnson & Jones'. Have a nice day and remember there is always someone else with a job that is more of a pain than yours. Now, if you haven't got a smile on your face and laughter in your heart, maybe you should apply for a job at 'Johnson & Jones'.

***

This guy was roasting a chicken on a rotisserie and had begun to hand-crank it to ensure all areas were evenly cooked. It was now getting golden brown and juices were causing some flames to lick the chicken as he turned it. Just then, a drunk stumbled into the guy's yard, looked at the scene and exclaimed, "Hey buddy, not only is your music box not making any music, but your monkeys on fire!

***

Three older ladies were discussing the travails of getting older. One said, "Sometimes I catch myself with a jar of mayonnaise in my hand in front of the refrigerator and can't remember whether I need to put it away, or start making a sandwich." The second lady chimed in, "Yes, sometimes I find myself on the landing of the stairs and can't remember whether I was on my way up or on my way down." The third one responded, "Well, I'm glad I don't have that problem; knock on wood," as she raps her knuckles on the table, then told them, "That must be the door, I'll get it!"

***

"My Dad always used to say that when you die, if you've got truly five or six real friends, then you've had a wonderful life."

***

The Tate Family

Do you know how many members of the TATE family belong to our congregation? There is old man DIC TATE who wants to run everything, while uncle RO TATE tries to change everything. Their sister, ADGA TATE, stirs up plenty of trouble with help from her husband, IRRI TATE. Whenever new projects are suggested, HESE TATE and his wife, VEGE TATE, want to wait until next year. Brother FACILI TATE is quite helpful in church matters. And a happy member is Mrs. FELICI TATE, Cousins COGI TATE and MEDI TATE always think things over and lend a helpful steady hand. And, of course, there is the bad seed in the family, AMPU TATE, who has cut himself off completely from the rest of the congregation.

***

Two elderly couples were enjoying friendly conversation when one of the men asked the other, "Fred, how was the memory clinic you went to last month?" "Outstanding," Fred replied. "They taught us all the latest psychological techniques: visualization, association. It was great." "Wow! What was the name of the clinic?" Fred went blank. He thought and thought, but couldn't remember. Then a smile broke across his face and he asked, "What do you call that flower with the long stem and thorns?" "You mean a rose?" "Yes, that's it!" He turned to his wife, and said, "Rose, what was the name of that memory clinic?"

***

"Enjoy the little things in life, for one day you may look back and realize they were the big things."

***

This is Wonderful!

The road to success is not straight, there is a curve called failure.
A loop called confusion, and speed bumps called friends.
Red Lights called enemies, and caution lights called family.
You will have flats called jobs, but if you have a spare called determination . . .
An engine called perseverance, and insurance called faith, and
A driver called Jesus; you will make it to a place called success!

***

What happened to honor among thieves?

Nick and Lou head out for a quick round of golf. Since they are short on time, they decide to play only 9 holes. Nick says to Lou, "Let's say we make the time worth the while, at least for one of us, and spot $5 on the lowest score for the day." Lou agrees and they enjoy a great game. After the 8th hole, Lou is ahead by 1 stroke, but cuts his ball into the rough on the 9th. "Help me find my ball; you look over there," he says to Nick. After 5 minutes, neither has had any luck, and since a lost ball carries a four-point penalty, Lou pulls a ball from his pocket and tosses it to the ground. "I've found my ball!" he announces triumphantly. Nick looks at him forlornly, "After all the years we've been friends, you'd cheat me on golf for a measly five bucks?" "What do you mean cheat? I found my ball sitting right here!" "And a liar, too!" Nick says, with amazement. "I'll have you know I've been standing on your ball for the last five minutes!"

***

Ideal Work Regulations The Modern Company

SICK DAYS:

We will no longer accept a doctor's statement as proof of sickness. If you are able to go to the doctor, you are able to come to work.

SURGERY:

Operations are now banned. As long as you are an employee here, you need all your organs. You should not consider removing anything. We hired you intact. To have something removed constitutes a breach of employment.

PERSONAL DAYS:

Each employee will receive 104 personal days a year. They are called Saturday and Sunday.

VACATION DAYS:

All employees will take their vacation at the same time every year. The vacation days are as follows: Jan. 1, July 4 & Dec. 25.

BEREAVEMENT LEAVE:

This is no excuse for missing work. There is nothing you can do for dead friends, relatives or co-workers. Every effort should be made to have non-employees attend to the arrangements. In rare cases where employee involvement is necessary, the funeral should be scheduled in the late afternoon. We will be glad to allow you to work through your lunch hour and subsequently leave one hour early, provided your share of the work is done enough.

OUT FROM YOUR OWN DEATH:

This will be accepted as an excuse. However, we require at least two weeks' notice, as it is your duty to train your own replacement.

RESTROOM USE:

Entirely too much time is being spent in the restroom. In the future, we will follow the practice of going in alphabetical order. For instance, all employees whose names begin with 'A' will go from 8:00 to 8:20, employees whose names begin with 'B will go from 8:20 to 8:40 and so on. If you're unable to go at your allotted time, it will be necessary to wait until the next day, when your turn comes again. In extreme emergencies employees may swap their time with a co-worker. Both employees' supervisors in writing must approve this exchange. In addition, there is now a strict 3-minute time limit in the stalls. At the end of three minutes, an alarm will sound, the toilet paper roll will retract, and the stall door will open.

LUNCH BREAK:

Skinny people get an hour for lunch as they need to eat more so that they can look healthy, normal size people get 30 minutes for lunch to get a balanced meal to maintain the average figure. Fat people get 5 minutes for lunch because that's all the time needed to drink a Slim Fast and take a diet pill. Sondra gets none.

DRESS CODE:

It is advised that you come to work dressed according to your salary, if we see you wearing $350 Prada sneakers and carrying a $600 Gucci bag we assume you are doing well financially and therefore you do not need a raise.

Thank you for your loyalty to our company. We are here to provide a positive employment experience. Therefore, all questions, comments, concerns, complaints, frustrations, irritations, aggravations, insinuations, allegations, accusations, contemplations, consternations or input should be directed elsewhere. Have a nice week.

Copied

***

A goober calls 911 on her cell phone to report that her car has been broken into. She is hysterical as she explains her situation to the dispatcher; "They've stolen the stereo, the steering wheel, the brake pedal and even the accelerator!" she cries. The dispatcher says, "Stay calm; An officer is on the way." A few minutes later, the officer radios in. "Disregard," he says. "She got in the back seat by mistake."

***

A Cabbie picks up a Nun. She gets into the cab, and notices that the very handsome cab driver won't stop staring at her. She asks him why he is staring. He replies; "I have a question to ask, but I don't want to offend you." She answers, "My son, you cannot offend me. When you're as old as I am and have been a nun as long as I have, you get a chance to see and hear just about everything. I'm sure that there's nothing you could say or ask that I would find offensive." "Well," he said, "I've always had a fantasy to have a nun kiss me." She responds, "Well, let's see what we can do about that; #1, you have to be single and #2, you must be Catholic." The cab driver is very excited and says, "Yes, I'm single and Catholic!" "OK" the nun says. "Pull into the next alley." The nun fulfills his fantasy with a kiss that would make a hooker blush. But when they get back on the road, the cab driver starts crying. "My dear child," said the nun, "Why are you crying?" The cab driver replies, "Forgive me but I've sinned. I lied and I must confess: I'm married and I'm Jewish." The Nun says, "That's OK sonny, My name is Kevin and I'm going to a Halloween Masquerade party."

***

MONEY

It can buy a House, But not a Home; It can buy a Bed, But not Sleep. It can buy a Clock, But not Time; It can buy you a Book, But not Knowledge. It can buy you a Position, But not Respect: It can buy you Medicine, But not Health. It can buy you Blood, But not Life; It can buy you Sex, But not love.

I tell you all this because I am your Friend, and as your Friend I want to take away your pain and suffering. So send me all your money and I will suffer for you. A truer Friend than me you will never find. CASH ONLY PLEASE!

***

As a Delta Qir Lines jet was flying over Arizona on a clear day, the co-pilot was providing his passengers with a running commentary about landmarks over the PA system. "Coming up on the right, you can see the Meteor Crater, which is a major tourist attraction in northern Arizona. It was formed when a lump of nickel and iron, roughly 150 feet in diameter and weighing 300,000 tons, struck the earth at about 40,000 miles an hour, scattering white, hot debris for miles in every direction. The hole measures nearly a mile across and is 570 ft. deep." From the cabin, a passenger was heard to exclaim, "WOW! It just barely missed the highway!"

***

NASA and the NAVAJO INDIANS

When NASA was preparing for the Apollo project, they did some astronaut training on a Navajo Indian reservation. One day, a Navajo elder and his son were herding sheep and came across the space crew. The old man, who spoke only Navajo, asked a question which his son translated. "What are these guys in the big suits doing?" A member of the crew said they were practicing for their trip to the moon. The old man got all excited and asked if he could send a message to the moon with the astronauts. Recognizing a promotional opportunity for the spin-doctors, the NASA folks found a tape recorder. After the old man recorded his message, they asked the son to translate it. He refused. So the NASA reps brought the tape to the reservation where the rest of the tribe listened and laughed, but refused to translate the elder's message to the moon. Finally, the NASA crew called in an official government translator. He reported that the moon message said, "Watch out for these guys, and I'm serious; they have come to steal your land."

***

I am growing older because

Old is when an all-nighter means not having to get up to go "potty."

Old is when your friends compliment you on your new alligator shoes and you're barefoot.

Old is when you don't care where your spouse goes as long as you don't have to go along.

Old is when you are cautioned to slow down by the doctor instead of by a policeman.

Old is when getting a little action means you don't have to take any fiber today.

Old is when "Getting Lucky," means you find your car in the Wal-Mart parking lot.

***

Doctor: "Does this medicine affect your memory at all?" "Yes". "And how does it affect your memory?" the doctor replied. Patient; "I forget." The doctor says, "You forget", "Can you give me an example of something that you have forgotten lately?"

***

Granddad's Story

I too, at times, have felt a great hate for those that have taken so much, with no sorrow for what they do. But hate wears you down, and does not hurt your enemy. It is like taking poison and wishing your enemy would die. I have struggled with these feelings many times." "It is as if there are two wolves inside me. One is good and does no harm. He lives in harmony with all around him, and does not take offense when no offense was intended. He will only fight when it is right to do so, and in the right way. But the other wolf, ah! He is full of anger. The littlest thing will set him into a fit of temper. He fights everyone, all the time, for no reason. He cannot think because his anger and hate are so great. It is helpless anger, for his anger will change nothing. Sometimes, it is hard to live with these two wolves inside me, for both of them try to dominate my spirit." The boy looked intently into his Grandfather's eyes and asked, "Which one wins, Granddad?" The Grandfather smiled and quietly said. "THE ONE I FEED!"

***

This old gentleman marries a beautiful 30 year-old blonde girl, and he is so excited. Just for safety's sake he went to his doctor. He says, "Doc, what should I do, I may get too excited." The Doctor says, "Yeah, I know, that's what I wanted to talk to you about. You'll have to really be careful. One of you may die with all of that excitement." "Oh yeah, I been thinking about that too Doc, well, if she dies she dies!"

***

This teenage boy got a date with a little neighbor girl. He went down to the local drug store and asked the owner for some advice. He said to the store owner, "I've got a hot date with a little gal that lives in our neighborhood. I want to make out with her as much as I can. Do you suggest I get her a one pound box of chocolates, a two pound box of chocolates, or a five pound box?" The store owner says, "Well son, if it was me and I wanted to have a real good evening, I'd get her the five- pounder." The little boy thanks him and heads out of the store. That night he goes to pick up his girl and was truly excited. He went and knocked on the door, and the girl was waiting for him. She said, "Sammy, before we go would you have a seat for a moment, I'd like for you to meet someone. She said this is my father and my mother. Dad . . . Mom . . . this is my date for tonight, this is Sammy." Well, they greeted each other and left. When they got outside the girl said to Sammy, "What did you think of my folks?" He replied, "Golly, I nearly fell out of my chair when your dad walked in. I sure didn't know he was the owner of the drug store down-town."

***

Little Johnny sat playing in the garden. When his mother came out to get him, she saw that he was slowly eating a worm. She turned pale. "No, Johnny! Stop! That's horrible! You can't eat worms!" Trying to convince him further she noted, "Now the mother worm is looking all over for her nice baby worm." "No, she isn't," said Johnny. "How do you know she's not?" said the mother, "Because I ate her first!" answered little Johnny.

***

Things a True Southerner Knows . . .

The difference between a hissie fit and a conniption fit. Pretty much how many fish make up a mess. What general direction cattywumpus is. That "gimme sugar" don't mean pass the sugar. When somebody's "fixin" to do something, it won't be long. The difference between Yankees and damn Yankees. How good a cold grape Nehi and cheese crackers are at a country store. Knows what "Well I Suwannee !" means. Ain't nobody's biscuits like Grandma's biscuits! A good dog is worth its weight in gold. Real gravy don't come from the store. The War of Northern Aggression was over states' rights, not slavery. When "by and by" is. The difference between "pert' near" and "a right fur piece." The differences between a redneck and a good ol'boy. Never to go snipe hunting twice. At one point learned what happens when you swallow tobacco juice. Never to assume that the other car with the flashing turn signal is actually going to make a turn. You may wear long sleeves, but you should always roll 'em up past the elbows. You should never loan your tools, pick-up, or gun to nobody. A belt serves a greater purpose than holding Daddy's pants up. Rocking chairs and swings are guaranteed stress relievers. Rocking chairs and swings with an old person in them are history lessons.

***

Money for Standing

The owner of a manufacturing firm decided to make a surprise tour of the factory. Walking through the warehouse he noticed a young man lazily leaning against a packing crate. The factory owner angrily said, "Just how much are you being paid?" The young man replied, "A hundred dollars a week." The owner pulled out his wallet, peeled off five $20 bills and shouted at the young man; "Here is a week's pay; now get out and don't come back!" Without a word, the young man stuffed the money into his pocket and left. The warehouse manager, standing nearby, stared in amazement. "Tell me," the boss asked him, "How long has that guy worked for us?" "He didn't work here," replied the warehouse manager, "He was just the Fed-Ex guy delivering a package."

***

Floyd wrote to his state comptroller to confess that he'd cheated on his income tax 15 years ago and hadn't been able to get a good night's sleep since. He enclosed a check for $25 and had the following note attached; "If I still can't sleep, I'll send in the balance."

***

Bill and Henry go golfing together one spring day, like they had done for a long time. Both of these fellows were rather crazy about golfing. They would go to almost any length to get a game in anytime it was possible. It was getting rather late for Bill to be getting home and his wife Melinda was a bit worried. Finally Bill came in the door and flopped in his easy chair. He was absolutely pooped out. His breathing was slow and he looked totally exhausted. Melinda said, "Where in the world have you been; you never get back from golfing this late, and why do you look so tired?" Bill replied, "Well, I had a little problem; I was doing really well, really well, and I looked around for Henry and he was lying on the ground; apparently he had a heart attack." Melinda said, "You actually should have been home earlier than usual after getting him into the hospital." Bill said, "Melinda, I didn't get him off the golf course for a few hours after he fell. I could tell he was dead; there was nothing I could do; I couldn't really help him and since I was doing so well with my game, I just kept playing; I guess I should have stopped but what took me so long was I'd hit the ball, then drag Henry; hit the ball, then drag Henry. I didn't think I was ever going to finish my game."

***

The Red Tater married the white tater and they had a little sweet tater and she married Dan Rather; now they got a common tater.

***

There was this young reporter who went to interview a sprightly senior who had reached his 99th birthday. At the end of his interview, the reporter said, "Boy oh boy, I hope I can come back next year and talk to you when you reach 100." "Why not?" the old-timer replied. "You look plenty healthy enough to me."

***

The heavy-set older lades in the community got together and decided they would start a new health program and lose weight at the same time. They joined a health club and the first morning they went to class and started with the basic exercises. Everyone in the class was doing great 1234 1234 1234 1234, but pretty soon they heard one poor little lady over in the corner going 911 911 911 911.

***

Shorty went in to the Wal-Mart store and told the clerk "I need 20,000 cockroaches." "My goodness," replied the clerk, "What in the world are you going to do with that many cockroaches?" "Well sir, I'm getting ready to move and my lease said I had to leave my apartment just the way I found it, so I thought I'd do my best to oblige them."

***

The old gentleman was all excited and he said to his buddy, "Boy oh boy, I got me a brand new watch and it's a honey." "Great," said his friend, "What kind is it?" "Well right now it is 3:00 p.m. right on the nose."

***

"Anybody know what they call a sleep walking Nun?" A little boy answered, "I guess they would call her a roaming Catholic."

***

"Why is a little dog like a little tree," asked the young girl. "Well," answered her friend, "Because they both have a little bark."

***

John and Paul, two brothers, were discussing John's car. John said to Paul, "I'm going to sell my car because it had over 100,000 miles on it." "That's a good idea," said Paul. John asked Paul if he would sell it for him. Paul said, "Sure." So the next day before Paul picked up the car to sell it, John got out a bunch of tools and turned the speedometer back to 21,000 miles. John said to Paul, "Did you find a buyer for my car?" Paul said, "I sure did but I did you a favor. He wanted the car real bad, but I didn't sell it to him." John said, "Are you crazy? Why didn't you sell him the car? Paul replied, "Because it only had 21,000 miles on it."

***

Mr. Jones, did you know there was no sugar until the 13th century, no coal fires until the 14th, no buttered bread until the 16th, no tea or soap until the 17th, no gas, matches or electricity until the 19th and no cars, canned or frozen food until the 20th century, now Mr. Jones, what was it you were complaining about?"

***

"Friends are the bacon bits in the salad bowl of Life."

***

The other day a lady had a telephone call from her grandson. He said, "Grandma, I want to wish you a happy birthday." He then asked me how old I was, and I told him 84." My little grandson was quiet for a few moments and then he said, "Grandma, did you start at age 1?"

***

During my 18 years in the tour business we did a lot of tours to Washington, D.C. A couple days during the tour we spent time in Pennsylvania, Pa. We visited several Amish farms; these really nice folks. We came up behind one of their buggies. He had a sense of humor, because attached to the back of the buggy was a hand painted sign that said, "Energy Efficient Vehicle, runs on oats and grass, caution, do not step in the exhaust."

***

This fellow was running through the country and taking people's lives as he went. One night he stopped at a farm house, and the front door was open. The folks trusted everyone so they never ever locked it. The man went in and went up the stairs to their bedroom. He opened the door and said, "Folks, I'm here to murder you." He looked straight at the lady and said, "Women go first, but before I kill you I want to know your name?" As she shook all over she said, "My name is Elizabeth." The man said to her husband, "What is your name?" The husband was shaking just as bad as his wife. He said, "My name is George, but all my friends call me Elizabeth." The murderer said, "Folks, this is your lucky night. My favorite aunt's name was Elizabeth, and because of that I'm going to let you live." And out the door he went, and that finishes this story.

***

My wife had a real good friend that had a terrible accident. She lost one of her legs and because of that she could not get a job. She was very disappointed. One day she came in and she was really excited, she said, "You'll never believe this, but I got a job this morning, I go to work tomorrow." My wife also was excited for her. My wife said "Well, that's great, where are you going to work?" She answered, "I am going to work at I-Hop."

***

This guy was just sitting on a bench near an intersection close to his home. All of a sudden there was a big crash. The police got there in a few minutes and investigated what happened. They looked over where the guy was sitting, so they went over to see if he saw what happened. "Say, mister, did you see what happened here just a few minutes ago?" The gentleman answered, thinking he was really doing some real investigating, "Well," he said, "The way I saw it, I'm pretty sure they hit each about the same time."

***

I decided, after quite a long period of thinking about this, to buy a dog. I'd wanted one for a long time; my wife just threw a fit. I think it was because it was a real special dog, or at least I thought it was. She said, "How much did you give for the dog?" I said, "I only paid $10,000 for it." Boy she really did get upset. She said, "Git out of here right now and go get your money back, we can't afford to pay that for a dog, and besides that we don't need it." Well, I left and came back in about 4 hours and I was really happy. I said, "Honey, I got rid of the dog, and boy did I do good. I traded it for 2, $5,000 cats. "It took me over 6 weeks for the knot to go down on my head."

***

A man and his wife were awakened at 3:00 a.m. by a loud pounding on the door. The man gets up and goes to the door where a drunken stranger, standing in the pouring rain, is asking for a push. "Not a chance," says the husband, "It is 3:00 in the morning!" He slams the door and returns to bed. "Who was that?" asked his wife. "Oh, it was just some drunk guy asking for a push," he answers. "Did you help him?" she asks. "No, I did not, its' 3:00 a.m. in the morning and it's pouring down rain out there!" "Well, you sure have a short memory," says his wife. "Can't you remember about three months ago when we broke down, and those two guys helped us? I think you should help him, and you should be ashamed of yourself!" "God loves drunk people too you know." The man does as he is told, gets dressed, and goes out into the pounding rain. He calls out into the dark, "Hello, are you still there?" "Yes, comes the reply from the dark. "Where are you?" asks the husband. "Over here on the swing," replied the drunk. "And I still need a push." I guess that proves that God loves drunk people too."

***

This young lady stepped up to the counter at one of the major airlines. She said to the attendant, "I would like very much for one piece of my luggage to go to New Orleans; one piece to New York; and the other piece to Billings, Montana." The attendant looked at her and said, "Young lady, we can't do that; they all have to go to the same place." "Well, I don't see why not, that's what happened last time." replied the young lady.

***

We had a power outage last weekend, and my PC, TV, and game console shut down immediately. It was raining, so I couldn't play golf. So, I talked to my wife for a couple of hours. You know what; she seems like a really nice person.

***

"At her age, a see-through nightgown won't help," said Henry.

"Yeah, that's right," replied Burt, "And besides that, her boyfriends are so old they couldn't see through it anyway."

***

The Coyote Principle

CALIFORNIA:

The Governor of California is jogging with his dog along a nature trail. A coyote jumps out and attacks the Governor's dog, then bites the Governor. The Governor starts to intervene, but reflects upon the movie "Bambi" and then realizes he should stop because the coyote is only doing what is natural. He calls animal control. Animal Control captures the coyote and bills the state $200 for testing it for diseases and $500 for relocating it. He calls a veterinarian. The vet collects the dead dog and bills the State $200 testing it for diseases. The Governor goes to the hospital and spends $3,500 getting checked for diseases from the coyote and not getting his bite wound bandaged. The running trail gets shut down for 6 months while Fish & Game conducts a $100,000 survey to make sure the area is now free of dangerous animals. The Governor spends $50,000 in state funds implementing a "Coyote Awareness Program" for residents of the area. The State Legislature spends $2 million to study how to better treat rabies and how to permanently eradicate the disease throughout the world. The Governor's security agent is fired for not stopping the attack. The state spends $150,000 to hire and train a new agent with additional special training with regard to the nature of coyotes. PETA protests the coyote's relocation and files a $5 million suit against the state.

TEXAS:

The Governor of Texas is jogging with his dog along a nature trail. A coyote jumps out and attacks his dog. The Governor shoots the coyote with his state-issued pistol and keeps jogging. The Governor has spent $ .50 on a .45 ACP hollow point cartridge. The buzzards eat the dead coyote, and the Governor continues his jogging.

AND THAT, MY FRIENDS, IS WHY CALIFORNIA IS BROKE AND TEXAS IS NOT!

***

My wife had been after me for several weeks to paint the seat on our toilet. Finally I got around to doing it while she was out. After finishing, I left to take care of another matter before she returned home. She came in and undressed to take a shower. Before getting in the shower, she sat on the toilet. As she tried to stand up, she realized the not-quite-dry epoxy paint had glued her to toilet seat. About that time, I got home and realized her predicament. We both pushed and pulled without any success whatsoever. Finally, in desperation, I undid the toilet seat bolts. My wife wrapped a sheet around herself and I drove her to the hospital emergency room. The ER Doctor got her into position where he could study how to free her. Try to get a mental picture of this. My wife tried to lighten the embarrassment of it all by saying, "Well, Doctor, I'll bet you've never seen anything like this before." The Doctor replied, "Actually, I've seen lots of them . . . I just never saw one mounted and framed." Wow! What a deal.

***

Missouri according to Jeff Foxworthy, Thank you Jeff

If you've had a lengthy telephone conversation with someone who dialed a wrong number, you may live in Missouri.
If you know several people who have hit a deer more than once, you may live in Missouri.
If you have switched from 'heat' to 'A/C' and back again in the same day, you may live in Missouri.
If you can drive 75 mph through 2 feet of snow during a raging blizzard without flinching, you may live in Missouri.
If driving is better in the winter because the potholes are filled with snow you may live in Missouri.
If you install security lights on your house and garage, but leave both doors unlocked, you may live in Missouri.
If you carry jumpers in your car and your wife knows how to use them, you may live in Missouri.
If everyone in your family has been on a 'float trip,' you may live in Missouri.
If the phrase "I'm going to the lake this weekend" has only one meaning, and everyone knows what you're talking about, you may live in Missouri.
If "Vacation" means driving to Silver Dollar City, Worlds of Fun or Six Flags, you might be from Missouri.
If you've seen people wear bib overalls to funerals you might be

from Missouri.

If you've ever said or heard it's not the heat, it's the humidity, you might be from Missouri.

If you think "deer season" is a national holiday, you might be from Missouri.

If your idea of a traffic jam is 10 cars waiting to pass a tractor, you might be from Missouri.

If you've seen farmers stop and remove their hat as a funeral passes by, you might be from Missouri.

If someone in a Home Dept. Store offers you assistance and they don't even work there, you may live in Missouri.

If you've worn shorts and a jacket at the same time, you many live in Missouri.

If you know what "Home of the throwed rolls" means, you may be from Missouri.

If you ever rode a school bus over an hour each way, you might be from Missouri.

If you failed World Geography in school because you thought Cuba, Versailles, California, Nevada, Houston, Cabool, Osceola, Louisiana, Springfield, and Mexico were cities in Missouri, and they are mind you, you might be from Missouri.

If you had school classes canceled because of cold, You're probably from Missouri.

If you had school classes canceled because of heat, You're probably from Missouri.

If you know that Richard F. Sunderwirth wrote the book, "Osceola, Missouri, The Burning of 1861," then you are from Missouri.

Thanks again, Jeff

***

The children of two actresses were talking. Marsha said, "Someone told me you have a new father, how is he?" Gina replied, "He's really nice. Come to my place; you can meet him. I'm sure you will like him Marsha. "Oh, Marsha said, I've already met him, he was my father too."

***

Georgia noticed her friend, Judy, who was standing a distance away, was having a conversation with another friend. Judging by their gestures, Georgia suspected that the conversation involved a secret. When the other woman left, Georgia walked over to Judy and asked, "What did she tell you? From your gestures it looked like it might be something juicy? "Now you know, Georgia, I never repeat gossip," said Judy. "All right," Georgia said with a sigh, "I understand." Judy whispered, "So, listen carefully the first time."

***

I love this Quote.

"A gun is like a parachute. If you need one, and don't have one, you'll never need one again.

***

A friend of mine was out on the golf course yesterday and accidently lost control of his golf cart and turned it over. He was laying there on the ground, when this nice very attractive lady came over and asked him if he was ok, and asked what his name was. He told her his name was Jack and that he wasn't hurt. She said she lived in a villa on the edge of the golf course and invited him to come over to the villa with her. He said "My wife won't like it." But she insisted that he go with her. She brought him a cold beverage and told him that he should use her shower and get cleaned up a bit. He said, "My wife won't like it." But she insisted and he did as she asked. Then she said we should go "Skinny Dipping" in the pool. He said "My wife won't like it." She said, "Your wife will never know. By the way, she said, "Where is your wife?" He said, "Well, by golly, the last time I saw her she was under my golf cart."

***

A couple of salesmen were flying to Chicago when all of a sudden the Captain spoke through the public address system. "Ladies and gentlemen, we've lost one of our engines, but there's nothing to worry about because we can still fly with three engines just fine." About an hour later the Captain came back on the system and said, "Ladies and gentlemen, we've just lost our second engine, but that also is really no big problem; we can still fly Ok with two engines." About another hour later the Captain came back on the system and said, "Ladies and gentlemen, let me have your immediate attention once again, we have lost the third engine, but let me assure you we can still fly safely with only one engine." The one salesman looked over at his friend and said, "Boy of boy, with the kind of luck we've been having lately, we'll probably lose the fourth engine and be up here all night."

***

"I don't believe it would be safe to have a woman join the armed forces." said John to his friend. "Well, why not," replied his buddy; women seem to be able to do about anything now days." Well," said John, "It wouldn't be good if it was my wife, because every time the commanding officer would holler charge, she would run off to Wal-Mart."

***

Paula packed seven pairs of underwear for each of her boys, as they went off to college. She said, "Boys, now that should work out just fine." One of the boys replied back, "No it won't, We'll need twelve pair." "No," said their mother, you'll need one pair for each day of the week." "Well, mom," We were figuring we need twelve, one for January, one for February, one for March, and so on."

***

One day Henry was having problems with his computer printer. It just simply was not working properly, so he decided he would take it to a local repair store who dealt in computers and printers. The service man was very friendly to Henry and when he told him what his problem was the guy said, "Well, your problem sounds to me like it needs to be cleaned. We charge $40 for doing a complete cleaning job; however, I have a suggestion that would probably work just fine. Why don't you go on back home; get your printer's manual out and read what it says about cleaning and do the job yourself. It will save you $40. Henry was pleasantly surprised at the repair man's idea. Henry says to the guy, "You know, that's really nice of you. Does your boss know that you suggest things like that, and lose a repair job?" "Oh yes," he replied, "He knows if you take it apart yourself, you'll probably have to bring it in to get it back together where it will run; and we charge a minimum of $100 to do that."

***

The telephone rang and Marjorie answered it. It wasn't for her so she started to hand it to her husband, Charlie. Charlie said, "Who is it," Marjorie replied, "Well, it's a baseball umpire and a couple of his friends and he wants to know if you'd like to have reservations, along with them, to some big game?" Charlie said to his wife, "Hang up, it's a crank call, there's no umpire in the world that has two friends."

***

Bill went back into the pet store and demanded his money back for the canary he'd just purchased. The store owner said, "Why do you want a refund, what's the problem," Bill answered, with a little disgust in his voice, "Well, this dumb bird has only got one leg." "I know that," replied the store owner. Bill said, "If you know that then give me my money." "Listen," said the owner, "You told me you wanted a bird that was a good singer, and that's the best singing bird I had. If you wanted a bird that danced, you should've said so."

***

Sam went into the book store and asked for a good book on love and marriage. The clerk said, "I'm sorry sir, if you want that you'll have to buy two separate books.

***

This gentleman went into the clothing store to buy a new suit. He told the clerk he really couldn't afford to spend very much on a suit this time. The clerk said, "Well, sir this is your lucky day, we just happen to have some suits for a great bargain; only $30." The gentleman said, "That's great, I'll take one." The clerk went and got the suit and the gentleman put it on. He said, "The color of this suit is just perfect; however, the left arm is a lot longer than the right arm." "Well," said the clerk, "That's why the suit is such a bargain. Just cock your left shoulder up a little, like this, and tuck this left lapel under your chin a bit, like this." The gentleman replied, "Ok, but the right leg is way too short." The clerk responded, "No problem, just keep your right knee bent a little at all times, walk like this, and no one will notice. Remember, that's why the suit is only $30." Finally, the fellow bought the suit, cocked his left shoulder into the air, tucked the suit's left lapel under his chin, bent his right knee, and limped out of the store toward his car. Two doctors happened to be walking by and one said to the other, "Look at that poor crippled fellow." The other doctor said, "Yeah, but doesn't his suit fit great."

***

This young couple was on their way to the wedding chapel to get married and on the way they were involved in a horrible automobile accident, and both died instantly. The next thing they knew they were standing at the Pearly Gates in front of St. Peter. They said, "We were just getting ready to be married when the accident occurred; do you think we could go ahead and get married up here before we settle into our new mansion? "Well," said St. Peter, "I'll have to go and do some checking around and see if I can make arrangements for that." He told them to have a seat and he would be back just as soon as he could find a minister. 1 day went by, and then another, and finally he came back after 5 days and said he arranged for the wedding to be on the following Sunday. The couple said that would be alright; however, they said to St. Peter, "During the time you were away making arrangements, we got into a pretty good sized argument and we want to know if it doesn't work out would we be able to get a divorce?" St. Peter answered them with a disgusted tone to his voice, "I really don't know if that would be possible. It took me 5 days to find a minister, and I don't think I might ever be able to find an attorney."

***

This ninety year old man went to the doctor concerned about his love life slowing down a bit. "Gosh, that's terrible, when did you first notice it?" said the doctor. "Well," said the old man, "Twice last night and once this morning."

***

There's a new drink out made with vodka and carrot juice. You get just as drunk as ever but you can see a whole lot better in the morning.

***

The other day I heard two people talking. One said, "Are you happy?" The other one said, "Yes," The first one then said, "Well, tell your face!" **Carl Hurley**

***

Ed would have been here earlier but he was in a department store when the power failed, and he was trapped on the escalator for 45 minutes.

***

"Sometimes humor does have a message. We tend to laugh at what is a truth, good or bad!"

***

One Sunday morning, an old cowboy entered a church just before services were to begin. Although the old man and his clothes were spotlessly clean, he wore jeans, a denim shirt and boots that were worn and ragged. In his hand he carried a worn-out old hat and an equally worn, dog-eared Bible. The church he entered was in a very upscale and exclusive part of the city. It was the largest and most beautiful church the old cowboy had ever seen. The people of the congregation were all dressed with expensive clothes and fine jewelry. As the cowboy took a seat, the others moved away from him. No one greeted, spoke to, or welcomed him. They were all appalled by his appearance and did not attempt to hide it.

As the old cowboy was leaving the church, the preacher approached him and asked the cowboy to do him a favor. "Before you come back in here again, have a talk with God and ask him what he thinks would be appropriate attire for worship in church." The old cowboy assured the preacher he would. The next Sunday, he showed back up for the services wearing the same ragged jeans, shirt, boots, and hat. Once again he was completely shunned and ignored. The preacher approached the cowboy and said, "I thought I asked you to speak to God before you came back to our church." "I did," replied the old cowboy. "And what was his reply?" asked the preacher. "Well, sir, God told me that he didn't have a clue what I should wear. He said he'd never been in this church."

***

**"A person that makes it doesn't use it.
A person that buys it doesn't need it.
A person that uses it doesn't know it.
What is it? ---- A coffin"**

***

Old Henry went into the police station and said to the officer on duty, "Gosh, officer, I'm in terrible shape." "Well, sir, said the on duty policeman, "At the scene you told the officer you were all right." "Yeah, said Henry, "But at the scene the cop shot the dog and even shot the horse; what would you have said?"

***

There were two old fellows sitting on the front porch visiting. All of a sudden a big ole frog jumped up on the porch and said to the guys, "If one of you guys would give me a kiss I'll turn into a beautiful princess, and be yours forever." One of the guys said, "Several years ago I might have taken you up on that offer, but, at my age I'll just keep you. I can have more fun with a talking frog."

***

Brenda and Linda were talking about this and that. Brenda said, "Linda, I just don't understand what it is that makes men so scared of commitment. Linda replied, "You're telling me; I dated this guy for 2 years and I finally had to give him an ultimatum." "Just what did you tell him?" said Brenda. "Well, I just told him, look you; you'd better tell me your last name or it's quits."

***

Miss Prim & Proper said to her Grandmother, "Granny you have really impressed me today." "What did I do to impress you?" said her Grandmother. "Well Granny, you have finally formed the habit of covering your mouth with your hand when you sneeze," replied Miss Prim & Proper. Her Grandmother said, "Why yes, of course I have; how else do you think I'm going to catch my teeth."

***

Did you hear about the fellow that married an Amish lady? It wasn't two weeks until he was driving her buggy.

***

Maynard was standing next to a big beautiful wishing well along with his wife. It wasn't long until his wife, for no particular reason, just simply fell in, head first. Maynard thought to himself; golly those things really do work!

***

This couple went to the doctor to have their yearly physical. The husband had his first and then he said to his wife," Honey, I think I'll go on home and then you can call me when you are finished." The doctor said to the wife. "You know I am glad he left for a little while because I really have some bad news for you." "What in the world is it?" she asked. The doctor replied, "He has a very serious disease, and it's critical for you to follow these specific instructions, or your husband will die." "Fix him three nutritious meals a day, take care of all the basic chores, no yard work whatsoever, and satisfy all of his sexual needs from this point forward, and I think his condition will improve greatly." "Well, thank you doctor so very much." She called her husband to come and get her, and on the way home he asked how his physical went." She said, "I've really got back news honey, you're going to die."

***

A Mafia Don makes a call

A Maafia Don calls his home. The butler picks up the phone and says "Hello."

Mafia Don "Give the phone to my wife."

Butler "Just a moment," The Butler comes back and says, "She is in the bathroom."

Mafia Don "I said I want to speak to her now."

Butler "I'm sorry she cannot come to the phone right now."

Mafia Don "If you don't get her on the phone in one minute, I am going to blow your head into smithereens."

Butler now scared "You do not understand; there is a man with her in the bathroom.

Mafia Don "What did you say?"

Butler Yes, it's true; there is a man in there with her.
Mafia Don "Listen carefully, I want you to take the gun from my closet and then shoot the both of them."
Butler scared out of his wits "I can't do that, I can never kill anyone."
Mafia Don "Do it right now."
Butler "No, I can't."
Mafia Don "If you don't do it right now, I will kill you and your family."
"Now, get on with it, I want to hear the shots, and don't forget to get rid of the gun."
Butler "Uh, all right."
Mafia Don The Mafia Don then hears the shots over the phone.
Butler badly shaken "I did it."
Mafia Don "Good work, what did you do with the gun?"
Butler "I threw it into the pool."
Mafia Don "What pool are you talking about? We don't have a pool." **"Is this 747-5478?"**

***

This pretty smart dog walked into the store and asked for the manager. The manager said, "I can't hire you. The sign says you have to be able to type." The dog jumped down, walked over to the typing table and typed a perfect letter. He took out the page and trotted over to the manager and gave it to him then jumped back on the chair. The manager was stunned, but then told the dog, "The sign says you have to be good with a computer." The dog jumped down again and went to the computer. The dog proceeded to demonstrate his expertise with various programs and produced a sample spread-sheet and database and presented them to the manager. By this time the manager was totally dumb founded! He looked at the dog and said, "I realize that you are a very intelligent dog and have some interesting abilities, However, I still can't give you the job." The dog jumped down and went to a copy of the sign and put his paw on the sentences that told about being an Equal Opportunity Employer. The manager said, "Yes, but the sign also says, that you have to be bilingual." The dog looked at him straight in the eye and said, "Meow."

***

Chicken Side off first...

Sam ran into one of his good friends in downtown New York City. Henry said, "Sam, what in the world are you doing up here?" "Sam said, Well, I'm on my way to see a Broadway play, and then I'm going to see the Statue of Liberty, and then. . ." No," said Henry, I understand that, but my question is; where is your wife, Betty?" "Oh," replied Sam, "She's at home; this is our 25th wedding anniversary and she didn't have to come, she'd been here before."

***

Mother was reading to her little girl, and the girl asked, "Mommy, do all fairy tales start with 'Once upon a time?' "Oh, no darling," Most of them begin with, 'Hi honey, I have to work late at the office tonight."

***

A wealthy man lay critically ill in the hospital. The doctor said, "Harold, there is only one way for you to survive this. You have to have a brain transplant; it's experimental and very expensive." Harold said," Money is no problem, can you get a brain?" "Yes, I think I can," replied the doctor. "I think we have possibly three available. We have one from a college professor for $25,000, one from a rocket scientist for $50,000, and one from a Washington D.C. bureaucrat for $100,000." "Harold said, "Why so much for the Washington guy? Well, said the doctor, it's never been used."

***

The chef at a family-run restaurant had broken her leg and came into the insurance office to file a disability claim. The agent asked the chef, "Why can't you work? It appears to me that is not a good reason." "Well, she replied, "I can't stand to cook."

***

The guy was just promoted to vice-president. He went home really excited and told his wife the good news. She said, "Oh, honey, Vice-presidents are a dime a dozen. The supermarket where we shop has so many vice-presidents they have one who's just in charge of grocery bags. The annoyed husband replied. "I'll call your bluff. Let's just call the store right now, and ask to speak to the vice-president in charge of bags." His wife said, "Ok, that's a deal." So they called the store and he said, "Could I please talk to the vice-president of bags?" The nice lady said, "Would you like paper or plastic?"

***

On his way home, Bob is taking a short-cut through a graveyard, in the middle of the night, when he is alarmed by a continuous tapping sound. As Bob moves closer to the source of the sound he finds a man sitting by a grave and tapping on a headstone. Bob notices that the man was adding the letter 'R' at the end of the name that was carved in the stone. Bob says to the man, "A little late for work like that, isn't it?" "Right" says the man, but I don't like it when someone spells my name wrong."

***

"Cash, check or charge," said the clerk. The lady said, "That will be charge." The clerk just happened to notice, as she was getting her credit card, there was a remote control for a television in her purse. He said, "Do you make a habit of carrying a TV control in your purse all the time." She said, "Oh no, my husband wouldn't come to the store to help me, so I figured this was the best way to get even."

***

Encouraging Words from Don Dunlap

The more sand that has escaped from the hourglass of our life, the clearer we should see through it. Age is a matter of mind; if you don't mind, it doesn't matter. Life is a GIFT, to live is an opportunity, to give is an obligation, and to grow old is a privilege. We don't stop playing because we are old; we grow old because we stop playing. So long as the heart receives messages of beauty, hope, cheer, and courage, you will be young. A man is not old until regrets take the place of dreams.

***

This guy was trying to lose weight. He had a tendency to grab sweets when he was bored. He and his wife devised a plan that whenever he's tempted to cheat on his diet, he should think of his wife, and how proud she is of him when he doesn't cheat on his diet. One night I overheard him tell some friends, "Boy, we designed a system that really helps me on my diet. Whenever I get hungry, I think about my wife and immediately lose my appetite."

***

"Did you know that tornados and divorces are an awful lot alike in the Ozarks Country? Someone's gonna lose a mobile home."

***

According to the Alaska Department of Fish and Game, while both male and female reindeer grow antlers in the summer each year, male reindeer drop their antlers at the beginning of winter, usually late November to mid-December. Female reindeer retain their antlers until after they give birth in the spring. Therefore, according to every historical rendition depicting Santa's reindeer, every single one of them, from Rudolf to Blitzen . . . had to be a girl. We should've known when they were able to find their way. Hey guys, remember it's Christmas . . . let them have a little fun.

***

A Merry Heart; the following is worth pondering.
If you woke up this morning with more health than illness . . . you are more blessed than the million who will not survive this week.
If you have never experienced the danger of battle, the loneliness of imprisonment, the agony of torture, or the pangs of starvation . . . you are ahead of 500 million people in the world.
If you can attend a church meeting without fear of harassment, arrest, torture, or death . . . you are more blessed than three billion people in the world.
If you have food in the refrigerator, clothes on your back, a roof overhead and a place to sleep . . . you are richer than 75% of this world.
If you have money in the bank, in your wallet, and spare change in a dish someplace . . . you are among the top 8% of the world's wealthy.
If your parents are still alive and still married . . . you are very rare, even in the United States and Canada.
If you holdup your head with a smile on your face and are truly

thankful . . . you are blessed because the majority can, but most do not.

If you can hold someone's hand, hug them or even touch them on the shoulder . . . you are blessed because you can offer a healing touch.

***

While taking a routine vandalism report at an elementary school, I was interrupted by a little girl about six years old. Looking up and down at my uniform, she asked, "Are you a cop?" "Yes, "I answered and continued writing the report. "My mother said if I ever needed help I should ask the police. Is that right?" "Yes, that's right." I told her. "Well, then," she said as she extended her foot toward me, "Would you please tie my shoe?" "Remember; God allows us to bring even the littlest of requests to Him in prayer."

***

As the waitress entered the restaurant, the manager demanded "Why are you late?" The waitress explained, "It was terrible; I was crossing the road when I witnessed a dreadful accident. A guy was hit by a speeding car, and he was lying there on the road, with his hands holding his fractured skull; he was a bloody mess." "Thanks to the good Lord, I had taken that first-aid course that you recommended." The manager asked, "How did you handle it?" The waitress replied, I sat on the ground and put my head between my knees so I wouldn't faint."

***

A woman was driving her old beat up car on the Highway with her 7 yr. old son, Little Johnny. She tried to keep up with traffic but they were flying by her. After getting caught in a large group of car's flying down the road she looked at her speedometer to see she was doing 15 miles over the speed limit. Slowing down, she moved over to the side and got out of the clump that soon left her behind. She looked up and saw the flashing lights of a police car. Pulling over she waited for the officer to come up to her car. As he did he said, "Ma'am do you know why I pulled you over?" Little Johnny piped up from the back seat, and said, "I do! because you couldn't catch the other cars!"

Chicken Side off first...

***

A beggar walked up to a well- dressed woman shopping on Rodeo Drive and said, "I haven't eaten anything in four days." She looked at him and said, "Gosh, I wish I had your will power."

***

Don't take Exlax with Flintstone vitamins. I did one time and I never in my life ever saw so much yabba dabba doo!

***

Kids take pot for a trip. We older folks keep pot under our bed so we won't have to take a trip.

***

At Thanksgiving with her folks, single Susie prayed the following prayer, "Oh Lord, I'm thankful for all the many blessing in my life. And, I'm not asking for this for myself; but please send my mother a son-in-law." "Oh yes, and bless this food to our bodies."

***

This guy went to the doctor to lower his sex drive. His doctor said, "Gee whiz, you're 85 years old, it's all in your head." "I know that, that's why I want it lowered."

***

It was time for winter once again. It came over the radio that they were expecting 6 to 8 inches of snow on Sunday. The announcer said, "Don't forget folks, in order for us to clean the streets really good on Monday, we want all of you with even street numbers to park your cars on the right side of the street. The ones with uneven numbers on Tuesday, park your cars of the left side of the street. The lady of the house looked at her husband and said, "It looks like to me, Horace, it would make more sense to just leave your car in the garage both days, rather than getting it out and moving it back and forth."

***

A pill a little hard to swallow

Sometime around the year 2006, mankind had advanced and found a way to package basic knowledge in pill form. It is now possible to buy pills that will give you all kinds of immediate knowledge about science, reading, history, geography, health, marriage, and just all kinds of stuff. It really was a wonderful new drug that was needed badly. A fellow was standing at a counter where the druggist was explaining how this new pill program would work. The fellow asked, "Do you have a pill that will help with math?" The druggist said, "Just a minute, let me go back to the storage area and see if I can find that type of pill." In a little while he came back and, WHAM! he slammed a whopping big pill on the counter. "Gee Whiz," said the fellow that wanted the pill, "Do I have to take one that big for it to help?" "I'm afraid that's what you'll have to do." As you probably know; math was always a little hard to swallow."

***

Sam just happened to look out in the street and notice that President Clinton was getting out of his car with a pig. He couldn't figure out what in the world the President was doing with a pig under his arm, so he asked. "Mr. President, I've got a question?" "Go ahead and ask it," replied the President. "Ok," said Sam, "Why do you have a pig under your arm." President Clinton politely answered, "Well sir, I got this for Hillary," Sam said, "You sure made a good trade."

***

"Who was the first person to look at a cow and say, "I think I'll squeeze these dangly things and drink whatever comes out?" The Dead Beat

***

Philip asked some of his friends over to his house for dinner. When the dessert was brought out Phil said, "Before I got married my mom taught me how to make two things really good; Lemon Pie and roast beef." One of his friends politely asked, "Which is this?"

***

My Aunt Zepha told me this little story many years ago, and she told it for the honest truth. She said, "Richard, one night some guy called me on the phone and absolutely made me so angry you wouldn't believe it." I said, "Aunt Zepha, What in the world did he do?" She replied, "He used the most vulgar language that I've ever heard, in my entire life. "So," she said, "I shouldn't have done this but I did, I just talked to him as bad or maybe worse than he talked to me." "Well then, what else happened," I said.

My aunt replied, "Before I completely finished talking he said back to me, 'did I call you or did you call me?' and he just hung up; but he never called again."

***

A little boy in pre-school really liked applesauce. One day they served applesauce in the lunch room. After the boy finished eating, he hollered out really loud, "More applesauce." "Who was that?" said the teacher over the loudspeaker. The little boy answered back, "It was God." The teacher said, "What did God say?" The little boy loudly said again said, "Give that little boy some more applesauce!"

***

"If you're not flexible most of the time it is real easy for one to get bent out of shape!"
RFS

***

A husband and wife got into a petty argument. Neither of them would admit the possibility that the other might be in error. To her credit, the wife finally said, "Look, I'll admit I'm wrong if you'll admit I was right." "Fine," said her husband. She took a deep breath, looked her husband in the eye and said. "I'm wrong." With a big gin, her husband replied. "You're right."

***

Two storks are sitting in their nest; a father stork and baby stork. The baby stork is crying and father stork is trying to calm him. "Don't worry, son. Your mother will come back. She's bringing people babies and making them happy."

The next night, it's father's turn. Mother and son are sitting in the nest, the baby stork is crying, and mother is saying "Son, your father will be back as soon as possible, but now he's bringing joy to new mommies and daddies."

A few days later, the stork's parents are desperate; their son is absent from the nest all night! Shortly before dawn, he returns and the parents ask him, "Where have you been all night?" The baby stork says, "Nowhere, just scaring the puddin' out of some college students!" **The Missouri Chigger**

***

"Gee whiz, it looks like a nudist camp to me." said Charley. "Well," said Margaret, are they boys or girls?" "I don't know" replied Charley, "They don't have any clothes on, I really can't tell."

***

An employee went in to see his supervisor and said to him, "I've really got a problem; my wife wants me to help her around the house tomorrow. She says we need to wash the windows, clean out the attic, straighten up the garage, and haul a bunch of stuff to the dump. Would it be possible for me to have the day off?" The supervisor looked at his scheduling chart and said, "Oh my no, we've got several folks already out for tomorrow on sick leave; I'm afraid it will not be possible." The employee shouted and said, "Boss, I knew I could count on you."

***

The doctor said to the father who just happened to be celebrating a little too much, "You've got a bouncing baby girl, here hold this light, here comes another one, and another one, and another one." The dad held on to the light and as quick as he could, ran out of the room. Finally after they determined there were no more babies they made the final count, they were the proud parents of two sets of twins. The dad came back into the room and the mother said, "Harold, where were you, why did you leave?" "Well, said Harold, I thought the light was attracting them."

***

"Jim, I'm really pleased with your progress," said Dr. Smith, "You've improved much more than your buddy Joe." "He's telling everyone that he is going to buy the Bank of America." Jim said, "Oh, He's so stupid; I told him over 100 times that I do not want to sell."

***

Byron finally went to the doctor, and after many years of pain, he found that he had been suffering with a broken leg for a long time. The doctor said, "Byron, how in the world did you happen to break your leg?" Byron said, "Well, 21 years ago, like I said, I worked on a farm where the farmer's daughter was the one that really was the boss. Every once in a while she would come up to me with a really big smile and say, "Byron, is there anything I can do for you?" "Several times over the years she would do the same thing over and over again, Byron is there anything I can do for you?" The doctor said, "Byron what has that got to do with a broken leg?" "Well," said Byron, "I was working on the top of the house putting on a new roof when it finally dawned on me what she had in mind, and that's when I fell off and broke my leg."

***

I remember well, listening to Kate Smith sing when I was a young man. Her confidence, her voice strength, and her ability to make gorgeous music was unbelievable . . . in my opinion!" I thought by printing this information it might bring back some pleasant memories and stir your emotions for America once again.

Frank Sinatra considered Kate Smith the best singer of her time, and said that when he and a million other guys first heard her sing "God Bless America" on the radio, they all pretended to have dust in their eyes as they wiped away a tear or two. Here is the story that gives the facts behind the first public singing of this beautiful 'tear jerking' song.

The time was 1940. America was still in a terrible economic depression. Hitler was taking over Europe and Americans were afraid we'd have to go to war. It was a time of hardship and worry for most Americans. This was the era just before TV, when radio shows were HUGE, and American families sat around their radios in the evenings, listening to their favorite entertainers, and no entertainer of that era was bigger than Kate Smith. Kate was also large; plus size, as we now say, and the popular phrase still used today is in deference to her, "It ain't over till the fat lady sings."

Kate Smith might not have made it big in the age of TV, but with her voice, coming loud and clear, over the radio, she was the biggest star of her time. Kate was also patriotic. It hurt her to see Americans so depressed and afraid of what the next day would bring. She had hope for America, and faith in her fellow Americans. She wanted to do something to cheer them up, so she went to the famous American song-writer, **Irving Berlin who also wrote "White Christmas"** and asked him to write a song that would make Americans feel good again about their country.

When she described what she was looking for, he said he had just the song for her. He went to his files and found a song that he had written, but never published, 22 years before – way back in 1917. He gave it to her and she worked on it with her studio orchestra. She and Irving Berlin were not sure how the song would be received by the public, but both agreed they would not take any profits from the song. The profits, if any, would go to the Boy scouts of America. Over the years, they have received millions of dollars in royalties from this song.

The premier of the song began with Kate Smith coming into the radio studio, with her orchestra and an audience. Ronald Reagan was among the audience and was moved beyond tears. She introduced the new song for the very first time, and starts singing. After the first couple of verses, with her voice in the background still singing, scenes are shown from the 1940 movie "You're in the Army Now." To this day, God Bless America still hopefully stirs our patriotic feelings and pride of our country.

Back in 1940, when Kate Smith went looking for a song to raise the spirits of her fellow Americans, I doubt whether she realized just how successful the results would be for the Americas during those years of hardship and worry . . . and for many generations of Americans to follow. Now that you know the story of the song, I hope you'll appreciate and treasure it more than ever before.

***

This rather goofy guy went into a restaurant, sat down and started crying. He said to the waitress, "My father just died." A few minutes later he received a telephone call. He started crying over again and it was almost worse than when he first came in. The waitress said to him, "What in the world is wrong this time?" He said, "Well, That was my brother, he said his Dad just died also."

***

There was this traveler who was hitchhiking on a dark night with rain and severe thunderstorms. He was out of the city limits waiting for a ride. Time passed but there was not a car in sight on the ghostly night. The wind was blowing hard and rain was lashing his face. He was tired, hungry, miserable and could hardly see anything in the darkness. Then he finally saw a ghostlike figure of a car slowly moving, inch by inch, towards him. He was desperate and so without waiting for usual formalities of asking permission, he took opportunity on the slow movement of the car, jumped in and closed the door after him. Only then he saw there was no one in the car, not even a driver. He could not hear the sound of the engine and yet the car was slowly moving forward. The traveler was terrified. He began to pray for his safety as he had heard a lot of ghost stories in this area. He was too scared to make a move and even try to jump out. So he sat frozen. Then all of a sudden, a hand from nowhere reached in from the front window to guide the car near a curve. The traveler was really frozen scared now. When the next curve came and the hand appeared from nowhere, he gathered his wits and jumped out of the slow moving car too fearful to see right or left, and he ran for his life. After what seemed like eternity he reached a small town and saw a bar at the side of the road. Scared, wet, and shocked, he barged into the bar and ordered 3 straight shots of whiskey on ice and gulped them down. Regaining his breath, he told everyone present in the bar of his experience with the ghost car. People realized he was not a drunk, shouting off his mouth. He was speaking the truth. All murmuring stopped and there was pin drop silence. The atmosphere became spooky. After about three quarters of an hour, Bill, John and Sam walked into the bar and Bill let out a roaring "Hey, John; Sam; look over there to your right, sitting at the counter. There sits that son-of-a-gun who rode in our car all the way into town, and we did all the pushing in the rain."

***

The Lone Ranger stopped for a drink. A Highway Patrolman came in and said, "You'd better give your horse a drink too." The Lone Ranger said, "Yeah, you're right." So Tonto went outside and began circling the horse. Another patrolman came in and says, "Who owns the horse outside?" The Lone Ranger answered and said, "It's mine, thank you." The patrolman said, "You'd better go out and check on it because you left your Indian running."

***

It was getting close to Christmas time. Mr. Jones went to the airport and was standing in front of the counter and said, "What in the world is that mistletoe hanging up over me for?" The clerk said to Mr. Jones, with a little smirk on his face, "Well, Mr. Jones, this is where you bring your luggage and kiss it goodbye."

***

This couple retired. One night he rigged the alarm clock so it would go off just a few minutes after they went to bed. Romantic music started playing. The husband put his arm around his wife and cuddled up a bit and said to her, "If I were forty years younger do you know what I'd do? His wife answered rather quickly, "Yes, you'd get up and go to work."

***

This gentleman went to the doctor and set up an appointment for two weeks in the future. He said, "Hey Doc, in two weeks I could be dead." The doctor answered and said, "Well, if that is the case have your wife give us a call and we'll cancel your appointment."

***

Dr. Kiddwamper said to his new patient, "Why do you think you don't sleep at night." "Well, because I'm trying to solve all the world's problems," said Mr. Brown. "Do you ever get them all solved?" said the doctor." "Yep, almost every time," says Mr. Brown. Dr. Kiddwamper replies, "Well then, why can' t you sleep?" Mr. Brown says, "I think it's those tickertape parades they have for me that keeps me awake."

***

"When they call the role in the Senate, the Senators don't know whether to answer, 'Present' or 'Not Guilty.'" Theodore Roosevelt

***

Some of us men can still think real fast.

An elderly Louisiana man owned a farm with a large pond behind the house. The pond was perfect for swimming, so he fixed it up real nice with picnic tables, horseshoe courts, and some apple and peach trees. One evening the farmer decided to go down to the pond to look it over as he hadn't been there for a while. He grabbed a five-gallon bucket to bring back some fruit. As he neared the pond, he heard voices shouting and laughing with glee. As he came closer, he saw it was a bunch of teenage girls skinny-dipping in his pond. When he made the women aware of his presence they all went to the deep end. One of the girls shouted to him, "We're not coming out until you leave!" The old man frowned, "I didn't come down here to watch you ladies swimming or make you get out of the pond and embarrass you." Holding the bucket up he said, "I'm here to feed the alligators."

***

WELCOME TO THE 21ST CENTURY!

Our Phones, Wireless . . . Cooking, Fireless. . . Cars, Keyless . . . Food, Fatless . . .Tires, Tubeless. . . Dress, Sleeveless. . . Youth, Jobless . . . Leaders, Shameless . . . Relationships, Meaningless . . . Attitude, Careless . . . Wives, Fearless . . . Babies, Fatherless . . . Feelings, Heartless . . . Education, Valueless . . .Children, Mannerless . . . Everything is becoming, LESS . . . but still our hopes are, Endless. . .

In fact we are, Speechless . . . Congress, Clueless . . . President is -- use your own opinion

Copied

***

"When you do the common things in life in an uncommon way, you will command the attention of the world." George W. Carver

***

As a senior citizen was driving down the freeway, his car phone rang. Answering, he heard his wife's voice urgently warning him "Charles, I just heard on the news that there's a car going the wrong way on Interstate 70. Please be careful!" Charles said, "It's not just one car. There's hundreds of them!"

***

"First you forget names, then you forget faces, then you forget to pull your zipper up, then you forget to pull your zipper down." Leo Rosenberg

***

Two elderly women were out driving in a large car, both could barely see over the dashboard. As they were cruising along they came to an intersection. The stoplight was red but they just went on through. The woman in the passenger seat thought to herself. "I must be losing my mind, I swear we just went through a red light." After a few more minutes they came to another intersection and the light was red again, and again they went right through. This time the woman in the passenger seat was almost sure that the light had been red, but was really concerned that she was mistaken. She was getting nervous and decided to pay very close attention to the road and the next intersection to see what was going on. At the next intersection, sure enough, the light was definitely red and they went sailing right through. She turned to the woman driving and said, "Mildred! Did you know we just ran through three red lights in a row! You could have killed us!" Mildred turned to her and said, "Oh, am I driving?"

***

"Friends are like Bras;
close to the heart and always there."

***

A guy was invited to some old friends' home for dinner. His buddy preceded every request to his wife by endearing terms, calling her Honey, My Love, Darling, Sweetheart, Pumpkin, etc. He was impressed since the couple had been married for sixty years. While the wife was off in the kitchen he said to his buddy, "I think it's wonderful that after all the years you've been married, you still call your wife those pet names." His buddy hung his head low. "To tell you the truth, I forgot her name about ten years ago."

***

Sally was bragging to her lady friend next door about her son, a college student. "Why, our son is so brilliant, every time we get a letter from him we have to go to the dictionary." Mary, her neighbor replied, "You're lucky," Every time we get a letter from ours, we have to go to the bank!"

***

The other day I heard two people talking. One said, "Are you happy?" The other one said, "Yes," The first one then said, "Well, tell your face!" **Carl Hurley**

***

London lawyer runs a stop sign and gets pulled over by a Glasgow copper. He thinks that he is smarter than the cop because he is a lawyer from London and is certain that he has a better education than a Jock cop. He decides to prove this to himself and have some fun at the Glasgow cop's expense! Glasgow cop says, "License and registration, please." London lawyer says, "What for?" Glasgow cop says, "Ye didnae come to a complete stop at the stop sign." London Lawyer says, "I slowed down, and no one was coming." Glasgow cop says, "Ye still didnae come to a complete stop, License and registration, please." Glasgow cop says, "The difference is, ye hyuvte come to complete stop, that's the law, License and registration, please!" London lawyer says, "What's the difference?" Glasgow cop says, "The difference is, ye huvte come to complete stop, that's the law, License and registration, please!" London lawyer says, "If you can show me the legal difference between slow down and stop, I'll give you my license and registration and you give me the ticket. If not, you let me go and don't give me the ticket." Glasgow cop says, "Sounds fair, Exit your vehicle, sir." The London lawyer exits his vehicle. The Glasgow cop takes out his baton and starts beating the living daylights out of the lawyer and says, "Dae ye want me to stop, or just slow doon?" **Copied**

***

After learning about our sugar-lade, fatty diets, Mrs. Johnson decided to serve a light meal with fresh fruit. When it was time for dessert, she asked her husband, "Do you want an orange or an apple?" "An orange or apple what," replied her husband.

***

"Enjoy life; it has an expiration date. Tell every friend that they are important to you. Tomorrow is NOT promised, so cherish your friends today . . . now Go!"

***

In my kindergarten class, one little boy was excitedly telling his class mates about his new baby sister. He then informed us that his mom was not going to have any more kids, "Yep, that's right," the little boy replied, "The dentist is going to help her; she is going to have her tooth tied."

***

New little song, to the tune of My Bonnie lies over the ocean.
My Bonnie lies over the gas tank; the height of it's contents to see;
She lit a match to assist her; Oh, bring back my Bonnie to me.

***

We got a Hen that lays 3 eggs on Friday and then takes the weekend off!

***

John wanted to buy an old still from a farmer. "Hey," said John, "What would you take for this old still?" The farmer said, $500 bucks." "If I give you $500 cash do I get 10% off?" said John. The old farmer didn't know how to figure too well so he went into town into the local café. "He said to the pretty waitress, "What would you take off for $500 bucks less 10%?" "Wow," said the waitress, "I'd take everything off but my ear rings."

***

Perfect Wings; a Great Story

Early in the spring, I noticed that a female bluebird was spending a lot of time on the ground, under my backyard bird feeder. This was somewhat unusual because the feeder has seed in it and the bluebird never flew any higher than the bird house on the garden fence post nearby, and even that was a struggle. My curiosity was aroused and I began watching the bird as she visited the feeder area. What I discovered became a timely lesson on tolerance and perseverance that I will long remember.

I learned that one of the bluebird's wings had been damaged and she couldn't fly very high. She had babies in the bluebird house on the fence that had to be fed. She had to feed them herself. I did see the male bluebird visit the nest frequently, so I know that he was helping to keep the baby birds fed. The mother bird came to the ground under the feeder to eat the seed wasted by other birds and the insects that accumulated around the dropped seed. She would drink and bathe in the small water dish that I put there for her. The other birds never tried to run her away from the feeder. She managed to feed herself and her babies despite her handicap. The birds grew up and I haven't seen the injured mother for a while now. I hope that she is healed and doing well.

The disabled bluebird could have given up, left her babies for someone else to feed and care for or probably die. She could have chirped loudly about her injury and cried for help. Instead, she quietly chose to do the very best job that she could despite her disability. Without perfect wings, it was hard for her to raise her family and keep herself alive, but she did. Her perseverance made me ashamed of the times that I have complained about work. The male bluebird could have shunned his mate and refused to help his family, but he didn't. He tolerated her less than perfect wings and pitched in with much needed help. The other birds at the feeder could have picked on the disabled bluebird and chased her away. But they were good neighbors, tolerating her presence at their feeder and allowed her to survive on their surplus food. Because of the tolerance and goodness of the others, five little bluebirds were permitted to live.

No one on this earth has perfect wings. Sometimes we give up and leave the task for someone else. Sometimes we complain loudly and bitterly about our problem and demand help from others. Sometimes we push others away when there is ample room for all. We can learn a lesson of life from the bluebirds. Do the job. Don't give up and leave the work for others. Accept others as they are. Success and happiness are not achieved until we forget ourselves and put others first. **By Joyce Harrison**

***

Two Indian families lived fairly close together, except there was a big valley between them. They couldn't hear each other, so when they wanted to talk they would send smoke signals. One morning one of the Indians wanted to talk to the other one, so he just sent his normal type of signal. The other Indian was in the process of sending a signal but rather than a normal signal he spilled a can of gasoline on the fire and his smoke signal was about the size of a huge building. The first Indian said to himself, "Wow, "I wish I could have said that."

***

Henry's dog was at the front door and wanted to come in. He realized that his wife was at the back door wanting in. His buddy said to him, "Which one are you going to let in first? "Well," said Henry, "I'm going to let the dog in first because at least when he came inside he'll probably stop barking."

***

Tony was a pretty smart little kid, and because of that he wanted to start school in the 3rd grade rather than the 1st grade. The superintendent said, "Well, if he wants to do that it will be Ok with me, but he has to take a special test first." The little kid and his mother both agreed that would be Ok. They all got set to take the test and the first question was, "What is 10 X 10?" asked the lady giving the test. The little fellow said, "100". "That's correct", said the lady. "Next question, "What is 200 divided by 10? "20" replied the little one. "That's correct." "Next question," "What does a cow have 4 of that your mother only has 2 of?" "Legs" said the boy. "That is correct, next question." "What does the superintendent, sitting over there have in his pants that you don't have much of in yours?" "Pockets", said the boy. The superintendent said, "Go ahead and put Tony in the 3rd grade, I missed 2 of those questions myself."

***

A friend of mine was at a college football game last fall when he heard a student challenge a senior citizen sitting next to him, saying it was impossible for the older generation to understand the younger generation. "You grew up in a different world," the student said loud enough for the whole crowd to hear. "Today we have television, jet planes, space travel, man has walked on the Moon, our spaceships have visited Mars, we even have nuclear energy, electric and hydrogen cars, computers with light speed processing and uh . . . Taking advantage of the pause in the student's litany, the elderly gentleman said, "You're right. We didn't have those things when we were young, so we invented them, you little twit? What the heck are you doing for the next generation?"

***

Chicken Side off first...

A little boy put a fairly hard puzzle together and did it at only 4 months of age. His dad said, "Boy," that was really good, because on the box it says 2 to 4 years.

***

It takes about 10 seconds for this next one to sink in

A little girl has some new shoes. She tries to put them on and she said, "They're too tight." Her mother replied, "Honey, pull your tongue out." The little girl did as her mother asked. The girl then said, "Mommy, their still too tight." **From Carl Hurley**

***

Charlie and Henry were wandering thru the cemetery. They came across the grave of one of their buddy's. The tombstone was leaning forward way too much, so someone had been nice and tied a wire onto the stone and pulled it back in place. Charlie said, "It sure looks like to me his stone is a bit crooked." "Yeah," replied Henry, "But it looks like he's doing Ok, he's already got his phone put in." **From Carl Hurley**

***

One of our city officials, Dan, got tired of the rat race, so he moved about as far away as he could get, away from everything and everybody. A few years later, one of his old friends found him living way up in Montana. His buddy said, "Dan, it sure is good to see you again, how come you're way up here, aren't you about ready to come home?" "No," said Dan, "I've got all I need up here; I've got my Bible, my Rosary and my dandelion wine." Dan then said, with a grin, "Rosary, get this nice man a glass of wine.

Carl Hurley

***

Sam, 89, and Lois, 84, were excited about their upcoming wedding. Out for a stroll one night, they stopped at a drugstore. Sam said to the druggist, "Do you sell heart medicine? The druggist replied, "Sure we do." Sam said, "How about medicine for circulation?" The druggist said, "We sure do." Sam asked, "Do you have medicine for rheumatism? The druggist said, "You can bet your bottom dollar." Sam said, "How about Medicine for memory? The druggist replied, "Definitely." Lois said to Sam, "Ask him if he's got vitamins and sleeping pills? Sam said, "Do you…the druggist heard her and said, "Of course, a large variety." Sam, "How about loose bowel and gas pills? "Oh, sure, replied the druggist. Sam said, "What about paraphernalia for diabetes? "Without question," said the druggist. The druggist finally said, "Sam; Lois; we sell medicine for about anything you can think of." Sam said, "Perfect! Splendid! We'd like to register here for our wedding gifts."

***

A man is driving down a road. A woman is driving down the same road from the opposite direction. As they pass each other, the woman leans out the window and yells, "Watch out, PIG." The man immediately leans out his window and yells, "Stupid!" They each continue on their way. When the man rounds the very next curve, he crashes into a huge pig in the middle of the road and totaled his car. **The moral of the story, If men would only listen.**

***

The funeral director sent a wire to a couple on vacation in Sweden. He said, "Hate to tell you this, but your mother-in-law has passed away, please advise what to do." The funeral director replied, "We can bury, cremate or embalm." The husband wired back and said, "Don't take any chances, do all three."

***

Horace and Betty Smith and her mother, were on vacation in Israel. The very first day they were there the mother-in-law passed away. Horace wired home to his local funeral director and said, "I've got bad news, my mother-in-law has died, and we need to know what we should do? The funeral director wired back and said, "Now, if you bury her there, it will be much cheaper because there will be no shipping by air to pay. If we cremate her here it will be $2,000; if we bury her, with a nice service, it will be $7,000." Horace wired back immediately and said, "We'll bury her at home, I'd rather pay the extra charges, I 've heard that on the third day over here in Israel there have been folks raised from the dead; I don't want to take any changes, so we'll see you tomorrow."

***

Johnny came home from school and told his mom and dad, "I

have some bad news and I have some good news." Dad said, "What's the bad news?" Johnny said, "I haven't done very well on my report card, I've flunked everything." Mom said, "What's the good news?" Johnny said, "I'm playing one of the wise men in the Christmas play."

***

The new bride said to her husband, "I've fixed one of you favorite desserts for tonight; coconut pudding; just wait until you see it." "Wow," her husband said, "that's great, but what's that big round lump in the middle." The wife answered, "That's the coconut."

***

There were four sophomores taking chemistry at a State University. All of them had an 'A' average so far. These four friends were so confident that the weekend before finals they decided to visit some friends and have a big party. They had a great time, but after all the partying they slept all day Sunday and didn't make it back to State until early Monday morning. Rather than taking the final then, they decided that after class they would explain to their professor why they missed it. They said they visited friends but on the way back they had a flat tire. As a result, they missed the final. The Professor agreed they could make up the final the next day. The guys were excited and relieved. They studied that night for the exam. The next day the Professor placed them in separate rooms and gave them a test booklet. They quickly answered the first problem worth 5 points. "Cool," they thought! Each one in separate rooms, they were all thinking this was going to be easy. Then they turned the page. On the second page was written . . . for 95 points . . . Which tire?

***

While driving down the highway recently I saw this on the T-shirt of a man on a motorcycle that pulled ahead of me: "If you can read this, my wife fell off."

***

The Judge said, "What terrible crime has this fellow committed?" The lawyer said, "Oh, none, He's the witness." A bystander said, "Where's the murderer? "He's out on bail."

***

This guy went into the restroom. Another guy, just standing by, laughed and said, "When you go in, you're Russian, while you are in there, European, and when you come out, you're Finnish."

***

'OLE BLUE.

A YOUNG COWBOY FROM MONTANA goes off to college. Half way through the semester, having foolishly squandered all his money . . . he calls home. "Dad," he says, "You won't believe what modern education is developing! They actually have a program here in Alabama that will teach our dog, Ole' Blue how to talk!" "That's amazing, "his Dad says. "How do I get Ole'Blue in that program?" "Just send him down here with $1,000." the young cowboy says "And I'll get him in the course." So, his father sends the dog and $1,000. About two-thirds of the way through the semester, the money again runs out. The boy calls home, "So how's Ole' Blue doing son?" his father asks. "Awesome, Dad, he's talking up a storm? He says, "But you just won't believe this . . . they've had such good results they have started to teach the animals how to read!" "Read!" says the father, "No kidding! How do we get Blue in that program?" "Just send $2,500, I'll get him in the class," The money promptly arrives. But our hero has a problem. At the end of the year, his father will find out the dog can neither talk, nor read. So he shoots the dog. When he arrives home at the end of the year, his father is all excited. "Where's Ole' Blue? I just can't wait to see him read something and talk." "Dad," the boy says, "I have some grim news. Yesterday morning, just before we left to drive home, Ole' Blue was in the living room, kicked back in the recliner, reading the Wall Street Journal, like he usually does." "Then Ole' Blue turned to me and asked, so, is your daddy still messing around with that little redhead who lives down the street?" The father went white and exclaimed, "I hope you shot that lying dog before he talks to your Mother!" "I sure did, Dad!" "That's my boy!"

The kid went on to law school, and now serves in Washington D.C. as a Congressman. ***Copied from the Missouri Chigger, Lowry City, Mo. - The article submitted to them by Mona Vance.***

***

Chicken Side off first...

A lady walks into the drugstore and tells the pharmacist she wants to buy some arsenic. He says, "What do you want with arsenic?" She said, "I want to kill my husband because he cheats on me by having an affair with another woman." The pharmacist says, "I can't sell you arsenic so you can kill your husband, lady, even if he is having an affair with another woman." So she reaches into her pocket and pulls out a picture of her husband having an affair with the pharmacist's wife. The pharmacist says, "Oh, I didn't realize you had a prescription!"

***

Two friends had been playing a round of golf every Saturday for a few years with one golfer always winning. One particular Saturday the match was closer than usual. In fact, it was tied when they came to the eighteenth. Try as he might, the losing golfer couldn't seem to pull out a victory, and started swearing and throwing his clubs. "Hey, calm down," said the winning golfer, "You played a great game and had me worried right up to the end." "That's why I'm so angry," said the losing golfer. "I cheated like crazy and still couldn't win?" **The Dead Beat**

***

Waiting for my first appointment with a new dentist, I noticed his diploma, which included his full name. I remembered a tall, handsome boy with the same name had been in my high school class some 30 years ago. However, when I met him I discarded the idea that his balding, gray-haired man with the deeply lined face could be my classmate. He was too old. Yet, I wondered if he was related to the boy I knew. So, after he examined my teeth, I asked him if he had attended the local high school and he had. "When did you graduate?" I asked him. "In 1971, why?" I was surprised, "You were in my class," I said. He looked at me closely and then asked, "What did you teach?"

***

"The problem with the designated driver program, it's not a desirable job, but if you ever get sucked into it, have fun with it. At the end of the night, drop them off at the wrong house."

Jeff Foxworthy

***

This guy, a dumb one, was on trial for armed robbery. The jury felt there was not enough evidence to convict him, so when they came out, the foreman of the jury announced, "Not guilty." "Wonderful" the prisoner hollered out. Does this mean I get to keep the money?"

***

"A study in the Washington Post says that women have better verbal skills than men. I just want to say to the authors of that study: "Duh" **Conan O'Brien**

***

"I think I must have married my sister," said the newlywed. "Why is that? asked his buddy. "Well, every time I get in bed she says, "Oh, brother."

***

Pierre, the Frenchman, went into a nice restaurant. After looking at the menu for a while he said to the waitress, "Do you have hog fries or maybe turkey fries?" The waitress said, "No, but we do have French fries." The waitress went over to her boss and said, "I wonder why that guy left so fast?

***

"Well, Honey, I've made up my mind. We can never get along, and besides that we don't meet each other's needs. "I've heard that in Las Vegas I can get $400 each time for making love." After finding the note left by his wife, he made the remark to a buddy friend, "Well, I guess if that is what she wants to do, that's what she'll have to do. But I don't see how in the world she'll ever get by on $800 a year."

***

"What do you call a grouchy German?
A sour Kraut! "

***

A traveler entering a small country store noticed a sign on the door warning, "Danger? Beware of dog?" Inside, he saw a harmless old hound dog asleep on the floor. "Is that the dog folks are supposed to beware of?" the traveler asked of Ole, the store owner. "Yep, dat's him," came the reply. The traveler couldn't help but be amused. "He doesn't look dangerous. Why the sign?" "Vell," Ole answsered, "Before I posted dat sign, people kept tripping over him."

***

"Mr. President, What do you have to say about 'Roe vs. Wade?" "Well, said the President, "I don't care how them folks get here, they are gonna have to go on back home."

***

Mr. John Sled had never been to a hospital. He had a severe problem and he was admitted. After being in there for a little while the nurse came into his room with a pan of warm water and a wash cloth. The nurse washed his face, behind his ears, the back of his neck and then handed him the wash cloth, and said, "Now it is your turn Mr. Sled," He took the cloth from her hand and began washing her face." Well, it did sound like that is what she wanted him to do.

***

I've really never found out whether you can or not. Can a person give a CAT-scan to a dog?

***

My wife and I got to the motel around mid-night and we were really tired. We didn't get much sleep. Apparently there was business going on in the room next to ours. We hadn't been in bed but a few minutes until we heard sounds from a candy salesman, "Oh, Henry, Oh, Henry, Oh Henry," and then it wasn't long until all we could hear was a little "snicker, snicker, snicker."

***

I just bought my wife a hot tub. Well, it's not a real one; it's an Ozarks hot tub: a wash tub and a bottle of Alka-Seltzer.

***

I really love being a daddy, even changing the diapers. Of course, I only change the baby every three to four days. Well, think about what the box of diapers says: "Holds up to 25 pounds."

***

One hot day, we were exploring the Scottish Highlands and stopped the car to let our aging collie out for some fresh air. With his tongue lolling, he lay panting on a grassy knoll while my husband spread his map over the car's hood, and, head in hands, proceeded to study it. Another car drove up, "Is he ill?" the driver asked in concern, "Can I help?" "Oh, no," I replied, "He's just getting old. He used to bound out of the car and jump all over me, ready for a romp in the grass." The stranger stared at me and hurriedly drove off shaking his head, he hadn't seen our dog.

***

Our dog, Mr. Hoover, suddenly bean barking daily at 4:00 a.m. and irritated my sleeping husband. John got up and searched the back yard for what might have disturbed this otherwise placid animal. For 3 days he found nothing amiss. Then the dog woke up the neighborhood at 3:00 a.m. with frantic barking. When John looked out the window, he discovered someone throwing pebbles to land near Mr. Hoover. John hurried outside and found the culprit. Crouching on the other side of the fence was our quiet neighbor, the last man you'd suspect of wrongdoing. My husband demanded to know what he was doing. "My mother-in-law is visiting," the embarrassed neighbor explained. "She says if she loses her beauty sleep one more night, she'll, for sure leave. I'm just trying to help her along."

***

A man hurried into a drug store on a recent Sunday morning and asked for change for a dollar. The druggist made change for the dollar and then said, "Here you are sir, and I hope you enjoy the sermon."

***

A little boy came home from school, and said, "Mommy I seen it, Mommy I seen it, Mommy I seen it, with my very own eyes!" "What in the world are you talking about?" said the little boy's Mother. What did you see son?" "I seen a miracle, yes, I seen a real miracle. Today in school, that real pretty teacher that I like so much, came into class and was just standing there teaching. All of sudden there was a little ole mouse came a runnin' across the room, Ms. Brown screamed, and that little ole mouse ran right up her dress." "Well, said his mother, "That wasn't a miracle." "No," said her son, "But Ms. Brown caught that little ole mouse between her knees and she squeezed a whole gallon of water, right outta that little ole mouse. Now that was a miracle if I ever seen one."

***

Why do they bury lawyers 8 feet underground? Because, down deep, they are not really too bad.

***

A young doctor had moved out to a small community to replace a doctor who was retiring. The older doctor suggested that the young one accompany him on his rounds, so the community could become used to a new doctor. At the first house a woman complains, "I've been a little sick to my stomach." The older doctor says, "Well, you've probably been overdoing the fresh fruit. Why not cut back on the amount you've been eating and see if that does the trick?" As they left, the younger man said, "You didn't even examine that woman? How'd you come to the diagnosis so quickly?" "I didn't have to. You noticed I dropped my stethoscope on the floor in there? When I bent over to pick it up, I noticed a half dozen banana peels in the trash. That was what probably was making her sick." "Huh," the younger doctor said, "Pretty clever. I think I'll try that at the next house." Arriving at the next house, they spent several minutes talking with a 30 year-old blond. She complained that she just didn't have the energy she once did and said, "I'm feeling terribly run down lately." "You've probably been doing too much work for the Church," the younger doctor told her. "Perhaps you should cut back a bit and see if that helps." As they left, the elder doctor said, "I know that woman well. Your diagnosis is almost certainly correct, but how did you arrive at it?" "I did what you did at the last house. I dropped my stethoscope and when I bent down to retrieve it, I noticed the preacher hiding under the bed." **The Dead Beat**

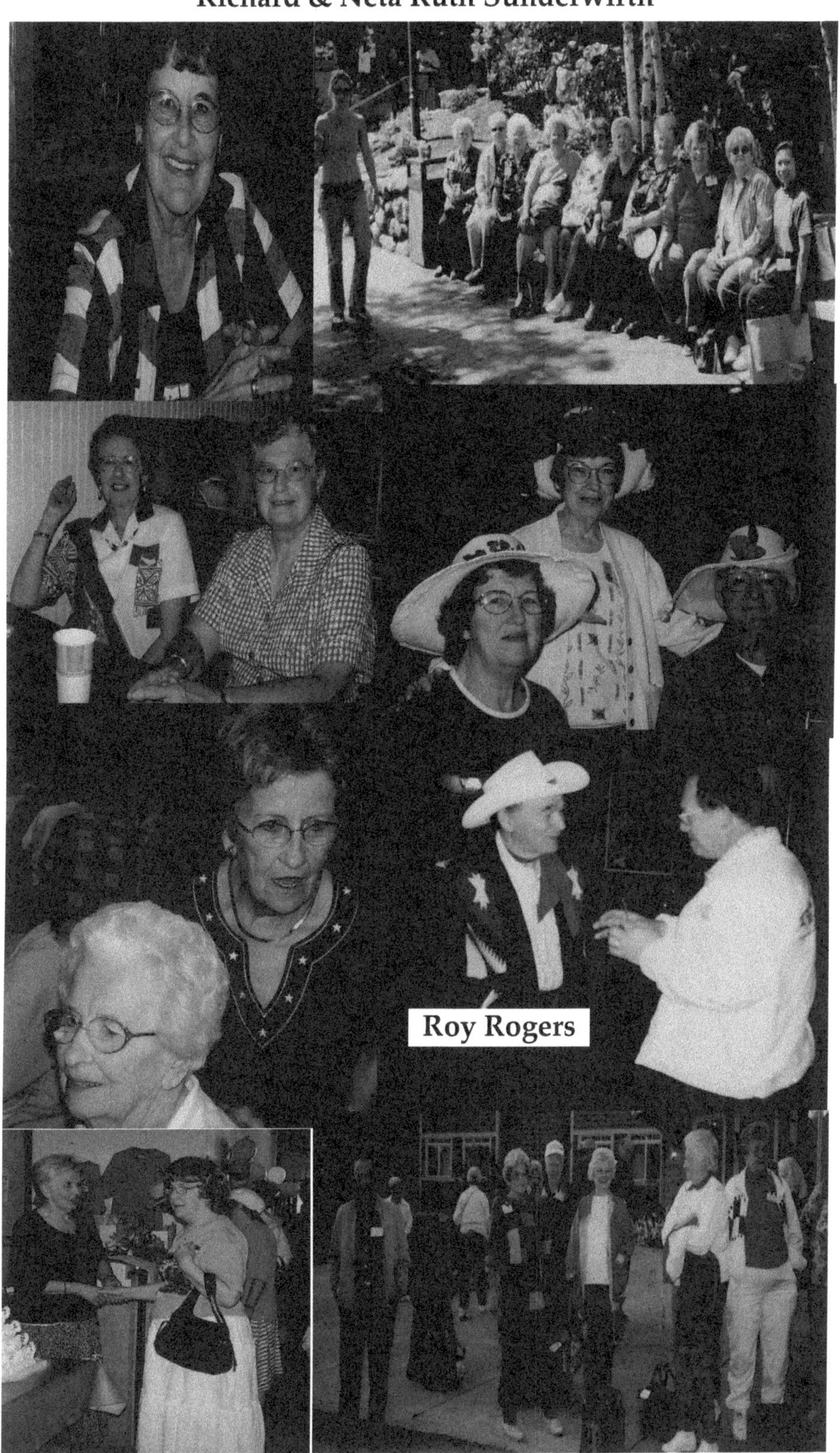

Roy Rogers

Chicken Side off first...

"Don't ever eat brown beans and onions together. The combination will give you tear gas!"

***

George was looking for a job; any kind of a job; he was desperate. As he was walking down the street he noticed a sign in a window and it said, "Toothbrush salesmen wanted." Well, he thought that might be a good job for him. He went in and asked, "Who do I have to see to get the job as a toothbrush salesman." The nice lady at the desk replied, "Well, sir, just come along with me and I'll take you to Mr. Johnson." George walked down the hall with the lady and she introduced him to Mr. Johnson. "Mr. Johnson, this is George and he'd like to be interviewed for that toothbrush salesman job that we have in the window." Mr. Johnson interviewed George and hired him on the spot. "Now, George, at the moment we have a contest going on and whoever sells the most brushes in a week wins a bonus of $1,000." "I think I can probably win that contest," George said. George picked up several cases of toothbrushes and left the building. One week later he came back and reported on his sales. By the time all the reports were turned in, George won the contest. Mr. Johnson called him up to the front of the room, presented him with the $1,000 and said, "George, how in the world did you sell over 5,000 toothbrushes? "Well, Mr. Johnson," said George, "It really wasn't too terribly difficult. I picked up a nice table, and two nice bowls, and filled one with chips and one with dip and headed to the front of the airport entrance. I set up my display and everyone that walked by me I said, "Would you nice folks like to have some free chips and dip? Of course, 99% of them said they would. After they had eaten their chips and dip, almost every time they would say, "Boy, this dip tastes a lot like horse manure." Then I would say to them, "You're absolutely right, would you like to buy a toothbrush?"

***

My mom used to say funny things like, "Johnny, if you fall out of that tree and break your leg, don't come running to me!"

Chicken Side off first...

There was a really big fire downtown last week, and a lady was on the 10th floor of the building that was on fire, and through the window she was hollering at the top of her voice, "Help, someone catch my baby, help me, somebody catch my precious little baby." Well, there just happened to be a Kansas City Chief's football player walking by, and he said, "Lady, throw down your baby, I'm a professional football star and I can catch your baby." The mother said, "Are you sure you can? It's a long way down there." The football star said, "Yes, I can catch your baby. I catch footballs, under pressure, and never miss." The mother said, "Ok, here comes my baby." She tossed her baby to the football player. Here the baby came, down, down, down, and sure enough, he caught the baby in his arms. By that time a huge crowd had assembled, and just as he caught the baby, the crowd went absolutely crazy with clapping and tons of singing their praises. When he heard the crowd roar he forgot he'd caught a baby and he threw it to the ground and hollered, TOUCH DOWN!

***

This man went to the doctor and said, "What's my problem Doc? I think I'm losing my mind. I can't remember anything." The doctor checked him over and said, "Well, sir, I'm afraid you have Alzheimer's disease." The man said, "What do you think I should do about it? The doctor replied, "It won't be that bad, just go home and forget about it."

***

There are two kinds of travelers; those who are really tired, and those who have no idea in the world, what condition they are in.

***

A young city slicker wanted to be a cowboy more than anything else. One summer, a rancher decided to give him a chance. "This is a lariat," the rancher said, handing the cowboy wannabe a rope on his first day. "We use it to catch cows." "I see," said the young man, examining it carefully. "What do you use for bait?"

***

Ralph said to Percy, "My wife's cooking is fit for a king. "Here King . . . here King."

Richard & Neta Ruth Sunderwirth

***

"Hey Sam, I've learned something today." Sam replied, "What in the world did you learn?" "Well," said Jonas, "My wife lost her Master Card." "Boy, that's not good," said Sam. "Oh, yes it is. I told the police to let whoever stole it just keep it, they are not spending near as much as my wife did."

***

Each week, our son, then in fourth grade, brought home his spelling word list to study. Part of his homework was to use each word in its own sentence. When finished, he would show his paper to me. I would admire his hard work. He had perfect penmanship, and the content of his sentences was always well thought out. One of his ten words for one particular week was depend. He wrote, "I can swim to the depend of the pool."

Cynthia Becktold

***

Tom came home from work and found his wife in bed with another man. As Tom walked through the door into the bedroom, Tom's wife said, "What in the world are you doing?" She looked over to the guy and said, "See, I told you he was dumb as a board."

***

There was an old man who was getting ready to celebrate his 93rd birthday. His two sons were discussing what they were going to get him for his birthday. John said, "Why don't we have a little fun with dad and see what he'll do." "What have you got in mind?" said David. "Well," replied John, "I know of a lady who is the lady of someone's evening. Why don't we have her come to dad's house about 8:00 p.m.; we'll be there, of course tomorrow evening and wish him a happy birthday with a silly offer, and see how dad handles it." So the next evening about 8:00 p.m. the doorbell rings and dad slowly gets up from his chair and worked his way over to the door. He said to the boys, "I wonder who in the world would be coming to my house at this time of evening? He opened the door and there stood a beautiful 30 year old blond, who quickly, with a twinkle in her eye said, "Happy birthday pop, I bring you super sex," The old man thought for a few moments and finally said, "That's awfully nice of you sweetie, I think I'll take the soup."

***

A continued story . . .
A couple of weeks later the old man got to thinking about what he'd said to the 30 year old blonde, who visited him on his birthday. He remembered going by where he thought she might be living, so he decided to get his walker and make his way to where she could be. Finally, he made it down the street, approximately 4 blocks, and made his way up the steep stairs to her front door. He knocked on the door and in a few moments the 30 year old blonde was standing in front of him. He said, "Sweetie, I got to thinking about what you said on my birthday and I thought I'd come down for a visit." She said, with NO twinkle in her eye, "Old timer, you've had it." Really quick he came back with this remark. "Golly, I have? What do I owe you?"

***

"Yes, I always try to have a positive attitude," Jerry said. "People ask if I ever wake up grumpy. I say, "No, I always let her sleep in."

***

"At my age, when a girl flirts with me in the movies, she's really just after my popcorn." **Milton Berle**

***

One night a wife found her husband standing over their baby's crib. Silently, she watched him as he looked at the sleeping infant. Reflected on his face was a range of emotions; disbelief, doubt, delight, amazement, enchantment, skepticism. Touched by this unusual display of deep and overt feelings, she slipped her arm around her husband's waist and said, with tear-filled eyes, "A penny for your thoughts." "It's amazing!" he replied. "I just can't figure out how anybody could make a crib like this for only $39.95."

***

My grandpa says he got in trouble at school once. The teacher called him in and said, "I think you and your cousin cheated on this test." Grandpa asked why she thought that. She said, "On the first question, 'Who was the first president,' both of you put 'George Washington.' On the second question, 'What year was the War of 1812 fought,' both of you put '1812.' On the third question, 'Who shot President Abe Lincoln,' you put 'I don't know,' and your cousin put, 'me neither.'"

***

"Remember in elementary school, you were told that in case of fire you have to line up quietly in a single file line from smallest to tallest. What is the logic in that? What . . . do tall people burn slower?" Warren Hutchenson

***

Did you know there are three ways to get something done? You can do it yourself; you can hire someone to do it for you; or you can forbid your kids to do it.

***

"The only difference between a rut and a grave is the depth."

***

Bobby Jones finally, after much thought, went to the doctor. After they called his name he went in to the inner-office and sat down. The doctor came in and said, "What can I help you with this morning?" Bobby said, "I've got a problem, no one ever listens to me." The doctor said, "NEXT".

***

The wit of Phyllis Diller

"Whatever you may look like, marry a man your own age. As your beauty fades, so will his eyesight."

"Housework can't kill you, but why take a chance?"

"Cleaning your house while your kids are still growing up is like shoveling the walk before it stops snowing."

"A smile is a curve that sets everything straight."

"The reason women don't play football is because 11 of them would never wear the same outfit in public."

"Best way to get rid of kitchen odors; Eat out."

"A bachelor is a guy who never made the same mistake once."

"I want my children to have all the things I couldn't afford. Then I want to move in with them."

"Most children threaten at times to run away from home. This is the only thing that keeps some parents going."

Chicken Side off first...

"Any time three New Yorkers get into a cab without an argument, a bank has just been robbed."

"We spend the first twelve months of our children's lives teaching them to walk and talk and the next twelve telling them to sit down and shut up."

"Burt Reynolds once asked me out. I was in his room."

"You know you're old if your walker has an airbag."

"What I don't like about office Christmas parties is looking for a job the next day."

"The only time I ever enjoyed ironing was the day I accidentally got gin in the steam iron."

"Old age is when the liver spots show through your gloves."

"My photographs don't do me justice – they just look like me."

"There's so little money in my bank account, my scenic checks show a ghetto."

"My mother-in-law had a pain beneath her left breast. Turned out to be a trick knee."

"Tranquilizers work only if you follow the advice on the bottle; keep away from children."

"The reason the golf pro tells you to keep your head down is so you can't see him laughing."

"You know you're old if they have discontinued your blood type."

Phyllis Diller

***

"We did a lot of cruises during the 18 years of touring.
Here is the top 11 of questions asked."
Does the elevator take us to the front of the ship?
Does the crew sleep on board?
Does the ship generate its' own electricity?
Is the water in the toilet salt or fresh?
How do we know which pictures are ours?
Do these stairs go up or down?
Is this island completely surrounded by water?
How will we know when we get to land?
What time is the midnight buffet being served?
What language do they speak in Alaska?
What do you do with the ice carvings after they melt?

***

Richard & Neta Ruth Sunderwirth

There were a couple of young boys that went fishing. They caught quite a lot of fish. Well, they were sitting around visiting about their catch when the State Game and Fish Warden came by and asked to see their fishing license. The one boy jumped up and took off running. He ran a long way really fast and then when he realized he had gone probably about a mile he slowed down and let the officer catch up. The officer said, "Young man I need to see your fishing license, do you have one?" The young boy replied, "Yep, I sure do." He got his billfold out and produced his valid fishing license. "Boy," said the warden, "you must be as dumb as a box of rocks. You had no reason to run from me when you knew you had a valid license. Why did you run?" The boy kinda chuckled to himself and said, "Yeah, I knew I had one but my buddy, and I don't even know his name, didn't have one."

***

A pirate was talking to a "Land-lubber" in a bar. The "Land-lubber" noticed that, like any self-respecting pirate, the guy had a hook in place of one of his hands, and a patch over one eye. The "Land-lubber" just had to know how the pirate got in such a bad shape. He asked the pirate, "How did you lose you leg?" The pirate responded, "I lost me leg in a battle off the coast of Jamaica." His new acquaintance was still curious so he asked, "What about your hand, did you lose it at the same time?" "No," said the pirate, "I lost it to the sharks off the Florida Keys." Finally, the "Land-lubber" asked, "I noticed you also have an eye patch. How did you lose your eye?" The pirate said, "I was sleeping on a beach when a seagull flew over and pooped right in me eye." The "Land-lubber" asked, "How in the world could a little seagull poop make you lose your eye." The pirate snapped and said, "It was right after I got me hook!"

***

From an airline flight attendant just after takeoff; "Your seat cushions can be used for a floating devise in the event of an emergency water-landing. If that should happen you may use and keep the devise, with our compliments."

***

A young fellow walked up to nice looking lady and said, "You're very pretty." She responded and said, "Thanks so much; I really wish there was something between us." "Me too," said the young fellow, "like what?" The lady looked him straight in the eye and said, "How about a wall?"

***

Sarah was reading a newspaper, while her husband was engrossed in a magazine. Suddenly, she burst out laughing. "Listen to this," she said. "There's a classified ad here where a guy is offering to swap his wife for a season ticket to the stadium." "Hmmm," her husband said, not looking up from his magazine. Teasing him Sarah said, "Honey, would you swap me for a season ticket?" "Absolutely not." he said. "How sweet." Sarah said, "Tell me why not?" He replies, "The seasons more than half over."

***

"I didn't say she was old, all I said was, if she was a car we'd have a really hard time getting parts for her."

***

Ruby was in the bathroom putting on some type of face cream. Her little five year old girl came in and said, "Mommy, what are you doing?" Her mother said, "Well, honey I'm trying to make myself pretty." The little one was watching intently when all of a sudden she noticed her mother was starting to rub it off with a towel, which of course was a normal thing to do, but not understood by the little girl. Little Judy said, "Mommy, what's the matter, are you giving up?"

***

Buford was talking to his buddy and he said, "Mutt, I'll bet you don't know what the fastest thing in the world is." "No, I don't have slightest idea," said his friend. "Well, guess," said Buford. "Ok," said Mutt. "I'll give it a shot; how about a blink?" "Nope," said Buford. Mutt said, "I know, its electricity, because you can flip a switch right in front you and it will turn on a light somewhere else in the room." "Nope, that's not it," replied Buford. "How about a speeding bullet?" said Mutt. "No, that's not it, do you give up?" laughed Buford. "I guess I do, but those things I mentioned are pretty darn fast." "Yes, I know that, but here's what it is; diarrhea," said Buford, "When you have diarrhea, and you're heading to the toilet, you ain't got time to blink, turn on a light, or shoot a gun, because it's already too late."

This lady went into a beautiful, well stocked store, absolutely loaded with all kind of crystal glassware, figurines, and a lot of other extremely valuable merchandise. The lady was blind; however, she had her seeing-eye dog with her. The dog appeared to be doing his job Ok, but all of a sudden she started swinging her dog around and around and around in the store, just barely missing the valuable items. The clerk didn't want to be unkind to her but she was scared out of her wits, thinking the dog was going to destroy a lot of things. She said to the lady "Is there anything I can help you with?" "Oh, no," said the lady, we're just looking around."

***

Big Johnnie finally decided he was going to go on a really good diet. Every morning he had been in the habit of eating a huge plate of hotcakes and sausage. So, this particular morning, he said to his wife, as he left the house, "Honey I'm going to pass on stopping at the good little café where I always eat my hotcakes. Dear Lord, if it be your will for me to eat my regular breakfast, let there be a parking spot right in front of the café. If there is no spot I will go on to work and know, for sure, I'm on the right track for my diet." After Big Johnnie circled the block 21 times, there just happened to be a spot right in front, so he stopped and had his breakfast. After he left, feeling really satisfied, he said, "Dear Lord, thank you, I didn't feel it would be your will for me to starve."

***

"Advice is what we ask for when we already know the answer, but we wish we didn't." Erica Mann Jong

***

A news reporter was interviewing Marvin concerning his family. He asked, "Where is your father at this time?" Marvin replied, "Well, he's in the state correctional facility for running moonshine." "Oh," said the interviewer. "How about your mother?" "She ran away from home several months ago; we haven't seen her for over 10 months." "Where is your sister? I know you have a sister." Johnnie lowered his head and said, "She's in prisor she was helping dad." "My my, that's too bad," replied terviewer. "You do have a brother don't you?" Johnnie answered, "Yes, I do, he's in Harvard University." "Well, what is he studying there?" "Oh, nothing, they're studying him."

***

A 70 year old woman started dating a 90 year old man. Her daughter was a bit concerned and so she asked, "Mom, is he a nice man? Do you really like him? Is he polite? Is he clean?" All of the answers were positive. At that point the daughter felt very comfortable. Mom said, "Yeah, but twice last week I had to slap his face." The daughter said, "Oh, Mom, was he mean to you? Did he try to do something improper? Did he insult you? What happened?" "Oh, nothing bad happened, I had to slap him, I thought he died."

***

I did a show in my hometown last week. They provided a limo for me. First time I ever rode in a stretch John Deere.

***

"Life is like a mirror.
Smile at it and it smiles back at you."

The Peace Pilgrim

***

There was a pretty bad automobile accident in front of Harold's house. It just happened to be a Jewish man that Harold knew from work. First thing after Harold reached the accident, he said, "Man alive; that was some deal, are you comfortable?" The Jewish man answered, "Oh yes, I make a good living."

***

Don't forget the magic of 1: Not a funny, but a good one.
The late Senator Couzens was at one time the richest member of the United States Senate, while Senator William Borah was reputedly the poorest. As Senator Couzins was leaving the Senate one day he put his hand in his pocket to take out some money, and discovered that he did not have a cent with him. He turned to Senator Borah, who was standing near him, and said, "Bill, can you lend me a dollar?" There are times when ONE counts. The margin of one vote cast by Senator Edward A. Hannegan of Indiana made Texas a part of the United States in 1845. As a matter of fact, California, Oregon, and Washington were also admitted to statehood by margins of ONE vote. Thomas Jefferson

and John Quincy Adams were each elected President by ONE vote in the Electoral College. Rutherford B. Hayes' election as President was contested and referred to an electoral commission. This commission confirmed his election by ONE vote. That vote was cast by a congressman from Indiana who had won his election by ONE vote. This congressman was a lawyer, and the ONE vote that elected him was cast by a client of his who was ill, but insisted on being taken to the polls to vote for him. NEVER UNDERESTIMATE THE POWER OF ONE! Have you ever wished that you had a better education? ONE hour a day spent on good reading of carefully selected books would mean about 50 pages a day. This would add up to 18,250 pages a year, and would represent the equivalent of 50 books of 350 pages each. A steady year of such reading would put you among the best informed men in your industry, your club, or your group of acquaintances.

Don't get bewildered about the complexity or magnitude of your job and your problems. Everything breaks down into a series of ONES. Take ONE step forward, and you are on your way. It's always the next ONE that counts.

***

Note to Son . . .

Dear Son . . . I am writing this letter real slow cause I know that you don't read really fast. We have moved since you were last here. Pa read in the paper where most accidents happen just a couple of miles of one's house. So he dislodged the tree logs that were keeping the trailer house parked and we rolled down the hill a ways. I won't be able to send you the address on account that the last folks that lived here took the number with them so they would not have to change their address. Grandpa fell in the hog trough last week trying to feed them, and was half chomped to death by those silly happy hogs. Those crazy geese that your Pa just had to have, got to pecking at the barrel of our Muskadine Wine and pecked a hole in it and those crazy geese drank it all. The way we found out what they did was we came home from the church house and found them out in the yard on their backs with their little webbed feet stiff up in the air. We couldn't eat them naturally since we did not know how or why they died, so we did what we thought was right, we went in the house and got some potato sacks and sat and plucked them poor dead geese naked. Then we took them down to the creek and threw them in, it was kinda sad though, there they were floating down the river with their little webbed feet straight up in the air. Upon returning to the house we smelled that Muskadine Wine and saw what they had done. Oh well, Pa said, that's what they get! So, we went in the house and started stuffing our mattresses and pillows with them feathers. Directly we heard some racket so we went outside to see what was going on and low and behold there came them crazy naked geese waltzing up the path.

Went to see your cousins in the city, they have a real nice house with green grass, but not much yard to park a car on though. They had a fancy room with a machine to wash your clothes. The first day we were there, I put in four of your pa's shirts and pushed the lever and have not seen 'em since. It rained twice that week, two days the first time and four days the next time.

You know that coat you wanted me to send you? Well, Aunt Sue said that it would be too heavy with all those large heavy buttons on it, so we cut them off and put them in the pockets, it should be there shortly. We got a letter, while we were gone, from the funeral home. It said that if we don't make the last payment on granny's funeral bill . . . Up She Comes! Your sister had her tenth kid yesterday morning. Have not heard what it was yet, so I don't know if you are an aunt or uncle. Your uncle Johnny fell in the hold vat out at the still last week. Some men tried to get him out, but he fought them off and drowned. They cremated him . . . he burned for three days. Got word a little while ago that three of your school chums went off the old Opossum Creek Bridge in a pick-up truck. One was driving, the other were in the back. The driver cranked his window down and got out, and swam to save the others, but failed to save them and they all drowned; it was said that it was on account that they couldn't get the tailgate down. Well, there's not much going on here, so I will say bye for now. Ma . . . P.S. I was gonna send you some money, but I already sealed the letter.

***

This lady went in to the new beauty shop. She had never been in there before, and she had never ever heard of the young man that did the work there. Just as she sat down in his chair she said to him, "Oh, I'm so nervous, I really don't know which end is up."

The young man was rather confused. He replied, "Well, Mrs. Jones, I would really appreciate it if you would tell me before I start to shampoo."

***

"I've been on a constant diet for the last two decades. I've lost 78 pounds. By all accounts, I should be hanging from a charm bracelet."
Erma Bombeck

***

"When I die," said the 12 year old grandson. "I hope I die, just like Grandpa did, in his sleep; not like the guy in the other car."

***

A man and his wife were having some problems at home, culminating in the silent treatment. This continued through the weekend. When the husband tried to set the alarm clock for the next morning, he couldn't get it to work right. Since his wife always got up first, he needed her to wake him at 5:00 a.m. for a morning business flight. Not wanting to be the first to break the silence, he wrote on a piece of paper, "Please wake me at 5:00 a.m." He placed the paper next to her bed on the night stand. The next morning the man woke up at 7:00 a.m. Furious, he was about to yell at his wife when he noticed a piece of paper on his night stand next to his bed. The paper said, "It's 5:00 a.m. Wake up dummy!"

***

"You look thin Margaret, are you on a diet?" said Mary. "Yes, I am," replied Margaret, "Every morning, when I first get out of bed, I take my night clothes off and I stand in front of a full length mirror; I turn around so I can see my entire body. That's when I get deathly ill and there is no way I can eat anything." Mary said, "What do you at lunch time?" Margaret answered quickly, I just think about what I saw in the morning, and there goes my appetite"

***

"Most folks are about as happy

as they make their minds up to be."
Abraham Lincoln

***

I really love Wal-Mart. Here in Missouri, it's like the Mall of America. A tornado hit the Wal-Mart in my hometown the other day. It left 300 housewives homeless.

***

"There is little difference in people, but that little difference makes a big difference. That little difference is attitude. The big difference is whether it is positive or negative." **W. Clement Stone**

***

An atheist was out fishing when suddenly his boat was attacked by the Loch Ness monster. The beast tossed him and his boat high in the air. Then it opened its mouth, ready to swallow both whole. Sailing head over-heels, the man cried out, "Oh, my God! Help me!" Amazingly, the boat got wedged in the monster's mouth as the atheist hung on for dear life. Then a booming voice came from above. "I thought you didn't believe in me!" "Come on, God give me a break!" the man pleaded. "Two minutes ago I didn't believe in the Loch Ness monster either!"

***

"What lies behind us and what lies before us, doesn't matter compared to what lies within us."
Ralph Waldo Emerson

***

Junk is the stuff you keep for 10 years in case you need it, and then you sell it two days before you really do.

***

Middle age is when you finally get your head on straight, and your body falls apart.

***

I invested everything I own in revolving doors and paper towels. I got wiped out before I could turn around.

***

The North won this battle, the North won there, etc. "Young man," said the ole boy from Mississippi, "I know the South had to win some of the battles." The guide replied, "Well sir, not as long as I'm the guide on this tour."

***

Here's a unique puzzle. Try it, you'll really be surprised, and you'll do it for your friends; guaranteed.
Pick a number between 2 and 9. Multiply that number by 9. Add those two digits together. Subtract 5. Take that number and with the letters ABCDEFG choose the letter that corresponds with your number. With that letter, name a country, with the last letter of country, name an animal, with the last letter of that animal, name a color. NOW WRITE DOWN YOUR ANSWER. Go to page 430 in this book and see if the answer relates to your answer. See, I told you, you would like it.

***

Freddie said to his mom, "Mommy, I want a pet goat." His mother said, "Freddie, if I've told you once I've told you a dozen times we can't have a goat." "Why can't we have a goat?" said Freddie. "Well, there are several reasons, but the main one is the odor, replied his mother." "Golly, gee mom, I really think he could get used to it," said Freddie.

***

Chicken Side off first...

"Obstacles are those frightening things you see when you take your eyes off your goal."
Henry Ford

***

As this couple was riding down the road, George looked over to his wife and said, "Honey, do you see that donkey over there in the field?" His wife answered, "Of course, do you think I'm blind," "No, No, I just wanted to ask you if he was among some of your relatives?" "Yes, yes, she said, by marriage."

***

Years ago there was a new detergent that came on the market. It was called New Blue Cheer. There was a tremendous television promotion on the air, and it went sorta like this; The TV producers displayed 3 tubs of hot water on the TV stage. He had previously asked them to bring the dirtiest article of clothing that their husbands wore. Now, in front of the audience he had each lady, by hand, wash each item of clothing in their tub. After the 1st one did her washing he held up a pair of socks that she had washed. He immediately started singing the new jingle. Washi, washi, washi, in new blue cheer, washi, washi, washi, till the water runs clear; run it by your nose, smells like a rose, it's NEW BLUE CHEER! Well, he went through the same thing with the 2nd contestant, and then he went to the 3rd one. As the lady held up a pair of her husband's dirty under shorts the hosts began singing his little jingle once again. Washi, washi, washi, in new blue cheer, washi, washi, washi, till the water runs clear. Run it by your nose, smells like a, G O L L Y ! washi, washi, washi, washi, washi, washi! ! !

***

The lady went to her doctor and said, "Oh doctor, every part of my body hurts, and it hurts so much." She touched her head and it hurts so much, she touched her other arm, it hurts so much, she touched her legs, and they hurt so much, she touched her stomach, and it hurts so much. Finally the doctor said, "I've been watching you as you touched each part of your body. I've determined that your problem is a fractured finger." "That will be $35.

Please." "Oh," said the lady, "that hurts so much also."

***

My boss isn't really bald; he just grew out of his hair. He used to use Head-n-Shoulders, now it's Mop-n-Glo.

***

A woman, obviously greatly agitated, rushed to see her doctor. "Doctor, when I woke up this morning and looked in the mirror, my hair was all frazzled, my skin was pasty, and my eyes were bloodshot and bugging out. I looked like a corpse! What's wrong with me?" "Well, I can tell you one thing," the doctor calmly replied. "There's nothing wrong with your eyesight."

***

Not a funny, but a good thought

"How many believe we're living in the last generation?" Much of the group voiced the following, "I don't think we can tell," "There's no way to tell," "The Bible says, only God knows," etc. "Well, I think all you have the answer, but it hasn't dawned on you as yet." The speaker continued. "We are all living in OUR last generation." Everyone had to agree. Yep, that's something to think about.

***

The phone rang at 2:00 p.m. When Mr. Smith answered, the voice on the other end of the line said. "I'm, Mr. Johnson, your new neighbor. If your dog doesn't stop barking I'm going to call the police." Then he hung up. At 2:00 p.m. the very next night Mr. Smith returned his neighbor's call. "This is Mr. Smith, your my new neighbor, we don't have a dog."

***

The teacher started the class; she told the class she wanted an essay that included a bit of Religion, Royalty, Sex and Mystery, within the essay. "I will need this by the end of the week," she said. In about 30 minutes Rupert came up to her desk and said, "Well Mrs. Smith, here is your essay." She said, "Are you sure you have the four subjects that I mentioned in it?" "Yep, I sure do" Rupert said. She looked it over and said, Rupert, you've done a good job, and it didn't take me long to read." Here's what it said: 'Holy Moses, said the Princess, pregnant again, who could it have been.'"

***

"He ought to be ashamed, he ought to be ashamed, he ought to be ashamed," said Billy. Billy was the one brother still living at home with his folks. Johnny, who was the other brother who was married, had 3 children, and not the best of jobs in the world, but he was working as much as was possible, stopped by for just a few minutes to see how his folks were getting along. "Billy, why were you hollering, he ought to be ashamed, he ought to be ashamed, when I drove up?" "Well, Billy said, "I was talking about you. Mom pays the rent and buys the groceries, dad bought my car and pays the insurance, our little sister does all the housework, keeps the cars clean, etc. and you don't give us anything. You outta be ashamed!"

***

This very elderly lady had a baby girl. She was so old that no one that knew her could possibly believe that she gave birth to a baby. One of her lady friends came over to see the new baby. After being there for at least 20 minutes, she asked, "Lois, I came over to see the little one, where is she?" "Well," replied Lois, "I knew that is what you came for, and all I've got to do is remember where I put her."

***

I sure felt sorry for John. Jim and John were in this department store and wanted to go to the basement and visit the tool department. When they got to the escalator, there was a sign that said; Dogs must be carried on the escalator. John turned to Jim and said, "Now where in Heaven's name are we going to get 2 dogs?"

***

Charley and his wife Treva, got on the elevator in Penny's department store. At the 2nd floor a beautiful 30 year old blonde got on, and I guess she was a knock out. Charlie couldn't keep his eyes off of her. Treva couldn't help but notice the spell that she had casted on Charlie. When the elevator stopped at the top floor, the blond started to step off, but stopped, turned, slapped Charlie with a good one. She said to Charlie, "I don't like to have my bottom pinched." Then she just walked away. Charlie turned to Treva and said honestly honey, I did not pinch her. Treva said, "I know, I did."

***

Young Mary was visiting her grand-parents farm. Investigating the chicken lot she came upon a peacock. She immediately ran to the house shouting. "Granny, Granny, come quickly. One of your chickens is in full bloom."

***

Ralph didn't want to do his homework, and his attitude about it was not good either. His dad thought he needed a little lecture. He said, "Son, when President Lincoln was your age, he studied by candle light and walked 10 miles to school every day." Ralph said to his father, "Dad when John F. Kennedy was your age, he was President."

***

Did you hear about the gal that was so skinny that after she swallowed an olive, 4 guys left town?

***

In life you learn to take the good with the bad, the bitter with the sweet, and the speaker with the dinner.

***

The other day I overheard two ladies talking in an antique store. Holding up a vase, one said, "I'd give anything for this, but not at this price."

***

Sam's wife was an excellent cook. She was especially good at making potato salad. Some new folks moved into the neighborhood and so Sam and Charlotte thought it would be nice to invite them over for dinner one evening. It came time for the dinner party and the new neighbors showed up right on time. The four of them sat around making small talk and during the meal Sam couldn't hold his tongue any longer. He didn't want to embarrass Charlotte, but he just couldn't hold it in. Sam said, "Folks I don't know what happened, but my wife really made a boo boo this evening with her potato salad. It is usually very good, as a matter of fact it's the best I've ever eaten anywhere." About that time Charlotte, under the table, kicked the fire out of Sam. Sam said, "No, I'm serious, she's the best there is with potato salad, but she sure screwed up this time." Charlotte said to Sam, "Would you please come into the kitchen for a minute and help me with dessert?" Sam got up and went into the kitchen with Charlotte. She said to Sam, "You idiot, I forgot to tell you, our neighbor wanted to bring something, so she brought the potato salad."

***

"If you always do what you have always done, you will always get what you've always got." Zig Ziglar

***

The CEO was scheduled to speak at an important convention, so he asked his assistant to write him a punchy 20-minute speech. When he CEO returned from the big event, he was furious. Cornering his assistant, he didn't hold back. "What's the idea of writing me an hour-long speech?! Half the audience walked out before I finished." "I wrote you a 20-minute speech," the assistant replied, baffled. "And I also gave you the 2 extra copies you requested."

***

"Your time is limited, don't waste it living someone else's life. Don't be trapped by dogma, which is living the result of other people's thinking. Don't let the noise of other's opinion drowned your own inner voice. And most important, have the courage to follow your heart and intuition, they somehow already know what you truly want to become. Everything else is secondary."

Steve Jobs

***

Richard & Neta Ruth Sunderwirth

This wedding anniversary drew a big crowd, because everyone in the community knew the couple well. The arranger of the affair asked one of their friends to do 4 songs for the event. The fellow that was asked to sing really knew the couple well, so he chose the following 4 songs. "Keep on the firing line," "One day at a time," "Nobody knows the trouble I've seen." and "Wasted years." **This might give you an idea if you ever have to sing at a wedding anniversary.**

***

My wife's an angel. You're lucky, mine is still living.

***

The Hypnotist

After the community sing-along led by Joyce at the piano, it was time for the star of the show-Horace the Hypnotist!

Horace explained that he was going to put the whole audience into a trance. "Yes, each and every one of you and all at the same time," said Horace. The excited chatter dropped to silence as Horace carefully withdrew from his waistcoat pocket a beautiful antique gold pocket watch and chain. I want you to keep your eyes on this watch," said Horace, holding the watch high for all to see. "It is a very special and valuable watch that has been in my family for six generations," said Horace. He began to swing the watch gently back and forth while quietly chanting "Watch the watch – "Watch the watch – "Watch the watch"—The audience became mesmerized as the watch swayed back and forth. The lights were twinkling as they were reflected from its gleaming surfaces. A hundred and fifty pairs of eyes followed the movements of the gently swaying watch. They were, beyond question, hypnotized. And then suddenly, the chain broke! ! ! The beautiful watch fell to the stage and burst apart on impact. "CRAP" said Horace. It took them three days to clean the Senior Citizens' Center and Horace was never invited there again.

***

A true story from the pages of the Manchester Evening News:

Last Wednesday a passenger in a taxi heading for Salford station leaved over to ask the driver a question and gently tapped him on the shoulder to get his attention. The driver screamed, lost control of the cab, nearly hit a bus, drove up over the curb and stopped just inches from a large plate glass window. For a few moments everything was silent in the cab. Then, the shaking driver said, "Are you OK? I'm so sorry, but you scared the daylights out of me." The badly shaken passenger apologized to the driver and said, "I didn't realize that a mere tap on the shoulder would startle someone so badly." The driver replied, "No, no, I'm the one who is sorry, it's entirely my fault. Today is my very first day driving a cab. I've been driving a hearse for the last 25 years."

***

Two buddies, Jasper and Joseph, worked together for years, but times got hard and they both lost their jobs. They decided they would go through the neighborhood and find some work. The first house they went to, the lady said, "Sure, I'll give you a job. All I need for you to do is to cut down that big dead tree in the backyard." They agreed on the price, $100 and they started working. The lady just happened to be looking out the kitchen window and noticed the tail end of some kind of, what appeared to be a tribal dance of some kind or something similar. After they finished cutting down the tree and cutting up the wood into smaller pieces Jasper went in to collect their money. The lady paid them and then she said as she smiled really big, "I'll tell you what I'll do, if you'll have your buddy do another one of those dances that he did a while ago, I'll give him another $100. I've never in my life seen anyone that could dance, jump, holler, and rollover like he did, it was fantastic. I don't know if he will or not, I'll ask him, "Hey Joe, for $100; would you cut off another toe?"

***

An older man was having problems with silent gas emissions. So he went to his doctor for relief. When the doctor asked what his problem was, he told him, "Doc, at the opera the other night I had 3 silent emissions. Last night at my poker game I had 6, and would you believe it, I've already had 3 since I came into your office, can you help me? The doctor replied, "Yes I can, the first thing I'm going to do is open those 2 windows behind you, and the second thing I'm going to check your hearing."

***

Two guys were going down the road and ran out of gas. They stopped at a farm house and asked if they could borrow or purchase some gasoline. The old farmer said, "Well sir, I've run out myself but I'll have some here on the truck first thing in the morning, but you're welcome to stay here tonight and I'll get your gas for you in the morning." The fellows said, "That will be just fine, we sure do appreciate your hospitality." "One of you can sleep here in the house with me," said the farmer, "and the other one can sleep in the barn with baby." "That will be fine, Charlie said to Tom, "I'll stay in the house, and Tom, you can sleep in the barn with baby." Everyone agreed on the arrangements. The next morning they got ready to leave and Charlie said to Tom, as he was coming out of the barn, "Who is that gorgeous 30 year old blond with you?" "Oh, said Tom, I'll let her introduce herself." She said, "I'm baby, and who are you?" "Well," said Charlie, "I'm Charlie, the fool that slept in the house last night."

***

"Did you hear about the lady of the night?
She wore really high heel shoes.
She didn't want to sell herself short."

***

Bill said to Warren, "Warren, I'm on two diets now, I think I can lose some weight." "Warren said, "Well, why in the world would you be on two diets? Bill replied, "I never could get enough to eat on just one."

***

Margie went in to the local grocery market. She said to the vegetable clerk, "I'd like to have a half a head of cabbage, please." The clerk said, "I wish I could do that but they won't let us cut one in half." Margie kept on insisting, she just wouldn't let up. The clerk said, "I tell you what I'll do, I'll talk to the manager." Well, the lady followed him into the back room. The clerk didn't notice her following him, but the manager did. The clerk said to the manager, "Hey boss, there's an old bag out in front that wants a half of a head of cabbage." The manager said, "Oh yes, we can do that, and there's a nice sweet little lady right her with you that would like the other half."

***

CBN studio, the Family Channel & Regent University

On Richard's Fun-Time Tours, once or twice a year, we would take a 10 day, Washington D.C. tour. That tour would include many other wonderful cities across the Eastern part of the U.S.A. One of our stops would be at CBN, 'The Family Channel' which housed, 'The 700 Club'. We would stay on the campus of CBN and have a fantastic luncheon, take a tour of the CBN TV studios also a live broadcast and spend one night at their beautiful 'Founders Inn'. Our adventures at this facility would begin at 9:30 a.m. and continue on until 1:00 p.m. The hostess, Margaret, would meet and greet us, as we drove up in front of the main building, would always say, "Richard, you are on time every time you come to see us. You are never early and you are never late." That would, of course, make me and everyone one on the motor coach feel good. When we first started going there, on one particular tour, I said to Margaret, "I have always tried to operate my tours with this thought in mind, using the 7-Ps. 'Proper Prior Planning Prevents Pitifully Poor Performance.' She thought that was great!

This stop also included 'Regent University,' on the same campus, which was a university that specialized in Law. The next year when we arrived, Margaret met us with this announcement. "I hope you don't mind but we have put your slogan on little walnut plaques and placed them on all of our desks in the TV production buildings, Regent University, Founders Inn, and every other desk we could find. We made one powerful addition to the plaque. For us it now reads: 'Proper Prior Planning PLUS PRAYER Prevents Pitifully Poor Performance.' "I remember this time so well." I told Margaret. "Your addition is great and I appreciate you using it at this huge facility." Neta Ruth and I still try to use this same slogan; now there are 9 P's in everything we do.

***

A motorcycle went by and it was really moving on. The local cop took out after it. Another cop joined in the chase. He got there a bit later than the first cop. The first cop said "The lady on the cycle was naked, but after I started in pursuit I found that she wasn't going quite as fast as I thought." "The second cop said, "Since we stopped her, we've got to charge her with something, how about, umm, no helmet; did she have on a helmet? First cop replied, "Golly, I'm sorry, I didn't even notice."

***

The hospital patient was really worried. She said to the doctor, "Doc, are you sure it's pneumonia? I've heard of cases where a doctor treated a patient for pneumonia and he ended up dying of something else?" "Don't worry," said the doctor, "When I treat a patient for pneumonia, they die of pneumonia."

***

Don't mess with Louisiana!

The President - - - ? - - - your choice was in the Oval Office when his telephone rang. "Hello, Mr. President," in a heavily accented Cajun voice said. "Dis' is Boudreaux, down here at Slim's in Kinder, I am callin' to tell ya'll dat we declaring war on ya!" "Well Boudeaux", The President replied, "This is indeed important news! How big is your army?" "Right now," said Boud, "dere's myself, my brother-in-law Thib my next-door-neighbor Bubba, and a few other gator huntn' buddies. Dat makes eight!"

The President paused, "I must tell you Boudreaux that I have one million men in my army waiting to move on my command." "Wow," said Boudreaux, "call ya back!" Sure enough, the next day, Boud called again. "Mr. President, da war is on? We got us some infantry equipment!" "And what equipment would that be Boudreaux?" the President asked. "We got us two combines, couple of 4 wheelers, a piroque, and Thib's John Deere." The President sighed. "I must tell you Boudreaux , that I have 16,000 tanks and 14,000 armored personnel carriers. Also I've increased my army to one and a half million since we last spoke." "Lord above", said Boud, "be getting back to ya cher." Sure enough, Boudreaux rang again the next day. "Mr. President, da war is still on! We got ourselves airborne! Bubba fixed his ultra-lite couple of shotguns in da cockpit, and four vets from the VFW signed up!" The President was silent for a minute then cleared his throat, "I must tell you Boudreaux that I have 10,000 bombers and 20,000 fighter planes. My military complex is surrounded by laser-guided, surface-to-air missile sites. And since we last spoke, I've increased my army to TWO MILLION!" "Oh Lord," said Boud, "I gonna call you back." Sure enough, Boudreaux called again the next day. "Mr. President! Sorry to tell you dat we have called off da war." "I'm sorry to hear that," said the President. "Why the sudden change of heart?" "Well sir," said Boudreaux, "We all sat down and had a long chat over a few beers, and come to think of it, dere's just no way our wives can make enough gumbo to feed two million prisoners."

***

There were 3 doctors going to a Christmas party. They were on I-70 about 40 miles from Kansas City and they had a flat tire. The first doctor got out of the car and said, "I checked the tire and it is flat. The second doctor jumped out of the car and said, "I will check the tire and see if it is really flat." He said to the 3rd doctor, "Yep, it looks like it is a flat. The 3rd doctor checked it over and said, "Yes, I believe you are both correct." The 3 all agreed; however, they felt they had better run some tests.

***

Santa Claus, the tooth fairy, an honest lawyer and an old drunk are walking down the street together when they simultaneously spot a hundred dollar bill. Who gets it? The old drunk, of course; the other three are mythical creatures.

***

One day a man answers his door and there's a snail at his doorstep. The man picks it up and throws it into the garden. 3 years later, he hears a knock on his door. Pretty faint knock, to say the least He opens the door and it's the same snail. He's now a little bigger And the snail says, "Hey, what was that all about?" He's got a pretty good memory also.

***

If you can eat the same food every day and be grateful for it, If you can understand when your loved ones are too busy to give you any time; If you can take criticism and blame without resentment; If you can resist treating a rich friend better than a poor one; If you can face the world without lies and deceit; If you can say honestly that deep in your heart you have no prejudice against creed; color or politics, . . . Then, my friend, you are almost as good as our little black, blue-eyed silver topped Shih-tzu dog,

REBEL. He's a Confederate dog, you know!

***

This fellow has only about six months to live. He goes to his doctor and says, "Doc, with only 6 months to live, what should I do; what should I do?" "Well," the doctor replies; "Go marry a 300 lb. woman, with 8 or 9 kids, and a mustache, and for some reason doesn't believe in deodorant. You won't really live any longer, but it will be the longest 6 months you ever lived."

***

**I'm going on a 30-day diet . . .
I'm gonna start in 30 days.**

***

When I'm an old lady and live with my kids.

When I'm an old lady, I'll live with my kids, and make their life happy and filled with such joy. I want to pay back all the joy they've provided returning each deed. Oh, they'll be so excited. **When I'm an old lady and live with my kids.**
I'll write on the walls with red, white, and blue and bounce on the furniture wearing my shoes. I'll drink from the carton and then leave it out. I'll stuff all the toilets and "oh" they'll shout. **When I'm an old lady and live with my kids.**
When they're on the phone and just out of reach, I'll get into things like sugar and bleach. Oh, they'll snap their fingers and then shake their head, and when that is done, I'll hide under the bed. **When I'm an old lady and live with my kids.**
When they cook dinner and call me to meals, I'll not eat my green beans or salad congealed. I'll gag on my oatmeal, spill milk on the table, and when they get angry, run fast as I'm able.
When I'm an old lady and live with my kids.
I'll sit close to the TV, through the channels I'll click. I'll cross both my eyes and see if they stick. I'll take off my socks and throw one away, and play in the mud til' the end of the day.
When I'm an old lady and live with my kids.
And later in bed, I'll lay back and sigh, and thank God in prayer and then close my eyes, and my kids will look down with a smile slowly creeping, and say, "She's so sweet when she's sleeping.
When I'm an old lady and live with my kids.

Copied

***

A rookie cop was asked in an examination what he would do to break up a crowd. He thought for a moment and wrote, and you can tell by his answer, that he knew a lot about the knowledge of human nature. He said he'd take up a collection.

***

This second grader went to borrow the phone. The Principal said, "May I help you son?" The boy replied, "Well, my mama said, "If I couldn't find my jacket tonight, not to come home. I was calling her to ask her where she wanted me go."

***

This psychic was jailed for false prophecies, but because he was only 4'7" tall and extremely slender, he was able to slip under the bars and make his escape. The newspaper headline the next day stated . . . "Small Medium at Large." The psychic was really happy he had escaped and soon was back in business in a new location. His first customer; however, was a plain clothes cop who had been searching for him. Before the psychic could escape, the detective hit the psychic with his fist to subdue him. After the arrest the cop was commended for **Striking a Happy Medium.**

***

The US Mint announced today that it has commenced a recall of the new Missouri quarter. Severe vending machine problems have forced the Mint to initiate the recall, much to the dismay of the general Missouri population. Mint officials state that they had no choice but to remove the much anticipated new quarter from circulation less than 24 hours after its release due to its inability to work in virtually all coin operated machines. Pay phones, Coke machines; vending machines of all types failed to accept the new tender. It seems that the duct tape holding the two dimes and the nickel together was getting stuck in the coin operated machine works.

***

What does it mean when a man is in your bed gasping for breath and calling your name? It means you didn't hold the pillow down long enough.

***

"Golf can be described as an endless series of tragedies obscured by the occasional miracle."

***

The patient sitting on the examining table told the doctor, "Gee, those oysters I ate don't seem to be agreeing with me." The doctor asked, "Were they fresh, as he palpated the man's stomach? "I'm not sure." said the patient. "Well, how did they look when you opened the shells?" inquired the doctor. The patient said, with a funny look on his face," What do you mean, opened the shells?"

***

A man walked into a lawyer's office and inquired about the lawyer's rates. "$50 for three questions," replied the lawyer. "Isn't that awfully steep?" asked the man. "Yes," the lawyer replied, "and what was your third question?"

***

Do you really want to find out, in your life, who is really the most loyal and loving? Put your favorite dog and your wife in the trunk of your car for 4 hours. Then open the trunk and see which one jumps in your arms; kisses you on the face, and seems thrilled to see you. **Robert Moore**

***

Two hillbillies struck up a conversation on the beach at Miami. One of them said, "I'm here on insurance money. I collected $10,000 for fire damage. "Me, too," the second hillbilly said. "But I got $20,000 for flood damage." There was a long, thoughtful pause and the first hillbilly said, "Tell me, how do you start a flood?"

***

Couldn't hurt, might help! Money Isn't Everything.
Money can buy a house but not a home. Money can buy a bed

but not sleep. Money can buy a clock but not time. Money can buy a book but not knowledge. Money can buy food but not an appetite. Money can buy position but not respect. Money can buy blood but not life. Money can buy medicine but not health. Money can buy sex but not love. Money can buy insurance but not safety. You see, money is not everything. Therefore; if you have too much, please send it to me. My name is . . . darn . . . I forgot my name. That seems to be happening more all the time.

Copied

***

The new librarian decided to change the book checkout procedure. Instead of writing the names of borrowers on the book cards herself, she asked the youngsters to sign their own names. "You are signing a contract instructing you to return the books on time," she explained. A 2nd grader brought 4 books to the desk and gave the librarian his name. She, in turn, handed him the 4 book cards to sign. The boy, obviously disgusted, laboriously printed his name and handed them back to her. Before the librarian could even start her speech he said, scornfully, "Our other librarian could write."

***

A hospital is a place where they keep you for three days if you have a big illness and three months if you have big insurance.

Copied

***

I'm having the time of my life

I'm the life of the party, even when it lasts until 8 p.m. I'm very good at opening child-proof caps with a hammer. . . I'm usually interested in going home before I get to where I'm going. I'm good on a trip for at least an hour without my aspirin, beano or antacid . . . I'm the first one to find the bathroom wherever I go . . . I'm awake many hours before my body allows me to get up. . . . I'm smiling all the time because I can't hear a word you are saying . . . I'm very good at telling stories, over and over and over and over . . . I'm aware that other people's grandchildren are not as bright as mine . . . I'm so cared for: long-term care, eye care, private care, and dental care . . . I'm not grouchy, I just don't like traffic, waiting, crowds, children, and especially politicians . . . I'm positive I did housework correctly before my mate retired . . . I'm sure everything I can't find is in a secure place . . . I'm wrinkled, saggy and lumpy, and that's just my left leg . . . I'm having trouble remembering simple words like . . . I'm now spending more time with my pillows than with my mate . . . I'm realizing that aging is not for sissies . . . I'm anti-everything now: anti-fat, anti-noise, anti-inflammatory . . . I'm walking more to the bathroom and enjoying it less . . . I'm going to reveal what goes on behind closed doors . . . absolutely nothing! . . . I'm sure they are making adults much younger these days . . . I'm in the initial stage of my golden years: SS, CD's IRA'S, AARP . . . I'm wondering . . . if you're only as old as you feel, how could I be alive at 150? . . . I'm supporting all movements now . . . by eating bran, prunes and raisins . . . I'm a walking storeroom of facts . . . I've just lost the storeroom . . . I'm a senior citizen and I think I am having the time of my life. **Copied, Patricia Ann**

***

One Hundred Years Ago, 1910

Only 14 percent of the homes in the U.S.A. had a bathtub. More than 95 percent of all births in the U.S.A. took place at home. The five leading causes of death in the U.S.A. were; Pneumonia and Influenza, Tuberculosis, Diarrhea, Heart disease, and Stroke. A 3-minute call from Denver to New York City cost $11.00. The average life expectancy in the U.S.A. was 47. There were only 8,000 cars in the U.S.A, and only 144 miles of paved roads. Only 8 percent of homes had a telephone. The maximum speed limit in most cities was 10 mph. Most women only washed their hair once a month and used borax or egg yolks for shampoo. The population of Las Vegas, NV was 30. Canned beer and iced tea hadn't been invented. Only 6 percent of all Americans had graduated from high school. Marijuana, heroin, and morphine were all available over the counter at the corner drugstores. According to one pharmacist, "Heroin clears the complexion, gives buoyancy to the mind, regulates the stomach and bowels, and is, in fact a perfect guardian of health." One in ten U.S.A. adults couldn't read or write. Eighteen percent of households in the U.S.A. had at least one full-time servant or domestic.

***

YOU REMEMBER THE REAL AMERICA, IF YOU CAN REMEMBER

When riots were unthinkable. **When** you left front doors open. **When** socialism was a dirty word. **When** ghettos were neighborhoods. **When** the Flag was a sacred symbol. **When** criminals actually went to jail. **When** you weren't afraid to go out at night. **When** taxes were only a necessary nuisance. **When** a boy was a boy, and dressed like one. **When** a girl was a girl, and dressed like one. **When** the poor were too proud to take charity. **When** the clergy actually talked about relationship with God. **When** clerks and repairmen tried to please you. **When** college kids swallowed goldfish, not beer. **When** songs had a tune, and the words made sense. **When** young fellows tried to join the Army or Navy. **When** people knew what the Fourth of July stood for. **When** you never dreamed our country could ever lose. **When** a Sunday drive was a pleasant trip, not an ordeal. **When** you bragged about your hometown, and home state. **When** everybody didn't feel entitled to a college education. **When** people expected less, and valued what they had more. **When** politicians proclaimed their patriotism, and meant it. **When** everyone knew the difference between right and wrong. **When** things weren't perfect, but you never expected them to be. **When** our Government stood up for Americans, anywhere in the world. **When** you knew that the law would be enforced, your safety protected. **When** you considered yourself lucky to have a good job, and proud of it too. **When** the law meant justice, you were in awe at the sight of a policeman. **When** you weren't too embarrassed to say that this is the best country ever. **When** America was a land filled with brave, proud, hardworking people!

Copied

***

"And ye shall dwell in the land that I gave to your fathers; and ye shall be my people, and I will be your God." Ezek. 36:28

***

"How do you account for your longevity?" asked the reporter, on Harvey's 100th birthday. Harvey said, "Well, you might call me a health nut. I never smoked, drank, always in bed and sound asleep by ten o'clock. I've always walked 3 miles every day, rain or shine, but I had an uncle who followed that exact routine and died when he was 62. "How come it didn't work for him," asked the reporter. "Well," said Harvey, "All I can say is that he didn't keep it up long enough."

***

Now this is a story that one similar has probably happened to you. It's kinda like the old adage that if anything can go wrong, it probably will.

This fellow found a shoe repair ticket in a suit that he hadn't worn for over two years. He told his wife that this would be wonderful because the shoes he was wearing now were about shot. He jumped in his car and made a mad dash for the shoe shop. He walked in with a smile on his face and told the shoe repair man that he's sorry he hadn't been in to pick up the shoes. The repair man looked at the ticket and told the man, "Well, I'll tell you what, those shoes will be ready a week from Tuesday." The man with the shoes started to jump up and down and ask for an explanation, but he thought he'd get a wild story. So a week from Tuesday will be the day as far as he knows now.

***

There was this 89 year old woman who found her husband in bed with another woman. She was so enraged that she dragged him to the balcony of their Miami high-rise and pushed him to his death. When she appeared in court the Judge asked her if she had anything to say in her own defense. "Well," she said, "I figured that if he could make love at 92, he could fly also."

***

This guy just returned from 2 weeks of vacation and asked for some more time off to get married. "Why didn't you get married while you were off?" The guy said, "What, are you nuts, and ruin my entire vacation."

***

Chicken Side off first...

After they'd brought their first baby home from the hospital, a young wife suggested to her husband that he try his hand at changing diapers. "I'm really busy, but I'll do it on the very next one." said the husband. The next time the baby was soiled, his wife said, "Honey, are you ready now to learn all about the changing process?" He looked at his wife, with a puzzled look on his face, and said, "Oh, I didn't mean the next diaper, I meant the next baby."

***

While waiting to board a plane in a small airport, we heard the ticket agent on the paging system. "Would the person who dropped his pants, please return to the ticket counter as soon as possible." After a pause, the same voice added, "The pants were on a hanger." Immediately, the entire airport crowd made a really big sound of relief.

***

This lady went to a self-defense meeting. A man charged through the group and grabbed her purse. The instructor said, to the lady, "Now after what we've learned, can you describe your assailant to us?" "Yes," replied the lady, he was 6 ft. tall, 185 lbs, had on a brown suit, blue socks, a scar on his chin and green eyes." The instructor nearly fell out of his chair, "My goodness lady, have you taken this course before, that was absolutely a marvelous description, and please tell us how you did it?" said the instructor. "Well, it wasn't too difficult, it was my husband, I forgot to give him the money to buy gas for the car."

***

After her son moved out, the mother decided to write her son and tell him that phones were so expensive she was going to write him instead of calling. The next day after her son received the letter he called her collect and said, "I just wanted to let you know, I received your letter, and I think that's a great money saving idea, thanks mom."

***

Upset with her husband she began to cry. That's when he said, "Susan, what's today's date? Boy did she blow up. He said, "What's wrong with what I said?" "Well," she said, "My name is Kathy."

***

Did you ever notice how some people will invest thousands in unknown stocks, but will be reluctant to put a dime in a beggar's cup, wondering if he is really blind?

***

Young girl from back in the sticks stood at the bank teller's window. The teller looked at her and also at the check she wished to cash and said, "Young lady, would you please identify yourself?" The girl pulled a small mirror from her handbag, glanced in it, and with relief said, "Yes, it's me all right."

***

The phone rang and the man rushed out of bed to answer it. "I'm sorry, you'll have to call the weather bureau for that information," he said. "Who was that, dear?" his wife asked. "Oh, just some guy who wanted to know if the coast was clear."

***

The boy from a small town met a lovely girl from Atlanta at a community dance, and he danced almost every dance with her, and, when the evening was over he asked her, "Would it be Ok if I could see you again, on my next trip to Atlanta?" "Oh yes," she replied. So he got out his notebook and asked, "What is your phone number?" She replied, " Capitol 2-1974. The young man paused for a minute and then asked, "How do you make a capital 2?"

***

MICROSOFT SHOULD MAKE CARS, GM SHOULD MAKE SOFTWARE.

At a recent computer exposition, Bill Gates reportedly compared the computer industry with the auto industry and stated: "If GM had kept up with technology like the computer industry has, we would all be driving twenty-five dollar cars that go 1000 miles to the gallon." In response to Bill's comments/General Motors issued a press release stating the following: "If GM had developed technology like Microsoft, we would be driving

cars with the following characteristics:

1. For no reason whatsoever, your car would crash twice a day.
2. Every time they repainted the lines on the road, you would have to buy a new car.
3. Occasionally, your car would die on the freeway for no reason, and you would accept this, restart, and drive on.
4. Occasionally, executing a maneuver such as a left turn would cause your car to shut down and refuse to restart; in which case you would have to reinstall the engine.
5. Only one person at a time could use the car, unless you bought 'Car95' or 'CarNT.' Then you would have to buy more seats.
6. Macintosh would make a car that was powered by the sun, was more reliable, five times as fast, and twice as easy to drive, but would only run on five percent of the roads.
7. The oil, temperature and alternator warning lights would be replaced by a single 'general car fault' warning light.
8. New seats would force everyone to have the same butt size.
9. The airbag system would say 'Are you sure?' before going off.
10. Occasionally, for no reason whatsoever, your car would lock you out and refuse to let you in until you simultaneously lifted the door handle, turned the key and grabbed hold of the radio antenna.
11. GM would require all car buyers to also purchase a deluxe set of Rand McNally road maps now a GM subsidiary, even though they neither need them nor want them. Attempting to delete this option would immediately cause the car's performance to diminish by 50 per cent or more.
12. Every time GM introduced a new model, car buyers would have to learn how to drive all over again because none of the controls would operate in the same manner as the old car.
13. You'd press the 'Start' button to shut off the engine.

The above was COPIED. No credit was given for the Author, that I could find

***

In the ear of the beholder. . .

A man goes to his doctor and says, "I don't think my wife's hearing is as good as it used to be, what should I do?" The doctor replies, "Try this test to find out for sure. When your wife is in the kitchen doing dishes, stand fifteen feet behind her and ask her a question, if she doesn't respond keep moving closer asking the question until she hears you." So, the man goes home and sees his wife preparing dinner. He stands fifteen feet behind her and says, "What's for dinner, honey?" He gets no response, so he moves to ten feet behind her and asks again. Still no response, so he moves to five feet, no answer. Finally he stands directly behind her and says, "Honey, what's for supper?" She replies, "For the fourth time, I SAID CHICKEN!"

***

Preparing for the most important presentation of his life, a sales rep decided to get help from a hypnotist. "I'll put a suggestion in your mind," said the hypnotist. "Just say 1-2-3, and you'll give the presentation of your life. However, do not say 1-2-3-4, because you'll freeze up and make a fool of yourself." The sales rep was ecstatic. He tried it at home and impressed his family. He tried it at work and got a standing ovation. Then came the big day, in the boardroom, the CEO signaled the sales rep to start. The sales rep whispered confidently under his breath, "One-2-3. Overhearing him the CEO asked, "What did you say 1-2-3-for?"

***

Have you heard about the Chinese restaurant that stays open 24 hours a day? It's called, "Wok Around The Clock."

***

A man was asked the question, "You're trapped in a room with a tiger, a rattlesnake and a lawyer. You have a gun with two bullets. What should you do?" "Well, said the man, you shoot the lawyer, twice."

***

"Doctor, how many autopsies have you performed on dead people?" The doctor replied, "All my autopsies are performed on dead people."

***

During a recent hot spell in Atlanta an older man collapsed on the street. Immediately a crowd gathered and began offering suggestions. "Give the poor man a drink of whiskey, a little old lady said. "Give him some air," a man called out. "Give him some whiskey," the little old lady cried again. Several other suggestions were made and the victim suddenly sat up and hollered, "Will all of you shut up and listen to the little old lady?"

***

PROVERBS

Once the game is over, the king and the pawn go back in the same box. Italian Proverb

A good laugh and a long sleep are the two best cures.
Irish Proverb

To change and to change for the better are two different things.
German Proverb

No one is as generous as he who has nothing to give.
French Proverb

Life is half spent before one knows what it is.
French Proverb

Fall seven times and stand up eight.
Japanese Proverb

Try not. Do or do not. There is no try.
Yiddish Proverb

The drowning man is not troubled by rain.
Persian Proverb

When the pupil is ready, the teacher will appear.
Native American Proverb

One kind word can warm three winter months.
Japanese Proverb

A constant guest is never welcome.
Unknown Proverb

A woman's appetite is twice that of a man's; her sexual desire, four times; her intelligence, eight times.
Sanskirt Proverb

An ounce of mother is worth a ton of priest.
Spanish Proverb

Be happy while you're living, for you're a long time dead.
Scottish Proverb

The less things change, the more they remain the same.

***

Uncle Amos was playing poker with the boys and was having so much fun that the time slipped by. When he looked at his watch, it was 5 a.m. He hated the thought of trying to explain to his wife at that hour. He jumped up, rushed to the phone and called her. When she answered, he hollered at the top of his voice, "Sweetheart, don't pay the ransom. I've escaped and will be home in thirty minutes."

***

A duck walks into a pharmacy. "Do you have any grapes?" he quacks. "No, I'm sorry, we don't, but the grocery store two blocks down sells grapes." The pharmacist replies with a smile. The next day, the same duck walks into the same pharmacy and asks "Do you have any grapes?" "No, two blocks down on the right." The pharmacist replies somewhat annoyed. The third day, the same duck walks back into the same pharmacy and asks the same question. Annoyed, the pharmacist says, "We don't sell grapes here. You've asked for grapes now for three days in a row. This is a pharmacy not a grocery store. If you come back in here tomorrow, and ask for grapes, I'm gonna nail your little webbed feet to the floor, NOW GET OUT!" The next day the same duck walks gingerly back into the same pharmacy. He nervously asks the pharmacist, "Do you have any NAILS?" "No," replies the pharmacist. "Whew! That's a relief," says the duck, "Then, do you have any grapes?"

***

There was a Kangaroo at the bar. After a few drinks he left the bar, did two flip flops over the counter, walked up the wall, walked across the ceiling and then went out the door. The guy sitting next to him at the counter said to the bartender, "Did you see that?" "The bartender said, "Yeah, I did but you eventually get used to it, he never does leave a tip."

***

"Here on this tour we have choices on our restroom stop. Some of you may want to get coffee, and some may want to just go to the restrooms. Some may want to get coffee and go to the restrooms, and some may, oh well, you know what I mean, because at our ages basically all we do with the coffee is rent it anyway."

***

My Favorite Animal

Our teacher asked what my favorite animal was, and I said, "Fried chicken." She said I wasn't funny, but she couldn't have been right, because everyone else laughed. My parents told me to always tell the truth. I did. Fried chicken is my favorite animal. I told my dad what happened, and he said my teacher was probably a member of PETA. He said they love animals very much. I do, too. Especially chicken, pork and beef. Anyway, my teacher sent me to the principal's office.I told him what happened, and he laughed, too. Then he told me not to do it again. The next day in class my teacher asked me what my favorite live animal was. I told her it was chicken. She asked me why, so I told her it was because you could make them into fried chicken. She sent me back to the principal's office. He laughed, and told me not to do it again. I don't understand. My parents taught me to be honest, but my teacher doesn't like it when I am. Today, my teacher asked me to tell her what famous person I admired most. I told her, "Colonel Sanders." Guess where I am now...

***

There were four ladies playing cards. One went to use the restrooms. She sat down and this new-fangled stool started playing music. The first song played was Jingle Bells, the second song was George Strait's latest country western. The next song took about 15 minutes to play. The ladies went up to check on their friend and as they walked into the restroom they walked through a puddle of water. One of the ladies said to her, "What have you been doing?" She answered, "Well, this new-fangled stool that plays music ended up playing 'The Star Spangled Banner' and I stood up and put my hand over my heart, and I'm sure you'll figure out the rest of the story."

***

Two old men went to the doctor and the first one said to him, "Doc, I can't see very well, and I need to be able to see, I like to play golf, as a matter of fact my memory is really bad also." The other man said, "Doc, "I've got arthritis so bad, I can hardly move around." The doctor said, "You guys had better stick together and between the two of you you'll be able to continue to play golf." One of you can hit the ball and the other can see where it went." So they thought they would give it a try. Next day they went out to play; one of them hit the ball, and the other one saw where it went. The guy that hit the ball asked the other guy, "Did you see where it went? "Yep, I did," but I'm sorry, I can't remember where it was."

***

Farmer Jones had this old bull that he'd had for a long time. The old bull wasn't worth anything anymore because he couldn't perform his duties. Farmer Jones went to the Vet and the Vet examined him, and said, "You know, Mr. Jones, I believe we can fix him up with some of our new medicine I've got, do you want to give it a try?" Farmer Jones said, "You betcha, if you think it will work?" Farmer Jones took the bull home, put him out in the pasture with the cow, and he did really well. He had a neighbor who had a bull with a similar problem and he was telling him about the new medicine. The neighbor said, "Well, what is the new medicine?" Farmer Jones said, "I don't know what it is, but it sure taste a lot like licorice?"

***

This gentleman was on this deserted island. A beautiful 30 year old blonde appeared on shore in a wet suit. They greeted each other and she said, "How long have you been here all alone?" He replied, "Lady, I've been here, all by myself, for a 10 long years." She unzipped one sleeve of her wet suit and pulled out a cigarette and asked him how long it had been since he had smoked a cigarette." He said, with excitement in his voice, "Oh my, it's been 10 long years." She unzipped the other sleeve and asked him, "How long has it been since you've had a big Baby Ruth candy bar." He replied once again, "Gee, it's been 10 terrible years." She unzipped the top of her wet suit a bit and said, "How long has it been since you played around?" He said, with more excitement than ever, "Oh my, don't tell me you've got a set of golf clubs down there."

***

This couple went on vacation, stayed in this great motel, and was really enjoying themselves. The next day they went to the check our counter to get their bill. In addition to the regular room rate, the gentleman at the desk presented him with an additional bill for $200. "Why in the world would you hand me another bill?" said the customer. "Well, I did carry your luggage to the room for you." said the clerk. That was all on your own, I didn't ask you to do that." "It was available," said the clerk. "That's not my fault," said the customer. "We had swimming pool for you, we had a nice continental breakfast for you, and also in-room movies for you," growled the clerk. The customer once again said, "We didn't use any of those things." "Well, that's not my fault, it was available, snarled the clerk again." The customer saw that he wasn't getting anywhere so he just presented the clerk with a bill for $200. The clerk said, "What in the world is that for?" "Well," said the customer," That's for kissing and hugging my wife." The clerk said, "I didn't do that!" Once again the customer replied, "That's not my fault, she was available."

***

John said, "Boy oh boy, I got in trouble this year when I went to Wisconsin." His buddy said, "What in the world happened to you?" "Well, I got locked up." "You got locked up, what did you do?" John replied, "I guess I ate way too much cheese."

***

George went to get a physical at his doctor's office. After they had visited for a bit the doctor said, "George I need to have you fill up that little cup over there in the corner." George replied, "You mean from way over here?"

***

"Why can't life's big problems happen when we're teenagers, and know everything?"

***

John and Henry decided they wanted to get in the funeral business. They took all their tests, filled out all the proper forms, did a little advertising, and finally it came time for their first funeral. They left the funeral home and on their way to the cemetery they had to go up a steep hill. They both forgot to secure the casket to the back of the coach. About the time they got to the top of the hill the casket broke loose, popped the back door open and out it went. John stopped the vehicle and both John and Henry started chasing the casket down the hill. The casket was going faster than they were, and it for sure was getting away from them. Henry looked way down to the bottom of the hill and noticed there was a **drug store** there. He hollered as loud as he possibly could, "Hey, open the front and back door, and in the meantime see if you've got anything at all that will stop a coffin?"

***

Charlie was driving down Main Street and all of a sudden he drove by a whole bunch of people standing in single file. He drove past about 50 of them until he finally lost count. Shortly thereafter he came to a standstill, and at the end of the line there was a funeral hearse, and then a big long black limousine, with a flat tire. Curiosity got the best of Charlie, so he stopped, walked over to the limo, tapped on the front door window, the guy rolled down the glass and Charlie said to him, "What's going on here." The man answered, "My mother-in-law is in the hearse; my dog killed her." Charlie said, "I'm so sorry for your loss." The man said, "Thank you." Charlie walked away and then turned around and came back and pecked on the glass again. "Is there a chance you'd loan me that dog for a while?" said Charlie. "Sure," replied the man, but you'll have to get in line."

***

Margaret was having a hard time getting her son to go to school. "Harold said to his mom, "Nobody likes me, the teachers, the kids, the superintendent wants me to drop out, I can't get along with the bus drivers, and besides that I don't like school!" "But you have to go to school," said his concerned mother. "You are healthy, you have a lot to learn, you have something to offer others, you are a leader, and besides, you are 55 years old and you are the Principal."

***

"Treat people as if they were what they should be, and you help them become what they are capable of becoming." Johann Wolfgang Lon Goethe

***

Two truck drivers applied for a job. "I'm Pete and this is my partner, Mike. When I drive he sleeps, really works good that way. And when I sleep he drives." The boss man said, "Well, I think we can probably use the both of you. I'll give you the oral test right now. It's 3 a.m. in the morning and you are loaded with nitroglycerin, and another semi-truck comes around the curve out of control at 80 miles an hour. What would you do if you were driving?" "Well," said Pete," I'd wake up Mike because he ain't never seen a big wreck like that before."

***

An elderly couple, both were 90, went to a lawyer to get a divorce. The lawyer said to the couple, "Why did you stay together so long and then finally decide to get a divorce?" "Well," said the husband, "We stayed together for the kids and the last one finally died last week."

***

A modern day Rip Van Winkle slept for 30 years, and then all of a sudden he awoke. He called his broker, with the aid of a computer, and said, "What's the stock market done since I've been asleep?" "Well," said the broker, "Your 100 shares of AT&T is now worth 9.5 million, General Motors now worth 8 million, and your oil holdings have increased to 27 million." Rip replied, "Wow, I've done alright! I'm rich." At that point the telephone operator interrupted his conversation and said, "Your 3 minutes are up, please deposit $50,000 dollars."

***

This big tall Texan was really proud of his ranch and his pride in everything he did. One day he gathered his new recruits together and said, "Which ever one of you can swim from one side of this small lake to the other side, will get his choice of $100,000 or my daughter's hand in marriage of 10 acres of my priceless land." Then he said, "Oh, by the way, the lake is filled with alligators. They are in there to show if you have enough courage to work on my ranch." About that time this one fellow hit the water like a bullet and swam to the other side and jumped out and ran back around the lake to where everyone was standing. The owner of the ranch said, "Man, I'm really proud of your guts, you can now choose your choice of No. 1, No. 2, or No. 3." The man with the guts said, "I'm not worry about No. 1-2-or 3, I just want to know who it was that pushed me in the lake. I'll show you guts when I knock the fire out of that jerk."

***

"Even if you are on the right track you'll get run over if you just sit there."

Will Rogers

***

A lady went to her doctor with a terrible earache. The doctor started pulling out a bunch of string. "Where did this all come from?" the doctor asked. "Well," replied the lady, "why don't you read the card." A dozen roses came out. The doctor said, "Gosh, no wonder you've got an earache."

***

"The trouble with a practical joke is that very often they get elected." Will Rogers

***

"I got into a squabble with my wife a couple of weeks ago," said Joe. "I told her 'what was what' in no uncertain terms." "How is she treating you now?" asked Tom. "Well," I don't know, I haven't seen her for two weeks, but I'm finally beginning to see a little out of my left eye."

***

This big Texas cowboy said to his friend, "I'll tell you what; my ranch is so big it takes me all day to get across it in my truck; what do you think about that?" His friend, from Iowa, responded, "I had a truck like that one time."

***

The little boy said, as he was handing his report to his parents, "Look this over real good, and see if I can sue for defamation of character."

***

"Is there any chance you could spare 5^{00} to help bury a famous politician?" "On my, yes," said his friend, here's 20^{00}; go bury four of them."

***

"The true measure of a man is how he treats someone who can do him absolutely no good."
Samuel Johnson

***

This elderly lady was walking down a rather dark alleyway. She came upon a fellow that said to her, "I'm gonna take all your money, give me your pocketbook. At first she was terrified and then she remembered what her preacher had preached about on Sunday. She said to the fellow, "Don't you think you should give some thought to Acts. 2:38?" The fellow hollered back to his friend who was standing behind him about 4 or 5 yards, "Let's get out of here quick, this lady has got an ax and 2, 38's."

***

The gentleman passed away and the wife went to the funeral director to set up the funeral. The director asked the lady what songs she would like to have sung. She said, "Well," I'm pretty sure he wanted Amazing Grace, and Jingle Bells." The funeral director said to her, "Are you sure he wanted Jingle Bells?" "Yes," she replied, "I've heard him mention that several times." "Ok," said the director. The day of the funeral came; the pastor preached and the singers sang. After the service the lady went up to the pastor, and said, "I'm so sorry, I'm sure the girls who sang must have been embarrassed with one of those songs." "Why is that?" said the preacher. "Well, right in the middle of Jingle Bells, I remembered what the song should have been; it was, When they ring those golden bells."

***

There was this female cat sitting down at the end of the alley. She was just singing up a storm. She was singing, "All I Want for Christmas is some baby kittens," and then she'd sing it over and over again. Way down at the other end of the alley there was a pretty frisky old Tom cat. When he heard the female cat singing it wasn't long till he took off down the alley toward her, and he was singing, at the top of his voice, "Here comes Santa Claus, Here comes Santa Claus."

***

"Good people do not need laws to tell them to act responsibly, while bad people will find a way around the laws."

Plato

***

Brian asked Mrs. Jones how old she was. Brian's mother stepped in and said, "Brian you don't ask how old someone is, it is not nice." Brian said, "Ok, how much do you weigh?" "Brian, you don't ask how much they weigh either." Brian said, "Ok, I found out anyway by looking on her driver's license, and I found out something else too, she made an F in sex."

***

Mr. Jones decided he would look at the Smith's house; it was up for sale. He found out the address and went to their house and knocked on the door. Mrs. Smith came to the door and he told her what he wanted. He said, "Mrs. Smith, would you be able to show me through the house?" She said, "Yes," and so she took him to all the rooms downstairs, then through the basement and then upstairs. While they were looking around Mrs. Smith says, "Mr. Johnson, the only bad thing about this property is that every afternoon about 3:00 p.m. we have a freight train that goes through here and it is really close to the house; it makes quite a noise, and the house shakes pretty bad." "Well," Mr. Jones said, "It is almost 3:00 now I'll just lay here on the bed and wait so I can hear and feel how much noise and shaking it makes." "About 2:45 Mrs. Smith's husband home from early work and hollers for his wife, "Honey, where are you." She says, "I'm upstairs in the bed room." So, her husband goes up the stairs and finds this stranger lying on the bed next to Mrs. Smith. He says, to the stranger, "What in the world are you doing on the bed with my wife?" Mr. Jones answers him very sheepishly, "Would you believe me if I told you we were waiting on the train?"

***

"If at first you don't succeed, you'll get a lot of free advice from folks who didn't succeed either."

Copied

***

The sheriff of a small mountain town was also the veterinarian. Late one night the phone rang and an excited voice asked, "Is Ron there? "Yes," his wife replied, Do you want him in his capacity of a vet or the sheriff?" "Both,"came the reply. We can't get our new bulldog to open his mouth." "What's wrong with that?" said Ron's wife. "Well, there's a burglar in it."

***

Chicken Side off first...

The squeaking wheel may get the grease, or it may be the first to be replaced.

***

Life is much like a bicycle. You don't fall off unless you stop pedaling.

***

The wife says, "I'll be ready in a minute dear." The husband replies, "Take your time, I've got to shave again anyway."

***

Do you know why Benjamin Franklin accomplished so much in his life time? He didn't have to answer the phone.

***

A middle-aged couple waiting in the funeral home's foyer to make arrangements for a deceased and honored elder, were met by a red-faced funeral director. He apologized for the piped-in music. The melody, richly orchestrated, was "Stranger in Paradise." **Leonard L. Levinson**

***

"Anyone who has never made a mistake has never tried anything new."

Copied

***

The repair man came to fix the big machine. "What do I owe you?" said the house owner. "Well," that will be $249." The owner said, "You mean to tell me you're going to charge that big price was just simply tapping on the machine." "Yes, said the repair man, $1^{00} for the part, and $248, for knowing where to tap."

***

A six-year-old boy told his father he wanted to marry the little girl across the street. The father being modern and well-schooled in handling children, hid his smile behind his hand. "That's a serious step," he said. "Have you thought it out completely?" "Sure," his young son answered. "We can spend one week in my room and the next in hers. It's right across the street, so I can run home if I get lonely in the night." "How about transportation?" the father asked. "I have my wagon and we both have our tricycles," the little boy answered. The boy had an answer to every question the father raised. Finally, in exasperation, the man asked, "What about babies? When you're married, you're liable to have babies, you know." "We've thought about that, too," "the little boy replied. "We're not going to have babies. Every time she lays an egg, I'm going to step on it."

***

A man was reading the paper when an ad caught his eye: Porsche! New! $100. The man thought that it was very unusual to sell a Porsche for $100, and he thought it might be a joke or a typo. He soon decided it was worth a shot. He went to the lady's house and sure enough, she had an almost brand new Porsche. "Wow!" the man said. "Can I take it for a test drive?" Unlike what he expected, he found that the car ran perfectly and took it back to the lady's house. "Why are you selling me this great Porsche for only $100?" "My husband just ran off with his secretary, and he told me I could have the house and the furniture just as long as I sold his Porsche and sent him the money."

***

A teacher asked her students to draw a picture of their favorite Old Testament story. As she moved around the class, she saw there were many wonderful drawings being done. Then she came across Johnny who had drawn an old man driving what looked like a station wagon. In the back seat were two passengers, both apparently naked. "It's a lovely picture," said the teacher, "But which story does it tell." Johnny seemed surprised at the question. "Doesn't it say in the Bible that God drove Adam and Eve out of the Garden of Eden?"

***

Jack Summers is a constructor at a building site. One day on the site there is a massive accident and Jack has both of his ears cut off. Jack goes through a time of deep depression, but thanks to the loving care of his family, he pulls through. After a time of therapy, Jack decides that he'll prove everybody wrong who thought that he was good for nothing. Jack goes into business, and becomes very successful. He becomes so successful that he decides that he needs an assistant. Jack was always very wary of new comers because of all the trauma he went through, so he decides to interview the applicants very thoroughly. He decides he'll ask them 1 question and that will be the basis of him accepting them. There are three applicants. The first, a man, very thoroughly qualified. He goes in for the interview and Jack says: "Do you notice anything strange about me?" The man says, "Of course, you've got no ears." Jack gets angry and throws the man out. The second, a woman, even more qualified goes in. Jack asks the same question and receives the same answer. She is kicked out. Before number 3 goes in he sees numbers 1 and 2 outside. They say to him that when Jack asks him the question, whatever he says, don't say that he's got no ears. With this in mind number 3 goes into the office. Jack says; "So, have you noticed anything strange about me?' Number 3 looks up and says; "Yes, you are wearing contact lenses." "Why," says Jack. "You're very observant. How did you know that?" "Well, you couldn't wear glasses without any ears could you?"

***

"Daddy, where did I come from?" the seven-year old asked. It was a moment for which her parents had carefully prepared. They took her into the living room, got out the encyclopedia and several other books, and explained all they thought she should know about sexual attraction, affection, love, and reproductions. Then they both sat back and smiled contentedly. "Does that answer your question?" her father asked. "Not really, I already knew all that stuff," the little girl said, "Marcia said she came from Detroit. I want to know where I came from."

***

A little old lady sold pretzels on a street corner for 25 cents each. Every day a young man would leave his office building at lunch time and, as he passed her pretzel stand, he would leave her a quarter, but would never ever take a pretzel. This went on for more than five years. The two of them never spoke. One day as the man passed the old ladies pretzel stand and left his quarter as usual, the pretzel woman spoke to him, "Sir, I appreciate your business, You are a good customer, but I have to tell you that the pretzel price has increased to 35 cents."

***

As most young, weak and smart kids are, Ken was picked on

constantly by the bullies in school. They stole his lunch; they beat him up and just down right made his life miserable. It took him a couple of weeks to find a way to get back at these bullies and when he found out what would get them back, he went all out. He was on the bus where he normally gets his lunch stolen when he brought out a bottle that had, what looked like, small brown balls in it. He then, making sure no one was looking, secretly took from his pocket some milk duds and started popping them in his mouth as obvious to the rest of the kids as possible making yum yum noises. The bus bully without asking snatched the jar from Ken's hand and asked "What's in the bottle that you are making such a big deal of?" "Well, they're smart pills." "Smart pills?" The bully asked. Then he opened the jar and popped a hand full of the foreign brown balls in his mouth. "Pweeuuweppblahhh!" he reacted. "What is this stuff? It tastes like rabbit poop!" "It is," says Ken, "see, you're getting smarter already."

***

"Certain things will catch your eye, but pursue only those that capture your heart."

***

Choices

Some people sit, some people try. Some people laugh, some people cry. Some people will, some people won't, some people do, and some people don't. Some people believe, and develop a plan. Some people doubt, never think that they can. Some people face hurdles, and give it their best. Some people back down, when faced with a test.

Some people complain of their miserable lot, Some people are thankful for all that they've got. and when it's all over, when it come to an end. Some people lose out and some people win.

We all have a choice, we all have a say. We are spectators in life, or we get in and play. Whatever we choose, how we handle life's game, the choices are ours; no one else is to blame.

***

At school, a boy is told by a classmate that most adults are hiding at least one dark secret, and that this makes it very easy to blackmail them by saying. "I know the whole truth," even when you don't know anything. The boy decides to go home and try it out. As he is greeted by his mother at the front door he says, "I know the whole truth." His mother quickly hands him $20 and says, "Just don't tell your father." Quite pleased, the boy waits for his father to get home from work, and greets him with, "I know the whole truth." The father promptly hands him $40 and says, "Please don't say a word to your mother." Very pleased, the boy is on his way to school the next day, when he sees the mailman at his front door. The boy greets him by saying, "I know the whole truth." The mailman drops the mail, opens his arms and says, "Then come give your FATHER a big hug."

***

The lawyer defending a man accused of burglary tried a creative defense: "My client merely inserted his arm into the window and removed a few trifling articles. His arm is not himself, and I fail to see how you can punish the whole individual for an offense committed by his limb." "Well put," the judge replied. "Using your logic, I sentence the defendants arm to one year's imprisonment. He can accompany it or not, as he chooses." The defendant smiled. With his lawyer's assistance he detached his artificial limb, laid it on the bench, and walked out.

***

There were three guys sitting behind three Christians at a football same. The men decided to antagonize the Christians, to get them to move. So the first one says to the others loud enough for them ahead to hear, "I think I want to move to California, I hear there are only 100 Christians living there." The second guy speaks up and says, "I want to move to Washington, there are only 50 Christians living there." He third guy speaks up and says, "I want to move to Idaho, there are only 25 Christian s living there . . ." One of the Christians turns around and looks all three men in the eye and calmly says, "Why don't you all go to hell, there aren't any Christians living there."

***

A man walks out of a bar totally hammered, only to be greeted by a snobby woman. She takes one look at him and says, "You sir, are drunk!" He looks back at her and says, "And you ma'am, are ugly. But when I wake up, I will be sober, and you'll still be ugly."

***

In the true spirit of Arkansas wisdom . . . A big city California lawyer went duck hunting in rural Arkansas. He shot and dropped a bird, but it fell into a farmer's field on the other side of a fence. As the lawyer climbed over the fence, an elderly farmer drove up on his tractor and asked him what he was doing. The litigator responded, "I shot a duck and it fell in this field, and now I'm going in to retrieve it." The old farmer replied. "This is my property, and you are not coming over here." The indignant lawyer said, "I am one of the best trial attorneys in the U. S. A. and, if you don't' let me get that duck, I'll sue you and take everything you own. The old farmer smiled and said, "Apparently, you don't know how we do things in Arkansas. We settle small disagreements like this, with the Arkansas Three Kick Rule." The lawyer asked, "What is the Arkansas Three Kick Rule?" The Farmer replied, "Well, first I kick you three times and then you kick me three times, and so on, back and forth, until someone gives up." The attorney quickly thought about the proposed contest and decided that he could easily take the old coot. He agreed to abide by the local custom. The old farmer slowly climbed down from the tractor and walked up to the city feller. His first kick planted the toe of his heavy work boot into the lawyer's groin and dropped him to his knees. His second kick nearly ripped the man's nose off his face. The barrister was flat on his belly when the farmer's third kick to a kidney nearly caused him to give up. The lawyer summoned every bit of his will and managed to get to his feet and said, "Okay, you old coot now it's my turn." I LOVE THIS PART The old farmer smiled and said, "Naw, I give up, you can have the duck."

***

"WELL, JUST KICK MY BEHIND"

Katie Couric, Charlie Gibson, Brian Williams and a tough old U.S. Marine Sergeant were captured by terrorists in Iraq. The leader of the terrorists told them he'd grant each of them one last request before they were beheaded and dragged through the streets. Katie Couric said, "Well, I'm a Southerner, so I'd like one last plate of fried chicken." The leader nodded to an underling who left and returned with the chicken. Couric ate it all and said, "Now, I can die content." Charlie Gibson said, "I'm living in New York, so I'd like to hear the song. 'The Moon and Me,' one last time." "The terrorist leader nodded to another terrorist who had studied the Western world and knew the music. He returned with some rag-tag musicians and played the song. Gibson was satisfied. Brian Williams said, "I'm a reporter to the end. I want to take out my tape recorder and describe the scene here and what's about to happen. Maybe, someday someone will hear it and know that I was on the job till the end." The leader directed an aide to hand over the tape recorder and Williams dictated his comments. He then said, "Now I can die happy." The leader turned and asked, "And now, Mr. U.S. Marine, what is your final wish? "Kick me in the behind,"said the Marine. **HE DIDN'T SAY BEHIND, BUT IT WAS SOMETHING REAL CLOSE.** "What?" asked the leader, "Will you mock us in your last hour?" "No, I'm NOT kidding. I want you to kick me in the behind," insisted the Marine. So, the leader shoved him into the yard and kicked him in the behind. The Marine went sprawling, but rolled to his knees, pulled a 9 mm pistol from inside his jacket and shot the leader dead. In the resulting confusion, he emptied his sidearm on six terrorists, then with his knife he slashed the throat on one, and with an AK-47, which he took, sprayed the rest of the terrorists killing another 11. In a flash, all of them were either dead or fleeing for their lives. As the Marine was untying Couric, Gibson, and Williams, they asked him, "Why didn't you just shoot them all in the first place? Why did you ask him to kick you in the behind?" "What," replied the Marine, "And have you all report that I was the aggressor ?" **Copied**

***

WHAT GOES AROUND . . . THIS IS NOT HUMOR, BUT A PRETTY DARN GOOD STORY.

His name was Fleming, and he was a poor Scottish farmer. One day, while trying to eke out a living for his family, he heard a cry for help coming from a nearby bog. He dropped his tools and ran to the bog. There, mired to his waist in black muck, was a terrified boy, screaming and struggling to free himself. Farmer Fleming saved the lad from what could have been a slow and terrifying death. The next day, a fancy carriage pulled up to the Scotsman's sparse surroundings. An elegantly dressed nobleman stepped out and introduced himself as the father of the boy Farmer Fleming had saved. "I want to repay you," said the nobleman. "You saved my son's life." "No, I can't accept payment for what I did," the Scottish farmer replied, waving off the offer. At that moment, the farmer's own son came to the door of the family hovel. "Is that your son?" the nobleman asked. "Yes," the farmer replied proudly. "I'll make you a deal. Let me take him and give him a good education. If the lad is anything like his father, he'll grow to a man you can be proud of." And that he did. In time, Farmer Fleming's son graduated from St. Mary's Hospital Medical School in London, and went on to become known throughout the world as the noted Sir Alexander Fleming, the discoverer of Penicillin. Years afterward, the nobleman's son was stricken with pneumonia. What saved him? Penicillin. The name of the nobleman? Lord Randolph Churchill. His son's name? Sir Winston Churchill. **COPIED** SOURCE UNKNOWN

***

One fine day, a bus driver went to the bus garage, started his bus, and drove off along the route. No problems for the first few stops. A few people got on, a few got off, and things went generally well. At the next stop; however, a big hulk of a guy got on. Six feet eight, built like a wrestler, arms hanging down to the ground. He glared at the driver and said, "Big John doesn't pay!" and sat down at the back of the bus. Did I mention that the driver was five three, thin, and basically meek? Naturally, he didn't argue with Big John, but he wasn't happy about it. The next day the same thing happened. Big John got on again, made a big show of refusing to pay, and sat down, and the next day, and the one after that, and so on. This grated on the bus driver, who started losing sleep over the way Big John was taking advantage of him.

Finally, he could stand it no longer. He signed up for body building courses, karate, judo, and all that good stuff. By the end of the summer, he had become quite strong; what's more, he felt really good about himself. So, on the next Monday, when Big John once again got on the bus and said, "Big John doesn't pay!" The driver stood up, glared back at the passenger, and screamed "AND WHY NOT?" With a surprised look on his face, Big John replied, "Big John has a bus pass."

***

WEBSTER'S BEST

ADULT: A person who has stopped growing at both ends and is now growing in the middle. **BEAUTY PARLOR:** A place where women curl up and dye. **CANNIBAL:** Someone who is fed up with people. **CHICKENS:** The only animal you eat before they are born and after they are dead. **DUST:** Mud with the juice squeezed out. **EGOTIST:** Someone who is ME-deep in conversation. **GOSSIP:** A person who will never tell a lie if the truth will do more damage. **LOVE:** When a girl puts on perfume and a boy puts on shaving cologne and they go out and smell each other. **MOSQUITO:** An insect that makes you like flies better. **SECRET:** Something you tell to one person at a time. T**OOTH-ACHE:** The pain that drives you to extraction. **YAWN:** An honest opinion openly expressed.

***

A young man, wanted to get his beautiful wife something nice for their first wedding anniversary. So, he decides to buy her a cell phone. She is all excited and she loves her phone. He shows her and explains to her all the features on the phone. The next day the wife goes to get her hair done. Her phone rings and it's her husband. "Hi, hon," he says, "How do you like your new phone?" "I just love it, it's so small and your voice is clear as a bell. But there's one thing I don't understand. How did you know I was at the beauty parlor?"

***

YOUR REAL NAME A farmer had so many children, he ran out of names, so he started naming his kids after something around the farm. The first day of school began and the teacher asked each child their name. When he got to one of the farmer's sons, the boy replied, "Wagon Wheel." The teacher said, "I need your REAL name, son," to which the boy replied, "It's Wagon Wheel, sir, really." The teacher, in a huff, said, "Alright young man ; march yourself right down to the principal's office THIS minute!" The boy got out of his chair, turned to his sister and said, "Come on, Chicken Feet, he ain't gonna believe YOU neither!"

***

Uncle Leroy got a job down at the Broom Factory. On his first day the straw boss Floor supervisor calls ol' Leroy into his little office and says, "You the new man huh? What is yer name?" Leroy replied "Leroy" The straw boss says "I don't call anyone by first names. It breeds familiarity and that leads to breakdown in my authority. I refer to all employees by their last name only; now what is your last name?" Leroy sort of smiles and says, "Darling" Its Leroy Darling?" The Straw Boss said, "Now Leroy the next thing . . . "

***

A goober was terribly overweight, so her doctor put her on a diet. "I want you to eat regularly for two days, then skip a day, and repeat this procedure for two weeks. The next time I see you, you'll have lost at least five pounds." When the goober returned, she had lost nearly 20 lbs. "Why, that's amazing!" the doctor said. "Did you follow my instructions?" The goober nodded, "I'll tell you, though, I thought I was going to drop dead that third day." "From hunger, you mean?" asked the doctor. "No, from all that skipping."

***

The guys at the barber shop asked me what actress I would like to be stuck in an elevator with. I told them the one who knows how to fix elevators. I'm old, tired, don't feel good, and besides that I need to go to the bathroom a lot.

***

The teacher wrote on the blackboard. "I ain't had no fun this summer at all." Then she asked a youngster in her class. "Susan, what would you suggest that I do to correct that statement?" Susan studied the sentence for a moment and replied, "I'd get another boyfriend."

***

"John, did you say you knew a perfect person?" After a long pause a meek looking fellow in the back of the room said, "Yep, it's my wife's first husband."

***

(Fourth baby's name was Henry. From Page 115.)

"Lord, keep your arm around my shoulder and your hand over my mouth. Amen."

Texas Prayer

***

The Texas Rancher

The Texas Department of Employment, Division of Labor Standards claimed a small rancher was not paying proper wages to his help and sent an agent out to investigate him.

texasbeyondhistory.net

GOVERNMENT AGENT: I need a list of your employees and how much you pay them.

RANCHER: Well, there's my hired hand who's been with me for 3 years. I pay him $200 a week plus free room and board. Then there's the mentally challenged guy. He works about 18 hours every day and does about 90% of all the work around here. He makes about $10 per week, pays his own room and board, and I buy him a bottle of bourbon every Saturday night so he can cope with life. He also sleeps with my wife occasionally.

GOVERNMENT AGENT: That's the guy I want to talk to - the mentally challenged one.

RANCHER: ...That would be me....

Gotta love those Texans...!

***

"I used to eat a lot of natural foods until I learned that most people die of natural causes."

NOT A FUNNY STORY, BUT REALLY A GOOD ONE

A store owner was tacking a sign above his door that read "Puppies For Sale," Signs like that have a way of attracting small children, and sure enough, a little boy appeared under the store owner's sign. "How much are you going to sell the puppies for?" he asked. The store owner replied, "Anywhere from $30 to $50." The little boy reached in his pocket and pulled out some change. "I have $2.37." he said, Can I please look at them?" The store owner smiled and whistled and out of the kennel came Lady, who ran down the aisle of his store, followed by five teeny tiny balls of fur. One puppy was lagging considerably behind. Immediately the little boy singled out the lagging limping puppy and said, "What's wrong with that little dog?" The store owner explained that the veterinarian had examined the little puppy and had discovered it didn't have a hip socket. It would always be limp. It would always be lame. The little boy became excited. "That's the little puppy that I want to buy." The store owner said "No, you don't want to buy that little dog. If you really want him, I'll just give him to you." The little boy got quite upset. He looked straight into the store owner's eyes, pointing his finger and said, "I don't want you to give him to me. That little dog is worth every bit as much as all the other dogs and I'll pay full price. In fact I'll give you $2.37 now, and 50 cents a month until I have him paid for. The store owner countered. "You really don't want to buy this little dog. He is never going to be able to jump and play with you like the other puppies." To this, the little boy reached down and rolled up his pant leg to reveal a badly twisted, crippled left leg supported by a big metal brace. He looked up at the store owner and softly replied. "Well, I don't run so well myself, and the little puppy will need some help at times, and someone who understands!" **Dan Clark**

***

Baked Beans

Once upon a time there lived a woman who had a maddening passion for baked beans. She loved them but unfortunately they had always had a very embarrassing and somewhat lively reaction to her. Then one day she met the man of her dreams, and fell in love. When it became apparent that they would marry she thought to herself, "He is such a sweet and gentle man, he would never go for this carrying on." So she made the supreme sacrifice and gave up beans. Some months later her car broke down on the way home from work. Since she lived in the country she called her husband and told him that she would be late. On her way home she passed a small diner and the odor of the baked beans was more than she could stand. Since she still had a couple or so miles to walk, she figured that she would walk off any ill effects by the time she reached home. So she stopped at the diner and before she knew it, she had consumed three large orders of baked beans. All the way home she putt-putted & putt-putted. Upon arriving home she felt reasonably sure she could control it. Her husband seemed excited to see her and exclaimed delightedly, "Darling, I have a surprise for dinner tonight." He then blindfolded her and led her to her chair at the table. She seated herself and just as he was about to remove the blindfold from his wife, the telephone rang. He made her promise not to touch the blindfold until he returned. He then went to answer the phone. The baked beans she had consumed were still affecting her and the pressure was becoming almost unbearable, so while her husband was out of the room she seized the opportunity, shifted her weight to one leg and let it go. It was not only loud, but it smelled like a fertilizer truck running over a skunk in front of a pulpwood mill. She took her napkin and fanned the air around her vigorously. Then, she shifted to the other cheek and ripped three more, which reminded her of cooked cabbage. Keeping her ears tuned to the conversation in the other room, she went on like this for another ten minutes. When the phone farewells signaled the end of her freedom, she fanned the air a few more times with her napkin, placed it on her lap and folded her hands upon it, smiling contentedly to herself. She was the picture of innocence when her husband returned, apologizing for taking so long, he asked her if she peeked, and she assured him that she had not At this point, he removed the blindfold, and she was really surprised! There were twelve dinner guests seated around the table to wish her a **"Happy Birthday! ! !"**

***

NOT A JOKE, BUT SOMETHING GOOD

Richard & Neta Ruth Sunderwirth

Suppose one morning you never wake up, do all your friends know you love them? I was thinking . . . I could die today, tomorrow or next week, and I wondered if I had any wounds needing to be healed, friendships that needed rekindling or three words needing to be said. Sometimes, "I love you," can heal & bless. Let every one of your friends know you love them. Even if you think they don't love you back, you would be amazed at what those three little words and a smile can do. Just in case I die tomorrow **. . . I LOVE YA !**

***

NOT A JOKE, BUT SOMETHING ELSE, TO MAKE YOU THINK

READ TO THE END

Near to the door, he paused to stand, as he took his class ring off her hand. All who were watching did not speak, as a silent tear ran down his cheek. And through his mind the memories ran, of the moments they walked, and ran in the sand. But now her eyes were so terribly cold, for he would never again have her to hold. They watched in silence, as he bent near, and whispered the words . . . "I love you," in her ear. He touched her face and started to cry, as he put on his ring and wanted to die. And just then the wind began to blow, as they lowered her casket into the snow. This is what happens to friends alive, when friends let friends drink and drive. Don't forget this powerful poem!

***

TRUTH LEARNED AS PARENTS

There is no such a thing as child proofing your house. A 4-year old's voice is louder than 200 adults in a crowded restaurant. Baseballs make marks on ceilings. When you hear the toilet flush and the words "uh-oh," it's already too late. A magnifying glass can start a fire even on an overcast day. Legos will pass through the digestive tract of a 4-year old. Play-Doh and microwave ovens should never be used in the same sentence. Tarzan can teach them many things that we don't want them to know. Garbage bags do not make good parachutes. Neither do umbrellas! Marbles in gas tanks make a lot of noise when driving. Always look in the oven before you turn it on. The spin cycle in the washing machine does not make earthworms dizzy. A good sense of humor will get you through most of the problems... Unfortunately, in retrospect.

***

REALLY BAD HEADLINES

March Planned For Next August – Blind Bishop Appointed To See – Lingerie Shipment Hijacked, Thief Gives Police The Slip – Latin Course To Be Cancelled , No Interest Among Students, Et Al. – Diaper Market Bottoms Out – Stadium Air Conditioning Fails, Fans Protest – Queen Mary Having Bottom Scraped – Henshaw offers Rare Opportunity to Goose Hunters.

***

A little boy went to the store with his grandmother and on the way home he was looking at the things she had purchased. He found a package of panty hose and began to shout out the words "Queen Size, Queen Size." He then turned to his grandmother and exclaimed, "Look Grandma, you wear the same size as our bed!"

***

COMFORT

It was one of the worst days of my life. The washing machine broke down, the telephone kept ringing, my head ached, and the mail carrier brought a bill I had no money to pay. Almost to the breaking point, I lifted my one-year-old into his high chair, and leaned my head against the tray, and began to cry. Without a word, my little son took his pacifier out of his mouth and stuck it in mine.

***

BASEBALL BASICS

At one point during a game, the coach said to one of his young players. "Do you understand what cooperation is? What a team is?" The little boy nodded in the affirmative. "Do you understand that what matters is whether we win together as a team?" The little boy nodded yes, "So," the coach continued, "When a strike is called, or you're out at first, you don't argue, curse or attack the umpire. Do you understand all that?" Again the little boy nodded yes. "Good," said the coach. "Now, please go over there and explain it to your mother."

***

The new employee stood before the paper shredder looking confused. "Need some help?" a secretary asked. "Yes," he replied. "How does this thing work?" "Simple," she said, taking the boss's important report from his hand and feeding it into the shredder. "Thanks, but where do the copies come out?"

***

A fourth-grade teacher was giving her pupils a lesson in logic. "Here is the situation." She said. "A man is standing up in a boat in the middle of a river, fishing. He loses his balance, falls in, and begins splashing and yelling for help. His wife hears the commotion, knows he can't swim, and runs down to the bank. Why do you think she ran to the bank?" A little girl raised her hand and said, "To draw out all his money."

***

OLD DOC CARVER

Old Dr. Carver still made house calls. One afternoon he was called to the Tuttle house. Mrs. Tuttle was in terrible pain. The doctor came out of the bedroom a minute after he'd gone in and asked Mr. Tuttle, "Do you have a hammer?" A puzzled Mr. Tuttle went to the garage, and returned with a hammer. The doctor thanked him and went back into the bedroom. A moment later, he came out and asked, "Do you have a chisel?" Mr. Tuttle complied with the request. In the next ten minutes, Dr. Carver asked for and received a pair of pliers, a screwdriver, and a hacksaw. The last request got to Mr. Tuttle. He asked, "What are you doing to my wife?" "Not a thing," replied old Doc Carver. "I can't get my instrument bag open."

***

- **WORLD'S BIGGEST LIES**
- The check is in the mail. * I'll respect you in the morning. I'm from your government, and I am here to help you. * It's only a cold sore. * You get this one, I'll pay next time. * My wife doesn't understand me. * Trust me I'll take care of everything. * Of course, I love you. * I am getting a divorce. * Drinking? Why no, Officer * I never inhaled. * It's not the money, it's the principle of the thing. * I never watch television except for PBS. * . . . but we can

still be good friends. * She means nothing to me. * Don't worry, I can go another 20 miles when the gauge is on "Empty." * I gave at the office. * Don't worry, he's never bitten anyone before. * I'll call you later. * We'll release the upgrade by the end of the year. * Read my lips; no new taxes. * I've never done anything like this before. * Now, I'm going to tell you the truth. * It's supposed to make that noise. * I "love" your new ______. * . . . then take a left. You can't miss it. * Yes, I did. * Don't worry, it's OK, I'm sterile.

***

As a new bride, Aunt Edna moved into the small home on her husband's ranch near Snowflake. She put a shoe box on a shelf in her closet and asked her husband never to touch it. For 50 years Uncle Jack left the box alone, until Aunt Edna was old and dying. One day when he was putting their affairs in order, he found the box again and thought it might hold something important. Opening it, he found two doilies and $82,500 in cash. He took the box to her and asked about the contents. "My mother gave me that box the day we married," she explained. "She told me to make a doily to help ease my frustrations every time I got mad at you." Uncle Jack was very touched that in 50 years she'd only been mad at him twice. "What's the $82,500 for?" "Oh, well that's the money I've made selling the doilies."

***

One day a man drove his secretary home after she fell quite ill at work. Although this was an innocent gesture, he decided not to mention it to his wife, who tended to get jealous easily. Later, that night the man and his wife were driving to a restaurant. Suddenly he looked down and spotted a high-heel shoe half hidden under the passenger seat. Not wanting to be conspicuous, he waited until his wife was looking out her window before he scooped up the shoe and tossed it out of the car. With a sign of relief, he pulled into the restaurant parking lot. That's when he noticed his wife squirming around in her seat. "Honey," she asked, "Have you seen my other shoe?"

***

CHICKEN FREEDOM

A man was having trouble getting his neighbor to keep his chickens fenced in. The neighbor kept talking about chickens being great creatures, and as such they had the right to go where they wanted. The man was having no luck keeping the chickens out of his flowerbeds, and he had tried everything. Two weeks later, on a visit a friend noticed his flowerbeds were doing great. The flowers were beginning to bloom. So the friend asked him how he managed to keep the birds away. "How did you make your neighbor keep his hens in his own yard?" "One night I hid half a dozen eggs under a bush by the flower bed, and the next day I let my neighbor see me gather them. I wasn't bothered after that."

***

I'm a counselor who helps coordinate support groups for visually-impaired adults. Many participants have a condition known as macular degeneration, which makes it difficult for them to distinguish facial features. I had just been assigned to a new group and was introducing myself. Knowing that many in the group would not be able to see me well, I jokingly said, "For those of you who can't see me, I've been told that I look like a cross between Paul Newman and Robert Redford." Immediately, one woman called out, "We're not THAT BLIND!"

***

As the family gathered for a big dinner together, the youngest son announced that he had just signed up at an army recruiter's office. There were audible gasps around the table, then some laughter, as his older brothers shared their disbelief that he could handle this new situation. "Oh, come on, quit joking," snickered one. "You didn't really do that, did you?" "You would never get through basic training," scoffed another. The new recruit looked to his mother for help, but she was just gazing at him. When she finally spoke, she simply asked, "Do you really plan to make your own bed every morning?"

***

THE VENTRILOQUIST

A young ventriloquist is touring the Southwest and stops to entertain in an Arkansas bar. He's going through his usual stupid redneck jokes, when a big burly guy in the audience stands up and says threateningly, "I've heard just about enough of your smart mouth hillbilly jokes; we ain't all stupid here in Arkansas!" Flustered, the ventriloquist begins to apologize, when the big guy interrupts him and says, "You stay out of this mister, I'm talking to the smart mouth little sawed off fella on your knee!"

***

Ever notice how a 4 year olds voice is louder than 200 adult voices? Several years ago, I returned home from a trip just when a storm hit, with crashing thunder and severe lightning. As I came into my bedroom about 2 a.m., I found my two children in bed with my wife, Karey, apparently scared by the loud storm. I resigned myself to sleep in the guest bedroom that night. The next day, I talked to the children, and explained that it was OK to sleep with Mom when the storm was bad, but when I was expected home, please don't sleep with Mom that night. They said OK. After my next trip several weeks later, Karey and the children picked me up in the terminal at the appointed time. Since the plane was late, everyone had come into the terminal to wait for my plane's arrival, along with hundreds of other folks waiting for their arriving passengers. As I entered the waiting area, my son saw me, and came running shouting "Hi Dad! I've got some good news!" As I waved back, I said loudly, "What's the good news?" "Nobody slept with Mommy while you were away this time!" Alex shouted. The airport became very quiet; everyone in the waiting area looked at Alex, then turned to me, and then searched the rest of the area to see if they could figure out exactly who his Mom was.

***

An acquaintance of mine who is a physician told this story about her then 4 yr. old daughter. On the way to preschool, the doctor had left her stethoscope on the car seat, and her little girl picked it up and began playing with it. "Be still, my heart," thought my friend, "My daughter wants to follow in my footsteps!" Then the child spoke into the instrument: "Welcome to McDonald's, May I take your order?"

***

A little girl asked her mother, "Can I go outside and play with the boys?" Her mother replied, "No, you can't play with the boys, they're too rough." The little girl thought about it for a few moments and asked, "If I can find a smooth one, can I play with him?"

***

Mary said, "I'm going to be a flight attendant. It's a good way to meet men." "There are a lot of jobs where you can meet men," replied Sandra. "That may be so, but they wouldn't be strapped in their seats."

***

A man called his mother in Florida. "Mom, how are you?" "Not too good," said the mother. "I've been very weak." The son said, "Why are you so weak?" She said, "Because I haven't eaten in 38 days." The man said, "That's terrible. Why haven't you eaten in 38 days?" The mother answers, "Because I didn't want my mouth to be filled with food if you should happen to call."

***

A lady was picking through the frozen turkeys at the grocery store, but couldn't find one big enough for her family. She asked a stock boy. "Do these turkeys get any bigger?" The stock boy replied, "No ma'am, they're dead."

***

What did the monkey say when his sister had a baby? "Well, I'll be a monkey's uncle."

***

"Most people would sooner die than think . . . in fact they do." **Bertrand Russell**

***

A lot of folks can trace their ancestors back hundreds of years, but can't tell where their kids were last night.

***

If you lend someone $^{\$}10^{00}$ and never see that person again, it's probably worth it.

***

The husband thought that he might have a car problem with his left blinker light, so he asked his wife to check. She got out of the car and he asked her if it was working. With a mischievous grin, she replied, "Yep, nope, yep, nope, yep, nope"

***

You're really getting old when your grandchild asks, what century were you born in?

***

With his request approved, the Fox News photographer quickly used a cell phone to call the local airport to charter a flight. He was told a twin engine plane would be waiting for him at the airport. Arriving at the airfield, he spotted a plane warming up outside the hangar. He jumped in with his bag, slammed the door shut, and shouted, "Let's go." The pilot taxied out, swung the plane into the wind and took off. Once in the air, the photographer instructed the pilot, "Fly over the valley and make low passes so, I can take pictures of the fires on the hillsides."
"Why?" asked the pilot. "Because I'm a photographer for Fox Cable News," he responded. "And I need to get some close up shots." The pilot was strangely silent for a moment, finally he stammered, "So what you're telling me is; you're NOT my flight instructor.
Copied

***

REMEMBER WHEN

- I want to go back to the time when . . . * Decisions were made by going "eeeny,meeny, miney, mo." * Mistakes were corrected by simply exclaiming, "do over!" * "Race issue," meant arguing about who ran the fastest. * Money issues were handled by whoever was the banker in "Monopoly." * Catching the fireflies could happily occupy an entire evening. * It wasn't odd to have two or three "best" friends. * Being old, referred to anyone over 20. * "Be careful, Mom's about to have a double, duck, fit." * The net on a tennis court was the perfect height to play volleyball and rules didn't matter. * The worst thing you could catch from the opposite sex was cooties. * It was magic when dad would "remove" his thumb. * It was unbelievable that dodge-ball wasn't an Olympic event. * Having a weapon in school, meant being caught with a slingshot. * Nobody was prettier than Mom. * Scrapes and bruises were kissed and made better. * It was a big deal to finally be tall enough to ride the "big people" rides at the amusement park. * Getting a foot of snow was dreams come true. * Abilities were discovered because of a "double-dog-dare." * Saturday morning cartoons weren't 30-minute ads for action figures. * No shopping trip was complete, unless a new toy was brought home. * "Oly-oly-oxen-free" made perfect sense. * Spinning around, getting dizzy and falling down was cause for giggles. * The worst embarrassment was being picked last for a team. * War was a card game. * Water balloons were the ultimate weapon. * Baseball cards in the spokes transformed any bike into a motorcycle. * Taking drugs meant orange-flavored chewable aspirin. * Ice Cream was considered a basic food group. * Older siblings were the worst tormentors, but also the fiercest protectors. * **If you can remember most or all of these, then you have LIVED!!!**

***

An old man and woman were married for many years. Whenever there was a confrontation, yelling could be heard deep into the night. The old man would shout, "When I die, I will dig my way up and out of the grave and come back and haunt you for the rest of your life!" Neighbors feared him. The old man liked the fact that he was feared. To everyone's relief, he died of a heart attack when he was 98. His wife had a closed casket at the funeral. After the burial, her neighbors, concerned for her safety, asked "Aren't you afraid that he may indeed be able to dig his way out of the grave and haunt you for the rest of your life?" The wife said, "Let him dig. I had him buried upside down, and I know he won't ask for directions."

***

BEAUTY COSMETICS

Todd's wife bought a new line of expensive cosmetics guaranteed to make her look years younger. After a lengthy sitting before the mirror applying the "miracle" products, she asked, "Darling, honestly, what age would you say I am?" Looking over her carefully, Todd replied, "Judging from your skin, twenty; your hair, eighteen; and your figure, twenty five." "Oh, you flatterer!" she gushed. "Hey, wait a minute!" Todd interrupted. "I haven't added them up yet."

***

• **GOVERNMENT VERBOSITY** Pythagorean theorem: 24 words. * The Lord's Prayer: 66 words. * Archimedes' Principle: 67 words. * The 10 Commandments: 179 words: * The Gettysburg Address: 286 words: * The Declaration of Independence: 1,300 words: * U.S. Government regulations on the sale of cabbage; 26,911 words: . . . and that says it all.

***

• **THIS ALSO, SAYS IT ALL** For the wife who says it's hot dogs tonight, because she is home with me, not with someone else. * For the teenager who is complaining about doing dishes, because that means she is at home & not on the streets. * For the taxes that I pay, because it means that I am employed. * For the mess to clean after a party, because it means that I have been surrounded by friends. * For the clothes that fit a little too snug, because it means I have enough to eat. * For my shadow that watches me work, because it means I am out in the sunshine. * For a lawn that needs mowing, windows that need cleaning, and gutters that need fixing, because it means I have a home. * For all the complaining I hear about the Government, because it means that we have freedom of speech. * For the parking spot I find at the far end of the parking lot, because it means I am capable of walking and that I have been blessed with transportation. * For my huge heating bill, because it means I am warm. * For the lady behind me in Church that sings off key, because it means that I can hear. * For the pile of laundry and ironing, because it means I have clothes to wear. * For weariness and aching muscles at the end of the day, because it means I have been capable of working hard. * For the alarm that goes off in the early morning hours, because it means that I am alive. * Finally . . . for too much E-mail, because it means I have friends who are thinking of me.

***

Mrs. Hopple, one of our tour members, was wearing a dress that was really too tight. She tried two different times to get up on the bus. Finally she reached around and unzipped her skirt in the back. That didn't quite do it so she unzipped it again a bit. Mr.

Florence was getting tired of waiting on her, so he just put his hands under her hips and calmly and gently helped her up on the bus. She turned around a slapped him pretty hard and said, "What makes you think you had a right to do that to me," Mrs. Hopple said. "Well," replied Mr. Florence, "I thought maybe I had the right to do it, after all; you unzipped my fly 3 times."

***

A circus owner runs an ad for a lion tamer and two people show up. One is a good-looking, older retired golfer in his late sixties and the other is a gorgeous blond in her mid-twenties. The circus owner tells them, "I'm not going to sugar coat it. This is one ferocious lion. He ate my last tamer so you two had better be good or you're history. Here's your equipment . . . chair, whip and a gun. Who wants to try out first?" The girl says, "I'll go first." She walks past the chair, the whip and the gun and steps right into the lion's cage. The lion starts to snarl and pant and begins to charge her. About halfway there, she throws open her coat revealing her beautiful scanty dressed body. The lion stops dead in his tracks, sheepishly crawls up to her and starts licking her feet and ankles. He continues to lick and kiss her entire body for several minutes and then rests his head at her feet. The circus owner's jaw is on the floor. He says, "I've never seen a display like that in my life." He then turns to the retired golfer and asks, "Can you top that?" The old golfer replies, "Yep, no problem, just get that lion out of there."

***

THERE WAS LIFE BEFORE THE COMPUTER

An application was for employment, A program was a TV show, A cursor used profanity, A keyboard was a piano. Memory was something that you lost with age, A CD was a bank account! And if you had a broken disk, It would hurt when you found out! Compress was something you did to garbage, Not something you did to a file, And if you unzipped anything in public, You'd be in jail for a while! Log on was adding wood to a fire, Hard drive was a long trip on the road, A mouse pad was where a mouse lived, And a backup happened to your commode! Cut – you did with a pocket knife, Paste – you did with glue, A web was a spider's home, And a virus was the flu!

I guess I'll stick to my pad and paper, and the memory in my head, I hear nobody's been killed in a computer crash, But when it happens they wish they were dead!

***

HOW SPECS LIVE FOREVER

When I was in my younger days, I weighed a few pounds less. I needn't hold my tummy in, to wear a belted dress. But now that I am older, I've set my body free; there's comfort of elastic, where once my waist would be. Inventor of those high-heeled shoes, my feet have not forgiven; I have to wear a nine now, but used to wear a seven. And how about those pantyhose, they're sized by weight, you see, so, how come when I put them on, the crotch is at my knees?

I need to wear these glasses, as the prints were getting smaller; and it wasn't very long on the inside, I'm the same old me, Just the outside's changed a bit.

***

THERAPY IS GOOD

My therapist told me the way to achieve true inner peace is to finish what I start. So far today, I have finished 2 bags of chips a piece of chocolate cake and 2 Snicker candy bars . . . I'm feeling better already.

***

Each evening bird lover Tom stood in his backyard, hooting like an owl, and one night, an owl finally called back to him. For a year, the man and his feathered friend hooted back and forth. He even kept a log of the "conversation." Just as he thought he was on the verge of a breakthrough in interspecies communication, his wife had a chat with her next door neighbor. "My husband spends his nights . . . calling out to owls," she said. "That's odd," the neighbor replied. "So does my husband."

***

HAVE A NICE NIGHT!

A fellow bought a new Mercedes and was out on the interstate for a nice evening drive. The top was down, the breeze was blowing through his hair and he decided to open her up. As the needle jumped up to 80 miles per hour he suddenly saw a flashing red and blue light behind him. "There ain't no way they can catch a Mercedes," he thought to himself and he opened her up further. The needle hit 90, 100, 110 and finally 120 with the lights still behind him. "What in the world am I doing?" he thought to himself and pulled over. The cop came up to him, took his license without a word and examined it and the car. "I've had a tough shift and this is my last pull over. I don't feel like more paperwork, so if you can give me an excuse for your driving that I haven't heard before you can go!" "Well," replied the man, "Last week my wife ran off with a cop, and I was scared to death, you were trying to catch me to bring her back!" "Have a nice night," said the officer.

***

A Minnesota couple decided to vacation in Florida during the winter. They planned to stay at the very same hotel where they spent their honeymoon 20 years earlier. Because of hectic schedules, it was difficult to coordinate their travel schedules. So, the husband left Minnesota and flew to Florida on Thursday. His wife would fly down the following day. The husband checked into the hotel. There was a computer in his room, so he decided to send an e-mail to his wife. However, he accidentally left out one letter in her e-mail address, and without realizing his error, he sent the e-mail. Well, it didn't go to the right place. Meanwhile, somewhere in Houston, a widow had just returned home from her husband's funeral. He was a minister of many years who was called home to glory following a sudden heart attack. The widow decided to check her e-mail, expecting messages from relatives and friends. After reading the first message, she fainted. The widow's son rushed into the room, found his mother on the floor, and saw the computer screen which read: "To: My Loving Wife; Subject: I've Arrived . . . Date: 16 May 2003 . . . I know you're surprised to hear from me. They have computers here now and you are allowed to send e-mails to your loved ones. I've just arrived and have been checked in. I see that everything has been prepared for your arrival tomorrow. Looking forward to seeing you then! Hope your journey is not as uneventful as mine was. P.S. Sure is hot down here!"

***

THREE-LEGGED CHICKENS

A man was driving along a rural road one day when he saw a three legged chicken. He was amused enough to drive a long side it for a while; as he was driving he noticed the chicken was running 30 mph. Pretty fast chicken, he thought. I wonder just how fast it can run. So he sped up and the chicken did too! They were now moving along the road at 45 mph! The man in the car sped up again, to his surprise the chicken was still running ahead of him at 60 mph!!! Suddenly the chicken turned off the road and ran down a long driveway leading to a farmhouse. The man followed the chicken to the house and saw a man in the yard and dozens of three legged chickens. The man in the car called out to the farmer "How did you get all these three legged chickens?" The farmer replied, "I breed 'em; Ya see it's me, my wife and my son living here and we all like to eat the chicken legs. Since a chicken only has two legs, I started breeding this three legged variety so we could all eat our favorite piece." "That's amazing!" said the driver. "How do they taste?" "Don't' rightly know, we ain't ever been able to catch one yet."

***

Once we had a real skinny guy take one of our Fall Foliage cruises. He made the remark to me, "You know, the way I got it figured if I eat 8 meals a day and then snack in between I can pay for the entire cruise with what I save on food at home."

***

"The beauty of the second amendment is that it will not be needed until they try to take it away."

President Thomas Jefferson

***

The 5th grade student was going through the dessert line at school and when he tried to take 4 or 5 cookies the teacher said,

"Johnny, only take one please, thank you." Well, when he got to the end of the line she was down there. He hollered back to his friend, "Hey Jimmy, take all the cookies you want, Mrs. Brown is watching the apples."

***

The traffic cop, with his notebook in hand, stopped a speeding motorist. "Name please," he said. The motorist said "Aloysius Sylvester Archambault." The cop put his book away and said, "Well, don't let me catch you speeding again."

***

A little boy was in a spelling bee. The teacher said, "Ok Timmy, please spell Mississippi for me. He said to the teacher, "Do you want the state or the river?"

***

Sam went in to the drug store and asked the clerk. "Can you fix me a big shot of castor oil so it wouldn't taste so terrible?" The druggist said he could and he asked Sam. "Would you like to have an ice cream soda while you wait?" Sam said, "Sure, don't mind if I do." In a little while the druggist came back and said to Sam, "Would that be all for you today?" Sam replied, "Yep, I'm just waiting on the castor oil." "You have already drunk you castor oil," said the druggist. "0h jumping grasshoppers, I wanted that for my brother Charlie."

***

An eagle was sitting on a tree resting, doing nothing. A small rabbit saw the eagle and asked him "Can I also sit like you and do nothing?" The eagle answered, "Sure, why not." So the Rabbit sat on the ground below the eagle and rested. All of a sudden a fox appeared, jumped on the rabbit and ate it. The moral of this story to be sitting and doing nothing, you must be sitting, somewhere very high up.

***

Little Johnny's father said, "Let me see your report card." Johnny replied, "I don't have it." "Why not," asked his father. Johnny said, "My friend Billy borrowed it. He wants to scare his parents."

***

Jimmy and Sarah were going to be new parents. They were both very excited. Jimmy asked Sarah if it would be alright for him to be the hospital delivery room with her when their little one was born. She told him, well, of course; that would be wonderful. Well, the time came for the baby to be born. Sarah went into labor; and Jimmy was standing there right by her side along with the nurse and the doctor. Jimmy asked the doctor if there was anything he could help with and the doctor said, "Not unless the lights would happen to go out, then you could hold a light for us." As luck would have it, sure enough the lights did go out. The nurse handed a flashlight to Jimmy and he was so proud to have something to do. All of a sudden the doctor said to Jimmy, "Here is a little one, oh, my, and here is another one, and here is another one." Then it got really dark in the delivery room. The doctor said to Jimmy, "Jimmy, where is the light? Where did you go?" All was quiet for a few moments and then from way back on the other side of the room little Jimmy said, "I'm over here in the corner Doc. I was afraid the light was attractin' them . . . so I thought I'd better get the heck out of the way."

***

"Have you ever tasted Rattlesnake?" asked Jimmy, "No," replied Johnny, "Well, just so you will know, it tastes a lot like Copperhead." "What does Copperhead tastes like? "Well, Johnny," "It tastes just like Alligator," replied Jimmy. "What does Alligator tastes like? "Johnny, it all tastes an awful lot like chicken," snorted Jimmy. Johnny said, "If all of it takes like chicken, I wonder why my folks spend so much money on all that those weird snake dinners and stuff?"

***

A young mother with three extremely active young boys was playing "cops and robbers" with them one afternoon in the backyard when a neighbor stopped by to borrow a cup of sugar. One little boy aimed his pistol at his mother and yelled "Bang! You're dead." She slumped to the ground in a heap. When she didn't get up right away, the neighbor hurried over to see if she had been hurt in the fall. As the neighbor bent over, the overworked mother opened one eye and whispered, "Shhh. Don't give me away. It's the only chance I get to rest."

***

"My husband is so self-centered and he's even really selfish," said Martha. "What do you mean?" replied Maxine. "Give me an example." "Well," said Martha, "He won two trips to Hawaii, and he took both of them."

***

The Commanding officer called all of his troops together out in front of their barracks. He said, "Gentlemen, I know it has been rough on all of you having to be out in the swamps for several days without changing underwear. I realize it had been extremely hot and steamy and I also know that we are going out on a similar mission in the morning. So, today we are going to get to change underwear." Everyone cheered, because they were all miserable in their present circumstances. The officer said, "John you change with Jim; Henry you change with Tom; George you change with Claude, and so it went."

***

There I was, sitting at the bar staring at my drink when a large, trouble-making biker steps up next to me, grabs my drink and gulps it down in one swig. "Well, whatcha' gonna do about it?" he says menacingly, as I burst into tears. "Come on, man," the biker says, "I didn't think you'd CRY. I can't stand to see a man crying." "This is the worst day of my life," I said. "I'm a complete failure. I was late to a meeting and my boss fired me. When I went to the parking lot, I found my car had been stolen and I don't have any insurance. I left my wallet in the cab that I took home, there I found my wife with another man and then my dog bit me." "So, I came to this bar to work up the courage to put an end to it all, I buy a drink, I drop a capsule in and sit there watching the poison dissolve, Then you show up and drink the whole thing! But enough about me, how's your day?

***

A helicopter carrying passengers suddenly loses engine power and the aircraft begins to descend. The pilot performs an emergency landing in the water, and tells the passengers to remain seated and to keep the doors closed, stating that in emergency situations, the aircraft is designed to stay afloat for 30 minutes, giving rescuers time to get to them. Just then a man gets out of his seat and runs over to open the door. The pilot screams at him, "Didn't you hear what I said?" The aircraft is designed to stay afloat as long as the doors remain closed?" "Of course I heard you," the man replied, "But it's also designed to fly, and look how well that one worked out for us!"

***

"Socialism is a philosophy of failure,
the creed of ignorance,
and the gospel of envy.
Its inherent virtue is the equal sharing of misery."
Winston Churchill

***

The husband went into the bedroom with a glass of water and two aspirins and handed them to his wife. She said, "Well, what did you bring me those for, I don't have a headache. I'm not sick." Her husband said, "Ah Ha, I got you."

***

There was a lady sitting at the ball game with an empty seat beside her. There weren't any other vacant seats. Someone asked her about it and she said, "Oh, it belonged to my husband, he died." "Well, I'd think one of your relatives or a friend would have wanted to use it." She said, "Oh they all insisted on going to the funeral."

***

President Clinton stopped in Arkansas to get gas. Hillary ran up and hugged some friend of hers. Bill said to Hillary, "Look where you'd have been if you'd married your friend, instead of me." Hillary said, "I was kinda wondering where you'd be, because if I'd married this friend he'd be the President."

***

We got a new chicken recipe, it's called Chicken Catchatori. "Well," said the friend, "We've got a new diet recipe, it is called Chicken Napoleon . There is not much meat on it because we just use the boney parts."

***

Henry went into the drug store to get some perfume for his wife's birthday. "It's gonna be a surprise," Henry said. "Yeah," said the clerk, "It's gonna be a surprise alright, she thinks she's gettin' a new car."

***

Does it hurt much?

A woman goes to the doctor who verifies that she is pregnant. This is her first pregnancy. The doctor asks her if she has any questions. She replies, "Well, I'm a little worried about the pain. How much will childbirth hurt?" The doctor answered, "Well, that varies from woman to woman and pregnancy to pregnancy and besides, it's difficult to describe pain." "I know, but can't you give me some idea?" she asks. The doctor says, "Grab your upper lip and pull it out a little." "Like this?" "A little more" "Rike diss?" "No, a little more . . . " "ike iss?" "Yes, does that hurt?" asks the doctor. "A wittle bit." "Well, now stretch it over your head."

***

A wife asked her husband "What do you like most? My pretty face, my sexy body or my personality?" Her husband looked at her from head to toe and replied, "I like your sense of humor."

***

You may be from Missouri . . . if . . .

1. you've ever used your ironing board for a buffet table.
2. your neighbors think you're a detective because a cop always brings you home.
3. your Grandmother has "Ammo" on her Christmas list.
4. your house doesn't have curtains but your truck does.
5. you have a complete set of salad bowls and they all say "Cool Whip" on the side.
6. your working TV sits on top of your non-working TV.
7. you've been involved in a custody fight over a hunting dog.
8. you have the local taxidermist on speed dial.
9. you come back from the dump with more than you took.
10. the biggest city you've ever been to is Wal-Mart.
11. a tornado hits your neighborhood and does $100,000 worth

of improvement.

***

Actual instruction labels

1. On a Bag of Fritos: You could be a winner. No purchase necessary. Details inside.
2. On a Bar of Dial Soap: Directions: Use like regular soap.
3. On A Hotel. Provided Shower Cap: Fits one head.
4. On a Frozen Dinner: Serving Suggestion: Defrost.
5. On Marks & Spencer Bread Pudding: Product will be hot after heating.
6. On Packaging for Rowenta Iron: Do not iron clothes on body.
7. On Boots Children's Cough Medicine: Do not drive car or operate machinery.
8. On Nytol a sleep aid: Warning: May Cause Drowsiness.
9. On a Japanese Food Processor: Not to be used for the other use.

***

Facts and other useless stuff

I went to a bookstore and asked the saleswoman, "Where's the self-help section?" She said, "If I tell you, it would defeat the purpose."

"If police arrest a mime, do they tell him he has the right to remain silent?"

On a T-shirt: I work hard because millions of folks on welfare depend on me.

Happiness is good health and a bad memory.

Poor planning on your part does not constitute an emergency on my part.

A robber broke into the police station and stole all the toilet seats and the police didn't have anything to go on.

Knowledge is not power until you apply the knowledge to yourself.

Nothing in the known universe travels faster than a bad check.

An actual comment left on a Forest Service comment card. "A small deer came into my camp and stole my bag of pickles. Is there any way I can get reimbursed? Please call."

How many men does it take to change a roll of toilet paper? We don't know, it's never happened.

The only two animals that can see behind itself without turning it's head are the rabbit and the parrot.

All of us could take a lesson from the weather. It pays no attention to criticism.

The early bird may get the worm, but the second mouse gets the cheese.
A used car is not always what it's jacked up to be.

***

One day some guys were doing a "Boxers or briefs" survey. They went to a 25 year old man and asked "Boxers or briefs?" He said briefs. They went to a 40 year old man and asked "Boxers or briefs?" He said "Boxers." They went to a 80 year old man and asked "Boxers or briefs?" And the old man replied "Depends."

***

Freddie noticed while leafing through an old photo album that his Grandmother was about 6 inches taller than his Grandfather. "Grandma, said Freddie," How in the world could you have fallen in love with a man 6 inches shorter than you?" "Well, Freddie, by the time we stood up it was too late."

***

Max stopped in front of the courthouse and just happened to notice that one of his friends, because of the wind, was having a bit of trouble trying to keep her hat on. She was holding it with both hands and her dress was flying everywhere, even above her head. Max said, "Mable, I don't mean to be nosey but, you are holding on to your hat and your dress is way up over your head. Don't' you think you should worry about that instead of your hat? "Naw", she said, "What you're looking at is 85 years old and my hat is brand new."

***

"Did you know that the greatest surprise on Christmas morning is: BATTERIES NOT INCLUDED!"

***

Here's one of the most frequent letters we got when we were operating at full speed, in the tour company. I don't think anyone gave it any thought after they wrote it and before they sent it. We always had to call them and let them know we got it.

"If you don't receive this letter with my check in it, please let me know and I'll send you another one."

***

I'VE BEEN TEACHING NOW FOR ABOUT FIFTEEN YEARS. I have two kids myself, but the best birth story I know is the one I saw in my own second grade classroom a few years back. When I was a kid, I loved show-and-tell. So I always have a few sessions with my students. It helps them get over shyness and usually, show-and-tell is pretty tame. Kids bring in pet turtles, model airplanes, pictures of fish they catch, stuff like that. And I never, ever place any boundaries or limitations on them. If they want to lug it in to school and talk about it, they're welcome. Well, one day this little girl, Erica, a very bright, very outgoing kid, takes her turn and waddles up to the front of the class with a pillow stuffed under her sweater. She holds up a snapshot of an infant. "This is Luke, my baby brother, and I'm going to tell you about his birthday." "First, Mom and Dad made him as a symbol of their love, and then Dad put a seed in my Mom's stomach, and Luke grew in there. He ate for nine months through an umbrella cord." She's standing there with her hands on the pillow, and I'm trying not to laugh and wishing I had my camcorder with me. The kids are watching her in amazement. "Then, about two Saturdays ago, my Mom starts going. 'Oh, oh, oh, oh! Erica puts a hand behind her back and groans. 'She walked around the house for, like an hour, 'Oh, oh, oh!' Now this kid is doing a hysterical duck walk and groaning. 'My Dad called the middle wife. She delivers babies, but she doesn't have a sign on the car like the Domino's man. They got my Mom to lie down in bed like this.' Then Erica lies down with her back against the wall. 'And then, pop! My Mom had this bag of water she kept in there in case he got thirsty, and it just blew up and spilled all over the bed, like psshhheewa!' This kid has her legs spread with her little hands miming water flowing away. It was too much! 'Then the middle wife starts saying 'push, push,' and 'breathe, breathe.' 'They started counting, but never even got past ten. Then all of a sudden, my little brother just plum fell out. He was covered in yucky stuff that they all said was from Mom's play-center, so there must be a lot of toys inside there. When he got out, the middle wife spanked him for crawling up there in the first place.' Then Erica stood up, took a big theatrical bow and returned to her seat. I'm sure I applauded the loudest. Ever since then, when it's Show-and-tell day, I bring my camcorder, just in case another 'Middle Wife' comes along. Now then, you have two choices . . . laugh and throw this away, or let someone read it from your book also, and then live every day as if it is your LAST chance to make someone happy!

***

A football coach walked into the locker room before a game, looked over to his star player and said, "I'm not supposed to let you play since you failed math, but we need you in there. So, what I have to do is ask you a math question, and if you get it right, you can play." The player agreed, and the coach looked into his eyes intently and asks, "Okay, now concentrate hard and tell me the answer to this. What is two plus two?" The player thought for a moment and then he answered. "4?" "Did you say 4?" the coach exclaimed, excited that he got it right. At that, all the other players on the team began screaming, "Come on coach; give him another chance!"

***

Sally was having some problems; not medical but mental. She went to a recommended Physiologist and told him she had to confide in someone. She said, "Doc, I've been seeing another doctor, well, to be truthful, I'm seeing another physiologist, 2 plumbers, and a bartender."

***

Margie, decided to surprise her husband, so she painted the back side of the house. She would have painted the front side next, but she wanted to keep it a secret for a while. When she finished, she cleaned her brushes, with a new powerful cleaner, and put her brushes away, and then dumped the paint can, full of solution, in the outside john. A little while before she started painting her husband, Ralph, went to the field to work. About 4:00 p.m. Ralph decided he had worked enough that day so he came to the house and rather than going inside to use the toilet he decided to use the outdoor one. Don't get ahead of the story now. He sat there for a while, enjoyed the peace and quiet, and then he finished and tossed his cigarette butte in the hole. The whole toilet, with him inside, blew up with a terrible explosion. He said to himself, "Self, it must have been something I had for breakfast, I've been telling Margie for several days to lay off that powerful pepper she puts on my eggs." Just so you'll know, Ralph wasn't hurt too bad but he didn't let Margie use that pepper any more.

***

Four fellow friends went hunting. After hunting for a while they decided it was time to go to bed and get an earlier start next morning. They went to their cabin and realized there were only 3 beds. Charlie lost the bed bid so he had to sleep with John. That didn't work because John snored too much, so he had to try and sleep with Sam. That didn't work either, so he had to try and sleep with Ben. He decided he had to get some sleep so just before he jumped in bed with Ben, he reached over and gave him a great big kiss and said, "Hi there sweetie pie." And you know what, he really got a good night's sleep, because poor old Ben sat on the side of the bed and didn't even consider trying to go to sleep with Charlie.

***

My old Granddaddy was accused of being involved with another woman. He told his wife, "Honey, I'll bring a picture, of the one you think I was with, and you'll know why I wasn't being unfaithful." Now, way back in those days they didn't make mirrors as yet; however, since old Granddaddy got around more that his wife he had seen one in a bar somewhere. His wife didn't even know a mirror existed. So, in a few days, he brought a mirror home with him and told his wife to look at her picture. She said, "Sugar Baby, I'm so sorry I accused you of being with another woman. I know you couldn't have had anything to do with a woman this ugly."

***

There was an Indian boy, who was so good with electrical gadgets, his reservation decided to put aside some money and send him to college. He was so grateful for his education that he decided to do something special for the reservation. He got a large moose head which had belonged to the tribe for some time. He attached it to a gate and wired it with brightly colored lights. After having done this he became known around the world, as the first person to wire a head for a reservation.

***

This old man, 85 years of age, was called down to the hospital. They said, "Congratulations Henry, you and your wife, have a bouncing 9-pound baby boy." Nine months later came a bouncing 8-pound baby girl; then one year later came another one. Henry said, "I'm so happy that my motor is still running." "Well," said the doctor, "You'd better check your spark plugs and change your oil, this one is black."

***

This very elderly lady went to her lawyer to visit about what she needed to do, moneywise, concerning her husband, who had just passed away. The lawyer said, "Mrs. Jones, your husband provided $100,000 for you when he died. He said in his will that you could give him a real nice funeral, I mean, a real nice funeral. You could spend $90,000 on his funeral and $10,000 to help around the house, etc." She said to the lawyer, "I'll get back with you this afternoon, after I consider his provision." About 2:00 p.m. the lawyer got the call, Mrs. Jones said, "I've decided what I want to do with the money. We'll spend $10,000 for the funeral, and I'll fancy up the house with the $90,000. Then when my death comes around I'll just let the state bury me."

***

Old Mr. Murphy went to the same movie, over and over and over again. One day one of his old buddies said to him, "Mr. Murphy, why in the world do you watch the same movie, over and over and over again? You've been doing that for a long time." "Well," he said, "In this particular movie there is a 30 year old blonde standing smak-dab in the front doorway of her home. The only thing she has on is a fabulous bathrobe. "Every day, there's a train that passes directly in front of her, just as that robe falls to the ground. One of these days that train is going to be late, and I want to be there as it goes by."

***

Mr. and Mrs. Perkins bought them a brand new car. One beautiful fall day Mrs. Perkins decided to take the new car on a drive. She picked up one of her lady friends and as they were going down the road, on a curve, she went a little too far over the center line to the left. Well, you know the rest of the story. The wrecker came and took her car to the garage and she had her friend take her home. That evening when her husband came home from work, she said, "Honey Bear, I've got some good news and I've got some bad news." "Well, what's the deal here," her husband said. She replied, "The good news is that the air-bags work." She fixed Mr. Perkins a really good dinner before she gave him the bad news.

***

There were two rather nutty fellows standing just outside of the County Nut House talking. Chuck said to Sam, "I am Napoleon Bonaparte!" Sam said, "Who told you that you were Napoleon Bona-what-ever? Chuck said, "Well, sir, God did!" Sam replied, with a little smirk in his voice, "I DID NOT!"

***

Down at the county jail they keep about 30 prisoners. The same old stories are told over and over again. The stories are told so much the fellows, to save time, have all of the stories numbered. The old man and the bat, for instance is No. 1, The old lady and the skunk, No. 2, and so on. One day, just recently, a brand new prisoner was brought in. After a few days and after hearing his buddies call off the stories by number, he shouted out, "No. 13" No one laughed or said a word. The new guy got a bit irritated and said, "What's the matter with number 13? I thought it was funny." One of the inmates replied. "Well, son, some people can tell'um and some people can't."

***

This particular family really liked to play golf. Minnie and Martin were sitting out on the porch one night and Minnie, out of the blue, asked her husband, "Martin, would you marry me again." He said, without thinking, "No, Rosie is left-handed." I think I left something out of this story. Maybe you can fill in what I left out.

***

This young college fellow just couldn't see to get along with girls. He just simply couldn't say the right things, at the right time. One of his buddies said to him. When you're dining, maybe you can get in the habit of saying nice things to them, when you ask them to pass something just say, "Mary, sugar, . . . would you please pass me the salt?" Jennifer, honey, would you please pass me the pepper?" He thought about it and it built up his confidence, so the next time he was out with a girl, he said, "Hey bag, would you pass me the tea."

***

A woman was waiting at the front door, ready to go shopping, with her arms full of coats. Her four little children stood by her side. Her husband, coming through the front door, asked why she was just standing there. "This time you put on the children's coats, she said, handing them to him, "and I'll go outside and honk the 'darn' car horn."

***

Boy, oh boy, the world is sure changing. I went to Blockbusters last night and rented a movie. Before the movie started it said on the screen, "This movie is formatted to fit your screen." Now, my question is this, "How in the world did they know how big my screen was?"

***

A Child's View of Retirement

After Christmas break, a teacher asked her young pupils how they spent their holidays. One small boy wrote the following; "We always used to spend Christmas with Grandpa and Grandma. They used to live here in a big brick house, but Grandpa got retarded and they moved to Florida. Now they live in a place with a lot of other retarded people. They all live in little tin boxes. They ride on three-wheeled tricycles and they all wear name tags because they don't know who they are. They go to a big building called a wrecked hall, but if it was wrecked, they got if fixed because it is alright now. They play games and do exercises there, but they don't do them very good. There is a swimming pool there. They go in it and just stand there with their hats on. I guess they don't know how to swim. As you go into their park, there is a doll house with a little man sitting in it. He watches all day so they can't get out without him seeing them. When they can sneak out, they go to the beach and pick up shells that they think are dollars. My Grandma used to bake cookies and stuff, but I guess she forgot how. Nobody cooks, they just eat out. They eat the same thing every night-early birds. Some of the people are so retarded they don't know how to cook at all, so my Grandma and Grandpa bring food into the wrecked hall and they call it "Pot Luck". My Grandma says Grandpa worked all his life and earned his retardment. I wish they would move back up here, but I guess the little man in the doll house won't let them out!"

***

This fellow took his car to the garage and told them to fix it. He said, "There is a big bumping noise every time I turn left or right. It goes kaboom . . . kaboom . . .etc. Well, the mechanics said they would do their best to find out what it was. The fellow left it there until the next morning and he went in to pick it up . . . if it was fixed. "Yep, we took care of it," they said." The fellow said, "What was wrong with it?" The mechanic kinda laughed and said, "Well, somebody had left a bowling ball in the trunk and every time you went to the right it would roll right, and every time you went left, it would roll back to the left. Is that enough said? NO CHARGE!"

***

I guess you know that my wife and I take a two week vacation every year. We both really look forward to it. My wife goes in May and I go in November.

***

One morning I woke up and my waterbed had burst. Then all of a sudden I realize I didn't have a waterbed . . . Nuff said.

***

You know folks, I have friends in low places.

***

I bought a brand new book the other day. The name of it is "Everything a man knows about women." It was 2 pages long.

***

How many men does it take to change a roll of toilet paper?
My wife says, "No one knows, none of them have ever done it."

***

I've got a really good joke for all the mind readers in this in this crowd . . . . Pause . . . "Did you get it?"

***

A businessman who had recently taken up golf and was devotedly pursuing his new hobby, came home and told his wife he finally had a winning day. "Did you break 100?" she asked. "No." he admitted, "but I found more golf balls than I lost."

***

Do you know how to start a rich man's parade? Roll a quarter down the street.

***

"My cousin thinks he's a chicken, said Bob."
"Well, did you tell him he was wrong?"
"Nope, because we need the eggs," replied Bob.

***

"We really have a lot to be grateful for," said Marvin. "Yes, we do," replied Jim. "Yeah, said Marvin, and it is really a blessed day when we get out of bed, and nothing new hurts."

***

"I went to a swimming class the other day," said Sally. Did you enjoy it? replied Linda. "Well, it wasn't bad at all, but I was a little upset when they told me to 'wear something loose,' if I had something loose, I wouldn't need to come to class in the first place."

***

Not too long ago, I got lost going to Bennett Springs. I stopped and asked a guy, "How do you get to Bennett Springs? The guy said, "Weeellll, most of the time my cousin takes me."

Carl Hurley

***

SOMEONE HAS WRITTEN THESE BEAUTIFUL WORDS. DO READ AND TRY TO UNDERSTAND THE DEEP MEANING OF IT. THEY ARE LIKE THE TEN COMMANDMENTS TO FOLLOW IN LIFE ALL THE TIME.

1. Prayer is not a "spare wheel" that you pull out when in trouble, but it is a "steering wheel" that directs the right path throughout.
2. So why is a car's windshield so large and the rear view mirror so small? Because our past is not as important as our future. So, look ahead and move on.
3. Friendship is like a book. It takes few seconds to burn, but it takes years to write.
4. All things in life are temporary. If it's going well, enjoy it, that won't last long. If it's going badly, don't worry, that won't last long either.
5. Old friends are gold! New friends are diamond! If you get a diamond, don't forget the gold! Because to hold a diamond, you always need a base of gold!
6. Often when we lose hope and think this is the end, God smiles from above and says, "Relax, sweetheart, it's just a bend, not the end!"
7. When God solves your problems, you have faith in His abilities; when God doesn't solve your problems, He has faith in your abilities.

8. A blind person asked St. Anthony, "Can there be anything worse than losing eye sight?" He replied, "Yes, losing your vision!"
9. When you pray for others, God listens to you and blessed them; sometimes, when you are safe and happy, remember that someone has prayed for you.
10. Worrying does not take away tomorrow's troubles, it takes away today's peace.

Copied

***

How do they keep Teflon stuck to the pan? How do they get that gooey stuff inside of twinkies?

***

Vanna White was really sick, so sick she almost died. She had an obstruction; she couldn't move her vowels.

***

This one particular young lady entered the wet T-shirt contest. Her breasts were two sizes. One large and one small, she did alright though; she came in first and third.

***

"My girlfriend and I split up over Religion," said Johnny. "She worshipped money and I didn't have any."

***

This guy took all of his worries to bed with him. The doctor suggested he take a waste basket and put it beside the bed. The doctor said, "When you come up with a worry just mentally throw it in the waste basket and get rid of it." Well, he tried that and he said it almost worked, but just about the time he was ready to doze off to sleep, he had to get up and empty the basket.

***

This woman went to the Physiologist and she said, "What am I going to do? What am I going to do?" "My husband thinks he's a refrigerator." What am I going to do?" "That's not too serious," said the doctor. "Oh, yes it is," says the lady, "He sleeps with his mouth open and the light keeps me awake all night."

***

A woman walked up to a little elderly man rocking in a chair his porch. "I couldn't help noticing how happy you look," she said. "What's your secret for a long happy life?" "Well, honey, I smoke three packs of cigarettes a day," he said. "I also drink a case of whiskey a week. I eat fatty foods, and never exercise." "That's amazing, "the woman said, "How old are you?" "Twenty-six," he said.

***

Mr. Salesman took his vacation this year and went to Hawaii. His wife got pregnant. When he got back home he was talking with some of his associates and he said, "I'll tell you one thing for sure, the next time I go on vacation I'm going to take her with me."

***

Did you hear about Olive?" the other reindeer. You might have to sing the song, to get the point.

***

My wife said, "Honey, we're going to build our next house, for sure, out of the same kind of wood that we used in our fireplace this year." Her husband said, "Why is that dear?" "You know dummy, that way no matter what, it wouldn't burn down."

***

Just our luck; my wife sent out our Christmas cards this year. Guess what, the first one we got back was from someone we forgot to send one to.

***

I hate the idea of going under the knife. So I was very upset when the doctor told me I needed a tonsillectomy. Later, the nurse and I were filling out an admission form. I tried to respond to the questions, but I was so nervous I couldn't speak. The nurse put down the form, took my hands in hers and said, "Don't worry. This medical problem can easily be fixed, and it's not a dangerous procedure." "You're right. I'm being silly," I said, "Please continue." "Good. Now," the nurse went on, "Do you have a living will?" [illegible]hat poor guy fell off his chair and out into the hallway. This was [illegible]t a good day for this guy.

***

"Seek out every opportunity for laughter that you can, for laughter is one of those things, like music and flowers, that God has given us to relieve the tensions that we undergo in life." Preston Bradley

***

A woman in my office, recently divorced after years of marriage, signed up for a refresher CPR course. "Is it hard to learn?" someone wanted to know. "Not at all," my co-worker replied. "Basically you're asked to breathe life into a dummy. I don't expect to have any problems. I did that for 32 years.

***

Desperate for a child, a couple asked their priest to pray for them. "I'm going on sabbatical to Rome," he replied. "I'll light a candle in St. Peter's for you." When the priest returned three years later he found the wife pregnant, tending two sets of twins. Elated, the priest asked to speak to her husband and congratulate him. "He's gone to Rome," came the harried reply. "To blow out that candle."

***

YES, THE PERFECT WIFE

An extraordinarily handsome man decided he had the responsibility to marry an extraordinarily beautiful woman so they could produce beautiful children beyond comparison. With that as his mission, he started his search. Soon, he met a farmer with three absolutely stunning daughters. He told the farmer of his mission and the farmer gave him permission to date his three daughters. After dating the eldest, the farmer asked for the man's opinion. He said, "She's just a weeeee bit, not that you can tell though, pigeon-toed." The farmer nodded and suggested the man date the middle daughter. After the date, the farmer asked for the man's opinion. He said, "She's just a weeeee bit, not that you can tell though, cross-eyed." The farmer nodded and suggested he date the youngster. The next morning, the man rushed to the famer, exclaiming, "She's perfect; she's the one I want to marry." So they were married. Months later, a baby was born. When the man visited the nursery, he was horrified to see their baby was nothing short of ugly. He rushed to the father-in-law, asking how such a thing could happen considering the beauty of the parents. "Well," explained the farmer. "I think you got in a little bit of a hurry in making your decision." "She was just a weeeee bit, not that you could tell though, pregnant when you met her."

***

This fellow said that he wanted a 'do it yourself' tax form. This form was very simple. It only had one question and one statement. The question was: "How much did you make." The statement was: "Send it in."

***

A man went to the hospital and had a very serious operation. Since the intensive care unit was full, they brought him back to his room. When he awakened, his doctor was sitting by his bed and all the shades were pulled down. He asked the doctor as to why the shades were pulled. His doctor replied, "I didn't want you to wake up and feel that the operation was a failure. There's a really big fire across the street."

***

Yes, God created Adam and Eve. After Eve was created God told Adam to give Eve a hug. Adam said, "What's a hug? God told him. He said to give her a kiss. Adam said, "What's a kiss? God told him, "Now, go out and populate the world." A few seconds later Adam came back and said. "God, what's a headache?"

***

This guy went out to fish. He cut a hole in the ice. This loud voice said, "There's no fish under the ice." and again, "There's no fish under the ice." and again. Finally the guy said, "Is that you God?" "No, I'm the manager of the ice skating rink."

***

John's wife asked her husband for a Jaguar, she asked him again and again. Then she said, "Honey, I sure would like to have a Jaguar." She kept insisting. Finally her husband got her one . . . and it ate her. Be careful what you ask for.

***

Richard & Neta Ruth Sunderwirth

This lady's parakeet died. The lady was just simply devastated. She was so sad, and just couldn't bring herself out of depression. A neighbor said, "Come on, I'll take you to the new musical down on Broadway. Maybe you can forget your problem and you'll get cheered up." Guess what was playing? Bye Bye Birdie.

***

A friend went to Florida and approached a fruit stand that advertised in large letters. **ALL THE ORANGE YOU CAN DRINK FOR $^{\$}1^{50}$.** It sounded like a good deal, so he parked his car, placed his $^{\$}1^{50}$ on the counter, enjoyed a freshly-squeezed glass of orange juice, and then eagerly awaited for a refill. "No refill," said the man behind the counter. "I don't understand, said the customer, Your sign says, All the orange juice you can drink for $^{\$}1^{50}$." "That's right," said the clerk, "And that's all you can drink for $^{\$}1^{50}$."

***

Mrs. Broomhandle, the teacher, said she was going to give all the kids off from school, if they could answer certain questions correctly. The first question, "Who was the first President?" said the teacher. "George Washington," "That's correct, you get Monday off," Second question; "Who said, Give me Liberty or give me death." Patrick Henry, "That's correct, you get Monday off." A little girl said, "No way, I'm Japanese and our culture tells us we cannot take off from learning, so even though I got the question correctly, I'll be here for school on Monday." The 3rd question, "Who was the 3rd President?" "Thomas Jefferson," said a little boy. "That's correct, you get off from school on Monday." The little boy said, "No, I'm Japanese also and I cannot take off either." From the back of the room a little boy hollered, with a little disgust in his voice, "Darn those Japanese," The teacher said, "Who said that." Little Johnny answered, "President Truman, April 14th, 1945, I'll see you on Tuesday," and out the door he went.

***

My husband, said the lady, is a big-time sports fan. Just recently he was watching a football game with our grandchildren. He had just turned 75 and was feeling a little wistful. "You know," he said to our grandson, Nick, "It's not easy getting old. I guess I'm in the fourth quarter now." "Don't worry, Grandpa," Nick said cheerily. "Maybe you'll go into overtime."

***

The racehorse owner asked his jockey why he hadn't ridden through the hole that had opened up on the final turn. "Well, sir, replied the jockey wearily, "Did you ever try to go through a hole that was going faster than you or your horse?"

***

The bookkeeper told his boss that he would have to have a raise. He concluded his request by noting that three companies were really after him. "What three companies are after you?" asked the boss. "Well," said the bookkeeper, it is the telephone, light, and water companies," was the reply.

***

Two guys were arguing about who was the best bear hunter. So they decided to go up into the woods, get a cabin, and prove to each other which one was the best. Well, that night one of the fellows decided to go outside for a little walk and all of a sudden he came upon a huge grizzly bear who started chasing him and continued right on his tail. Finally they came to the cabin; the guy opened the door and quickly got behind it. Just as he came in he hollered to his buddy, "Here's my bear, you skin him and I'll go out and get another one."

***

Mrs. Peterson said to her husband, "Clark, if I've told you once I've told you a hundred times, we've got company coming to see us Saturday evening, and you need to take a bath." Clark replied, "Look it is only Thursday and I have plenty of time. You know that I usually only take a bath on Saturday." Mary Lu said, "Clark you'll fool around and we'll all have to take a bath on the same evening." "Yeah, you're probably right, said Clark, but what if they don't come?"

***

"Why are you laughing so hard Harold?" asked the wife. "Well, I'm telling myself a joke." replied Harold. "Yeah, why are you laughing so loud and hard?" asked his wife. "Well," he said, "I guess it's because this is the first time I've heard it."

***

MARY POPS IN!

One stormy day, Mary Poppins was walking down a dirt road. She became very tired from walking, and decided to rest at a nearby motel. As she walked inside, she put her umbrella on the umbrella rack, then asked the clerk behind the counter for a room. "Hello, I would like a room just for tonight." Mary Poppins said to the clerk. "Well, you're just in luck because we have one room left," he replied. Mary Poppins looked very pleased. After the man handed her the keys to the room he then added, "By the way, would you like room service to bring you something to eat?" "Why, certainly, "Mary Poppins answered, "I'd like some cauliflower, Swiss cheese, and eggs, thank you very much." "Okay, we'll send the order right up." He said. So Mary Poppins went up to her room, and as the man said, room service brought her cauliflower, eggs, and Swiss cheese. The next day, as Mary Poppins was checking out of the motel, the man asked her how she enjoyed her meal. "Well," she started, "The cauliflower was good, and so was the cheese, but the eggs weren't very tasty." "Please feel free to write your comments down and put them in our suggestion box for the owners to see," the man said in response. So, Mary Poppins wrote down her suggestion and put it in the box. She grabbed her umbrella, then off she went. The clerk was very curious about her comments. So he walked over to the suggestion box to read what she had written. He read: Supercauliflowercheesebuteggswere quiteatrociuos. Mary Poppins.
Copied

***

BUBBA AND BILLY BOB

Bubba and Billy Bob, who are from Arkansas, travel to Kansas to visit a relative. They are driving in their pickup when they see a sign on a store which reads, "Suits $^{\$}5^{00}$ each, Shirts $^{\$}2^{00}$ each, Trousers $^{\$}2^{50}$ per pair." Bubba says to Billy Bob, "Lookie here! We could get a gob of these, take'em back to Arkansas, sell them to our friends and make a fortune. Now, when we go in there, you be quiet, okay? Just let me do the talkin', cause if they hear your accent they might think we are ignorant and not wanna sell that stuff to us." They go in and Bubba says, "I'll take 50 of them suits at $^{\$}5^{00}$ each, 100 of them shirts at $^{\$}2^{00}$ each, and 50 pair of them trousers at $^{\$}2^{50}$ each. I'll back my pickup up and . . . " The owner of the shop interrupts, "You are from Arkansas,

aren't you?" "Well, yeah," says a surprised Bubba, "How could you tell that?" The owner says, "Because this is a drycleaners."
From Bonnie

***

THIS ONE IS NOT A JOKE! TEN TOP REASONS TO GO TO THE EMERGENCY ROOM Thanks to Golden Valley Memorial Hospital Healthcare, Clinton, Missouri www.gvmh.org

1. Loss of consciousness.
2. Signs of heart attack that last more than 3 minutes. These include: pressure, fullness, squeezing, or pain in the center of your chest; tightness, burning or aching under the breastbone; chest pain with lightheadedness.
3. Signs of a stroke, including; sudden weakness or numbness of the face, arm or leg on one side of the body; sudden dimness or loss of vision, particularly in one eye; loss of speech or trouble understanding speech or talking; sudden severe headaches without cause; unexplained dizziness, unsteadiness or sudden falls, especially when accompanied by any of these other symptoms.
4. Severe shortness of breath.
5. Bleeding that does not stop after 10 minutes of direct pressure.
6. Poisoning after calling poison control.
7. Unexplained stupor, drowsiness or disorientation.
8. Coughing or vomiting up blood.
9. Severe persistent vomiting.
10. Suicidal or homicidal feelings or thoughts.

Knowing an emergency from a non-emergency, can save you time and money.

***

There were two country representatives who came to visit the USA and they were accompanied on a tour of the country by one of the USA Senators.

There was a representative from Israel, one from India, and a USA Senator. They started out across the countryside when, after about 4 hours of traveling, their car broke down. They stopped by a farm house where the farmer told them no problem. They could stay with him all night until the next day when they could get their car repaired. He told them; however, that he only had two extra single beds available, but one of them could sleep on a nice cot in the barn. So, the gentleman from Israel volunteered and went to the barn. In a few minutes there was a knock on the door; there stood the Jewish fellow who said he didn't want to cause a problem, but there was no way he could sleep in a barn with a pig. The gentleman from India volunteered to go to the barn. In a few more minutes there was another knock on the door; there stood the fellow from India. He said he didn't want to cause a problem, but there was no way he could sleep in a barn with a cow, because that was their sacred animal. So then the Senator from Washington, D.C. volunteered to go to the barn. In a few minutes there was another knock on the door. There stood the cow and the pig. **End of story**

***

When you take a shower
and your knees don't get wet,
it might be time
to consider going on a diet?

***

Did you know that a Rooster says, Cock a Doodle Doo, and an ole Hen says, any Old Dude will do?

***

"Now, doctor, isn't it true,
when a person dies in his sleep, he doesn't know
about it until the next morning?"

Grin and Groan

***

Chicken Side off first...

1. Everyone has a photographic memory. Some don't have film.
2. Save the whales. Collect the whole set.
3. A day without sunshine is like, well, night.
4. Change is inevitable, except from a vending machine.
5. I just got lost in thought. It was unfamiliar territory.
6. When the chips are down, the buffalo is empty.
7. See it all, done it all, can't remember most of it.
8. I feel like I'm diagonally parked in a parallel universe.
9. Those who live by the sword get shot by those who don't.
10. He's not dead, he's electroencephalographically challenged.
11. He's always late. His ancestors arrived on the June Flower.
12. You have the right to remain silent. Anything you say will be misquoted, then used against you.
13. I wonder how much deeper the ocean would be without sponges.
14. Honk if you love peace and quiet.
15. Pardon my driving. I am reloading.
16. Despite the cost of living, have you noticed how it remains so popular?
17. Nothing is foolproof to a sufficiently talented fool.
18. Atheism is a non-prophet organization.
19. He who laughs last, thinks slowest.
20. If all the world is a stage, where is the audience sitting?

***

"Doctor, before you performed the autopsy, did you check for a pulse?" "No." "Did you check for blood pressure?" "No." "Did you check for breathing?" "No." "How can you be so sure, Doctor?" "Because his brain was sitting on my desk in a jar." "But could the patient have still been alive nevertheless?" "It is possible . . . that he could have been alive and practicing law somewhere."

***

The side effects of Viagra

An elderly woman goes to the doctor and asks his help to revive her husband's sex drive. "What about trying Viagra?" asks the doctor. "Not a chance" says Mrs. Murphy. "He won't even take an aspirin for a headache." "No problem," replies the doctor. "Drop it into his coffee, he won't even taste it. Try it and come back in a week or so, to let me know how everything went." A week later Mrs. Murphy returns to the doctor and he inquires as to how her love life has been since the little pill. "Oh it was terrible, just terrible doctor." "What happened?" asks the doctor. "Well, I did as you advised and slipped it in his coffee. The effect was immediate. He jumped straight up, swept the cutlery off the table, at the same time ripping my clothes off and then proceeded to make passionate love to me on the tabletop. It was terrible." "What was terrible?" said the doctor, "Was the sex not good?" "Oh no doctor, the sex was wonderful, the best in 25 years, but we'll never be able to show our faces in McDonald's again."

***

Henry was running through the city park one day and met his doctor. The doctor said, "Henry what are you doing? You're going to kill yourself." Henry replied, "No, I'm doing exactly what you said to do, by the way, meet my new 30 year old bride." The doctor said, "Hello, now let's get back to my instructions to you." Henry stopped the doctor and said, Doc, you told me to get a hot mama and be cheerful." "No, I didn't, said the doctor, "I said you have a heart murmur, be careful!"

***

HOME REMEDIES

1. If you are choking on an ice cube, don't panic. Simply pour a cup of boiling water down your throat and presto! The blockage will be almost instantly removed.
2. Clumsy? Avoid cutting yourself while slicing vegetables by getting someone else to hold them while you chop away.
3. Avoid arguments with the missus about lifting the toilet seat by simply using the sink instead.
4. High Blood pressure sufferers; simply cut yourself and bleed for a while, thus reducing the pressure in your veins.
5. A mouse trap, placed on top of your alarm clock will prevent you from rolling over and going back to sleep when you hit the snooze button.
6. If you have a bad cough, take a large dose of laxatives, then you will surely be afraid to cough.

Have a bad toothache? Hit your thumb with a hammer, then you will forget about your toothache.

***

"Attitude is extremely important, because it determines altitude!"

***

Little Johnny asked his Grandma how old she was. Grandma answered, "39 and holding." Johnny thought for a moment and then asked, "And how old would you be if you let go?"

***

Mrs. Johnson was called to serve for jury duty, but asked to be excused because she didn't believe in capital punishment and didn't want her personal feelings to prevent justice from running it's proper course. But the public defender liked her thoughtfulness and tried to convince her that she should serve on the jury. "Madam," he explained. "This is not a murder trial! It's a simple civil lawsuit. A wife is bringing this case against her husband because he gambled away the $12,000 he had promised to use to remodel the kitchen for her birthday." "Well, okay," agreed Mrs. Johnson, "I'll serve. I guess I could be wrong about capital punishment after all."

***

A Pastor, who was previously a sailor, was very aware that ships are addressed as "she" and "her." He often wondered what gender computers should be addressed as. To answer that question, he set up two groups of computer experts. The first was composed of women, and the second of men. Each group was asked to recommend whether computers should be referred to in the feminine gender, or the masculine gender. They were asked to give 4 reasons for their recommendation. The group of women reported that the computers should be referred to in the masculine gender because;

1. In order to get their attention, you have to turn them on.
2. They have a lot of data, but are still clueless.
3. They are supposed to help you solve problems, but half the time they are the problem.
4. As soon as you commit to one, you realize that, if you had waited a little longer you could have had a better model.

The men, on the other hand concluded that computers should be referred to in the feminine gender because:

1. No one but the Creator understands their internal logic.
2. The native language they use to communicate with other computers is incomprehensible to everyone else.
3. Even your smallest mistakes are stored in long-term memory for later retrieval.
4. As soon as you make a commitment to one, you find yourself spending half your paycheck on accessories for it.

Copied

***

Here's a few thoughts for your consideration.

1. Why do overlook and oversee mean opposite things?
2. If horrific means to make horrible, does terrific mean to make terrible?
3. Why isn't 11 pronounced onety one?
4. "I am." is reportedly the shortest sentence in the English language. Could it be that "I Do." Is the longest sentence?
5. If lawyers are disbarred and clergymen defrocked, doesn't it follow that electricians can be delighted, musicians denoted, cowboys deranged, models deposed, tree surgeons debarked and dry cleaners depressed?
6. Do Roman paramedics refer to IV's as "4"s"?
7. Why is it that if someone tells you that there are 1 billion stars in the universe you will believe them, but if they tell you a wall has wet paint you will have to touch it to be sure?
8. If people from Poland are called "Poles," Why aren't people from Holland called "Holes?"
9. If a pig loses its voice, is it disgruntled?
10. Why do women wear evening gowns to nightclubs? Shouldn't they be wearing night gowns?
11. If love is blind, why is lingerie so popular?
12. When someone asks you, "A penny for your thoughts," and you put in your two cents in, what happens to the other penny?
13. Why is the man or woman who invests all your money called a broker?
14. Why do croutons come in airtight packages? It's just stale bread to begin with.
15. When cheese gets it's picture taken, what does it say?
16. Why is a person who plays the piano called a

pianist, but a person who drives a race car not called a racist? Copied

***

Recently, Julie Andrews is reportedly to have done a concert for AARP, at which she sang her hit from 'The Sound of Music', but the words had been altered. Here are the new words to this tune.

Maalox and nose drops and needles for knitting, Walkers and handrails and new dental fittings, Bundles of magazines tied up in strings, These are a few of my favorite things. Cadillacs and cataracts . . . hearing aids and glasses, Polident and Fixodent and false teeth in glasses, Pacemakers, golf carts and porches with swings, These are a few of my favorite things. When the pipes leak, When the bones creak, When the knees go bad, I simply remember my favorite things, and then I don't feel so bad.

Hot tea and crumpets and corn pads for bunions, No spicy hot food or food cooked with onions, Bathrobes and heat pads and hot meals they bring, These are a few of my favorite things. Back pains, confused brains and no fear of 'sinnin', Thin bones and fractures and hair that is 'thinnin', and we won't mention our short shrunken frames, If we can remember our friends and their names. When the joints ache . . . when the hips break, When the eyes grow dim, Then I remember the great life I've had, and then I don't feel so bad!

Copied

***

The Genie

A guy is walking along a Florida beach when he comes across a lamp partially buried in the sand. He picks up the lamp and gives it a rub. A genie appears and tells him he has been granted one wish. The guy thinks for a moment and says, "I want to live forever." "Sorry," said the genie, "I'm not allowed to grant eternal life." "OK, then, I want to die after our Government balances the budget and eliminates the National debt.

"You crafty little guy," said the genie.

***

I'm overworked

People remind me sometimes that I look tired, and for years, I've blamed it on middle age. Smoking, diet, bad blood, pollution and a lack of vitamins all played a part in my being tired. Now I'm reading in the news some other reasons why I'm about to give in, give out or give up. By using some mathematics and government statistics, I find the real reason why I'm so tired. I'M OVERWORKED! The working population of this country is approximately 200 million strong, and 84 million of these are retired, leaving 116 million to do the work. There are 75 million in school. That leaves 41 million to do the work. Out of that number, 22 million are government employees, and we all know what that means. That leaves 19 million to do the work. 4 million are in the armed forces, leaving 15 million to do the work. However, there are 14,800,000 million who are employed in the state, city and county governments. Now there are only 200,000 to do the work, and out of that number 188,000 are sick or in the hospitals, leaving 12,000 to do the work. Reports show that 11,998 are in jails and prisons, leaving just 2 persons to do the work . . . you and me, and you're sitting there reading this article.

NO WONDER I'M TIRED! **Copied**

***

THIS IS ESPECIALLY FOR THOSE OF YOU WHO THOUGHT YOU'D HEARD EVERYTHING. THE FOLLOWING SENTENCES ARE EXAMPLES OF CREATIVITY IN FILLING OUT FORMS. THESE STATEMENTS WERE FOUND ON ACTUAL INSURANCE FORMS WHERE DRIVERS ATTEMPTED TO SUMMARIZE THE DETAILS OF AN ACCIDENT IN THE FEWEST POSSIBLE WORDS.

1. Coming home I drove into the wrong house and collided with a tree I don't have.
2. The other car collided with mine without giving warning of its intentions.
3. The pedestrian had no idea which way to run, so I ran over him.
4. A truck backed through my windshield into my wife's face.
5. A pedestrian hit me and went under my car.
6. The guy was all over the road. I had to swerve a number of times before I hit him.

7. In my attempt to kill a fly, I drove into a telephone pole.
8. I pulled away from the side of the road, glanced at my mother-in-law, and headed over the embankment.
9. I had been driving for 40 years when I finally fell asleep at the wheel and had an accident.
10. To avoid hitting the bumper of the car in front, I hit the pedestrian instead.
11. My car was legally parked as it backed into the other vehicle.
12. An invisible car came out of nowhere, struck my car, and then vanished.
13. I told the police that I was not injured but on removing my hat I found that I had a fractured skull.
14. I thought my window was down but I found out it was up when I put my head through it.
15. I saw a slow-moving, sad-faced old man as he bounced off the roof of my car.
16. The indirect cause of the accident was a little guy in a small car with a big mouth.
17. I was thrown from the car as it left the road. I was later found in a ditch by some stray cows.
18. The telephone pole was approaching fast. I was attempting to swerve out of its way when all of a sudden it struck the front end.
19. I was on my way to the doctor with rear end trouble when my universal joint gave way causing me to have an accident.

Copied

***

FRETTIN'

I'se been frettin' 'bout de future, and de things dat I'se been told; 'bout what happens to us folkses, when we starts to gittin' old. But I took a little journey, to de eastern part of state; gazed at all dat pretty scenery, 'til de time was gittin' late.

Sakes alive what gorgeous colors; like de rainbow in de sky; I just cain't explain my feelin's, but I couldn't help but cry.

As I stared at dem big mountains, trees and flowers everywhere; from my heart there welled up praises 'cause my Lord had put 'em dere.

Now, I'se ain't frettin' any longer, for here's one thing dat I see; if my good Lord made dem mountains, He can shore take care of me.

Richard M. "Pek" Gunn, Nashville, Tn.

***

For many years Mr. John Dunn wanted to be an Insurance Salesman. Well, he took the test and passed, and they sent him to Washington, D. C. to work. Before he left home his mother told him, "Now John, don't you dare forget to write home to your mother. I don't like to be in the dark about how you're getting along." "Well," John said to his mother, "You know I wouldn't do that, I'll write to you ever chance I get." After a week or so he took off for Washington, got settled in his new housing, and got checked in at the office. There was only one problem and that was for several weeks he forgot about writing to his mother. This was a big company office and they had lots of people coming and going. One day the company got a letter in the mail and they didn't know where it went so they just pitched it. Another week or so went by and John's mother called and gave whoever answered the phone holy heck. She said, "He works there and you'd better find him." Well, John just happened to be in the office that day and was in the back using the restroom. The man thought he might as well, at least, holler down the hall and see if he might be there. He hollered really loud, "Is there a John in here anywhere? John hollered back, and said "Yep, my name is John." "Are you Dunn?" the man asked. "John hollered back and said, "Yes, I'm Dunn." "Well, hurry up and get out of there and C**ALL YOUR MOTHER!"**

***

There was a guy from Texas every thing's big in Texas that went to New York on business. When got to his office building he hadn't been in there very long until he had to use the restroom. He asked the fellow he was talking to if he had a restroom. The fellow said, "Go down the hall and make a right and then a left and go through that door into the restroom." Well, that's what he did, but rather than turning a right and a left he made two turns to the right, opened the door, and fell 15 feet, smak-dab in the middle of a big swimming pool. He began screaming and really making a big fuss. Someone hollered at him from way up above in the building and said, "Are you Ok?" "Yes," he said, "I'm Ok, but don't let anyone flush this darn thing."

***

"After a certain age, if you don't wake up aching in every joint, you are probably DEAD."

Tommy Mein

***

Two, not so bright, fellows are walking down different ends of a street toward each other and one is carrying a sack. When they meet, one says, "Tommy Ray, what'cha got in th' bag?" "Jus' some chickens." "If I guess how many are in there, can I have one?" "Good golly yes, I'll give you both of them." "OK. Umm-mmmmm . . . , five?"

***

Mama always said
Don't count your chickens before they hatch . . . Don't kick a dog when he's down, Beauty is only skin deep . . . What goes around comes around.

Every cloud has a silver lining . . . Every dog has his day,
Don't judge a book by its cover . . . Save for a rainy day.

Don't put all your eggs in one basket . . . A stitch in time saves nine,
Practice what you preach . . . Make hay while the sun shines.

You can lead a horse to water . . . But you can't make him drink,
Two wrongs don't make a right . . . You are what you think.

Count your blessings every day . . . And fill your life with love,
For every gift we're given . . . Comes from the Father above.

Courtesy from "Courage for the Chicken Hearted, Becky Freeman

***

The Urine Sample
One time I got sick and landed in the hospital. There was this one nurse that just drove me crazy. Every time she came in, she

would talk to me like I was a little child. She would say in a patronizing tone of voice," And how are we doing this morning?" Or "Are we ready for a bath?" or "Are we hungry?" I had had enough of this particular nurse. One day at breakfast, I took the apple juice off the tray and put it in my bedside stand. Later I was given a urine sample bottle to fill for testing. So, you know where the juice went! The nurse came in a while later, picked up the urine sample bottle, looked at it and said, "My, my, it seems we are a little cloudy today." At this point, I snatched the bottle out of her hand, popped off the top, and gulped it down, saying, "Well, I'll run it through one more time; maybe I can filter it better this time!" The nurse fainted; I just smiled.

***

**"Sometimes I pretend to be normal;
but it gets boring;
so I go back to being me."**

***

Did you know that 40 pounds can really make you feel better, especially if you see it on someone you almost married!

***

Did you hear about the two hunters that one of them got lost in the forest. They told each other earlier, "If either one of us gets lost, we'll fire into the air 3 times, and the other one will come a running." Well, that happened, one got lost, and fortunately he was found. The one that was lost told his buddy, "I didn't think you were ever going to get here, I was almost out of arrows."

***

Middle age is when your wife tells you to pull in your stomach and you already have."

***

Three men were stranded on a deserted island. There was a Medical doctor, a carpenter, and one that was not too bright. They wandered around for several days and thought they were not going to be rescued; and besides that they were starving. As they were walking around, the doctor stumbled onto a funny looking bottle with a cork in the top. The carpenter said, "That looks just like one of those Jeannie bottles. Let's pull the cork and maybe we'll be lucky. Well, they were; she hopped out of the bottle and said, "I can give you each 1 wish, and 1 wish only. The carpenter said that he wished for a million dollars, and to be back in his workshop back home. The doctor said he wished for his living room and a big meal waiting. The not so bright one thought for a little bit and said he sure wished those other guys were back with him, he was so lonesome.

***

"How old would you be if you didn't know how old you were?"
Satchel Page

***

A couple went for their yearly checkup. The doctor saw the man first and asked him how he'd been feeling. "I have one problem, Doc, the first time my wife and I make love, everything is perfect, but the second time I really sweat a lot." The doctor completed his exam on the man, and then called his wife in. The doctor says to his wife, "Your husband says the first time you folks make love it is perfect, but the second time he sweats terribly. Do you know why that would be?" "Yeah, she said, "The old goat, the first time is in December and the second time is in July."

***

Dolly Parton and Princess Diana were playing cards. They enjoyed themselves immensely; however, every time they played Princess Diana would win. I can't figure that out said Dolly. Every time I play with someone back home I usually win most of the time. Princess Diana laughed and said, "Well, Dolly, you know a royal flush will beat a pair anytime."

***

"I hate this dull town," a teen-age boy complains to his parents. "I want action: I want to make real money. I want to meet pretty women. I can't do any of that here, so I'm leaving. Before he gets down the street, his father calls to him. The boy shouts back. "Don't try to stop me Dad, my minds made up." "I'm not trying to stop you," his father yells, "I want to go with you."

***

"Do you think," asked the man taking the poll, "That the terms of Congressmen and Congress-women, should be limited?" "No way," said the young man. I think they should stay in jail as long as everyone else does."

***

Copper Wire Discovered

After having dug to a depth of ten feet last year outside of New York City, New York scientists found traces of copper cable dating back 100 years. They came to the conclusion that their ancestors already had a telephone network more than 100 years ago. Not to be outdone by the New Yorkers, in the weeks that followed, a Los Angeles, California archaeologist dug to a depth of 20 feet somewhere just outside Oceanside. Shortly after, a story in the L.A. Times read: "California archaeologists report a finding of 200 year old copper cable, having concluded that their ancestors already had an advanced high-tech communications network a hundred years earlier than the New Yorkers." One week later, a local newspaper in Warrenton, Missouri reported the following. "After digging down about 30 feet deep in his pasture in Missouri, Bubba, a self-taught archaeologist, reported that he found absolutely nothing. Bubba has, therefore, concluded that 300 years ago, Missouri had already gone wireless."

The Dead Beat

***

"Life without God is like an unsharpened pencil . . . It has no point!"

***

A young lady was engaged to be married. "But dad, I really don't want to leave you and mother." "Honey, I don't want to stand in the way of your happiness, take her with you." said her dad.

***

There was this ole boy that moved to Montana. He really liked it there for several reasons. Not many folks around, plenty of room to ride his horse, and the wide open space really turned him on. One day he went to town, the towns are a long way apart out in that country, and stopped to get himself a Pepsi Cola. While he was standing next to the pop cooler a beautiful 30 year old young lady stepped up to get her a Pepsi also. He said, "I see you like Pepsi, I always serve Pepsi at my parties. Is there are chance you'd like to come to my party, out at the ranch?" She replied, "Well, I don't know, I might." He said, "We'll have dinner in the main dining hall, there will be a lot of huggin', kissin', and we'll have a lot of fun." She asked, "What should I wear?" The cowboy said, "It don't make no difference what you wear, cause there won't be nobody there but you and me." **NOW, THE REST OF THE STORY I CAN'T REMEMBER.**

***

"Do you recall the time that you examined the body?" asked the lawyer. The medical examiner replied." "The autopsy started around 8:30 p.m." "And Mr. Dennington was dead at the time?" said the lawyer. "Oh my NO," said the examiner, "He was sitting on the table wondering why I was doing an autopsy."

***

"Are you qualified to give a urine sample?" "Yes, I have been since early childhood."

***

This guy's shirt was soaking wet when he picked up his date. "Why in the world is your shirt wet?" she asked. The guy answered, "Well, the label inside says, wash and wear."

***

WHY MEN ARE NEVER DEPRESSED

Men are just happier people . . . What do you expect from such simple creatures? Your last name stays put . . . The garage is all yours . . . Wedding plans take care of themselves . . . Chocolate is just another snack . . . You can be President . . . You can never get pregnant . . . You can wear a white T-shirt to a water park . . . Car mechanics tell you the truth . . . The world is your urinal . . . You never have to drive to another gas station restroom because this one is just too icky . . . You don't have to stop and think of which way to turn a nut on a bolt . . . Same work, more pay . . . Wrinkles add character . . . Wedding dress $5,000. Tux rental, $100 . . . People never stare at your chest when you're talking to them . . . New shoes don't cut, blister, or mangle your feet . . . One mood all the time . . . Phone conversations are over in 30 seconds flat . . . You know stuff about tanks . . . A five-day vacation requires only one suitcase . . . You can open all your own jars . . . You get extra credit for the slightest act of thoughtfulness . . . If someone forgets to invite you, He or she can still be your friend . . . Your underwear is $8.95 for a three-pack . . . Three pairs of shoes are more than enough . . . You almost never have strap problems in public

. . . You are unable to see wrinkles in your clothes . . . Everything on your face stays its original color . . . The same hairstyle lasts for years, even decades . . . You only have to shave your face and neck . . . You can play with toys all your life . . . One wallet and one pair of shoes, one color for all seasons . . . You can wear shorts no matter how your legs look . . . You can 'do' your nails with a pocket knife . . . You have freedom of choice concerning growing a mustache . . . You can do Christmas shopping for 25 relative on December 24, in 30 minutes.

***

Men are just happier people with nicknames

If Laura, Kate and Sarah go out for lunch, they will call each other Laura, Kate and Sarah. If Mike, Dave and John go out, they will affectionately refer to each other as Fat Boy, Bubba and Wildman.

***

Eating out

When the bill arrives, Mike, Dave and John will each throw in $^{\$}20$, even though it's only for $^{\$}32^{50}$. None of them will have anything smaller and non will actually admit they want change back. When the girls get their bill, out comes the pocket calculators.

Money

A man will pay $^{\$}2^{00}$ for a $^{\$}1^{00}$ item he needs. A woman will pay $^{\$}1^{00}$ for a $^{\$}2^{00}$ item that she doesn't need, but it's on sale.

Bathrooms

A man has six items in his bathroom; toothbrush and toothpaste, shaving cream, razor, a bar of soap, and a towel. The average number of items in the typical woman's bathroom is 337. A man would not be able to identify more than 20 of these items.

Arguments

A woman has the last word in any argument. Anything a man says after that is the beginning of a new argument.

Future

A woman worries about the future until she gets a husband. A man never worries about the future until he gets a wife.

Marriage

A woman marries a man expecting he will change, but he doesn't.

Chicken Side off first...

A man marries a woman expecting that she won't change, but she does.

Dressing Up

A woman will dress up to go shopping, water the plants, empty the trash, answer the phone, read a book, and get the mail. A man will dress up for weddings and funerals.

Natural

Men wake up as good-looking as they are ever going to get. Women somehow deteriorate during the night.

Offspring

Ah, children. A woman knows all about her children. She knows about dentist appointments and romances, best friends, favorite foods, secret fears and hopes and dreams. A man is vaguely aware of some short people living in the house.

Thought for the day

A married man should forget his mistakes. There's no use in two people remembering.

***

A rather shallow gentleman took his wife to St. Louis on their twenty-fifth wedding anniversary, so that they could stay overnight in a hotel for the first time in their lives. When the bellboy showed them to their room, a look of disappointment came over the wife's face. "What's the matter?" the husband asked. The wife pointed at the twin beds and said, "When you said we were going to stay in a nice hotel, I didn't think we'd have to share a room with somebody else."

***

READ TO THE END, SEE IF YOU REMEMBER THIS LADY!

We need to be reminded.

As General Eisenhower said at the time "We need to GET as many photos as we can, so no one can ever say this did not happen"

Irena Sendler – Born 1910, Died May 12, 2008 in Warsaw, Poland.

During WWII, Irena got permission to work in the Warsaw ghetto, as a Plumbing- Sewer specialist. She had and ulterior motive.

Irena smuggled Jewish infants out in the bottom of the tool box she carried. She also carried a burlap sack in the back of her truck, for larger kids.

Irena kept a dog in the back that she trained to bark when the Nazi soldiers let her in and out of the ghetto. The soldiers, of course, wanted nothing to do with the dog and the barking help cover the kids; infant noises.

During her time of doing this, she managed to smuggle out and save 2,500 kids/infants. Ultimately, she was caught, however, and the Nazi's broke both of her legs and arms and beat her severely.

Irena kept a record of the names of all the kids she had smuggled out, in a glass jar that she buried under a tree in her back yard. After the war, she tried to locate any parents that may have survived and tried to reunite the family. Most had been gassed.

Those kids she helped got placed into foster family homes or adopted.

In 2007 Irena was up for the Nobel Peace Prize. She was not selected.

In MEMORIAM – 65 YEARS LATER.

It is now more than 65 years since the Second World War in Europe ended. This story is in memory of the six million Jews, 20 million Russians, 10 million Christians and 1,900 Catholic priests, who were murdered, massacred, raped, burned, starved and humiliated!

HOLOCAUST to be 'a myth', It's imperative to make sure the world never forgets, because there are others who would like to do it again.

Please Google IRENA on your computer and see how many books have been written about this precious lady's life. Also you can find her full autobiography of her life's story. I noticed when looking up her story it said she rescued 25,000 children; however, the story where I obtained this said 2,500. One of these figures has to be incorrect. If 2,500 is the correct number, it is still an absolute miracle. May God's richest blessing be with you for reading this story! **COPIED**

***

Here is a song I sang while on tour with my tour members. It was sung to the tune of "Side by Side"- I have no idea who wrote this little funny song.

1. We got married last Friday, My girl was right there beside me. Our friends were all gone; we were alone, side by side.
2. We were so happily wed din; She got ready for bed then, Her

pretty blond hair, she placed on a chair, side by side.

3. Such beautiful teeth, when she smiled, She looked so sweet, like a child, She then took them out, Nothing left but her snout, side by side.
4. One glass eye so tiny; One hearing aid so small, She then took one leg off, and placed it there by the wall.
5. I stood there broken hearted, Most of my girl had departed, I slept on the chair; There was more of her there, side by side.

***

Dead Penguins – I never knew this!

Did you ever wonder why there are no dead penguins on the Antarctica? Where do they go?

Wonder no more! It is a known fact that the penguin is ritualistic bird which lives an extremely ordered and complex life. The penguin is very committed to its family and will mate for life as well as maintain a form of compassionate contact with its offsprings throughout its life.

If a penguin is found dead on the ice surface, other members, family and social circle have been known to dig holes in the ice using their vestigial wings and beaks, until the hole is deep enough for the dead bird to be rolled into, and buried.

The male penguins then gather in a circle around the fresh grave and all sing in unison:

"Freeze a jolly good fellow."

"Freeze a jolly good fellow."

"Ah hah, got you! I read all the way through and was really sucking it up, of course, until I got to the last line, but so were you."

***

Little Johnny was left to fix lunch. When his mother returned with a friend, she noticed that Johnny had already strained the tea. The two women then slipped their tea happily while having lunch. "Was it hard finding the tea strainer in the kitchen?" Johnny's mother asked. "I couldn't find it Ma, so I used the fly swatter," he replied. His mother nearly fainted, so Johnny hastily added: "Don't get excited, Ma, I used the old one!"

***

Here is another song I sang while on tour. It was sung to the tune of "Are you Lonesome Tonight" Once again, I have no idea who wrote this funny little song. I did change quite a few of the words, to make it work for me.

Pre-announcement; If you know this song and you would like to join in with me, please don't do it. I can hardly get through it myself. Thank You!

1. Are you bloated tonight, are your bowels feeling just right? Did you bring your Mylanta® or Tums®? Does your memory stray to that bright sunny day? When you had all your teeth and your gums?

2. Is your hairline receding, your eyes growing dim? Hysterectomy for her and Prostate for him? Does your back give you pain, do your knees predict rain? Tell me, dear are you bloated tonight?

3. Is your blood pressure up, your cholesterol down? Are you eating your low-fat cuisine? All that oat bran and fruit, Metamucil to boot, keeps you just like a well-oiled machine.

4. If it's football or baseball, he sure knows the score. Yes, he knows where it's at, but forgets what it's for. So, your gall bladder's gone, but your gout lingers on, Tell me dear, are you bloated tonight?

5. When you're hungry, he's not. When you're cold, then he's hot. Then you start that old thermostat war. When you turn out the lights, he goes left, you go right. Then you get his great symphonic snore.

6. He was once so romantic, so witty and smart, but he turned out to be just a cranky, old . . . feller. So, don't take any bets, it's as good as it gets. Tell me dear, are you bloated tonight?

***

"Life is Unpredictable . . .
. . . Prepare for it!"

Turn to page 351.

Religious Humor!

***

The **Preacher** and the bus driver both died and went to heaven. The bus driver goes in first. The **Preacher** can't understand, "I was the **Preacher**." St. Peter said, "Well, when folks sat in your church they all went to sleep, when they got on his bus they all started praying."

***

This man didn't make it to Heaven; he ended up in hell. He was met by the old devil himself. He said to the man, "You have 3 gates to choose from to go in through." The fellow smelled coffee so he decided to take the gate on the right, it was the one filled with a vast amount of garbage and 1000's of folks were standing drinking coffee. He went in and got a cup of delicious coffee and it wasn't 5 minutes until the devil said, "Ok you guys, coffee break is over." "Everybody go back to standing on your head."

***

Dad and mom and their little boy, Johnny, went to church on Sunday morning. Dad gave Johnny 25 cents to put in the offering. Johnny said, "Daddy, why are we putting money in that bag?" Dad said, "We're giving it to Jesus." When they got home from church Johnny said to his folks, "I didn't have to put my 25 cents in the offering, I've still got it." Dad said, "Son, why didn't you put it in like I told to do." Johnny replied, "Well, because he never did show up."

***

"The greatest financial adventure in the bible was what, asked the **Minister**?" "Do you give up," he said. "It was Noah; he floated his stock during the time of the great liquidation."

***

Two bums were walking down the street and they met a Catholic Nun whose arm was in a sling. "What's wrong with your arm Sister?" asked the one bum. "It's broken in three places," the Sister replied. "How did that happen?" asked the first bum. "I slipped in the bathtub," answered the Sister. After leaving, the first bum asked his friend, "What's a bathtub?" "Heck, I don't know," said his friend, "I'm not Catholic."

This may be new to a lot of Catholic folks, but now in the big cities they have an express line for folks in a hurry. It's called toot n' tell.

***

The Sunday school teacher was reviewing a lesson and asked her class if anyone knew who led the children of Israel out of Egypt. There was no answer, so she pointed to a little boy in the back row. "Do you know, Johnnie?" she asked. "Well, I'll tell you one thing for sure; Johnnie replied, "It wasn't me because we just moved here last week."

***

"Realize that it's never too late.
Do ordinary things in an extra-ordinary way.
Have health and hope and happiness.
Take the time to wish upon a star."

***

John came to Osceola looking for the Osceola City Cemetery. He stopped down at the local service station and asked where it was located. The attendant said, "Well, you just stay on this road right here, you can't miss it. It will be on your left side of the road, as a matter of fact it is located right in the dead center of town."

***

At a big church event our **Minister** stood chatting with a young couple thinking he had recently christened their baby. "So, are you two finally getting some sleep at night." said the **Minister**. With their stuttering reply, he realized his error. They were the couple he had married 3 weeks earlier.

***

This very religious doctor and lawyer were discussing how they were going to leave this world. They both said, "We want to be on a cross just like Jesus was!" There was a young gentleman standing by where the doctor and lawyer were discussing their demise. "Hey, you guys can do that, because I want to be in the middle, where Jesus was, and it would really be nice if you two would be on either side. You know! Like Jesus between two thieves." said the young gentleman.

***

The Johnson family invited their **Preacher** and wife to dinner, and it was little Sam's job to set the table. When it came time to eat, Sam's mother asked with surprise, "Why didn't you give Mrs. Smith any silverware, dear?" I didn't think it was necessary, don't you remember mom, dad told us the last time they were here she ate like a horse."

***

"Keep this in mind: Whatever you are full of, comes out, when you are bumped."

***

There were two Irish brothers who owned a farm and always argued over whether their favorite animal, Sally, was a donkey or a mule. Finally, they brought the animal to Father O'Malley, their local **Priest**. "The Bible says that this animal is an ass," said Father O'Malley, which settled the brothers' argument. Unfortunately, the day after the brothers returned to the farm they discovered that old Sally had died. As they were digging the grave, the **Priest** passed by and asked, "What are you doing this fine morning, digging a post hole?" The brothers answered, "Not according to the Bible."

***

"My daddy has all the money in the world," said Jimmy. Little Charles said, "Well, my daddy has all the love in the world." Ralph said, "My dad owns all of hell." Charles and Jimmy both chimed in at the same time and said, "What do you mean he owns all of hell?" Ralph replied, "My dad, he's a **Preacher**, and he went to a business meeting last at the church, and when he came home I heard him tell mom that they gave him hell."

***

"Find the pace of life that works best for you. Always marching to someone else's beat is like living a charade. Don't be too over-extended with an-

other. Get in step with your own parade."

***

The ladies were down at the local bank, and they were counting and sorting the money at the end of their shift. One of the ladies said to the others, "These $500 bills have been in the finest casinos." Another lady spoke up and said, "These $100 bills have been in the finest theatres, and amusement centers." The third lady said, "Well, my husband is a **Minister** and he says these $1.00 bills have been in the finest churches."

***

"If we ever forget that we're one nation under God, then we will be a nation gone under."

Ronald Reagan

***

I will never forget our daughter, Laneta, reminding us about the time, she and Rick were **Minister**ing in the ghettos of a large city. Neta Ruth and I were visiting in her Sunday school class. Laneta wanted to show us what the kids had been learning. Most of the children had never been to Sunday school in their lives, until they started going to this church. She said to the children, "Now, this is my mom and dad; I want someone in this class, to tell them about our learning the names of the first four books of the New Testament. Can anyone here do that for me?" Little Joe stuck his hand up promptly and said, "Ms. Laneta, I can do it, please let me, I promise I know what they are, please." She said, "Ok, Joe, what are they?" Little Joe stood up, stuck his chest out, and said, "Matthew, Mark, Luke and, and, and, and, 'with gusto' said, Rrrrrr ob . . . ert." Laneta said, "No, Joe, I'm so sorry, it wasn't Robert, it was John." Little Joe was so disappointed, that he loudly blurted out; this is all he knew to say, "Oh, sh . .." This was the only way the little fellow knew to express his personal disappointment with himself, at this point in his Sunday school education. Neta Ruth and I felt so sorry for him, because he was extremely proud of what he had learned. This was just a typical story of the ghetto. The kids didn't know it but, all three of us, laughed silently, because it was funny. All of the class learned a lot about the Lord, while they sat under Laneta's teaching.

***

Reverend Brown found himself wondering whether there were any golf courses in Heaven. He even began to ask the question in his prayers. One day, in answer to his prayers, he received a direct answer from Heaven. "Yes," said the voice from up above, "There are many excellent golf courses in Heaven. The greens are always in first-class condition, the weather is always perfect, and you always play with the best people there." "Oh, thank you," responded **Reverend** Brown. "That is wonderful news." "Yes, isn't it?" replied the messenger. "And we've got you down for a foursome next Saturday."

***

Be Thankful!

Be thankful that you don't already have everything you desire. If you did, what would there be to look forward to?

Be thankful when you don't know something, for it gives you the opportunity to learn.

Be thankful for the difficult times. During those times you grow.

Be thankful for your limitations, because they give you opportunities for improvement.

Be thankful for each new challenge, because it will build your strength and character.

Be thankful for your mistakes. They will teach you valuable lessons.

Be thankful when you're tired and weary, because it means you've made a difference.

It's easy to be thankful for the good things. A life of rich fulfillment comes to those who are also thankful for the setbacks.

Gratitude can turn a negative into a positive. Find a way to be thankful for your troubles, and they can become your blessings.

Experience is a hard teacher. It gives the test first and then the lesson.

The Be Thankful Nuggets came from:
www.milkeysFunnies.com

***

A Sunday school teacher was teaching her class about the difference between right and wrong. "All right, children, let's take another example," she said. "If I were to get into a man's pocket and take his billfold with all his money, what would I be?" Little Harold, the **Pastor**'s son, raised his hand, and with a confident smile, he blurted out, "You'd be his wife!"

***

"Remember, mistakes are a by-product of doing something right!"

***

Every day the **Minister**'s secretary was twenty minutes late. Then one day she slid snugly in place only five minutes late. "Well," said the **Minister**, "This is the earliest you've ever been late."

***

"Death is for certain, Predictable . . . . . Prepare for it!" From page 345.

John 3:16

***

The **Pastor**'s son said to his mother, "I've decided that I want to be a **Preacher**, like dad, so that I can clean up the mess the world is in." "That's just wonderful," replied his mother. "You can go upstairs and start with your room."

***

"If you jump to conclusions, don't expect a happy landing."

***

One day the phone rang at our church. The secretary answered it. The person on the line said, "Let me speak to the head hog." The secretary replied, "Excuse me, what did you say, the head hog? Sir, I'll have you know we refer to our **Pastor** as the honored **Reverend** Matthew Jones, and besides he's not here right now "Well," said the caller, "I wanted to talk to him because I plan to donate $100,000 to the church building fund." "Hold on just a minute, I think I hear the big pig coming this way right now."

***

Little Marie was running down the hall, just outside the door going into the main church sanctuary. The **Pastor** was walking toward her and plainly heard her say a bad bad word. He said to her, "Honey, that was not a nice word to use, I'll give you 25 cents to never say it again." Marie stopped short and said, "I'll tell you what **Preacher**, I've got another word I could use that would be worth at least $2.00.

***

One Sunday morning **Reverend** John advised his congregation, "Next week I plan to preach about the sin of lying. In preparation for my message, I want you all to read Mark 17: 3." The following Sunday the **Reverend** asked for a show of hands from those who had read Mark 17:3. Every hand went up. **Pastor** John smiled and announced, "Well, Mark has only sixteen chapters; I will not proceed with my message on the sin of lying."

***

"Don't feel you are disloyal to your grief, by seeking joy"

***

"Oh, **Pastor**, I almost committed a crime. The **Pastor** replied, "What in the world did you almost do?" "I started to steal a man's coat," replied the fellow; however, when you preached on the 4th commandment about being a little too friendly with another, I remembered where I left my coat."

***

Attitude

"The longer I live, the more I realize the impact of attitude on life. Attitude, to me, is more important than facts. It is more important than the past, than education, than money, than circumstances, than failures, than successes, than what other people think or say or do. It is more important than appearance, giftedness, or skill. It will make or break a company; a church; a home. The remarkable thing is we have a choice everyday regarding the attitude we will embrace for that day. We cannot change our past; we cannot change the fact that people will act in a certain way. We cannot change the inevitable. The only thing we can do is play on the one string we have, and that is our attitude; I am convinced that life is 10% what happens to me and 90% how I react to it. And so it is with you; we are in charge of our Attitudes." **Charles Swindoll**

***

Richard & Neta Ruth Sunderwirth

A new missionary started his first year on the field of ministry. The first year when he got a cup of coffee and it didn't taste good, he threw out the whole cup. The second year, if a fly happened to land in his coffee he would take his spoon, dip out the fly, throw it away, and continue drinking his coffee. The third year, if a fly landed in his coffee, he would just simply get the fly by the wings, hold it up and say, spit it out, spit it out.

***

"Being nobly born matters little if one is not nobly remembered."

***

"God can take your tears and make rainbows."

***

If I had my life to live over; (READ THIS CAREFULLY)
"If I had my life to live over; I'd dare to make more mistakes next time. I'd relax; I would limber up, I would be sillier, I wouldn't take things so seriously. I would look for the best side in very situation; I would take more chances, I would take more trips. I would climb more mountains. I would swim more rivers; I would eat more ice cream and less beans, I would perhaps have more actual trouble, but I would have fewer imaginary ones. I'd love more and gripe less; you see, I am one of those people who live sensibly and sanely, hour after hour, day after day. I'd start each day knowing that my way is not always the only way; Oh, I've had my moments, and if I had it to do over again, I'd have more of them. In fact, I'd try to have nothing else; just moments, one wonderful moment after another, instead of living so many years ahead of each day. I have been one of those persons who never goes anywhere without a thermometer, a hot water bottle, a raincoat and a parachute. If I had to do it again, I'd travel lighter than I have in the past. If I had my life to live over, I would start barefoot earlier in the spring and stay that way later in the fall. I would go to more dances; I would ride more merry-go-rounds, I would pick more daisies, and I'd cherish each day, love my God and live my life to the fullest. If I had my life to live over again."
COPIED, and added to by Richard.

***

There were three Baptist churches in the community, and they all had a terrible problem with bats. The bats would come in, just hang around, and really bother everyone. The **Pastor**, of the first church, decided he would just shoot them and they would all be gone. The folks came the next Sunday, after the shooting, and the bats were there again. The **Pastor** of the second church decided he would just poison them and they would all be gone. His folks came the next Sunday, after he poisoned them, but the bats were still there. The **Pastor** of the third church really gave this problem some serious thought. He decided he would baptize them, let them join the church, and guess what? He ain't seen them since!

***

The **Minister** was invited over for dinner one Sunday after church. He was asked to say the blessing over the meal. After a very brief prayer, little Johnny said approvingly, "You don't pray very long when you are hungry, do you?"

***

The new young **Pastor** arrived at his church and the first thing he wanted to do was start off with a little humor. He said to the folks, "I want you all to know I'm really happy to be here. I want you to know that we welcome all denominations . . . and that can be in 10's, 20s, 50s, or even 100 dollar bills." I never found out what they group had to say about it, but the last time I heard he was still their **Pastor**.

***

One Sunday morning in the Primary class the teacher told them it would nice if they would create a masterpiece that related to the Bible. As she wandered around the room looking at the pictures, she came to little Wanda Sue. "Wanda Sue," she said, "What is your masterpiece going to be?" Wanda Sue replied, "Well, I'm going to paint a real fancy picture of God." The teacher said, "But honey, no one knows what God looks like." With all the confidence in the world, Wanda Sue said, "They will when I'm finished."

***

A lady, of the night, came to church one Sunday evening. Several of the church folks had been inviting her for a long time to come and visit. They were all surprised to see her, so the song leader thought he would be nice to her and he said, "We're so glad to see you here tonight Lucy Sue, I'm going to let you pick out the next 3 hymns. "Would you like to do that Lucy Sue?" said the song leader. Lucy Sue smiled real big and said, "Yeah, I'm glad to be here; I'll take him, him, and him.

***

"Grief can take care of itself, but to get the full value of a joy you must have somebody to divide it with."
Mark Twain

***

Miss Sweet Potato Pie, the local beauty queen, was seated in the front row of the church balcony and suddenly felt dizzy during the service. Just as the **Minister** started to pray she lost her balance and fell over the railing. There she hung, over the top of the congregation below, as they all stood in prayer. A lot of her very private undergarments were in full view. Before the church could look up the **Minister** said, "If you turn to stare at this damsel in distress, God will strike you blind," One guy nudged his friend and whispered, "I think I'll risk one eye."

***

A test of faith (Don't Miss This One!)

I was listening to a Christian radio station one Sunday afternoon. A lady called in and said to the **Minister** that was speaking on talk radio that day. "**Pastor**, I was born blind, and I've been blind all of my life. I don't mind so much, but I have some well-meaning sisters in Christ who tell me that if I had more faith I could be healed." The radio **Minister** asked her, "Tell me sister, "Do you happen to have one of those white canes?" "Yes, I do," she replied. "Well then, let me tell you this; the next time someone tells you that, hit him or her on the head with your cane and say, 'If you had more faith that wouldn't hurt;' have a nice day."

***

"Be, thankful for what you have; you'll end up having more. If you concentrate on what you don't have, you will never, ever have enough."
Oprah Winfrey.

***

A brand new **Preacher** came to the church. It was his first Sunday and he wanted to make a good impression on his church members. He preached on whiskey, he preached on tobacco, he preached on dancin', and then he got to preachin' on money. He told them about paying their tithes, he preached on offerings and he preached on the widow's mite. After church he asked one of the older fellows in the church, as they were coming out the front door, "How did you like my sermon? How about the widow's mite? One of the young fellows piped up and said, "Well **Preacher**, I don't know a lot about that, but I do know the widows that will, and the widows that won't, but I sure don't know about the widows that might!"

***

Who was Haym Solomon? This story is great! Don't forget this one.

Read this fascinating history of the $1.00 bill all the way to the end of the article. You'll be glad you did!

On the rear of the One Dollar bill, you will see two circles. Together, they comprise the Great Seal of the United States. The First Continental Congress requested that Benjamin Franklin and a group of men come up with a Seal. It took four years to accomplish this task and another two years to get it approved. If you look at the left-hand circle, you will see a Pyramid. Notice the face is lighted, and the western side is dark. This country was just beginning. We had not begun to explore the west or decided what we could do for Western Civilization. The Pyramid is uncapped, again signifying that we were not even close to being finished. Inside the Capstone you have the all-seeing eye, and ancient symbol for divinity. It was Franklin's belief that one man couldn't do it alone, but a group of men, with the help of God, could do anything.

"IN GOD WE TRUST" is on this currency. The Latin above the pyramid, ANNUIT COEPTIS, means, 'God has favored our undertaking.' The Latin below the pyramid, NOVUS ORDO SECLORUM, means, 'a new order has begun.' At the base of the pyramid is the Roman numeral for 1776. MDCCLXXVI.

If you look at the right-hand circle, and check it carefully, you will learn that it is on every National Cemetery in the United States. It is also on the Parade of Flags Walkway at the Bushnell, Florida National Cemetery, and is the centerpiece of most heroes' monuments. Slightly modified, it is the seal of the President of the United States, and it is always visible whenever he speaks, yet very few people know what the symbols mean. The Bald Eagle was selected as a symbol for victory for two reasons: First, he is not afraid of a storm; he is strong, and he is smart enough to soar above it. Secondly, he wears no material crown. We had just broken from the King of England. Also, notice the shield is unsupported. This country can now stand on its' own. At the top of that shield there is a white bar signifying congress, a unifying factor. We were coming together as one nation. In the Eagle's beak you will read, 'E PLURIBUS UNUM' meaning, 'from many – one.' Above the Eagle, we have the thirteen stars, representing the thirteen original colonies, and any clouds of misunderstanding rolling away; again, we were coming together as one.

Notice what the Eagle holds in his talons. He holds an olive branch and arrows. This country wants peace, but we will never be afraid to fight to preserve peace. The Eagle always wants to face the olive branch, but in time of war, his gaze turns toward the arrows.

An untrue old-fashioned belief says that the number 13 is an unlucky number. This is almost a worldwide belief. You will almost never see a room numbered 13, or any hotels or motels with a 13th floor. But think about this: America, which relies on God not a number to direct and lead, boldly chose: 13 original colonies . . . 13 signers of the Declaration on Independence . . . 13 stripes on our flag . . . 13 steps on the pyramid . . . 13 letters in 'Annuit Coeptis' . . . 13 letters in 'E Pluribus Unum'. . . 13 stars above the Eagle . . . 13 bars on that shield . . . 13 leaves on the olive branch . . . 13 fruits, and if you look closely, 13 arrows. And finally, notice the arrangement of the 13 stars in the right-hand circle. You will see that they are arranged as a STAR OF DAVID. This was ordered by George Washington who, when he asked Haym Solomon, a wealthy Philadelphia Jew, what he would like as a personal reward for his services to the Continental Army, Solomon said he wanted nothing for himself, but he would like something for his people. The Star of David was the result. Few people know it was Solomon who saved the Army, through his financial contributions . . . then died a pauper. Haym Solomon gave $25 million dollars to save the Continental Army, money that was sorely needed to help realize America's freedom and independence from England.

Therein lies America's Judeo-Christian beginning. Most American children do not know any of this. They are not taught because their history teachers do not know this either.

***

Three clergymen were deep in a discussion of the best positions for praying while a telephone repair man worked nearby. "Kneeling is definitely best, "claimed one. "No," another contended. "I get the best results standing with my arms outstretched to Heaven." "You're both wrong," the third argued. "The most effective prayer position is lying on the floor facedown"

The telephone repairman could contain himself no longer. "Hey, guys," he interrupted, "The best prayin' I ever did was while hangin' upside down from a telephone pole, and I mean to tell you, I WAS PRAYIN'."

***

"Dear Santa, I've been good . . . I have been really good . . . I haven't been quite as good as I should have been . . . as a matter of fact I've been rather bad at times." He started over about 6 times trying to write the letter to Santa. He thought for a couple of minutes and then he took off running down the street to the local Catholic church. He ran down the aisle to the alter, and took the statue of Mary, and with all the strength he could muster, he drug it up the stairs, into a side room, and put it in the closet and shut the door. He sat down, and wrote, "Dear Santa, If you ever want to see your Mother again, you'd better bring me something really nice for Christmas."

***

"When Christmas is over," said a merchant to a **Minister**, "It's our job to rid this store completely of Christmas in a day." "Well," said the **Minister**, "I've bigger job; to keep Christmas in the hearts of my people for a lifetime."

***

Hearing his dad preach on Justification, Sanctification, and all the other anctions, the Sunday school teacher asked the little boy if he'd done his lesson, "Son, what does procrastination mean." "I really don't know, said the boy, but I know one thing, our church probably believes in it."

***

In the Garden of Eden, Adam asked God, "Why did you make Eve so beautiful?" God said, "To attract your attention Adam." Adam then said, "Why did you give her such a sweet personality?" "God answered again, "So you would love her." Adam thought about this for a while. "Why then, did you make her so dumb? asked Adam. God replied, "So she would love you."

***

"Love me when I least deserve it, because that's when I really need it."
Swedish Proverb

***

A **Minister**, a **Priest**, and a **Rabbi** went for a hike one very hot day. They were sweating and exhausted when they came upon a small lake. Since it was fairly secluded, they took off all their clothes and jumped in the water. Refreshed, the trio decided to pick a few berries while enjoying their "Freedom." As they were crossing an open area, along came a group of ladies from town. The men ran for cover, with the **Minister** and **Priest** covering their privates and the **Rabbi** covering his face. After the ladies were gone and the men had retrieved their clothes, the **Minister** asked the **Rabbi** why he covered his face and not his privates. The **Rabbi** replied, "I don't know about you guys, but in MY congregation, it's my face they would recognize." **The Dead Beat**

***

A Baptist deacon had advertised a cow for sale. "How much are you asking for her?" inquired a prospective purchaser. "A hundred and fifty dollars," said the deacon. "And how much milk does she give?" "Four gallons a day," he replied. "But how do I know that she will actually give that amount?" asked the prospective purchaser. "Oh, you can trust me," reassured the advertiser, "I'm a Baptist deacon." "I'll buy her then," replied the other. "I'll take her home and bring you back the money later. You can trust me, I'm a Presbyterian elder." When the deacon arrived home he asked his wife, "What is a Presbyterian elder?" "Oh," she replied, "A Presbyterian elder is about the same as a Baptist deacon." "Oh, dear," groaned the deacon, "I'll never get my money!"

***

"I've learned people will forget what you said, people will forget what you did, but people will never forget how you made them feel."
Maya Angelou

***

The new **Preacher** visited one of his deacons. As he walked through the front door, he heard the deacon in the back of the house holler, "Who in the "blankety blanket is it son?" The son tells his dad it is the new **Preacher**. The deacon came out into the living room and greeted their guest. The **Preacher** said, "My goodness, I thought I heard you use a very bad word, but I'm sure you didn't, I just misunderstood. You see, when I hear a really bad word it just gives me cold chills down my back." Before he could stop his son, the son said, "Boy, it's a good thing you didn't show up a few minutes ago. If you'd heard the word my dad used, when he was trying to change a tire, you wouldn't have thawed out until spring."

***

Father George was opening his Christmas cards one December morning. Out of one of the cards came a single sheet of paper and on it was written only one word; "Fool," The following Sunday, in church, **Father** George announced to the assembled congregation, "I have known many people who have written notes to me and forgotten to sign their names. But this week I received a note from someone who signed his name and had forgotten to write a letter."

***

Answers to life's problems . . . just in case!

When we say:	**God says:**	**His Word says:**
It's impossible	All things are possible	Luke 18:27

I'm too tired	I will give you rest	Matthew 11:28-30
Nobody really loves me	I love you	John 3:16-John 3:34
I can't go on	My grace is sufficient	2 Corinthians 12:9-Psalms 91:15
I can't figure things out	I will direct your steps	Proverbs 3:5-6
I can't do it	You can do all things	Philippians 4:13
I'm not able	I am able	2 Corinthians 9:8
It's not worth	It will be worth it	Romans 8:1
I can't forgive myself	I forgive you	1 John 1:9-Romans 8:1
I can't manage	I will supply all your needs	Philippians 4:19
I'm afraid	I have not given you a spirit of fear	2 Timothy 1:17
I'm always worried	Cast all your cares on Me	1 Peter 5:7
I'm not smart enough	I give you wisdom	1 Corinthians 1:30
I'm all alone	I will never leave you or forsake you	Hebrews 13:5

***

Ol' Fred had been a faithful Christian and was in the hospital, near death. The family called their **Preacher** to stand with them in prayer. As the **Preacher** stood next to the bed, Ol' Fred's condition appeared to deteriorate and he motioned frantically for something to write on. The **Pastor** lovingly handed him a pen and a piece of paper, and Ol' Fred used his last bit of energy to scribble a note, then he died. The **Preacher** thought it best not to look at the note at that time, so he placed it in his jacket pocket. At the funeral, as he was finishing the message, he realized that he was wearing the same jacket that he was wearing when Ol' Fred died. He said, "Ol' Fred handed me a note just before he died. I haven't looked at it, but knowing Fred, I'm sure there's a word of inspiration her for all of us." He opened the note, and read. "Hey, you're standing on my oxygen tube."

***

Sam was a **Preacher** but golf was his passion. It had rained every weekend for a month and he was dying to play a round. Sunday was the first sunny day in weeks. So he called his head deacon and told him an emergency had called him away. Church would have to be cancelled. He realized he couldn't play at a local course – someone might recognize him, so he drove two counties away and teed up on a course he'd never played before. Meanwhile, Saint Peter was watching Sam from Heaven. He called the angel on weekend duty and said, "I've got a **Preacher** who canceled church to play golf. Come here and administer appropriate punishment." The angel appeared as Sam was teeing off on hole 4, par 3. The ball lofted and landed precisely in the hole. "You gave him a hole-in-one." Peter asked incredulously, "You call that punishment?" "Yes," the angel replied. "Who can he tell about it?"

***

A **Minister** parked his car in a no-parking zone in a large city because he was short of time and couldn't find a space with a meter. Then he put a note under the windshield wiper that read; "I have circled the block 10 times. If I don't park here, I'll miss my appointment." The **Minister** left this note: FORGIVE US OUR TRESPASSES. When he returned, he found a citation from a police officer along with this note. "I've circled this block for 10 years. If I don't give you a ticket, I'll lose my job. LEAD US NOT INTO TEMPTATION."

***

Love to all!

There are moments in life when you miss someone so much that you just want to pick them from your dreams and hug them.

Dream what you want to dream; go where you want to go; be what you want to be, because you have only one life and one chance to do all the things you want to do.

May you have enough happiness to make you sweet, enough trials to make you strong, enough sorrow to keep you human, enough hope to make you happy.

Always put yourself in others' shoes. If you feel that it hurts you, it probably hurts the other person, too.

The happiest of people don't necessarily have the best of everything; they just make the most of everything that comes along their way.

Happiness lies for those who cry; those who hurt, those who have searched, and those who tried, for only they can appreciate the importance of people who have touched their lives. Love begins with a smile, grows with a kiss and ends with a tear.

The brightest future will always be based on a forgotten past; you can't go on well in life until you let go of your past failures and heartaches.

When you were born, you were crying and everyone around you was smiling. Live your life, loving God, so that when you die, you're the one who is smiling and everyone around you is crying.

***

"When I stand before God at the end of my life, I would hope that I would not have a single bit of talent left, and could say I used everything you gave me."

Erma Bombeck

***

Little Johnny went in to see the inside of their new church, and the **Preacher** asked him if he knew where God was. Johnny said, "Mr. **Preacher**, I don't have the slightest idea where he is." The **Preacher** said, "Are you sure you don't know where he is? Do you, by chance, happen to know where your friend Jimmie is? Johnny fibbed a bit and said, "No sir, I don't know," and out the front door he went. When he finally ran into Jimmie he said, "We've got to get out of here, we're in trouble." "What's the matter," said Jimmie. "Well," replied Johnny, "God's missing and they think we had something to do with it."

***

The Harmonica

"Thanks for the harmonica you gave me for Christmas," little Joshua said to his uncle the first time he saw him after the holidays. "It's the best present I ever got." "That's great," said his uncle. "Do you know how to play it?" "Oh, I don't play it," the little fellow said. "My mom gives me a dollar a day not to play it during the day and my dad gives me five dollars a week not to play it at night.

***

Three expectant fathers, were pacing the floor of the Baptist General hospital. Finally the doctor came out and told one man that he was the father of two healthy sons. "That's great, because I work at the Double Tree Hotel." After some time the doctor came in a told the second man he was the father of three beautiful girls. "That's wonderful because I work for 3-M Company." The third expectant father said, "I'm getting out of here, I work for 7-up."

"The Amish don't have the problems the Native

Chicken Side off first...
Americans have . . .
because there is no Bureau of Amish Affairs."

***

A Sunday school teacher asked the class to suggest a hymn to sing. One boy said, "Let's sing the laundry song?" The teacher said, "What one is that?" The boy replied, "You know, 'Bringing in the sheets.'" A girl piped up and said, "It's not sheets, dummy, it's cheese, bringing in the cheese."

***

Years ago, in America, sermons were long and tedious. A circuit-riding judge visited a church one Sunday knowing the **Preacher** would be long-winded. After the service the **Preacher** asked the judge what he thought of the sermon. "It was wonderful. It was like the peace of God." The **Preacher** was flattered and said, "I scarcely hoped to achieve that. How can you make that comparison?" The judge replied, "Easily, It was like the peace of God that passes understanding."

***

Life

Life is a series of problems. Either you are in one now, you're just coming out of one, or you're getting ready to go into another one.

The reason for this is that God is more interested in your character than your comfort. God is more interested in making your life Holy than He is in making your life happy.

We can be reasonably happy here on earth, but that's not the goal of life. The goal is to grow in character, in Christ likeness.

Some think that life is just hills and valleys . . . you go through a dark time, then you go to the mountaintop, back and forth. That is not true.

Rather than life being hills and valleys, it's kind of like two rails on a railroad track, and at all times you have something good and something bad in your life.

No matter how good things are, there is always something bad that needs to be worked on. And no matter how bad things are in your life, there is always something good you can thank God for.

You can focus on the good things, life your family, your overall purpose, your wonderful blessings, or you can focus on your problems.

If you focus on your problems, you're going into self-centeredness,' which is my problem, my issues, my pain.' But one of the easiest ways to get rid of pain is to get your focus off yourself and onto God and others.

You must learn to deal with both the good and the bad of life. Life's not fair. You must ask yourself, am I going to live for a perfect situation, a perfect life, or am I going to be driven by God's purposes for my life. Am I going to live for me or for the wonderful things that God has allowed me to have, and for the precious ones around me.

Am I going to be driven by pressures? Guilt? Bitterness? Materialism? Or am I going to be driven by God's purposes for my life?

When I get up in the morning, I should sit on the side of my bed and say, God, If I don't get anything else done today, I want to know You more and love You better. I must realize that I wasn't put on this earth just to fulfill a to-do-list. God is more interested in what I am that what I do. That's why we're called human beings, not human doings.

Happy moments, PRAISE GOD . . . Difficult moments, SEEK GOD . . . Quiet moments, WORSHIP GOD . . . Painful moments, TRUST GOD . . . Every moment, THANK GOD!

Rick Warren

***

"Old friends are Gold! New friends are Diamonds. If you get a diamond don't forget the Gold! Because to hold a Diamond, you always need a base of Gold"

***

A business man moved into a new location on the Country Club Plaza. He was delighted with the floral arrangements sent to him. However, he was puzzled to notice that one had a ribbon on it reading, "Rest in Peace." So he phoned the florist and asked for an explanation. There was a long silence and then the florist blurted out, "Oh no, there's a grave at the cemetery with a spray that says, "Good luck on your new location."

***

After God created Adam, the Lord talked with him and said, "Adam, are you happy in this paradise?" Adam replied, "Yes, Lord, it's wonderful, but I'm lonely." God said, "I will give you a helpmate. She will be beautiful, a perfect companion, a good cook and she will never nag you." Adam said, That's great, but what will it cost me?" The Lord replied, "An arm and a leg." Adam thought about that for a moment, then said, "What will you give me for a rib?"

***

"How far you go in life depends on your being tender with the young, compassionate with the aged, sympathetic with the striving and tolerant of the weak and strong; because someday in your life you will have been all of these."

George Washington Carver

***

In a domestic relations court the judge listened intently to both sides in a case against an elderly former **Pastor** who was charged by his wife for nonsupport. After all the evidence was in, the judge told the defendant, "You haven't taken proper care of his woman, so I'm going to give her $500 a month." The defendant beamed with pleasure and said, "Judge you know I love this women, and have for many years, but I really don't have any money to spare, and I sure do appreciate what you're doing for her. As a matter of fact I'll give her a few dollars from time to time myself."

***

In an adult Sunday School class the lesson was from Genesis and was centered on Abraham who lived for a time in Beersheba. A class member asked the teacher, "Please tell me how far it is in actual miles from Dan to Beersheba. I've always heard the expression 'from Dan to Beersheba.'" Another member said, "Do you mean to tell me that Dan and Beersheba are places? I always thought they were husband and wife, like Sodom and Gomorrah."

***

"Worrying does not take away tomorrow's troubles, it takes away today's peace."

***

When the **Pastor** finished his long lesson he asked, "Are there any questions?" A little fellow in the back of the room said, "What time is it?"

***

"God, grant me the serenity to accept the things I cannot change, courage to change the things I can, and the wisdom to know the difference."

Reinhold Niebuhr

***

The **Pastor** of a local church was introducing the guest speaker, who was a Professor of Expository, preaching at a seminary. The **Pastor**'s tongue slipped when he said, "I'm happy to introduce the Professor of Suppository Preaching." No doubt the congregation heard a very 'moving' sermon that Sunday!

***

A drunken man staggers into a Catholic church and sits down in a confession box and says nothing. The bewildered **Priest** coughs to attract his attention, but still the man says nothing. The **Priest** then knocks on the wall three times in a final attempt to get the man to speak. Finally, the drunk replies: "Ain't no use a knockin' mate, there's no paper in this one either."

***

At a drugstore, a wife wanted to buy some shaving lotion for her **Pastor** husband. "What kind?" asked the clerk. "Well, he's 75 years old. Have you got any of that Old Spouse?"

***

At a monastery the annual Fish and Chip Festival was being held. A visitor told the Abbot he'd like to congratulate the chef on the good food. The Abbot said, "There's your man, in the brown robe." The visitor went over and asked, "Are you the fish friar?" "No, I'm the head chip monk."

***

Chicken Side off first...

In a certain city there were two brothers who were known for their shady business practices. Year by year they grew richer and richer at the expense of associates and others in the community. At last one of the brothers died and the remaining brother tried to find a **Minister** to conduct the funeral of the deceased. Finally the brother told one **Minister** that he would pay him a large sum if he would conduct his brother's funeral, with the condition that in the eulogy he would call him a saint. The **Minister** thought about the proposition and finally being a pragmatist decided he would accept the offer and conduct the funeral on the condition that he paid in advance. The **Minister** decided the large sum would pay for a new roof on the church. The funeral chapel was packed with curious business people wondering what the **Minister** would say about the despised man. In the eulogy the **Pastor** said, "The man lying before you in the coffin was a cheat, a deceiver, a rotten no-good, but compared with this brother he was a saint."

***

"A baby is God's opinion that life should go on."
Carl Sandburg

***

This past summer was exceptionally dry in some parts of the country. How dry? It was so dry the Baptist resorted to sprinkling. The Methodist used a damp cloth for baptism and the Presbyterians gave out rain checks!

***

St. Peter was sitting at the Pearly Gates when two guys wearing dark hoodies, and sagging pants, arrived. St. Peter looked out through the Gates and said, "Wait here. I'll be right back." St. Peter goes over to God's chambers and tells him who is waiting for an entrance. God says to Peter: "How many times do I have to tell you? You can't be judgmental here. This is Heaven. All are loved. All are brothers. Go back and let them in!" St. Peter goes back to the Gates, looks around, and lets out a heavy sigh. He returns to God's chambers and says, "Well, they're gone." "The guys wearing hoodies?" said God. "No, The Pearly Gates" replied St. Peter.

***

The church went on a mini-trip down through the country. This lady got off the bus to take a few pictures. It wasn't too long until here she came running back toward the bus. When the driver saw her he closed the door. "What's the matter?" the folks in the bus hollered. The driver said, "We don't let ladies back on the church bus with a bare behind."

***

"And don't ever forget, for even a day, how special you are!"

***

The Remembered Kiss *Don't miss this story Mr. Jerome Burk was a funeral director, for many years.*

The First Presbyterian Church . . . which is twenty years older and three times as stylish as the Second in my hometown . . . gave its annual Spring Fair last week and of course I went. Not entirely for business reasons, either. Church fairs are like wakes. You meet so many old friends at them, hear so many good stories and, pick up so much interesting gossip.

There was the usual array of catch-dollar devices, tables filled with fancy work, booths displaying home-baked cakes and pies and cookies, a candy bar; and, right where you couldn't miss it, a stand with a great tray of pastel-colored sugar puffs, staffed by four pretty girls and bearing a sign which read "Buy a Kiss – 20 cents."

Those candy kisses retail for about two cents apiece at almost any confectioners; so you didn't have to be a cost accountant to figure that the church was not losing much by those transactions. I laid my coins on the counter, received a puckered pink confection from a smiling girl and bit into the thing, which was almost as substantial as a soap bubble. Then suddenly a memory called me like the echo of a voice heard far away, and the blaring words and tune of "Black Magic" coming over the loudspeaker were mystically transmuted to "A Baby's Prayer at Twilight" played by a military band . . . and I was back again, at a different fair, a charity bazaar held more than fifty years ago. I forget the object for which it was held, except that it was connected in some way with the War Effort, the first World War, the "war to end all wars," you know.

They sold kisses at that fair too. Not sticky-sweet confections, but luscious, warm-lipped osculations from the mouths of pretty girls –"For Charity . . . $1.00". Some of the girls went peddling tickets through the crowd; the rest stood in the booth and kissed all comers in exchange for the checks.

"Boughten" kisses, whether for sweet charity or otherwise, never had much appeal for me but I took a ticket or two just for the sake of appearances . . . With no intention of cashing them, you understand. Or, anyway that's what I told my wife.

Right ahead of me as I shuffled through the crowd was Jonah Pettigrew. Whoever thought up that name for him had a gruesome sense of humor. He was short, almost dwarfish, and his stature was further decreased by a spinal scoliosis which gave him a hunch-backed appearance. As if that weren't enough, his mouth was deformed by a harelip. No tailor could cut clothes to drape effectively on that poor, misshaped body; no mustache could disguise that cleft lip

Life had been cruel to Jonah from childhood. His schoolmates had tormented him unmercifully; his teachers shrank from him involuntarily. The only consolation that the unfortunate child could find was in solitude. No wonder that he grew up hating everyone and everything, or that be plied his trade of money-lender with a lack of pity that would have put old Shylock to shame. Indeed, he must have had a fellow feeling for the Jew of Venice who, after he had been reviled and insulted, was besought to lend money to the very ones who had made mock of him in public.

I was surprised to see him at the bazaar that night. Perhaps he had come to see how his debtors spent the money he lent them at compound interest. And when a girl gave him a gorgeous smile and asked, "Won't you take a ticket, sir? Only a dollar," I was thunderstruck to see him drag a leather purse from his pocket, painstakingly undo its fastenings, and fish out a dollar bill.

The smile that made his deformed mouth seem even more disfigured was a grimace of pure cynicism as he walked to the "Kisses for Sale" booth and laid his ticket on the counter. "Watch 'em welch on this," he muttered loud enough for me to hear.

Sarah Jane Corbet, the prettiest girl in town, was in charge of the booth, and with her were Sue Hampton and Emily Frye, both of whom were more than merely easy to behold. There was a fourth girl there, too; one who obviously did not "belong." A woman could have told in detail just where she failed to measure up, a man could only sense that there was something lacking. Her clothes were not quite right, she wore her makeup – girls then were just beginning to experiment with rouge and lipstick which had recently become respectable – with an air of self – consciousness and the manner of her booth mates toward her was decidedly not cordial. Then I recognized her. Ana Palenzeke, the pretty little Polish war refugee who worked as a maid for Mrs. Lemuel Cushing. What was she doing in a booth staffed by daughters of the socially elect? I had my answer almost as I asked myself the question. "One of your customers, Ana," Sarah Jane said curtly as Jonah laid his kiss ticket on the counter. The announcement was an order such as one might expect a superior to give an inferior, and obviously was intended to be taken as such.

If Ana were revolted by the deformed face that leered up at her she never showed it. Her smile was warm and welcoming; her eyes were bright with friendly laughter, as she leant across the counter, took Jonah's cheeks between her pink palms and covered his poor, crippled mouth with hers.

Jonah staggered like a man hit with a blackjack. For a moment he swayed drunkenly, then walked away unsteadily, as if the solid floor beneath him had no substance.

I met Sarah Jane later that evening at the soda fountain. "Having a good time, Mr. Burke?" she asked brightly, "Very" I told her, then added, "but I'm puzzled, Sarah Jane." She raised plucked eyebrows at me. "Yes?" "How does it come that Ana Palenzeke was in the booth with you and Sue and Emily." "Oh that!" The dimples each side of her pretty mouth deepened as she smiled at me, "You see, Mother was afraid we might be called upon to kiss some – well, you know – some undesirable characters – drunken men or laborers, or something like that; so she got Mrs. Cushing to send Ana to fill in for us in emergencies. Wasn't that just too perfectly clever of Mother?" "Quite," I agreed, as I felt something like a swarm of tiny, ice-cold red ants go crawling up my spine and into my scalp. The monstrous thing these women had done to little, defenseless Ana was shocking enough. But that they saw no impropriety in doing it was absolutely appalling. I said good night to Sarah Jane – a little curtly, I'm afraid – and hurried home to take a drink of honest whiskey. The ice cream sodas of the charity bazaar had suddenly begun to nauseate me.

Ana Palenzeke died the very next winter. "Spanish" Influenza; no one knew who or where her family was, or if she had a family. Her savings bank book showed a balance of $41.53. Silas Hickey, the local funeral director, had the city contract that year, and lost money on every case. I was about to call him and offer to take Ana off his hands when Jonah Pettigrew forestalled me.

"I've made arrangements with the Board of Overseers for you to take the case, Mr. Burke," he told me. "They were only too glad to get rid of the cost and gave me an order on Hickey for you to get the body. If he raises any objections, tell him I'll see that he'll get the same fee that the city would have paid him."

"All right," I answered. "Would you like to select a casket now, Mr. Pettigrew?" We went through my display room, but it was not until we came to the new silver bronze, I'd let a salesman talk me into buying, that he was satisfied. "Finest thing you've got in stock, ain't it?" he asked.

"Yes sir, but it's pretty expensive." "I didn't ask you the price," he broke in, "I asked you if you have anything better." "No I haven't. Neither has anyone else." "Then that's what I want, and everything to go with it. The finest dress you've got in the house, the best embalmin' you can do, the best music – a Solemn High Mass of Requiem with a full choir, Mr. Burke."

I was about to ask him if he realized what he was letting himself in for, when he hurried on: "She was the only – the only – girl who ever kissed me in all my life, Mr. Burke. I can't remember that my mother ever kissed me; neither did my sister, As for other women – ha!" The gall and wormwood of an embittered life were concentrated in the exclamation. "But she kissed me; did it as if she wanted to, not as if she were takin' a dose of castor oil. You don't know what the memory of that kiss has meant to me, Mr. Burke. Think of it – fifty years old, and never kissed by a woman till that little dead girl did it! I've got almost a half million dollars, Mr. Burke, but I wouldn't trade the memory of that kiss for all of it, nor for ten times as much. D'yue think I'd let the girl who's given me that lovely memory to live with, be buried in the potter's field, or in anything less than the best I can afford? Oh, Burke, Burke you'll never understand!"

He was sobbing like a brokenhearted child as he left my office. But he came back, again and again before the funeral just to look at little Ana in the casket – as if forever to implant each tiniest detail of her appearance in his memory.

I am sure he was not disappointed, for we took a very special pride in the embalming of that good, sweet- natured girl.
For all his ill-stared nature, and for all his outward ugliness, the inner Jonah Pettigrew was a man of gentle sensitivity. When he paid his bill, he placed a like amount in trust at my bank – to be used, anonymously, for the funeral of some dear, good person who would otherwise be buried in Potter's Field.

It is from such appreciation of one's service . . . from the knowledge that our work has been of real usefulness in the everyday lives of our neighbors . . . that the Funeral Profession gains its finest rewards.

Copyrighted by the Dodge Company and is a reprinted with permission from the Dodge Magazine. Read this story again!

***

"Prayer is not a 'spare wheel' that you pull out when in trouble, but it is a 'steering wheel' that directs the right path throughout the journey."

***

There was a Boy Scout, a **Preacher**, a politician and a doctor took a flight to Chicago to a special meeting. Before they'd been in the air for very long, about an hour, the Captain came on the sound system and said, "Ladies and gentlemen, we have a serious problem with our engines and we only have 3 parachutes left for you to use. Let me have your attention: everyone on the plane that received your parachutes upon boarding are now free to jump;" so they did. Now, the only ones left to jump were the **Preacher**, the Boy Scout, the doctor, and the politician, but there were only 3 available parachutes. The Boy Scout said, "I'm very young and I think the **Preacher** should go first because there are many folks that need to hear his sermons," so he jumped. Then the little Boy Scout said, "I'm young and there is a chance I might survive without the chute, I think the doctor should go now because he can save many lives." Before anyone could do anything, the politician boldly said, I think I should go now because I'm a brilliant Senator from Washington, D.C. and the people need me, and so, he grabbed the parachute and jumped. Well, that left the Boy Scout and the doctor. The doctor said, "Son, I've had a good life and you're young and your life is all ahead of you. You should go ahead and jump now." The Boy Scout said, "Don't worry Doc, we can both jump. That brilliant Senator, from Washington, D.C. jumped, using my knap sack."

***

"If you wake up on the wrong side of the bed . . . climb right back in and get out the other side . . . after all , why should all the rest of us have to deal with a crab."

***

There was an Evangelist in downtown Philadelphia who needed to know where the post office was located, so he asked a newsboy for information. The newsboy said, "Go this way two blocks and then turn to the right and you'll see the post office in front of you." Well, the Evangelist thanked the boy for his information and then said, "You seem like a bright young fellow. Do you know who I am?" "Nope," said the boy. The **Preacher** replied, I'm the **Preacher** who is holding a revival in the big tent down the street. If you come tonight, I'll show you the way to Heaven." "Aw, go on now, said the boy, You don't even know the way to the post office, how in the world would you know how to get to Heaven?"

***

Two women were talking and one of the ladies asked the other one, "What's it like being a Christian?" The other lady replied, "It is like being a pumpkin. God picks you from the patch, brings you in, and washes all the dirt off of you. Then He cuts the top off and scoops out all the yucky stuff. He removes the seeds of doubt, hate, and greed. Then He carves you a new smiling face and puts His light inside of you to shine for all the world to see." "The pumpkin story is nice," said the first lady, "but the real difference is that the pumpkin didn't have any choice but to come in when picked. To become a Christian you must make the decision to become the clean pumpkin by asking the Lord to forgive your sins and come into your heart, because you believe in John 3:16. The pumpkin just takes a chance."

***

"If you don't have something nice to say, then

don't say anything at all . . . yes, this does mean that some people may never speak, but . . . SO BE IT!"

***

One Sunday morning a young **Preacher** was preaching and he hit almost every person in the Bible, and finally he said, "Now, what am I going to do with Zechariah?" A little boy on the front row said, "Here **Preacher**, I've been here long enough, you can give him my seat."

***

"For my heart rejoiced in all my labor; and this was my reward from my labor!" Ecclesiastes 2:10

***

"Isn't God wonderful? Isn't God wonderful?" said the **Minister**. "Yes, siree' making the same number of men as women. A man for every woman and a woman for every man, you can hardly improve on that." A young man around 22 or 23 said, "I don't want to improve on it, I just want to get in on it."

***

The Power of a Letter

Most of us remember John Wayne as an actor. You may not know what happened to him before he died. **This is that story!**

Robert Schuller's teenage daughter, Cindy, was in a motorcycle accident and had to have her leg amputated. John Wayne was a big fan of Robert Schuller. He heard Rev. Schuller say on one of his programs that his daughter had been in an accident and had to have her leg amputated. John Wayne wrote a note to her saying: "Dear Cindy, sorry to hear about your accident. Hope you will be all right." Signed, John Wayne. The note was delivered to her and she decided she wanted to write John Wayne a note in reply. She wrote: "Dear Mr. Wayne, I got your note. Thanks for writing to me. I like you very much. I am going to be all right because Jesus is going to help me. Mr. Wayne, do you know Jesus? I sure hope you know Jesus, Mr. Wayne, because I cannot imagine Heaven being complete without John Wayne being there. I hope, if you don't know Jesus, that you will give your heart to Jesus right now. See you in Heaven." And she signed her name. She had just put that letter in an envelope, sealed it, and written across the front of it John Wayne: when a visitor came into her room to see her. He said to her, "What are you doing?" She said, "I just wrote a letter to John Wayne, but I don't know how to get it to him." He said, "That's funny, I am going to have dinner with John Wayne tonight at the Newport Club down at Newport Beach.

"Give it to me and I will give it to him." She gave him the letter and he put it in his coat pocket. There were twelve of them that night sitting around the table for dinner. They were laughing and cutting up and the guy happened to reach in his pocket and felt that letter and remembered. John Wayne was seated at the end of the table and the guy took the letter out and said, "Hey, Duke, I was in Schuller's daughter's room today and she wrote you a letter and wanted me to give it to you. Here it is." They passed it down to John Wayne and he opened it. One of them said, "Hey, Duke, what is the matter?" He said and can't you hear him saying it, "I want to read you this letter." He read the letter. Then he began to weep. He folded it, put it in his pocket, and he pointed to the man who delivered it to him and said, "You go tell that little girl that right now, in this restaurant, right here, John Wayne gave his heart to Jesus Christ and I will see her in Heaven." Three weeks later, John Wayne died.

END OF A WONDERFUL STORY ABOUT A GREAT MAN!

***

"It's all about quality of life, and finding a happy balance between God, Family, Friends and Work"

Philip Green

***

The young **Minister** hadn't been at the Main Street Church in downtown Kansas City, very long. It was Sunday morning, and time for his sermon once again. He got up said the following; "What a fine, good looking bunch we have here this morning. I usually tell everyone that, but this time I really mean it."

***

Richard & Neta Ruth Sunderwirth

"If your religious experience does not change you, then you should change your religion."
Elbert Hubbard

***

The new **Minister** of the church went to visit a family of his congregation that he'd never met. They offered him a drink. He said, "My goodness, do you know who I am or why I'm here? The member said, "No, but if you know where you live we'll be more than happy to take you home."

***

"Judge each day not by the harvest you reap, but by the seeds you plant."
Robert Louis Stevenson

***

Reverend. John Buford was out hunting one day, and all of a sudden he realized he was being chased by a big ole black bear. The bear chased him up against a big rock bluff and there was not a place for **Reverend** Buford to go. He looked the bear straight in the eye and said, "I'm a Christian, I rebuke you in the name of our Lord and Savior." The bear looked at **Reverend**. Buford, and said, "Well, I'm a Christian bear so, before I have you for lunch I will say the blessing."

***

A few more Church Bulletin Announcements

Don't let worry kill you – let the church help.

Thursday night – Potluck supper; Prayer and medication to follow

For those of you who have children and don't know it, we have a nursery downstairs.

The rosebud on the altar this morning is to announce the birth of David Alan Belzer, the sin of **Reverend** and Mrs. Julius Belzer.

This afternoon there will be meetings in the south and north ends of the church. Children will be baptized at both ends.

Tuesday at 4:00 p.m. there will be a meeting of the 'Little Mothers Club'. All ladies wishing to be 'Little Mothers' will meet with the **Pastor** in his study.

This being Easter Sunday, we will ask Mrs. Lewis to come forward and lay an egg on the altar.

The service will close with 'Little Drops of Water'. One of the ladies will start quietly and the rest of the congregation will join in.

***

Ed, when did you stop singing in the choir? "Well," said Ed. When they insulted me, you see, I missed one week and they all thought we had the organ tuned."

***

"Laughter is the jam on the toast of life. It adds flavor, keeps it from being too dry, and makes it easier to swallow!" **Diane Johnson**

***

Safety Tips

1. Do not ride in an automobile; they cause 20 percent of all fatal accidents.
2. Do not stay at home; 17 percent of all accidents happen there.
3. Do not walk in the street; 15 percent of all accidents happen to pedestrians.
4. Do not travel by air, rail or water; 16 percent of all accidents result from these activities.
5. Only .001 percent of all accidents happen in church.
6. FINAL TIP: It sounds like we should spend most of our time in church.

Copied

***

These 3 fellows died and went to the pearly gates of Heaven. St. Peter met them and said, "If you can each answer one of these questions you can go right in." St. Peter asked the first fellow, "Can you tell me what Easter is all about?" First guy said, "Well, it is when you put out the pumpkins, then dress up like a monster, and go ask for candy." St. Peter replied, "No, you can't come in." He asked the second fellow, "What is Easter?" The second guy said, Well, that's when ole Santa Claus comes down the chimney and . . ." St. Peter said, "No you can't come in." Then he asked the third fellow about Easter. The fellow said, "Well, when Christ died on the cross," St. Peter thought, well at least we're going to have one out of three know the answer. The fellow continued with his explanation. . . . and if he comes out of the grave and sees his shadow."

***

A friend of mine attended a Christian college where the tradition was to deliver a box of notes nightly from the men's dorm to the women's dorm and vice versa. My friend would write his fiancé a note every night and close it with an inspirational Scripture reference. One night, he meant to write the reference II Corinthians 5:1, which says: "Now we know that if the earthly tent we live in is destroyed, we have a building from God, an eternal house in heaven, not built by human hands." Unfortunately, he referenced I Corinthians 5:1 which says; "It is actually reported that there is sexual immorality among you, and of a kind that does not occur even among pagans . . ."

***

Nails and Temper A great bit of advice, read slowly and absorb.

There once was a little boy who had a really bad temper. His father gave him a bag of nails and told him that every time he lost his temper, he must hammer a nail into the fence. The first day the boy drove 37 nails into the fence. Over the next few weeks, as he learned to control his temper, the number of nails hammered daily gradually dwindled down.

Finally the day came when the boy didn't lose his temper at all. He told his father about it and the father suggested that the boy now pull out one nail for each day that he was able to hold his temper. The days passed and the young boy was finally able to tell his father that all the nails were gone.

The Father took his son by the hand and led him to the fence. He said, "You have done well, my son, but look at the holes in the fence. The fence will never be the same. When you say and do things in anger, they leave a scar just like this one. You can put a knife in a man and draw it out. It won't matter how many times you say I'm sorry, the wound is still there. Make sure you control your temper the next time you are tempted to say something you will regret later or maybe even for the rest of your life.

Author Unknown

***

The story of Noah

Ending his sermon, a **Preacher** announced that he would preach on Noah and the Ark on the following Sunday, and gave the scriptural reference for the congregation to read ahead of time. A couple of boys noticed something interesting about the placement of the story in the Bible. They slipped into the church and glued two pages of the pulpit Bible together. The next Sunday, the **Preacher** got up to read his text. "Noah took unto himself a wife," he began, "and she was "– he turned the page to continue – "three hundred cubits long, fifty wide and thirty high." He paused, scratched his head, turned the page back, read it silently, and tuned the page again. Then he looked up at his congregation and said, "I've been reading this old Bible for nearly fifty years, and sometimes I'm more baffled than ever before."

***

The **Priest** was hearing confessions. A member of his church came in with 3 sins. The **Priest** said, "You're forgiven, but be sure and put $5.00 in the basket as you're leaving." Another person came in with her story, but she only had 2 sins. The janitor was in the back of the church and when he heard her confession he hollered out. "Might as well go out and do another one, they are going 3 for $5.00 this week."

***

"If you cannot pray over a thing, and cannot ask God to bless you in it, don't do that thing. A secret that you would keep from God is a secret that you should keep from your own heart."

***

Wonderful Quotes

1. If you feel far away from God, guess who moved?
2. Fear knocked. Faith answered. No one was there.
3. What you are is God's gift to you. What you become is your gift to God.
4. I am God's melody of life and He sings His song through me.

5. We can never really go where God is not, and where He is, all is well.
6. No matter what is happening in your life, know that God is waiting for you with open arms.
7. God promises a safe landing, not a calm passage.
8. Do your best and then sleep in peace. God is awake.
9. God has a purpose and plan for me that no one else can fulfill.
10. The will of God will never take you to where the grace of God will not protect you.
11. We are responsible for the effort, not the outcome.
12. We set the sail; God makes the wind.
13. Begin to weave and God will give you the thread.
14. Sometimes when God says "no", it's because He has something better in store for you.
15. The talk ahead of us is never as great as the power behind us.
16. Prayer; don't bother to give God instructions, just report for duty.
17. It's my business to do God's business and it's His business to take care of my business.
18. Serenity is not freedom from the storm, but peace amid the storm.
19. How come you're always running around looking for God? He's not lost.
20. God put me on earth to accomplish a number of things; right now I'm so far behind I will live forever.
21. I'd live life in the fast lane but I am married to a speed bump.

***

In this little community, every year, the folks would have a Masquerade party, on Halloween. There was one fellow that decided he would have some real fun and dress up like the devil. Halloween night came, he was dressed up in his bright red suit, which even included a big long tail, and yes, he really looked the part. He was headed for the party and he just happened to pass by a small country church that was having an old time revival meeting. He jumped in the front door, with all the vim and vinegar he could muster; ran to the front and said, with gusto, "Boo, I'm the devil." There was a little old man sitting on the front pew and he didn't move a muscle. He just looked up and said, "Well, you don't scare me one little bit." The devil jumped a little closer to the old man and said, "Why do you say that old man?" The old man calmly replied, "Because I'm married to your sister and she don't scare me either."

***

"If you want to make an apple pie from scratch, you must first create the Universe."

***

The Good Samaritans

A guy was in a bar about as drunk as it is possible to get. A couple of guys notice his condition and decide to be good Samaritans and take him home. First they stand him up to get to his wallet, so they can find out where he lives, but he keeps falling down. He fell down an additional eight more times on the way to the car, each time with a real thud. After they get him to his house, he falls down another four times just getting him to the door. His wife comes to the door, and one guy says, "We brought your husband home." The wife says, "Oh that's really nice of you, but where is his wheelchair?" **Copied**

***

"In the 60s' people took acid to make the world weird. Now the world is weird and people take Prozac to make it normal."

***

After the fall in the Garden, Adam was walking with his sons, Cain and Abel. They passed by the fruit trees of the garden. "Boys," said Adam, "That's where your mother ate us out of house and home."

***

The **Preacher** was wired for sound with a lapel mike, and as he preached, he moved briskly about the platform, jerking the mike cord as he went. Then he moved to one side, getting wound up in the cord and nearly tripping before jerking it again. After several circles and jerks, a little girl in the third pew leaned toward her mother and whispered, "If he gets loose mommy, will he hurt us?"

***

A father was reading Bible stories to his young son. He read, "The man named Lot was warned to take his wife and flee out of the city, but his wife looked back and was turned to salt." His son asked, "What happened to the flea?"

***

A mother took her little boy to church. While in church the little boy said, "Mommy, I have to pee." The mother said to the little boy, "It's not appropriate to say the word 'pee' in church. So, from now on whenever you have to 'pee' just tell me that you have to 'whisper'." The following Sunday, the little boy went to church with his Father and during the service said to his Father, "Daddy, I have to whisper." The Father looked at him and said, "Okay son, why don't you whisper in my ear."

***

There were three couples that died and went to Heaven. When they got to the Pearly Gates they met St. Peter and he said, "How did you folks all happen to arrive here at the same time?" "Well," said one of the folks, "We were in a terrible automobile accident and we all ended up here with you." St. Peter said, "That's too bad you all had to go at one time. In order for you get into Heaven I have to know your wives first names, and then I'll check to see if you are OK to come in. St. Peter said to the first lady, "And what is your name?" She answered, "My name is Penny." St. Peter said, "You just can't come in because your name proves that you are obsessed with money." And he asked the next lady, "And what is your name?" She answered, "My name is Candy." St. Peter said, "You can't come in either because you are obsessed with sweets." Well, the last wife looked at her husband, and he looked back at her and said, "Honey, we might as well head out of here; we don't stand a chance either, since your name is Fanny."

***

Man was Complaining . . .
Oh Lord, please have mercy on me; I work so hard; in the meantime my wife stays at home. I would give anything if you would grant me one wish "Switch me into my wife." She's got it easy at home and I want to teach her a lesson of how tough a man's life

is. As God was listening he felt sorry for this soul and granted his wish. Next morning the "new woman" wakes up at dawn, makes lunch boxes, prepares breakfast, wakes up the kids for school, puts a load of clothes in the washer, takes the meat out of the freezer, drives the kids to school; on his way back stops at the gas station, cashes a check, pays the electricity and phone bills, picks up some clothes from the cleaners, then quickly goes to the market. It was 1:00 p.m. already. He made the beds, took the clothes out of the washer and puts another load in, then vacuumed the house, made some rice, went to pick up the kids from school, and has an argument with the kids. As soon as he got home he fed the kids, washed the dirty dishes, he hung the damp clothes he had washed on the chairs because it was raining outside. He helped the kids with their homework, watched some TV while he ironed some clothes, prepared dinner, he gave the kids a bath and put them to sleep. At 9:00 p.m. he was so tired and he went to bed. Of course, there were some more duties and somehow he managed to get them done and finally fell asleep. The next morning he prays to God once again: "Oh Lord, what was I thinking when I asked you to grant my wish, I can't take it anyone. I beg you please switch me back to myself, please oh please." Then he heard God's voice speaking to him, saying; Dear son, of course I'll switch you back into yourself but there's one minor detail, you will have to wait 9 months because last night you got pregnant.

***

Every summer the **Minister**ial alliance would have a nice social get-together. Next door there just happened to be a local brewery that was having a brewery society meeting at the same time. Somehow the orders for the watermelons got mixed up and the **Minister**ial social just happened to get the ones ordered by the brewery meeting folks. The **Minister**'s watermelons were spiked with a heavy blend of strong alcohol. Before anyone could stop the affair, the **Minister**s were into the watermelons full force. The guys from the brewery society noticed what had happened and one said, "What are we going to do." The other guy said, "Nothing, it's too late. We'll just pretend it didn't happen." Before the social was over the Catholic **Priest** had collected little chunks of the watermelon and was squeezing them through a handkerchief into a glass and sipping the juice slowly. The Jewish **Rabbi** was trying to buy an extra melon to take home. The Episcopalian was gnawing on the rind, the Methodist is asking for 4[ths], the Baptist was going from plate to plate and collecting the seeds, and the Pentecostals were taking a drink, then shouting, "Praise the Lord, we've finally reached the promise land."

***

A beautiful story . . . makes you understand that things happen for a reason!

The brand new **Pastor** and his wife, newly assigned to their first ministry, to reopen a church in suburban Brooklyn, arrived in early October excited about their opportunities. When they saw their church, it was very run down and needed a lot of work. They set a goal to have everything done in time to have their first service on Christmas Eve.

They worked hard, repairing pews, plastering walls, painting, etc. On December 18th they were ahead of schedule and just about finished. On December 19th a terrible tempest; a driving rainstorm hit the area and lasted for two days. On the 21st, the **Pastor** went over to the church. His heart sank when he saw that the roof had leaked, causing a large area of plaster about 20 feet by 8 feet to fall off the front wall of the sanctuary just behind the pulpit, beginning about head high.

The **Pastor** cleaned up the mess on the floor, and not knowing what else to do but postpone the Christmas Eve service, headed home. On the way he noticed that a local business was having a flea market type sale for charity, so he stopped in. One of the items was a beautiful, handmade, ivory colored, crocheted tablecloth with exquisite work, fine colors and a Cross embroidered right in the center. It was just the right size to cover the hole in the front wall. He bought it and headed back to the church.

By this time it had started to snow. An older woman running from the opposite direction was trying to catch the bus. She missed it. The **Pastor** invited her to wait in the warm church for the next bus which was coming in about 45 minutes. She sat in a pew and paid no attention to the **Pastor** while he got a ladder, hangers, etc., to put up the tablecloth as a wall tapestry. The **Pastor** could hardly believe how beautiful it looked and how that it covered up the entire problem area.

Then he noticed the woman walking down the center aisle. Her face was white as a sheet. "**Pastor**," she asked, "Where did you get that tablecloth?" The **Pastor** explained. The woman asked him to check the lower right corner to see if the initials, EBG were crocheted into it there. They were. These were the initials of the woman, and she had made this tablecloth 35 years before, in Austria.

The woman could hardly believe it as the **Pastor** told how he had just gotten "The Tablecloth." The woman explained that before the war she and her husband were well-to-do people in Austria. When the Nazis came, she was forced to leave. Her husband was going to follow her the next week. He was captured, sent to prison and never saw her husband or her home again.

The **Pastor** wanted to give her the tablecloth; but she made the **Pastor** keep it for the church. The **Pastor** insisted on driving her home. That was the least he could do. She lived on the other side of Staten Island and was only in Brooklyn for the day for a housecleaning job.

What a wonderful service they had on Christmas Eve. The church was almost full. The music and the spirit were great. At the end of the service, the **Pastor** and his wife greeted everyone at the door and many said that they would return. An older gentleman, whom the **Pastor** recognized from the neighborhood continued to sit in one of the pews and stare, and the **Pastor** wondered why he wasn't leaving.

The man asked him where he got the tablecloth on the front wall because it was identical to one that his wife had made years ago when they lived in Austria, before the war and how could there be two tablecloths so much alike? He told the **Pastor** how the Nazis came, how he forced his wife to flee for her safety and he was supposed to follow her, but he was arrested and put in a prison. He never saw his wife or his home again all the 35 years between.

The **Pastor** asked him if he would allow him to take him for a little ride. They drove to Staten Island and to the same house where the **Pastor** had taken the woman three days earlier. He helped the old man climb the three flights of stairs to the woman's apartment, knocked on the door and he saw the greatest Christmas reunion he could ever possibly imagine. **A TRUE STORY; SUBMITTED BY PASTOR ROB REID.**

***

The scriptures tell us about a happy heart, "A merry heart does good like a medicine; A merry heart makes a cheerful countenance; But he that is of a merry heart hath a continual feast.

***

I didn't used to finish sentences, but now I ...

Copied

***

I used to think I was indecisive,
but now I'm not too sure.

Copied

***

Two men were shipwrecked and landed on a deserted island. One of them decided it was time to pray, so he started, "Dear Lord, I've broken most of the Ten Commandments, I've been a horrible sinner, I've treated my wife badly at times, plus no telling what else. If you'll spare us I'll promise to" . . . the other guy hollered and said, "Hold on a minute, don't commit yourself, I think I see a boat."

***

"Dear Pastor" Letters From Youngsters

Dear **Pastor**, I know God loves everybody, but He never met my sister. Age 8

Please say in your sermon that Peter Peterson has been a good boy all week. I am Peter Peterson. Age 9

My father should be a **Minister**. Every day he gives us a sermon about something. Age 11

I'm sorry I can't leave more money in the plate, but my father didn't give me a raise in my allowance. Could you have a sermon about a raise in my allowance? Age 10

My mother is very religious. She goes to play bingo at church every week even if she has a cold. Age 9

I would like to go to Heaven because I know my brother won't be there. Age 8

I hope to go to Heaven someday, but later than sooner. Age 9

Please say a prayer for our Little League team. We need God's help, or a new pitcher. Thank You! Age 10
My father says I should learn the Ten Commandments. But I don't think I want to because we have enough rules already in my house. Age 10
Are there any devils on earth? I think there may be one in my class. Age 10
How does God know the good people from the bad people? Do you tell Him or does He read about it in the newspapers? Age 9
I liked your sermon on Sunday, especially when it was finished. Age 11

***

A Heartwarmer: "Get To . . ."

Did you ever have something that someone said hit you like a ton of bricks? That happened to me at 8:05 p.m. on Thursday, January 18, 2001. It is a day I will never forget.

I need to back track a little here, so you will understand where I am coming from. In September of 1996, I walked through the doors of Marian College as an adult student going to college for the first time, at 44 years of age. It has always been a dream of mine to go to college, but that didn't lessen the butterflies in my stomach, or my lack of confidence. Today I have completed 96 credits and I have 33 more to go. I've come a long way from that first night 52 months ago. It was during one of my current marketing classes that my instructor, Pam Schlenvogt, told us about "Get To: and I just can't get it off my mind.

She told us that we walk through life making choices. Some of them are good, and some of them not so good, but hopefully we learn something from all of them. She told us that night a little about attitude and how it affects us. She gave us a hand-out called "LIFE IS AN ATTITUDE; and walked us through Accountability, Tenacity, Truth, Integrity, Trust, Understanding, Dedication, and Excellence. She also told us that we cannot choose what happens to us. But we can choose our attitudes toward each situation; first brick. If we walk through life on the path we have chosen feeling as though we HAVE to do this or we HAVE to do that, eventually we might feel overwhelmed. She then told us about changing our attitude and looking at the opportunities presented to us each day. If we look at those opportunities or challenges with a "GET

TO" instead of a "HAVE TO" we might enjoy the journey just a little bit more; second brick.

I decided to make a conscious effort over the next couple of days to exchange the words "HAVE TO" with "GET TO" in my conversations with friends, co-workers, and family, but most of all in my thoughts, and something amazing happened. I noticed all the things I "GET TO" do and started appreciating the opportunities and challenges on my path.

JUST IMAGINE

I GET TO, go to school to fulfill my dream. I GET TO, go to work when so many people can't. I GET TO, do the laundry, thankful for a washer and dryer. I GET TO, play with my cat who is so thankful for the attention. I GET TO, say a prayer, I have freedom of speech. I GET TO, remember the things that make me happy. I GET TO, spend time with a friend, who needs my help. I GET TO, read a book, I still have my sight.

I give you a challenge. With every thought and conversation for the next day or two, change the words "I HAVE TO" with the words "I GET TO" and see if it makes a difference in your day. **Lesleigh Ann Scaefer**

***

A local **Minister** received a call from the Internal Revenue Service asking about a member of his church. The agent said, "Mr. Johnson stated on his income tax return that he gave $4,000 dollars to your church building fund this past year, is that correct? "I don't have the receipts right here in front of me, but if he didn't he will," said the **Minister**.

***

"When there is nothing left but God, that is when you find out that God is all you need!"

***

Little Joey blurted out with a loud whistle in Church. His mother said to Joey, "Why in the world did you do that?" Joey replied back, "Well, I've asked the Lord, in my prayers, to help me learn how to whistle, and I guess He just decided to do it right then."

***

"God always gives His best

to those who leave the choice to Him."
Jim Elliot

***

The Cabby and the Preacher
A cab driver who had worked all his life in Kingston, Jamaica reaches the Pearly Gates and announces his presence to St. Peter, who looks him up in his Big Book. Upon reading the entry for the cabby, St. Peter invites him to grab a silk robe and a golden staff and to proceed into Heaven. A **Preacher** is next in line behind the cabby and has been watching these proceedings with interest. He announces himself to St. Peter. Upon scanning the **Preacher**'s entry in the Big Book, St. Peter furrows his brow and says, "Okay, we'll let you in, but take that cloth robe and wooden staff." The **Preacher** is astonished and replies, "But I am a man of the cloth. You gave that cab driver a gold staff and a silk robe. Surely I rate higher than a cabby." St. Peter responded matter-of-factly: "Here we are interested in results. When you preached, people slept. When that cabby drove his taxi, people prayed and some even found God before the meter was turned off!"

***

At church last Sunday the **Minister** ask Tony, who said he was going to be celebrating his 50th wedding anniversary, how in the world he managed to stay married to the same woman for all those years. Tony replied, "Wella, I'va tried to treat her nicea, spenda da money on her, but besta of all is, I tooka her to Italy for our 25th anniversary!" The **Minister** responded, "Tony, you are an amazing inspiration to all of the husbands here today. Please tell us what you are planning for your wife for your 50th anniversary?" Tony proudly replied, "I'ma gonna go pick her upa."

***

Old Mr. Jackson was a rich man near death. He was grieved because he'd worked so hard for his money, and he wanted to be able to take it to heaven. An angel heard his concern and appeared to him and said, "Mr. Jackson, sorry, but you can't take your wealth with you." Mr. Jackson pled with the angel. Later the angel reappeared and told the wealthy man that he could take one suitcase. Overjoyed, the man found his largest case and filled it with gold bars. When he finally died and showed up in heaven, St. Peter saw the suitcase and said, "Hold on, you can't bring that in here." Mr. Johnson explained to St. Peter that he had permission. Sure enough, the saint checked the record and verified the man's story. "But," St. Peter added, "I am supposed to check the contents before letting it through." So St. Peter opened the suitcase to discover what was too precious to leave behind. He couldn't believe his eyes, He said, "We don't really don't need any more of this, but I guess we can always use a little more pavement?"

***

"There are people in the world so hungry, that God cannot appear to them except in the form of bread."

Mahatma Gandhi

***

This is no joke, but certainly worth reading.

Psalm 46:10 "Be still, and know that I am God: I will be exalted among the heathen, I will be exalted in the earth." Verse 11: The Lord of hosts is with us; the God of Jacob is our refuge." In the mist of all the busyness, noise, and posturing, we need to be still and know that He is God and will never leave or forsake us and will be that refuge when difficult times are upon us.

***

One day in school, around Christmas time, the teacher was telling the children about the birth of Christ. She asked Joyce if she knew what Jesus's mother's name was." "Mary," she quickly answered. "Ok, that is correct. Now then, Sammy, do you know the name of Jesus's father?" Sammy blurted out, "Virg." The teacher said, "No, I don't think that is right." Sammy said, "Well, I think it is; ever since I was a little kid, I've heard every body talk about the Virgin and Mary."

***

There was a religious lady that had to do a lot of traveling for her business, so naturally she did a lot of flying. Flying made her extremely nervous, so she always took her Bible along with her to read since it helped relax her on the long flights. One time, she was sitting next to a man. When he saw her pull out her Bible, he gave a little chuckle, smirked and went back to what he was doing. After a while, he turned to her and asked, "You don't really believe all that stuff in there do you?" The lady replied, "Of course I do. It is the Bible." He said, "Well, what about the guy that was swallowed by the whale?" She replied, "Oh, Jonah; Yes, I believe that, it is in the Bible." He asked, "Well, how do you suppose he survived all that time inside the whale?" The lady said, "Well, I don't really know. I guess when I get to heaven, I will ask him." "What if he isn't in Heaven?" the man asked sarcastically. "Then you can ask him," replied the lady.

***

A **Minister** was asked to give a talk at a local women's health club. His wife asked about his topic, but he was too embarrassed to admit that. You see, he had been asked to speak about sex. Thinking quickly, he said, I'm talking about sailing. "Oh, that's nice," replied his wife. The next day at the grocery store, a young woman, who had attended the club meeting lecture, recognized the **Minister**'s wife. "That was certainly an excellent talk your husband gave yesterday," she said. "He really has a unique perspective on the subject." Somewhat surprised, the **Minister**'s wife replied, "Gee, funny you should think so, he's only done it twice. The first time he threw up, and the second time his hat blew off."

***

Yes, it really does pay to tithe.
There were two men shipwrecked on a desert island. One was a churchgoer and the other wasn't. The very minute they got stuck on the island, the non-believer began screaming and yelling, "We're going to die! There's no water, no food! We're going to die! The believer was calmly propped against a palm tree, which drove the other guy crazy. "Don't you get it? We're going to die! What's wrong with you? "You don't understand," said the churchgoer, "I make one hundred thousand dollars a week." "What difference does that make, in a situation like this? asked the non-believer. "We're on a desert island, we're going to die." The believer smiled and said, "You just don't get it. I make one hundred thousand dollars a week, and I tithe. My **Pastor** will find me!"

***

"Apparently I did not proofread the Sunday bulletin as well as I thought," said the **Preacher** to his wife. I thought when I prepared it, I checked it over, but I guess I didn't." His wife said, "Well, what did it say?" "I certainly was surprised when I looked at the bulletin when I entered the church this morning. It said, Come and visit with us during our coffee hour in the lower level of the church. Come down and say hell to our **Pastor**."

***

"When you reach the end of your rope, you will find the hem of His garment."

***

There was a very young girl that took skating lessons from the local rink. She did extremely well and many folks stopped to ask her name. "Well," she would say, "I'm **Pastor** Smith's daughter." As she advanced in this particular sport, she really became very popular. More and more folks would come up to and say, "Do you live around here? and what is your name?" Just as usual she would say, "I'm **Pastor** Smith's daughter." One day her mother heard her say that and she said to her. "Honey, I believe it is time for you to just simply say, "My name is Susie Smith." One more time her mother heard her say, I'm **Pastor** Smith's daughter. This time her mother got a little bit rough with her and said, "Honey, I insist that you say when they ask you your name, say 'I'm Susie Smith." Susie replied to her mother, "Ok, mom, if you insist." A few days later a reporter came into the skating rink and was there to interview little Susie. He went over to where he thought she might be and said, "Are you **Pastor** Smith's daughter?" She answered with a sigh, "Well, for years I thought I was, as a matter of fact my mother insisted that I'm not, my name; however, is Susie Smith."

***

I think this is hilarious! I never heard creation explained this way before!

In the beginning . . . God created the Heavens and the Earth and populated the Earth with broccoli, cauliflower and spinach, green and yellow and red vegetables of all kinds, so

Man and Woman would live long and healthy lives. Then using God's great gifts, Satan created Ben and Jerry's Ice Cream and Krispy Crème Donuts. And Satan said, "You want chocolate with that?" And Man said, "Yes!" and Woman said, "And as long as you're at it, add some sprinkles." And they both gained 10 pounds, and Satan smiled. And God created the healthful yogurt that Woman might keep the figure that Man found so fair. And Satan brought forth white flour from the wheat, and sugar from the cane and combined them. And Woman went from a size 6 to a size 14. So, God said, "Try my fresh green salad." And Satan presented Thousand-Island Dressing, buttery croutons and garlic toast on the side. And Man and Woman unfastened their belts following the feast. God then said, "I have sent you heart healthy vegetables and olive oil in which to cook them." And Satan brought forth deep fried fish and chicken-fried steak so big it needed its own platter. And Man gained more weight and his cholesterol went through the roof. God then created a light, fluffy white cake, named it "Angel Food Cake," and said, "It is good." Satan then created chocolate cake and named it "Devil's Food." God then brought forth running shoes so that His children might lose those extra pounds. And Satan gave cable TV with a remote control so Man would not have to toil changing the channels. And Man and Woman laughed and cried before the flickering blue light and gained many pounds. Then God brought forth the potato, naturally low in fat and brimming with nutrition. And Satan peeled off the healthful skin and sliced the starchy center into chips and deep-fried them. And Man again gained pounds. God then gave lean beef so that Man might consume fewer calories and still satisfy his appetite. And Satan created McDonald's and its 99-cent double cheeseburger. Then said, "You want fries with that?" and Man replied, "Yes! and super-size them!" And Satan said, "It is good." And Man went into cardiac arrest. God sighed and created quadruple bypass surgery. And that is it . . . so far!

***

Did you know that Moses had no problems with constipation? The reason I know that is because God told him to take two tablets and go into the wilderness.

***

A priest, a Pentecostal preacher, and a rabbi . . . all served as

Chaplains at a local university. They would get together two or three times a week for coffee and to talk shop. One day, someone made the comment that preaching to people isn't really all that hard. A real challenge would be to preach to a bear. One thing led to another, and they decided to do an experiment. They would go out into the woods, find a bear, preach to it, and attempt to convert it. Seven days later, they all came together to discuss the experience. Father Flannery, who had his arm in a sling, was on crutches, and had various bandages on his body and limbs, went first. "Well," he said, "I went into the woods to find me a bear. And when I found him, I began to read to him from the Catechism. Well, that bear wanted nothing to do with me and began to slap me around. So I quickly grabbed my holy water, sprinkled him and; Holy Mary Mother of God, he became as gentle as a lamb. The bishop is coming out next week to give him first communion and confirmation."

Reverend Billy Bob spoke next. He was in a wheelchair, had one arm and both legs in casts, and had an IV drip. He said, "Well, brothers, you KNOW that we don't sprinkle! I went out and I found me a bear. And then I began to read to my bear from God's HOLY WORD! But that bear wanted nothing to do with me. So I took hold of him and we began to wrestle. We wrestled down one hill, up another and down another until we came to a creek; So I quickly DUNKED him and BAPTIZED his hairy soul. And just like that, he became as gentle as a lamb. We spent the rest of the day praising Jesus."

The **Priest** and the **Reverend** both looked down at the **Rabbi**, who was lying in a hospital bed. He was in a body cast and traction with IVs and monitors running in and out of him. He was in really bad shape. The **Rabbi** looked up and said, "Looking back on it now boys, I have decided that circumcision may not have been the best way to start."

***

The **Pope** came into the U.S.A for a very important meeting. He knew where the location of the building was; however, in New York City, sometimes it is very difficult to get where you are going. Finally the **Pope** decided to get a Taxi. He hailed one down and jumped in the back seat. He told the driver where he wanted to go, but the driver seemed to be going in circles. The **Pope** said,

"Driver, please let me drive, I think I know where this address is." Well, they changed places and they were going again. The **Pope** was driving so fast he got a ticket. The policeman pecked on the Taxi's front window glass and asked the **Pope** to roll down his window. The **Pope** did as the policeman requested.

About the time the **Pope** started rolling down the window the Policeman recognized who it was. He pardoned himself and told the **Pope** he would be right back. He went to his patrol car and called the Mayor and the Chief of Police. I stopped this car and, Wow! The guy in the back seat must really be somebody. I didn't know quite for sure what I needed to do. The Mayor said, "Why do you think he must really be somebody?" "Well," said the Cop, you're not going to believe this, but the **Pope**, the Catholic **Pope** is driving him around."

***

The Important Things Life Teaches

One night, at 11:30 P.M., and older African American woman was standing on the side of an Alabama highway trying to endure a lashing rain storm. Her car had broken down and she desperately needed a ride. Soaking wet, she decided to flag down the next car. A young white man stopped to help her . . . generally unheard of in those conflict filled 1960's. The man took her to safety, helped her get assistance and put her into a taxicab. She seemed to be in a big hurry! She wrote down his address, thanked him and drove away. Seven days went by and a knock came on the man's door. To his surprise, a giant console color TV was delivered to his home. A special note was attached. It read: "Thank you so much for assisting me on the highway the other night. The rain drenched not only my clothes but my spirits. Then you came along. Because of you, I was able to make it to my dying husband's bedside just before he passed away. God bless you." Sincerely, Mrs. Nat King Cole **Gordon Steele**

***

"Health nuts are going to feel stupid someday, lying in hospitals, dying of nothing."

***

"The difference between a rut and a grave, is the depth."

***

"Therefore, as God's chosen people, holy and dearly loved, clothe yourselves with compassion, kindness, humility, gentleness and patience." Colossians 3:12

***

The **Preacher** went to Chicago for a meeting. While there he ran into one of his classmates from Joliet, Illinois. The classmate said to him, "Why don't we go next door and have a drink." "Oh no." said the **Preacher**, I don't drink." The classmate insisted so finally the **Preacher** said, "Well, I guess I'll go in with you, but I still want you to know, I don't drink." Finally his buddy convinced him to have just one with him. "Ok," said the **Preacher**, I'll have one of them things they call a Mar, a Marti, a Martina." The buddy said to the bartender, "I'll have a scotch on the rocks and my buddy here will have a Martini." The bartender looked up and said with a smile, "Oh, there's my good friend the **Preacher**, when did you get back in town?"

***

Reverend Billy Graham, Oral Robert, and Jerry Falwell, died and went to Heaven. When they got to the pearly gates St. Peter said, "Fellows it is really great to have you here, but we've got a little problem. Your accommodations are not quite ready yet. If you'll hold up right here, next to the Chamber of Hell, we'll have your mansion ready shortly." In a little while St. Peter called for the guard to bring them on in. The guard said, "It might be a little difficult. Billy has just about got everybody saved; Oral, has just about got everybody healed; and Jerry has just about got enough money raised to air-condition the place.

***

Two **Ministers** died and went to Heaven. St. Peter greeted them and said, "Your condos aren't quite ready yet. Until they are finished, you can return to earth as anything you want to be. "Fine," said the first **Minister**, "I've always wanted to be an eagle soaring over the Grand Canyon." St. Peter said to the second **Minister**, "What would you like to be?" He said, "I'd like to be a real cool stud." Poof, their wishes were granted. When the condos were finished, St. Peter asked an assistant to bring back the two **Ministers**. "How will I find them?" replied the assistant. "Well," St. Peter said, "One of them is soaring over the Grand Canyon as an Eagle; the other one may be a little hard to locate; he's somewhere in Detroit, on somebody's snow tire."

***

"For a Christian, this question is one of the most thrilling questions than can be asked, "Please, teach me about Jesus."

Pastor Mike Banks

***

One Sunday, the **Minister**, was invited over to the Brown's house for dinner. He arrived and, while visiting with one of the children, he asked, "Well," what do you think we're going to have for dinner? Little Johnny answered, "I think we're going to have goat." The **Minister** replied, "Wow, that's quite different. Do your folks have that very often? "No, not that I can remember," said little Johnny, "But I heard mom and dad talking the other day about inviting you over, and dad said, 'We might as well have the old goat for lunch this next Sunday, because we've got to do it sometime.'"

***

The truth about the Bible; This was copied and I don't know who the "I" is in the story facts.

I thought this was so interesting I had to pass it along. During a question and answer session at a recent speaking engagement, a university student asked me, "Why do you believe that the Bible is the inspired word of God?" Now this is a very interesting question, and probably one of the most important questions any Christian could ask themselves. What is so special, so unique about the Bible that Christians believe it is literally the inspired word of God?

In answering this student's question, I encouraged him to consider the following facts about the Bible. First, the Bible is not just one single book. This is a more common misconception than many people realize, especially with people who do not come from a Judeo-Christian background. Rather than being a single book, the Bible is actually a collection of 66 books, which is called the canon of scriptures. These 66 books contain a variety of genres; history, poetry, prophecy, wisdom literature, letters, and apocalyptic, just to name a few.

Second, these 66 books were written by 40 different authors. These authors came from a variety of backgrounds: shepherds, fishermen, doctors, kings, prophets, and others. And most of these authors never knew one another personally.

Third, these 66 books were written over a period of 1,500 years. Yet again, this is another reminder that many of these authors never knew or collaborated with one another in writing these books.

Fourth, the 66 books of the Bible were written in 3 different languages. In the Bible we have books that were written in the ancient languages of Hebrew, Greek, and Aramaic; a reflection of the historical and cultural circumstances in which each of these books were written. And finally, these 66 books were written on 3 different continents; Africa, Asia, and Europe. Once again, this is a testament to the varied historical and cultural circumstances of God's people.

Think about the above realities; 66 books, written by 40 different authors, over 1,500 years, in 3 different languages, on 3 different continents. What's more, this collection of books shares: a common story line – **the creation, fall, and redemption of God's people; a common theme – God's universal love for all of humanity; and a common message – salvation is available to all who repent of their sins and commit to following God with all of their heart, soul, mind and strength.**

In addition to sharing these commonalities, these 66 books contain no historical errors or contradictions. God's word truly is an amazing collection of writings!

After I had shared the above facts with this student, I offered him the following challenge. "If you do not believe that the Bible is the inspired word of God, if you do not believe that the Bible is of a supernatural origin, then I challenge you to a test. You must choose 66 books, written by 40 different authors, over 1,500 years, in 3 different languages, written on 3 different continents; however, they must share a common storyline, a common theme, and a common message, with no historical errors or contradictions."

I went on to say, "If you can produce such a collection of books, I will admit that the Bible is not the inspired word of God."

The student's reply was almost instantaneous, he emphatically stated, "But that's impossible!" "Ok then, it must be, beyond question; it does bear the mark of Divine inspiration," I said to the young man . . . and yes, he agreed. The next time you encounter someone who says the Bible could not be the inspired word of God, all you have to do is go through the solid information above, and challenge them to come up with such a collection that will match those perimeters.

***

Little Suzy gave the **Preacher** 25 cents, as he was coming out the front door of the church, after the Sunday morning service. The **Preacher** said to Little Suzy, "Well honey, that's very nice of you to do that for me." Suzy replied back, "Yes, I felt a little bit sorry for you because dad told me you were the poorest **Preacher** he'd ever heard."

***

This little boy was in the lobby of the church. He looked up and saw a beautiful plaque hanging on the wall. He said to a nice lady that just happened to be standing next to him, "What does the plaque mean, that's hanging up there?" "Oh," she said, "That's in memory of folks that have died in the service." "I understand," said the little boy; "Was it in the morning service or in the evening service?"

***

Little Johnny won a beautiful parrot in Sunday School this past Sunday. His dad was delighted that he had answered so many of the teacher's questions correctly. Johnny took the parrot home in a little cage and told his mom and dad he was going to take it down to the basement and tidy it up a little bit. After about 30 minutes dad began to worry about Johnny, so he went to the basement to check on him. When he got down there he was really shocked because the parrot was on the carpenter's bench dead. He said, "Son, what in the world happened to your parrot? Little Johnny replied, "Well dad, I tried to give him a bath, but he wouldn't hold still, but I think he was dead when I took his head out of the vice."

***

How True!

The paradox of our time in history is that we have taller buildings, but shorter tempers; wider freeways, but narrower viewpoints; we spend more, but have less; we buy more, but enjoy it less.

We have bigger houses and smaller families; more conveniences, but less time; we have more degrees, but less sense; more knowledge, but less judgment; more experts, but less solutions; more medicine, but less wellness.

We have multiplied our possessions, but reduced our values. We talk too much, love too seldom and hate too often.

We've learned how to make a living, but not a life; we've added years to life, not life to years.

We've been all the way to the moon and back, but have trouble crossing the street to meet the new neighbor.

We've conquered outer space, but not inner space; we've cleaned up the air, but polluted the soul; we've split the atom, but not our prejudice.

We have higher incomes, but lower morals; we've become long on quantity, but short on quality.

These are the times of tall men, and short on character; steep on profits, and shallow on relationships.

These are the times of world peace, but domestic warfare; more leisure, but less fun, more kinds of food, but less nutrition. These are days of two incomes, but more divorce; of fancier houses, but broken homes. It is a time when there is much in the show window and nothing in the stockroom; a time when technology can bring this letter in print, and a time when you can choose either to pass it on, and make a difference, or just forget about it.

***

**"Today is what I make it!
The choice is mine alone."**

***

Next Sunday a special collection will be taken to defray the cost of the new carpet. All those wishing to do something on the new carpet will come forward and do so.

***

Chicken Side off first...

Little brother and sister, about 5 years old, got extremely dirty playing out in the mud. Mother said, "Take off all your clothes, we've got to get you both cleaned up." Little girl looked at her brother and then herself and said, "Golly mom, now I know what the difference is between the Methodist and the Baptist."

***

Something to think about

There are many reasons why God should not have called you. But do not worry. You are in good company. Remember no one is perfect. Only God himself exhibits perfection.

Moses stuttered - David's armor did not fit -John Mark was rejected by Paul - Timothy had ulcers - Hosea's wife was a prostitute – Amos' only training was in the school of fig-tree pruning - Jacob was a liar – David had an affair – Solomon was too rich – Jesus was too poor – Abraham was too old – David was too young – Peter was afraid of death – Lazarus was dead – John was self-righteous – Naomi was a widow – Paul was a murdered – So was Moses – Jonah ran from God – Miriam was a gossip – Gideon and Thomas both doubted.

***

The ladies of the church have cast off clothing of every kind. They can be seen in the church basement on Saturday afternoon.

***

A bean supper will be held on Tuesday evening in the church hall. Music will follow.

***

At the evening service tonight, the sermon topic will be "What is Hell?" Come early and listen to our choir practice.

***

Bill goes to Heaven. At the Pearly Gates of Heaven . . . "And who might you be?" inquires St. Peter. "It's me, Bill Clinton, formerly the President of the United States and Leader of the Free World." "Oh, Mr. President, what may I do for you?" ask St. Peter. "I'd like to come in," replies Bill Clinton. "Sure," says the Saint. "But first, you have to confess your sins. What bad things have you done in your life?" Mr. Bill bites his lip and answers, "Well, I tried marijuana, but you can't call it 'dope-smoking' because I didn't inhale. There were inappropriate extramarital relationships, but you can't call it 'adultery' because I didn't have full 'sexual relations.' And I made some statements that were misleading, but legally accurate, but you can't call it 'bearing false witness' because, as far as I know, it didn't meet the legal standard of perjury." With that, St Peter consults the Book of Life briefly, and declares, "Okay, here's the deal. We'll send you somewhere it is hot, but we won't call it 'Hell'. You'll be there indefinitely, but we won't call it 'eternity'. And when you enter, you don't' have to abandon all hope, just hold your breath waiting for it to freeze over.

***

"Religions and Fire"

During a recent ecumenical gathering, a secretary rushed in shouting, "The building is on fire!" The METHODISTS gathered in the corner and prayed. The BAPTISTS cried, "Where is the water?" The QUAKERS quietly praised God for the blessings that fire brings. The LUTHERANS posted the fire was evil. The ROMAN CATHOLICS passed the plate to cover the damage. The JEWS posted symbols on the doors hoping the fire would pass. The CONGREGATRIONALISTS shouted, "Every man for himself!" The FUNDAMENTALISTS proclaimed, "It's the vengeance of God!" The EPISCOPALIANS formed a procession and marched out. The CHRISTIAN SCIENTISTS concluded that there was no fire. The PRESBYTERIANS appointed a chairperson who was to appoint a committee to look into the matter and submit a written report. The PENTECOSTALS started shouting, "We did something wrong! We're in the fire." The secretary grabbed the fire extinguisher and put the fire out.

***

The Sunday school teacher asks, "Now, Johnny, tell me frankly do you say prayers before eating?" "No sir,' little Johnny replies, "I don't have to. My mom is a good cook."

***

Terri asked her Sunday School class to draw pictures of their favorite Bible stories. She was puzzled by Kyle's picture, which showed four people on an airplane. She asked him which story it was meant to represent. "The flight to Egypt," said Kyle. "I see, and that must be Mary, Joseph, and the Baby Jesus," Miss Terry said. But who's the fourth person?" "Oh, that's Pontius-the Pilot."

After the christening of his baby brother in church, little Johnny sobbed all the way home in the back seat of the car. His father asked him three times what was wrong. Finally, the boy replied, "That **Priest** said he wanted us brought up in a Christian home, and I want to stay with you guys!"

***

After a church service on Sunday morning, a young boy suddenly announced to his mother, "Mom, I've decided to become a **Minister** when I grow up." "That's okay with us, but what made you decide that?" "Well," said the little boy, "I have to go to church on Sunday anyway, and I figure it will be more fun to stand up and yell than to just sit there and listen."

***

A boy was watching his father, a **Pastor**, write a sermon. "How do you know what to say?" he asked. "Why, God tells me." "Oh, then why do you keep crossing things out?"

***

A little girl became restless as the **Preacher's** sermon dragged on and on. Finally, she leaned over to her mother and whispered, "Mommy, if we give him the money now, will he let us go?"

***

A six year old little girl was overheard reciting the Lord's Prayer at a church service, "And forgive us our trash passes, as we forgive those who passed trash against us."

***

It was Palm Sunday and Sue's five year old son had to stay home from Church, with a neighbor, because of strep throat. When the family returned home carrying palm branches, he asked what they were for. His mother explained, "People held them over Jesus' head as he walked by." "Wouldn't you know it," the boy fumed. "The one Sunday I don't go, Jesus shows up!"

***

At the beginning of a children's sermon, one girl came up to the altar wearing a beautiful dress. As the children were sitting down around the **Pastor**, he leaned over and said to the girl, "That is a very pretty dress. Is it your Easter dress?" The girl replied almost directly into the **Pastor's** clip-on mike, "Yes, and my Mom says it's a bitch to iron."

***

"While we are free to choose our actions, we are not free to choose the consequences of our actions."

***

A father is in church with his three young children, including his five-year-old daughter. As was his custom, he sat on the very front row so that the children could better see all that was going on. During this particular service, the **Minister** was performing the baptism of a tiny infant. The little five-year-old girl was most enthralled by this, observing that he was saying something and pouring water over the infant's head. With a quizzical look on her face, the little girl turned to her father and asked, "Daddy, why is he brainwashing that little baby?"

***

Who's Hands?

A basketball in my hands is worth about $19. A basketball in Michael Jordan's hands is worth about $33 million. It depends whose hands it's in - - - A baseball in my hands is worth about $6. A baseball in Mark Mcquires hands is worth $19 million. It depends whose hands it's in. - - - A tennis racket is useless in my hands. A tennis racket in Pete Sampras' hands is a Wimbledon championship. It depends whose hands it's in. - - - A rod in my hands will keep away a wild animal. A rod in Moses' hands will part the mighty sea. It depends whose hands it's in. - - - A sling shot in my hands is a kid's toy. A sling shot in David's hand is a mighty weapon. It depends whose hands it's in. - - - 2 fish and 5 loaves of bread in my hands is a couple fish sandwiches. 2 fish and 5 loaves in God's hands will feed thousands. It depends whose hands it's in. - - - A nail in my hands might produce a birdhouse. A nail in Jesus Christ's hands will produce salvation for the entire world. It depends on shoes hands it's in. - - -As you see now it depends whose hands it's in. So put your concerns, your worries, your fears, your hopes, your dreams, your family and your relationships in God's hands because - - - It depends whose hands it's in!

***

Chicken Side off first...

Your Inspiration: I Asked God!

I asked God for Strength . . . And He gave me difficulties to make me strong . . . I asked God for Wisdom . . . and He gave me problems to solve . . . I asked God for Prosperity . . . and He gave me a brain and brawn to work . . . I asked God for Courage . . . And He gave me danger to overcome . . . I asked God for Love . . . And He gave me troubled people to help . . . I asked God for Favors . . . And He gave me opportunities . . .I received nothing I wanted . . . And I received everything I needed!

***

YOUR QUICK INSPIRATION FOR THE DAY; Be Happy Today!

We convince ourselves that life will be better after we get married and have a baby, then another one. Then we are frustrated that the kids aren't old enough and we'll be more content when they are. After that, we're frustrated that we have teenagers to deal with. We will certainly be happy when they are out of that stage. We tell ourselves that our life will be complete when our spouse gets his or her act together, when we get a nicer car, are able to go on a nice vacation, or when we retire. The truth is, there's no better time to be happy than right now. If not now, when? Your life will always be filled with challenges. It's best to admit this to yourself and decide to be happy anyway. Happiness is the way. So, treasure every moment that you have and treasure it more because you shared it with someone special, special enough to spend your time with . . . and remember that time waits for no one. **SO, STOP WAITING, UNTIL**. . . our Car or home is paid off . . . you get a new car or home . . . your kids leave the house . . . you go back to school . . . you lose ten pounds . . . you gain ten pounds . . . you finish school . . . you get a divorce . . . you get married . . . you have kids . . . you retire . . . summer comes, etc.

***

Thought for the day: "Work like you don't need the money; Love like you've never been hurt and dance like no one's watching."

***

MISCELLANEOUS CHURCH OBSERVATIONS

1. Some people are kind, polite, and sweet-spirited until you try

to get into their pews or their favorite church parking spot.
2. Many folks want to serve God, but only as advisers.
3. It is easier to preach ten sermons than it is to live one.
4. We were called to be witnesses, not lawyers.
5. When you get to your wit's end, you'll find God lives there.
6. People are funny. They want the front of the bus, middle of the road, and the back of the church.
7. Opportunity may knock once, but temptation bangs on your door for years.
8. Quit griping about your church; if it was perfect, you couldn't belong.
9. The phrase that is guaranteed to wake up an audience; "And in conclusion."
10. If the church wants a better **Pastor**, it only needs to pray for the one it has.
11. To make a long story short, don't tell it.
12. Some minds are like concrete, thoroughly mixed up and permanently set.
13. I don't know why some people change churches. What difference does it make which one you stay home from.
14. A lot of church members are singing "Standing on the Promises," while they are just sitting on the premises.

***

Yesterday, Today & Tomorrow

There are two days in every week that we should not worry about. Two days that should be kept free from fear and apprehension. One is YESTERDAY, with its mistakes and cares, its faults, and blunders, its aches and pains. Yesterday has passed, forever beyond our control. All the money in the world cannot bring back yesterday. We cannot undo a single act we performed. Nor can we erase a single word we've said. Yesterday is gone!

The other day we shouldn't worry about is TOMORROW with its impossible adversaries, its burden, its hopeful promise and poor performance. Tomorrow is beyond our control. Tomorrow's sun will rise either in splendor or behind a bank of clouds, but it will rise. And until it does we have no stake in tomorrow, for it is yet unborn.

This leaves only one day, TODAY. A person can fight the battles of just one day. It is only when we add the burdens of yesterday and tomorrow that we break down. It is not the experience of today that drives people mad, it is the remorse for something that happened yesterday, and the dread of what tomorrow may bring. Let us therefore, LIVE ONE DAY AT A TIME.

***

A woman arrived at the Gates of Heaven. While she was waiting for Saint Peter to greet her, she peeked through the Gates. She saw a beautiful banquet table. Sitting all around were her parents and all the other people she had loved and who had died before her. They saw here and began calling greetings to her. "Hello, how are you? We've been waiting for you, Good to see you." When Saint Peter came by, the woman said to him "This is such a wonderful place! How do I get in?" "You have to spell a word," Saint peter told her. "Which word?" the woman asked. "Love." The woman correctly spelled "Love" and Saint Peter welcomed her into Heaven.

About a year later, Saint Peter came to the woman and asked her to watch the Gates of Heaven for him that day. While the woman was guarding the Gates of Heaven, her husband arrived. "I'm surprised to see you," the woman said. "How have you been?" "Oh, I've been doing pretty well since you died," her husband told her." "I married the beautiful young nurse who took care of you while you were ill. And then I won the lottery. I sold the little house you and I lived in and bought a big mansion. And my wife and I traveled all around the world. We were on vacation and I went water skiing today. I fell and hit my head, and here I am. How do I get in?" "You have to spell a word," the woman told him. "Which word?" her husband asked. With a little grin on her face the woman said, "Czechoslovakia."

***

"God so loved the world that . . .
He did not send a committee"

***

Sitting on the side of the highway waiting to catch speeding drivers, a State Highway Patrol sees a car puttering along at 22 M.P.H. He thinks to himself, *"This driver is just as dangerous as a speeder!"* So, he turns on his lights and pulls the driver over. Approaching the car, he notices that there are five old ladies; two in the front seat and three in the back seat; all wide eyed and white as ghosts.

The driver, obviously confused, says to him. "Officer, I don't understand, I was doing exactly the speed limit! What seems to be the problem?" "Ma'am," the officer replies, you weren't speeding, but you should know that driving slower than the speed limit can also be a danger to other drivers; slower than the speed limit?" "No sir, I was doing the speed limit exactly . . . twenty-two miles an hour!" The old woman says proudly. The Patrol officer, trying to contain a chuckle explains that "22" was the route number, not the speed limit. A bit embarrassed, the woman grinned and thanked the officer for pointing out her error. "But before I let you go, Ma'am, I have to ask . . . Is everyone in this car OK? These women seem awfully shaken and they haven't muttered a single peep this whole time," the officer asks with concern. "Oh, they'll be all right in a minute officer. We just got off of Route "99."

***

A ten-year-old, under the tutelage of her grandmother, was becoming quite knowledgeable about the Bible. Then one day she floored her grandmother by asking, "Which Virgin was the mother of Jesus; the Virgin Mary or the King James Virgin?"

***

A Sunday school class was studying the Ten Commandments. They were ready to discuss the last one. The teacher asked if anyone could tell her what it was. Susie raised her hand, stood tall, and quoted, "Thou shall not take the covers off thy neighbor's wife."

***

Last week I took my children to a restaurant. My six-year-old son asked if he could say grace. As we bowed our heads, he said, "God is good, God is great, thank you for the food, and I would even thank you more if mom gets us ice cream for dessert, and liberty and justice for all. Amen!" Along with laughter from the other customers nearby, I heard a woman remark. "That's what's wrong with this country; kids don't even know how to pray. Asking God for ice cream! Why, I never!" Hearing this, my son burst into tears and asked me. "Did I do it wrong? Is God mad at me?" As I held him and assured him that he had done a terrific job and God was certainly not mad at him, an elderly gentleman approached the table. He winked at my son and said, "I happen to know that God thought that was a great prayer." "Really?" my son asked. "Cross my heart." Then in a theatrical whisper the gentleman added indicating the woman whose remark had started this whole thing, "Too bad she never asks God for ice cream. A little ice cream is good for the soul sometimes." Naturally, I bought my kids ice cream at the end of the meal. My son stared at his for a moment and then did something I will remember the rest of my life. He picked up his sundae and without a word walked over and placed it in front of the woman. With a big smile he told her, "Here, this is for you. Ice cream is good for the soul sometimes, and my soul is already good."

***

One Sunday they were having a church dinner, and when the **Preacher** came in with his food it looked like it was beans. A little boy said to his dad, "Hey dad, I believe the **Preacher** brought beans for the dinner; ain't that something?" His dad said, "Yes son, looks like he did." A lady was sitting there close to the little boy's dad and she said to him, "Son, why were you so concerned about the **Preacher** bringing beans? "Well," he said, "I didn't think he could because I heard my daddy tell someone one time that our **Preacher** didn't know beans."

***

I am told that the muscles of the face are capable of over 250,000 different combinations of expressions. And one of the most useful is a smile. Fulton J. Sheen used to say, "A smile across the aisle of a bus in the morning could save a suicide later in the day." That statement is true. We all need the healing medicine "of the heart" that a smile, even from strangers, provides. And for some, that medicine can save lives. English essayist Joseph Addison put it this way: "What sunshine is to flowers, smiles are to humanity." Don't say you can't make a difference! Don't ever say you have nothing to give. Each of us can give a smile, spontaneously and sincerely. Its value may not be at once recognized, but be assured that it will be felt. My friend, Marion, sent me this anonymous poem about passing along a smile:

Smiling is infectious; you catch it like the flu. When someone smiled at me today, I started smiling too. I passed around the corner and someone saw my grin. When he smiled I realized I'd passed it on to him. I thought about that smile, then I realized its worth, A single smile, just like mine, could travel around the earth. So, if you feel a smile begin, don't leave it undetected; Let's start an epidemic quick, and get the world infected!

***

THE DEAD MULE

A **Pastor** went to his church office on Monday morning and discovered a dead mule in the church yard. He called the police. Since there did not appear to be any foul play, the police referred the **Pastor** to the health department. They said since there was no immediate health threat that he should call the sanitation department. The manager said he could not pick up the mule without authorization from the mayor. Now, the **Pastor** knew the mayor was not too eager to receive call. The mayor had a bad temper and was generally hard to deal with, but the **Pastor** called him anyway. The mayor did not disappoint the Pastor. He immediately began to rant & rave at the **Pastor** and finally said, "Why did you call me anyway? Isn't it your job to bury the dead?" The **Pastor** paused for a brief prayer and asked the Lord to direct his response. He was led to say, "Yes, Mayor, it is my job to bury the dead, but I always like to notify the next of kin first!"

***

"Dusty Bibles lead to dirty lives."

***

"The Son"

Years ago, there was a very wealthy man who, with his devoted young son, shared a passion for art collecting. Together they traveled around the world, adding only the finest art treasures to their collection. Priceless works by Picasso, Van Gogh, Monet and many others adorned the walls of the family estate.

The widowed elder man looked on with satisfaction, as his only child became an experienced art collector. The son's trained eye and sharp business mind caused his father to beam with pride as they dealt with art collectors around the world. As winter approached, war engulfed the nation, and the young man left to serve his country. After only a few short weeks, his father received a telegram. His beloved son was missing in action. The art collector anxiously awaited more news, fearing he would never see his son again.

With days, his tears were confirmed. The young man had died while rushing a fellow soldier to a medic. Distraught and lonely, the old man faced the upcoming Easter holidays with anguish and sadness. The joy of the season, a season that he and his son had so looked forward to, would visit his house no longer. On Easter morning, a knock on the door awakened the depressed old man.

As he walked to the door, the masterpieces of art on the walls only reminded him that his son was not coming home. As he opened the door, he was greeted by a soldier with a large package in his hand. He introduced himself to the man by saying, "I was a friend of your son. I was the one he was rescuing when he died. May I come in for a few moments? I have something to show you." As the two began to talk, the soldier told of how the man's son had told everyone of his father's love of fine art. "I'm an artist," said the soldier, "and I want to give you this." As the old man un-wrapped the package, the paper gave way to reveal a portrait of the man's son. Though the world would never consider it the work of a genius, the painting featured the young man's face in striking detail. Overcome with emotion, the man thanked the soldier, promising to hang the picture above the fireplace. A few hours later, after the soldier had departed, the old man set about his task.

True to his word, the painting went above the fireplace, pushing aside thousands of dollars of paintings. And then the man sat in his chair and spent Easter gazing at the gift he had been given. During the days and weeks that followed, the man realized that even though his son was no longer with him the boy's life would live on because of those he had touched. He would soon learn that his son had rescued dozens of wounded soldiers before a bullet stilled his caring heart. As the stories of his son's gallantry continued to reach him, fatherly pride and satisfaction began to ease the grief. The painting of his son soon became his most prized possession, far eclipsing any interest in the pieces for which museums around the world clamored. He told his neighbors it was the greatest gift he had ever received. The following spring, the old man became ill and passed away. The art world was in anticipation.

With the collector's passing, and his only son dead, those paintings would be sold at an auction. According to the will of the old man, all of the art works would be auctioned on Easter Sunday, the day he had received his greatest gift. The day soon arrived and art collectors from around the world gathered to bid on some of the world's most spectacular paintings. Dreams would be fulfilled this day; greatness would be achieved as many would claim "I have the greatest collection." The auction began with a painting that was not on any museum's list. It was the painting of the man's son. The auctioneer asked for an opening bid. The room was silent. "Who will open the bidding with $100?" he asked. Minutes passed. No one spoke. From the back of the room came, "Who cares about that painting? It's just a picture of his son.

Let's forget it and go on to the good stuff." More voices echoed in agreement. "No, we have to sell this one first," replied the auctioneer. "Now, who will take this picture?" Finally, a friend of the old man spoke. "Will you take ten dollars for the painting? That's all I have. I knew the boy, so I'd like to have it." "I have ten dollars. Will anyone go higher?" called the auctioneer. After more silence, the auctioneer said, "Going once, going twice, Gone." The gavel fell. Cheers filled the room and someone exclaimed, "Now we can get on with it and we can bid on these treasures!" The auctioneer looked at the audience and announced the auction was over.

Stunned disbelief quieted the room. Someone spoke up and asked, "What do you mean it's over? We didn't come here for a picture of some old guy's son. What about all of these paintings? There are millions of dollars of art here. I demand that you explain what's going on here." The auctioneer replied, "It's very simple. According to the will of the father, whoever takes the son . . . gets it all!" Just as those art collectors discovered on that Easter day, the message is still the same, the love of a Father, a Father whose greatest joy came from His Son who went away and gave his life rescuing others. And because of that Father's love . . . whoever takes the Son gets it all. **Bill Cromie, Md, MBA. Department of Surgery Section of Pediatric Urology, MC 4056 University of Chicago , 5841 S. Maryland Ave. Chicago, Ill. 60637, Received from Scott Neville.**

***

Today you will find plenty of occasions to pass along a heart-felt smile. Remember . . . it's the second best thing you can do with your lips!

***

Chicken Side off first...

A new lady in town came to church one Sunday to visit. She told someone she had moved there from New Orleans and her name was Gladys Dunn. They visited a bit and then they both went into the auditorium and sat down. She appreciated the pretty sanctuary and the music by the choir, but the sermon went on and on and on. Worse, it wasn't very interesting at all. Glancing around, she saw many people in the congregation nodding off. Finally the service was over, and she turned to a sleepy-eyed gentleman who was sitting next to her. She extended her hand, and said, "I'm Gladys Dunn." "You and me both" he replied, "I think I went to sleep several times during that book report."

***

I hate splits in churches but it happens sometimes. In this particular church the **Pastor** had done some things that the majority of the folks did not agree with. On his last Sunday he came to the pulpit made some opening remarks then said, "The one that called me here has now called for me to leave." The Sunday school superintendent got up almost immediately and said to the folks, "Could we please turn to page 445 and sing, 'What a friend we have in Jesus."

***

Giving Blood Not a funny; but a great story.

Some years ago, when I worked as a volunteer at Stanford Hospital, I got to know a little girl named Liz who was suffering from a rare and serious disease. Her only chance of recovery appeared to be a blood transfusion from her 5 year old brother, who had miraculously survived the same disease and had developed the antibodies needed to combat the illness. The doctor explained the situation to her little brother, and asked the boy if he would be willing to give his blood to his sister. I saw him hesitate for only a moment before taking a deep breath and saying, "Yes, I'll do it if it will save Liz." As the transfusion progressed, he lay in bed next to his sister and smiled, as we all did, seeing the color returning to her cheeks. Then his face grew pale and his smile faded. He looked up at the doctor and asked with a trembling voice, "Will I start to die right way?" Being young, the boy had misunderstood the doctor; he thought he was going to have to give his sister all of his blood. Greater love has no man than that he lay down his life for his friends. **True Story**

My mother was a rather plump lady who laughed a lot, who ate a lot of popcorn almost every evening, and a very spiritual lady as well. She was getting along in years so I, in my wonderful wisdom, I said to Mom, "Did you know in the Bible it says 'Our bodies are a temple of the Holy Spirit.' Mom, don't you think you ought to cut back on the popcorn, just a wee bit." She quickly replied, "Richard, why be a temple when you can be a cathedral!"

***

Did you know, when you cross Holy Water with prune juice you really get a good Religious experience?

***

A **Priest** is walking down the street one day when he notices a very small boy trying to press a doorbell on a house across the street. However the boy is very short and the doorbell is too high for him to reach. After watching the boy's efforts for some time, the **Priest** moves closer to the boy's position. He steps smartly across the street, walks up behind the little fellow and, placing his hand kindly on the child's shoulder leans over and gives the doorbell a solid ring. Crouching down to the child's level, the **Priest** smiles benevolently and asks, "And now what, my little man?" To which the boy replies, **"Now we run!"**

***

There was a very special meeting scheduled for Friday evening. "We have all the seats reserved in the front section for all the **Ministers**." said the host **Minister**. "Oh yes, he said, I forgot to tell you, the Pastors from the Lutheran church said they would not be able to be here, so, we will not prepare for them. If they do show up please bring up three chairs for them, because we don't want to leave them out." Well, the service started and just about the time the **Minister** said an opening prayer, the boys in the back saw the 3 Lutheran **Ministers** come in, so one boy said to another one, "The **Preacher** said we don't want to leave them out, so they must be something special. Let's give them a good welcome." Just as the **Ministers** started up the isle toward the front of the church, the boys in unison shouted, "Let everyone please stand and everyone please give three cheers for the Lutherans."

***

George, a **Pastor,** known for his lengthy sermons, noticed Ralph get up and leave during the middle of his message. He returned just before the conclusion of the service. Afterwards George asked Ralph where he had gone. "I went to get a hair-cut," was his reply. "But," said the **Pastor,** Why didn't you do that before the service?" "Because I didn't need one then."

***

"Have a good day, unless you have made other plans."

***

There was a new young Catholic **Priest** who just graduated from the seminary; he was sent to a church to be under the supervision of the **Priest** who had been there for several years. The older **Priest** told the new graduate to sit in the confession booth next to him and listen to how he handled each situation. The young **Priest** sat and listened for several days. The older **Priest** said to the new graduate, "Now, you're going to take confessions for a few days and I'll listen in and let you know how I think you're doing." The graduate agreed that would be fine and so they started doing that the first thing the next morning. Several folk came in for confession and the young man did his job fairly well. The senior **Priest** called him aside and said, "You did rather well; however, I believe a bit of your wording should be changed somewhat." "Ok," said the young man. "Listen carefully now son, when someone gives you a confession that is really quite a story, one that is almost unbelievable, you should say something like this, tisk, tisk, tisk, rather than "Wow."

***

"The tongue weighs practically nothing . . . But so few people can hold it back."

***

Josh felt that things were not going the way he wanted them to go in his relationship with Janie. So, he decided to take her a beautiful bouquet of flowers and a large box of candy. When Janie saw the lovely gifts, she was so excited that she threw her arms around Josh and gave him a warm hug and kiss. Suddenly, he turned and began running down the steps of her porch. "Where are you going, Josh? Have I embarrassed you? Have I offended you?" "Oh no," came the reply. "I'm going for some more flowers and candy!" **A lead-in story, to illustrate a point, from the Guido Evangelistic Assn. Inc.**

***

This young church youth **Pastor** died and went to heaven. When he got to the pearly gates St. Peter was there to greet him. St. Peter said, "Son lets add up your points and see if this is really where you belong. "Ok," said the young **Pastor**. "How many points do I need?" "Well son, you'll need 1000." "Now," said St. Peter, "tell me what you've done." The young **Pastor** replied, "I've driven the church bus for quite some time." St. Peter said, "That's 45 points." "I've served on the church board." "That's 25 points." "I've mowed the grass each week." "That's 10 points." "I've taught 2 different classes." "That's 20 points." "Wow," said the youth **Pastor,** That's really not very many points, the only way I'm going to make it to Heaven is by the Grace of the Lord." St. Peter said, "That's 900 points, come right on in."

Thanks for the good story, Kenneth - RFS

***

"There is no self-made,
you will reach your goals
only with the help of others."
George Shinn

***

This old man had been a Christian most of his life. He had never ever bought a lottery ticket. He just didn't quite know whether he should or not. One day he decided he would try it just once. He went down to his local service station and said, "I think I'll try one of those there lottery ticket things." It turned out he won $500,000 dollars. He was really excited and he just couldn't figure how he was going to tell his **Pastor**. One of his friends said, "Now, be real gentle when you tell the **Preacher**, you don't want to scare or shock him with the news." "Ok," said the old man. Well, he went down to the church parsonage and asked to see his **Pastor**. When the **Pastor** came to the door they exchanged greetings. The old man said, "**Pastor** John, I've got some news I thought you'd like to know about. I've just won the lottery, $500,000 dollars." "Oh my, Oh dear me, said the **Pastor,** What are you going to do with that amount of money?" The old man said, "Well, I don't really need it, so I'm going to give the church one half, and the other half I'm going to give to you." It is a sad story to be such a good one, but the **Pastor** died right there on the spot. It just goes to show you, you'd better be careful when you shock your **Pastor**.

***

"Human nature seems to endow every man with the ability to size up everybody but himself."

***

John: "My Grandfather was touched on the shoulder with a sword by Queen Victoria and made a knight." Sam: "That's nothing. My Grandfather was touched on the head with a tomahawk by an Indian and made an angel."

***

There were two very elderly ladies that always sat in the front pew of the church, close enough to be heard by the **Minister**. One Sunday, one of the women said loudly enough to be heard above the singing of a hymn: "The organist is playing the hymn too fast." Looking at her friend's hymnal, the other lady responded: "What difference does it make? you're not singing the right hymn anyway."

***

John and Mary were enroute headed to the Cayman Islands. While standing on deck John looked out toward the sea and said, "Wow, there is a lot of water out there." Mary replied, "Yeah, and that's just the top of it."

***

"A smile is a curve that can set a lot of things straight."

***

The **Minister** was laboring earnestly to inspire his congregation with the example of the "Apostle Whom Jesus Loved." As he grew more eloquent, he leaned across the pulpit and said: "What this church needs is more Johns!"

***

The **Preacher** and his secretary went to New Orleans to a church convention. There was only one motel room left in the entire city. The only thing they could do was stay in the same room. "Why don't we just go ahead and get the room; we'll do absolutely nothing wrong, nobody will know, and everything will be Ok." said the **Preacher**. When they got to the room there was only one bed and no roll-a-way either. The secretary said, "Well, we both know we're not going to do anything wrong, let's just jump in bed, pretend we're man and wife for the night, and before we know it, it will be morning." They agreed that would work out fine, but there would be no reason to tell anyone, no one at all. "We'll just pretend we're man and wife," said the secretary. They went to bed and in about an hour the secretary said, "Would you be kind enough to get up and get me another blanket, I'm cold." The **Preacher** jumped out of bed and got the blanket. In about another 2 hours she said, "Would you please get up and get me another blanket." Well, he got up and got another blanket. In about another 2 hours she said, I'm still cold, would you get me another blanket." He firmly said to his secretary, "Didn't we say we were going to pretend we were man and wife?" She replied, "Yes dear." He said, "Get up and get you own darn cotton pickin' blanket, and stay asleep . . . see you in the morning."

***

"Blowing out the other fellow's candle won't make yours shine any brighter."

***

John Jones dreamed that hc died and went to Heaven. He knocked at the gate and St. Peter called out: "Who is there?" "This is John Jones, may I come in?" "Are you mounted?" asked St. Peter from within. "No," said John, I am afoot." "Well, you cannot come in here unless you are mounted," came the reply. John was greatly disappointed and started back down the hill. He had not gone far when he met his old **Pastor** coming up to the gate. "What is the matter, John," greeted the **Pastor,** "Could you not get in?" "No, sir, they will not let me in unless I am mounted." "Well, that is strange I am not mounted either." "Then it will be no use of your trying to get in," replied John. "I will tell you what we will do, suggested the **Pastor,** You get down on your all-fours and let me ride you, then we both will get in." This was agreed to, and they proceeded to the gate. The **Pastor** knocked and St. Peter asked who was there. The **Pastor** told him, and then came the question, "Are you mounted?" "Yes, I'm mounted," replied the **Pastor**. The voice came back, "All right, just hitch your horse outside and come on in!"

***

"People are like tea bags. They don't know their own strength until they get into hot water."

***

A man suffering from insomnia asked a friend how he slept so well every night. "Do you count sheep?" he inquired. "No" replied the friend. "I talk to the Shepherd."

***

This young man went out looking for a job. He went everywhere but nobody needed any help. He was about to give up, when at the next place, the boss was really nice and said he could probably use him. He said, "I've got to ask you a few questions. Do you mind getting up early in the morning? Do you enjoy working around people? Do you have transportation to get to work? Do you go to church? I know I'm not supposed to ask that but I'd just like to know."

"Oh yes," said the young man, we're Catholic. We are rooted and grounded in God's word. My folks teach classes." He continued on telling the boss, in detail, about what a good religious family they were. As a matter of fact when the boss asked the next question in jest, the young boy replied, "Yes sir, we're so religious my mother was a nun and my daddy was a **Priest**."

***

A LITTLE PRAYER

Dear Lord, so far today I'm doing all right. I haven't gossiped, lost my temper, been grumpy, greedy, nasty, selfish, or over-indulgent. However, I am going to get out of bed in a few minutes, and I will need a lot more help after that.

***

"It requires no musical talent to always be harping on something."

***

THE BIBLE IN FIFTY WORDS THE SIMPLICITY OF THE GOSPEL

God made, Adam bit, Noah arked, Abraham split, Joseph ruled, Jacob fooled, Bush talked, Moses balked, Pharaoh plagued, People walked, Sea divided, Tablets guided, Promise landed, Saul freaked, David peeked, Prophets warned, Jesus born, God walked, Love talked, Anger crucified, Hope died, Love rose, Spirit flamed, Word spread, God remained.

***

ON THE COUNT OF THREE, I WANT YOU TO LOOK TO THE.

1. Person on your left . . . and say . . . "Isn't God good!"
2. On the count of 3, look to the right . . . and say . . . "I'm so glad to see you."
3. On the count of 3, look to the left and right . . . and say . . . "Aren't you glad you don't look like me."
4. From here on down: Great things to think about . . .
5. Your past is not a part of your future unless you want it to be.
6. Turbulence is inevitable . . . misery is optional . . . you choose each day.
7. As Steve Marin so eloquently said. "This is a sing-a-long, but there are no lyrics, so good luck."
8. When the rolls are served up yonder, I'll be there.
9. A nice noisy buffet is when Big Ugly Fat Fellers are Eating Together.

Did you know; you have to have 2 mountains to make a valley, start climbing!

***

SOMETIMES WE'RE KINDA LIKE THE FELLOW THAT KNEW ENOUGH ABOUT THE CARPENTER BUSINESS TO BE DANGEROUS.

Joe stopped by one of his friends to give him a hand. The carpenter said to Joe, "Do you know anything about doing this?" Joe said, "Yeah, I can do about anything." Well, the carpenter said, "I need these 80 - 2 x 4s cut into 8 ft. lengths." So, Joe went home and got his chain saw and marker and started in to cut the boards. He marked off the first one at 8 ft. cut it off and laid the 1st one over in a stack. Then he marked off the next one of the last one and then put the 2nd one over on the stack. Then he marked off the next one and put the 3rd one over on the stack. He kept doing that until he ran out of boards. When he finished he had boards all the way from 8 ft. all the way up to 9 & ½ ft. He should have marked everyone off of the original. The moral of the story is this: Read your Bible every day, but don't keep adding to it, where the story ended before, or the story will get a little longer each time you tell it.

***

"We cannot teach God anything, we must learn from Him."

Pastor Mike Banks

***

Isn't it great to remember who is really in control, and that; "The Word of the Lord endures forever. And this is the Word which by the Gospel is preached unto you." (1 Peter 1:25) Sometimes we need the reminder of just WHO is really in control. No matter what happens in today's world the following will always be true.1. The Bible will still have all the answers. 2. Prayer will still be the most powerful thing on Earth. 3. The Holy Spirit will still move. 4. God will still honor the praises of His people. 5. There will still be God-anointed preaching. 6. There will still be singing of praise to God 7. God will still pour out blessings upon His people. 8. The will still be room at the Cross. 9. Jesus will still love you. 10.Jesus will still save the lost when they come to Him.
(John 3:16) For God so loved the world, that He gave His only begotten Son, that whosoever believe in Him should not perish, but have everlasting life. (John 3:17) For God sent not his Son into the world to condemn the world; but that the world through him might be saved. (Copied)

***

"Go talk to people who don't have faith, and they will quickly tell us why they don't go to church!"

Pastor Mike Banks

***

"Many churches today are exclusive rather than inclusive!"
Pastor Mike Banks

***

As this was the Sunday immediately following Christmas, the Sunday school teacher asked her Primary Class if they would like to say their Christmas verses again. Little Margie waved her hand enthusiastically, so the teacher said she could come forward. Margie recited: "I'm a cute little girl, with a cute little figure; stay away boys, til' I get a little bigger!"

***

A father's Day composition written in a Sunday school class of eight-year olds: "My father can climb the highest mountain or swim the biggest ocean. He can fly the fastest plane and fight the strongest tiger. He can do anything. But most of the time he just takes out the garbage."

***

Johnny received a perfect attendance record for his first year in Sunday school. As he proudly showed his parents, his dad questioned: "and what have you learned after attending Sunday school so regularly?" "I learned that I should sit down and shut up!"

***

"God becomes a reality . . . When there is a necessity."

The list of prizewinners at a church picnic was announced and included: "Mrs. Smith won the ladies rolling pin throwing contest with a throw of 75 feet. Mr. Smith won the 100-yard dash."

***

This man went to a revival meeting, really got excited. The Lord really spoke to the man. He came home and told his wife all about his experience. He said to his wife, "I'm going fishing today and I know the Lord will take care of me and give me some nice fish." He got in the boat but noticed there was a tiny hole in the bottom about the size of a dime. After a while the water starting rising higher in the boat. The fellow stood up in the boat and began singing, "Jesus never fails; Jesus never fails." You know what happened, I would think. Yep, you got it. The fellow almost drowned. The moral of the story is this: **Don't expect the Lord to do everything for you when you can take care of it yourself.**

***

I was so embarrassed. When I was a kid my mother used to buy clothes from the Army Surplus store. I was so embarrassed. She bought me a new set of clothes. I was so embarrassed. One day we were having something really special at school. I was so embarrassed. I went to school that day dressed like a Japanese General. **Carl Hurley**

***

**"Many people will walk in and out of your life . . .
but only true friends
will leave footprints in your heart."**

***

The **Preacher** had two gals that loved him very much. One was sorta homely, no, she was really homely, but boy could she sing and play the piano. The other gal was absolutely beautiful but she couldn't sing or play a lick. Since he was going to be a **Preacher**, he decided it might be better if he married the one that could help him in church by singing and playing. They went on their honeymoon and the next morning he got up and turned on the lights and said to his new wife, "Honey, Honey, Honey, get up quick and find a good piano and sing me a song."

***

**"God gives every bird its food . . .
But He does not throw it into its nest."**

***

SOMETHING TO THINK ABOUT

A woman was testifying at a prayer meeting: "I ain't what I ought to be; and I ain't what I'm gonna be; but anyway, I sure ain't what I was."

***

Value Not a funny . . . but a great story
A well-known speaker started off his seminar by holding up a $20 bill. In the room of 200, he asked, "Who would like this $20 bill?" Hands started going up. He said, "I am going to give this $20 to one of you but first, let me do this." He proceeded to crumple the dollar bill up. He then asked, "Who still wants it?" Still the hands were up in the air. "Well," he replied, "What if I do this?" And he dropped it on the ground and started to grind it into the floor with his shoes. He picked it up, all crumpled and dirty. "Now who still wants it?" Still the hands went into the air. "My friends, you have all learned a very valuable lesson. No matter what I did to the money, you still wanted it because it did not decrease in value. It was still worth $20. Many times in our lives, we are dropped, crumpled, and ground into the dirt by decisions we make and the circumstances that come our way. We feel as though we are worthless. But no matter what has happened or what will happen, you will never lose your value in God's eyes. To Him, dirty or clean, crumpled or finely creased, you are still priceless to Him. Psalm 17:8 states that God will keep us, "as the apple of His eye." **THOUGHT: The worth of our lives comes not in what we do or who we are, but by WHOSE WE ARE!**

***

It was a cold winter's day that Sunday. The parking lot to the church was filling up quickly. I noticed as I got out of my car, fellow church members were whispering among themselves as they walked in the church. As I got closer, I saw a man leaned up against the wall outside the church. He was almost lying down as if he was asleep. He had on a long trench coat that was almost in shreds and a hat topped his head, pulled down so you could not see his face. He wore shoes that looked 30 years old, too small for his feet, with holes all over them, his toes stuck out. I assumed this man was homeless, and asleep, so I walked on by through the doors of the church. We all fellow-shipped for a few minutes, and someone brought up the man lying outside. People snickered and gossiped, but no one bothered to ask him to come in, including me. The church service began. We waited for our **Minister** to take his place and to give us the Word, when the doors

to the church opened. In came the homeless man walking down the aisle with his head down. People gasped and whispered and made faces. He made his way down the aisle and up onto the pulpit, where he took off his hat and coat. My heart sank. There stood our **Preacher**; he was the "homeless man." No one said a word. The **Preacher** took his Bible and laid it on his stand, "Folks, I don't think I have to tell you what I am preaching about today."
Leon Hart

***

Why doesn't the fellow who says "I'm no speechmaker," let it go at that instead of giving a demonstration? **Kin Hubbard**

***

The secret of life is to make the best of whatever comes along. Make every day fresh and new. Go in search of knowledge and experience. Let your questions and your answers reconcile . . . and do your best to remember; the best kind of learning curve is an educated smile.

***

In the story of your life, write the best book you can. Have pages on understanding and tales of overcoming hardships. Fill your story with romance, adventure, poetry, and laughter. Make each chapter reflect time well spent. Meet your obligations, but take time to greet your aspirations. If you live up to your potential, you'll never have to live down any disappointment.

***

"There is no satisfactory substitute for brains, but in some cases silence does pretty well."

***

Nothing wastes more energy than worrying. The longer one carries a problem, the heavier it gets. Don't take things too seriously. Live a life of serenity, not a life of regrets.

***

"No time for your health today; no health for your time tomorrow."
An Irish Proverb

***

You'll figure out what to do when difficulties arise. Problems come and go as naturally as the seasons. One solution to remember is that it can sometimes be better to do the wrong thing for the right cause, than the right thing for the wrong reason.

***

"If you are sick and tired of living in the fast lane; change lanes."

***

We got home from church and it was terrible around our dinner table for a little while. Dad criticized the Pastor's message. Mother thought the organist made a lot of mistakes. My sister thought the soloist sang way too loud. My little brother thought the song leader was way too ugly to be leading the song service. I don't know what is wrong with my family. I thought it was a darn good show for a dime.

***

Saturday afternoon the little boy answered the phone, "Hello," said the boy. The person on the other end of the line said, "Is my husband there?" "Nope," replied the little boy. The person on the line said, "How did you know that, how can you say before I even told you who I am?" "Doesn't make no difference lady, there ain't nobody's husband here," replied the little boy.

***

"An ounce of mother and father is worth a pound of clergy."

Old Spanish Proverb

***

"When folks become as concerned about their sick souls as they are about their sick bodies, then the churches will be just as crowded as the doctor's office."

***

Asked what he'd learned at Sunday School, the ten-year-old began, "Well, our teacher told us about when God sent Moses behind the enemy lines to rescue the Israelites from the Egyptians. When they came to the Red Sea, Moses called for the engineers to build a pontoon bridge. After they had all crossed, they looked back and saw the Egyptian tanks coming. Quick as a flash, Moses radioed headquarters on his walkie-talkie to send bombers to blow up the bridge and he saved the Israelites." "Bobby," exclaimed his startled mother, "Is that really the way your teacher told that story?" "Well, not exactly, but if I told it her way, you'd never believe it!"

***

"People seldom lose their religion by a "blow-out." Usually, it is just a "slow leak."

***

There was a boy named Odd. Children teased him all through school and everywhere he went. In spite of all the bad treatment he stuck out his chest and refused to be bothered. As he grew up they still made fun of him, even after he became a successful attorney. Finally as an old man, he wrote out his last wishes. "I've been the butt of jokes all my life," he said. "I'll not have people making fun of me after I'm gone," so he instructed that his tombstone not bear his name. Days and days, after his death, people noticed the large completely blank stone and said, "My my, isn't that odd?"

***

"Some minds are like concrete, all mixed up and permanently set."

***

Run for your life *(This one is a real funny!)*
It might not have been funny! Two gas company servicemen, a senior training supervisor and a young trainee were out checking meters in a suburban neighborhood. They parked their truck at the end of the alley and worked their way to the other end. At the last house a woman looking out her kitchen window watched the two men as they checked her gas meter. Finishing the meter check, the senior supervisor challenged his younger co-worker to a foot race down the alley back to the truck to prove that an older guy could outrun a younger one. As they came running up to the truck, they realized the lady from that last house was huffing and puffing right behind them. They stopped immediately and asked

her what was wrong. Gasping for breath, she replied. "When I saw two professional gas men running away as hard as you two were, I figured I'd better run too!"

***

"People are funny. They spend money they don't have, to buy things they don't need, to impress people they don't like."

***

"Many folks today claim to be Creatures of Circumstance rather than Creators of their own Circumstance!"

RFS

***

"Give us, Lord, a bit o' sun, A bit o' work and a bit o' fun; Give us in all the struggle and sputter, Our daily bread and a bit o' butter; Give us health, our keep to make, An' a bit to spare for others' sake; Give us, too, a bit of song, And a tale, and a book to help us along. Give us, Lord, a chance to be, Our goodly best, brave, wise and free, Our goodly best for ourself, and others, "Til' all men learn to live as brothers."

An old English Prayer

***

"Keep Smiling"

***

Enjoyable community service through-out my life time to date;

I had the privilege and I felt honored, to serve on the Osceola School Board, the Osceola City Council, operated the swimming pool, MC'd Rodeo Daze for many years, and about anything else that had a microphone on it, a member of the First Assembly of God Church Board in Osceola, Missouri, on the Advisory Board of Evangel College in Springfield, Mo., the Board of Business and Economics of Central Missouri State University in Warrensburg, Missouri, an officer in the Chamber of Commerce, produced the first 4-color map of the new Truman Lake, Vice-President of W.P.I. Recording Company, President of the local Optimist Club,

Lt. Governor of Optimist International, board member of St. Clair County Friends of Hospice, a featured speaker for 2 years at the Governor's Conference on Tourism in Oklahoma City, and for 10 years wrote a column, "Did You Know?" in the St. Clair County Courier Newspaper in Osceola, Missouri.

I just realized, why . . . I'm tired!

"GOD HAS BEEN GOOD TO US . . . Neta Ruth and I have been blessed"

Two words of advice, especially for anyone that has ever thought about writing a book; **DO IT!**

A few words, for anyone who thinks they will probably never write a book. Either way here is what you should do; **STARTING TODAY.**

With very little effort, from this point forward, every funny story, every tragedy, anything and everything interesting, almost anything that happens to you that is the least bit exciting or not exciting, write it down, date it, and throw it into a bushel basket and forget about it until you're ready to start writing.

If you never write a book it will still be neat to look through your basket, just for the fun of it. If you do decide to write your book, your memoirs. A story of the facts or experiences in a person's own life. Then, because of the little tiny effort you've taken to throw your stuff into the basket, the biggest part of your book is already finished, and is already in date order. All you have to do, at that point, is go through the basket and start writing. If you should happen to end up as President of the United States, or the head basketball coach at Missouri University, or just a good ole boy or girl, then, if you want, you can let someone else write your book for you; they've already got the stuff.

GOOD LUCK! I CAN HARDLY WAIT TO READ YOUR BOOK.

* **Answer to an earlier question** on page 243:
An orange Kangaroo from Denmark.

About The Authors

by: Meredith Anderson (Publisher)

Richard and Neta Ruth Sunderwirth

Wow! What can one say about this dynamic duo? The dictionary describes a duo as: "a pair of people ..., especially in music or entertainment."

Married for over 56 years, this happy couple has contributed to the joy, happiness and entertainment of thousands, perhaps hundreds of thousands of people during their lives.

Folks of deep Christian belief and rich moral fiber, they have spent their lives in the business of enriching other people's lives.

Richard has always enjoyed a good story or joke to share and brighten the day of another...

Oh, what am I going on for? Read this book. It tells the story of these two wonderful people and their family better than I could ever hope to.

Chicken Side off first...

A Real Treat for History Buffs

Author and historian, Richard F. Sunderwirth has released his very popular New book,

<u>OSCEOLA, MISSOURI, THE BURNING OF 1861</u>

on Amazon.com.

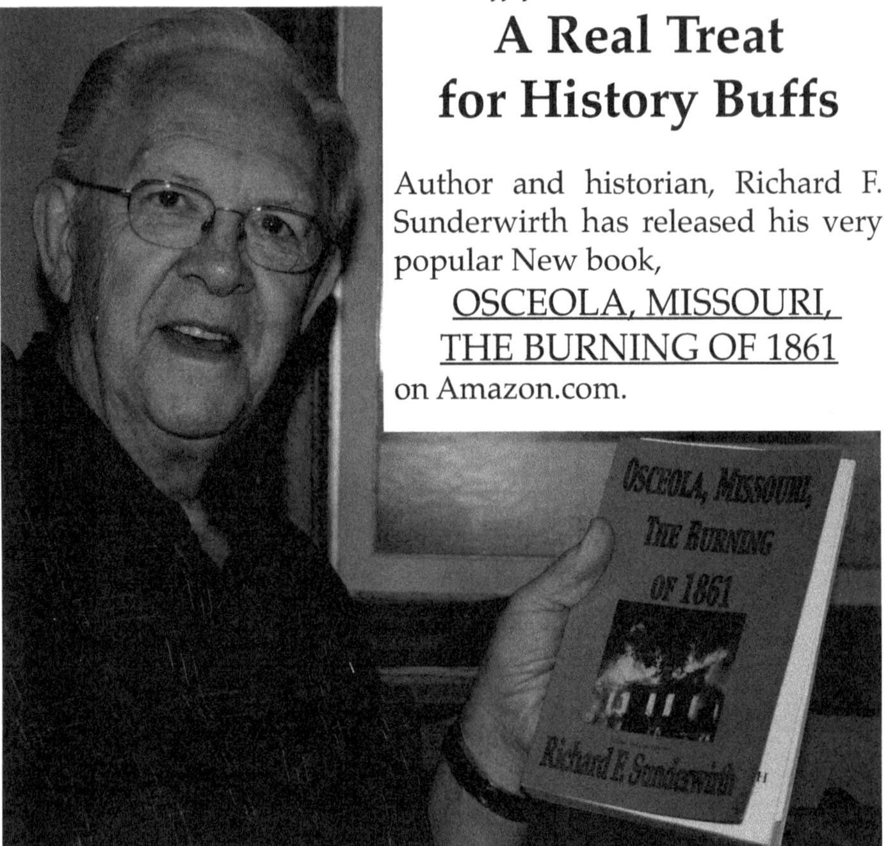

"As the sun went down Sunday night," concluded the brigade correspondent, "Osceola, Missouri, was a heap of smoldering ruins."

Well over two thousand people were left homeless and perhaps the fairest city in Missouri had been utterly wiped from the face of the earth this September afternoon.

Union Brigadier General Jim Lane left Osceola, Missouri with wagon loads of plunder and headed for Kansas, leaving old age, and helpless innocents to keep vigil over the dead and wounded.

Life blood and tears marked the spot which only a few short hours before had been peaceful, contented, happy homes."

Historian Hildegarde Rose Herklotz said, "Lane's troops were no better than an armed and organized banditti. The destruction of Osceola was a case of wanton devastation."

The Kansas Union Brigadier General, Jim Lane raided the city and burned it to the ground after plundering, ravaging and killing many of the inhabitants.

When no gold was found in the bank's vault, a dozen citizens were lined up against a wall and shot.

Richard F. Sunderwirth, a native of Osceola, has presented us with one of the finest narratives on the events of that fateful day in September 1861 when Union General James Lane rode into town with a large military complement and demanded that the townspeople turn over all their worldly goods to his army.

Osceola, a wealthy town located on the banks at the confluence of the Sac and Osage Rivers was totally unprepared and unprotected.

A city of commerce and wealth with a population second only to Kansas City at the time was robbed, pillaged, murdered and turned into a pile of smoldering rubble.

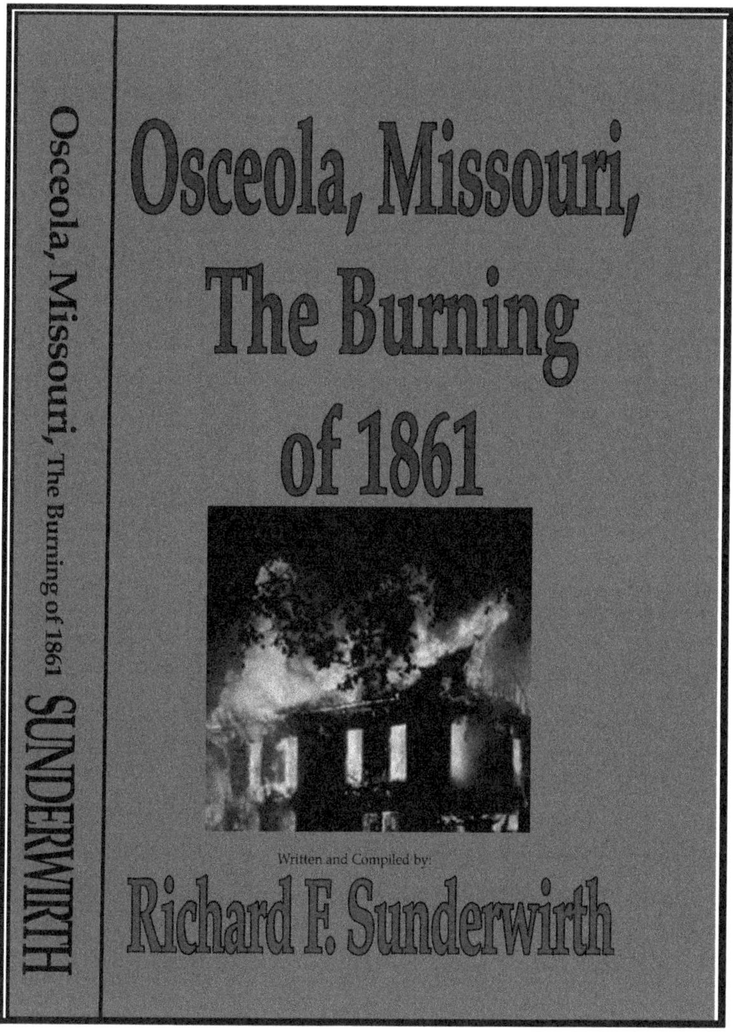

Chicken Side off first...

Dr. Kent Ingle has a new inspirational book.

Dr. Kent Ingle

THIS ADVENTURE CALLED LIFE DISCOVERING YOUR DIVINE DESIGN

Richard F. Sunderwirth wrote:

Today, especially families and youth are in a crisis! So many are dysfunctional. The parents struggle, the kids rebel, and because of this, there is constant turmoil. If you believe, accept and practice what the scripture (BIBLE) says in Proverbs 22.6 "Train up a child in the way he should go, even when he is old he will not depart from it." Parents and their children will have a much better opportunity for success and have a greater balance in their lives. The outlines and suggestions described in this book can and will produce a far greater future for you, your children and grandchildren, than you can possibly imagine. This small, yet powerful book can help eliminate the turmoil that is prevalent today.

I highly recommend this book because I know the author personally; he is my nephew, I've watched him grow from infancy and he has proven by what he's written, a record of strength, stability, courage, and a home life that is to be memorable in every way.

-- JON GORDON, best selling author of

THE ENERGY BUS AND THE SEED wrote:

"You will either live your life by design or default and this book will help you find the best and highest design for your life." -- MARK SANBORN, best selling author of THE FRED FACTOR

Dr. Kent Ingle is the President of Southeastern University. Previously, he served as the Dean of the College of Ministry at Northwest University in Kirkland, Washington. He has also served eight years as a college professor and fifteen years as a pastor. Prior to entering professional ministry, Kent spent ten years as a television sports anchor for NBC and CBS.

JON GORDON

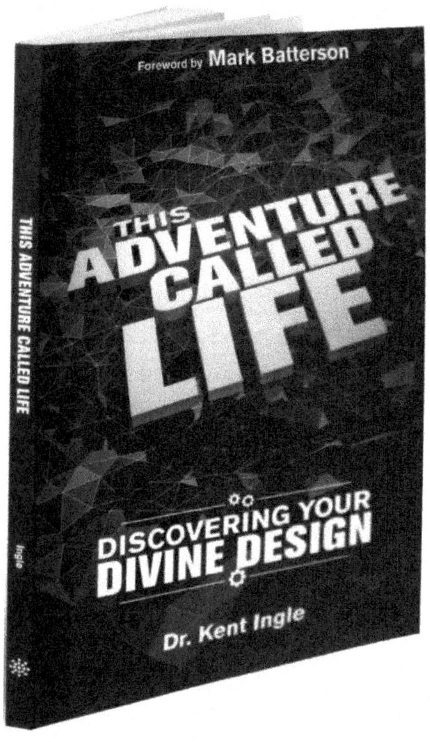

YOU CAN DECIDE TO BECOME ALL GOD CREATED YOU TO BE.

This Adventure Called Life: Discovering Your Divine Design embodies the timeless message of Ephesians 2:10 - you are God's masterpiece. Through its pages, Dr. Ingle unpacks the steps of the creative process that God has crafted into the journey of life. He expounds on God's ongoing handiwork in us to develop and refine the strengths and gifts of our divine design. God has created you with the potential to attain greatness that is more valuable than power, position, or prestige. This greatness is about living a life of significance and meaning. If we allow God to unleash our divine design, we'll embark on an adventure far greater than we could have ever imagined.

"If you've had a nagging feeling about changing something in your life, this book will help you make the change before you have to, rather than because you have to."
Dr. Kent Ingle

You can find this book at:
www.influenceresources.com
www.kentingle.com
www.myhealthychurch.com

Dr. Kent Ingle is the son of Gail and the late Joe Ingle. Gail lives in Osceola, Missouri and is faithfully involved in Piano Ministry and has been for many years. Gail is the sister of Richard F. and Jim D. Sunderwirth.

Chicken Side off first...

Western History Fans, Here's something for you...

Linda Pool Anderson

Award winning novelist and historian Linda Anderson has released her new book on Amazon.com.

Charles Barnhill, Deputy US Marshal

is now available after eight years of research, writing and rewriting.

After the Civil War, the Indian Territory became a sanctuary for villains seeking refuge from the law of their native state. At that time the law of the land was written in such a manner as to prevent non-Indian outlaws from being arrested or prosecuted by Indian courts, so the territory was the perfect place for white criminals to hide.

In 1875 President Grant appointed Judge Isaac Parker to the bench over the Western District of Arkansas and the lawless face of the west began to change. Parker's jurisdiction covered a land area of 74,000 square miles, including 13 counties of Arkansas and all of the Indian Territory. Judge Parker sentenced 161 men to hang, more than any other court in the land. Hanging was the only penalty for murder and rape but only 79 met their fate at the end of a rope.

This book chronicles the efforts of Charles Barnhill and his brothers, Abel and James, devoted peace officers, who spent almost two decades in the service of the court of the Western District of Arkansas from 1879 until the venerable court was closed in 1896, its legendary authority divided and spread over several federal jurisdictions. Known among outlaws as "the Bible believing marshal," Charley never took the life of a fugitive, although he was involved in many gun battles and was wounded multiple times in the performance of his duty. The quintessential Christian lawman, husband, father, brother and son, he performed his duties with fellow notable lawmen, Heck Thomas, Bass Reeves, and Tyner Hughes.

Budd Johnson, U. S. Marshals Service - Retired wrote:

My wife and I are both retired United States Marshals and recently finished reading Charles Barnhill Deputy U. S. Marshal. Mrs. Linda Anderson's account of Deputy Barnhill transported us back to rough and callous times of Indian Territory of the 1870's. Mrs. Anderson did an outstanding job of researching the role of a deputy U. S. marshal right down to the office work, the U. S. District Court at Fort Smith which had jurisdiction of the District of Western Arkansas and Indian Territory.

Mrs. Andersons' depiction of life on the scout was amazingly accurate down to the methodology, the hiring of guards, cooks and possemen. Her portrayal of deputy marshals read like a movie in our minds eye. We could almost smell the smoke from the campfire and taste the cooking bacon in the skillet. It was that good. Likewise, Mrs. Anderson's account of Charles Barnhill as a lawman of compassion and deep seated religion depicted the true character of the man and the family.

For any student of American history, frontier or territorial law, the U. S. Marshals Service or anyone wanting a great read, this is your book. I'd lend you ours, but we are re-reading it already. Do yourself a favor and get the book.

Budd Johnson

Donetta Garman

Growing Up Ugly is a moving memoir about coming of age and realizing the beauty in this life we are all searching for is within our grasp.

Join the author, Donetta Garman, as she drifts in and out of consciousness after suffering a medical emergency and recalls some of the events in her unusual but loving childhood. After a traumatic birth, Donetta was left homely, clumsy, and awkward. Growing up, she learned to cope with being "ugly" by laughing at herself and trying to help hold the family together.

While her family climate was dysfunctional, the cohesiveness of it was undeniable, and Garman's story is infused with intense love and resilience of a peculiar but fiercely devoted family. With the help of her family, children, husband, friends and God, Donetta finds that beauty really is only skin deep and there is a "swan" just waiting to escape all of us.

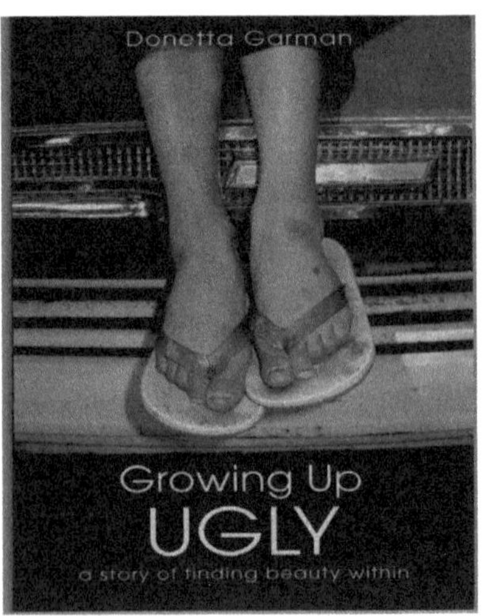

Reviewed by Paula Friedrichsen for Crossmap.com & PositivelyFeminine.com
"Growing Up Ugly" is a fast paced, completely engrossing memoir. Full of twists and turns, it almost reads like a novel. Garman doesn't offer up "self-help" suggestions--or go on yards about the lessons to be learned from her experiences. She simply tells the story of her sometimes difficult, sometimes wonderful childhood, while occasionally sharing her

own personal growth with readers. The day I received this book in the mail I had a stack of eight books to read and review. Yet there was just something about the title (and the interesting cover art) that compelled me to read this book first, and I'm so glad I did! I would recommend this book to anyone desiring a quick, easy, and entertaining read. Also, "Growing Up Ugly" would be helpful and encouraging for those who have struggled with alcohol or prescription drug addiction personally, or with a loved one.

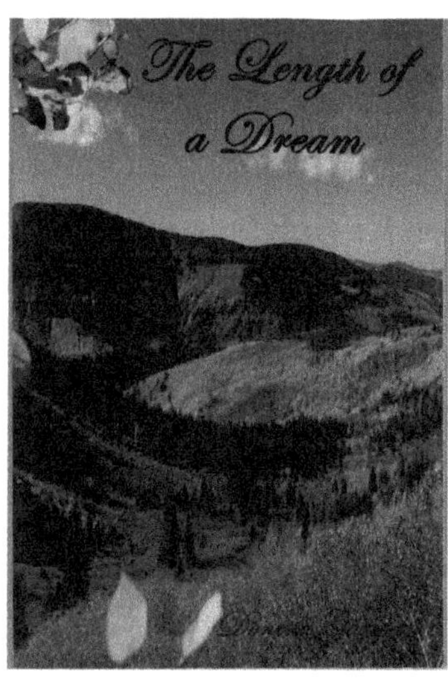

The Length of a Dream is an inspirational, historical novella set in the time period right after the end of the Civil War. The story takes place in a small frontier town in Colorado.

When a man named Joshua rides into the little western town of Uptop and meets Hannah Fain Mullins, the woman at the well, the community is in for a big change. Meanwhile, Hannah's husband, Flint, has been captured by Indians and as he makes his way home and survives many hardships and adventures, he rediscovers his faith in God. Follow the lives of these frontier men and women as they fight to survive the harsh realities of the west, while exploring the length of their dreams.

Reviewed by Cindy Bauer, Inspirational Fiction author. **Set in the late 1800's,** The Length of a Dream is the story of Hannah Fain and Flint Mullins, Hannah's husband. They lived in Uptop, Colorado. Two years earlier, Flint had gone to buy cattle so they could start their own herd, but he was attacked by renegade Ute Indians.

Hannah is left fending for herself and winds up taking a job at the local saloon working in the kitchen and rents the cabin out that she and Flint built to a new preacher, who has shown up in Uptop and decided it's the perfect place to set up church.

Meanwhile, Flint is alive and well. The Ute Indians merely wanted his cattle to feed on during the forthcoming winter, sure to be a hard one. Because of his blonde hair, his life is spared.

While on his journey to head home to Hannah, who surely believes him to be dead, he comes across a wagon belonging to a young black boy and his deceased, slave mother. The slaves had since been freed. He helps the boy bury his mother and together they climb into the wagon. Flint is going to find him a home where "his kind" are staying, hopefully at Fort Garland, which is along the way to Uptop.

Without giving away too much of the story, based on accurate historical research, Ms Garman has written a well-told, captivating, story in **The Length of a Dream.** With lively dialogue, depicted accurately for the era, you'll be sure to keep turning the pages to find out what happens to this family next.

A Must Read!

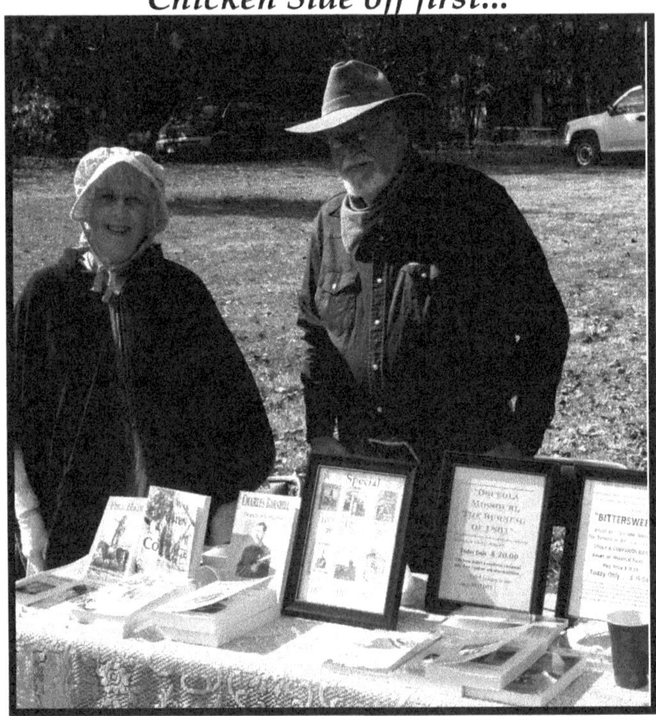

Authors, Linda and Meredith (Andy) Anderson

Award winning Christian writers, Linda and Meredith Anderson write primarily "True" history that they take from boring facts to an exciting read. All of their books are free of scenes that would limit their audience.

They attend many shows each year and council fellow authors in regards to writing and publishing. All of their books can be found at amazon.com.

More Than A Job,
An Adventure
Meredith "Ike" Anderson

If you want a good adventurous read This Is The Book. I loved this book! I was impressed by the raw emotions I felt as I read each page, the realistic youthful response and the fantastic imagery. After reading the first 4 pages I was hooked. I am rather inclined to identify with the youthful Pete, I cared about his story. I identified him without the author stating his age. I feel this Young Adult book should be marketed to the youth of this country. It would really blow their socks off! I consider this book to be right up there with the Alex Rider series. Ike has shown us what a true Hero is. All I can say is that this book is fantastic. I should mention that the Title grabbed me, but I usually don't read a lot of Historical Fiction. However I can easily see this book being made into a movie some day. More Than A Job, An Adventure is a great book for anyone. ***G.P. Jankowski***

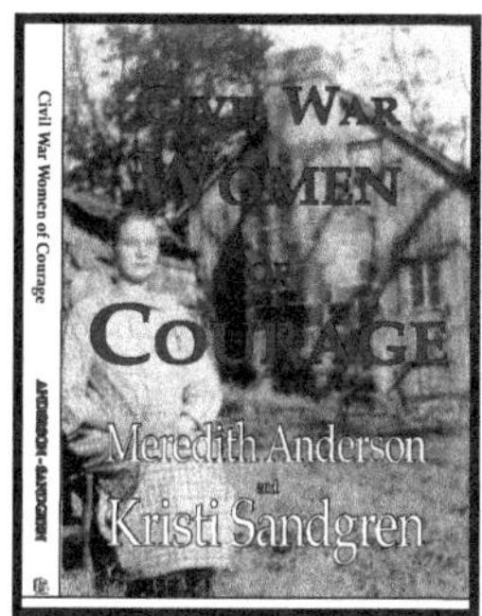

Common Complaint: *Nobody writes about women in the Civil War. What happened to the women?"*

Civil War, Women of Courage is a collection of exciting true stories based on actual evens reported in letters and newspapers during our nation's greatest conflict.

These thirteen stories of women, ages 11 to 24, will entertain and interest readers of all levels. It's nonstop adventure from the streets of Baltimore to the Indian-ravaged frontier of Minnesota and across the battlefields of the South.

"This is a wonderful book! Written in a way to entertain and at the same time, it delivers plenty of history. I Couldn't put it down. The lady who wrote the review on the back of the book was right on target."

Three Feathers, **Northern Cherokee Nation**

Sixth grader, Jayde R. of Sage Creek Elementary wrote: "I read **WHISPERING OAKS THE CURSE** and it was fun, interesting and exciting from page one to the end. I loved it! My favorite part was the ***wish fairy*** Millie. How long before the next book?"

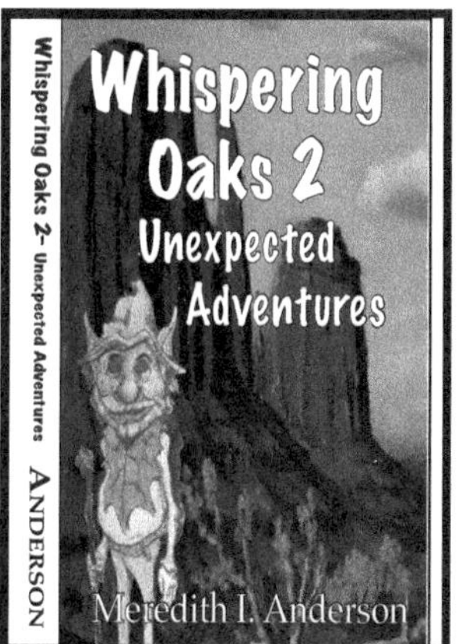

"**Whispering Oaks 2, Unexpected Adventures** is an excellent and entertaining story, written in the style of Mark Twain and other authors of the 19th century. Every chapter turns a corner and takes the reader on a new adventure within the scope of this magical adventure."

Dr. Nikki Hansen
Weber State University

Chicken Side off first...

A Chef's Aid at the age of 14, the author has always wanted to write a little cook book. This one not only has his favorite recipes (pages 96-97) and a few from friends, but also a sample of his and his wife's literary works to entertain any reader or cook.

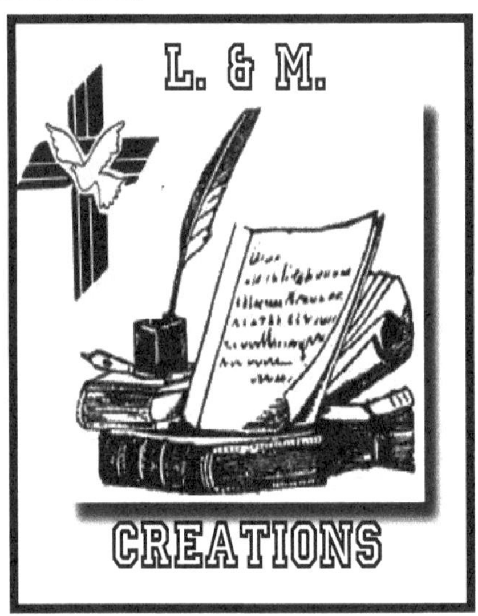

If Richard has inspired you to write YOUR BOOK, and you would like a guiding word or some help, please do not hesitate to call on us. We are as close as your phone:

Meredith "Andy" Anderson fisherman.anderson@ juno.com
Linda Anderson linda.skymama@gmail.com
Our phone is: 417-664-0012

Bittersweet

by Linda Cushman

Available on amazon.com

"The original idea for this wonderful book came after the author read Richard Sunderwirth's book, The Burning."

Meredith Anderson

Anna Lea Pepper is a feisty, independent, determined woman with a mind of her own. With war between the states looming on the horizon, she's even more determined to protect all that she holds dear: her land and family.

When her husband, James, goes off to fight with the Missouri State Guard in the War of Northern Aggression, she is left to tend to their farm at Dry Fork Creek and raise their two children, eleven-year-old Pearl and fourteen-year-old Philip.

One day, after Anna Lea and her children finish up their chores on the farm, Anna hears a sound that makes her heart freeze with an unfamiliar fear. Drums boom, and there's the sound of feet trampling the ground. Then she sees them coming down the hill in an endless stream of blue, some on horseback, others marching on foot to the constant rattle of fife and drums -- Northern soldiers. Captain Allan Saunders of the Federal Army informs her that General Nathaniel Lyon and his troops will be camping at her home. It is the first of a series of events that will thrust her full-force into the violence and turmoil of war. Anna Lea builds walls of resentment around her heart that have to be torn down when she is forced to rely on help from unexpected sources: an Osage Indian family and the very same Federal captain who camped on the Pepper farm at the start of the war. Anna Lea soon learns life can sometimes be Bittersweet.

Author Linda Cushman and her husband, Gary, live in rural Polk County, Missouri, on the farm that is the setting for Bittersweet. She raises cattle and writes in her spare time.

You can order an autographed book or contact the author at:

Linda Cushman
3543 Hwy 83
Bolivar, Mo. 65613